D0848883

GOETHE'S NOVELS

Also published by Macmillan

LESSING: THE FOUNDER OF MODERN GERMAN LITERATURE
by H. B. Garland

Goethe's Novels

HANS REISS

University of Miami Press
Coral Gables, Florida

Published in Great Britain by Macmillan and Co Ltd
This edition published 1971 by
University of Miami Press

Library of Congress Catalog Card Number 74–145426
ISBN 0–87024–198–2

Manufactured in Great Britain

For my Wife

Contents

ABBREVIATIONS USED IN NOTES

W.A.	*Goethes Werke* (Weimarer or Sophien-Ausgabe).
G.A.	*Goethes Werke* (Artemis-Gedenkausgabe).
H.A.	*Goethes Werke* (Hamburger Ausgabe).
ÉG	*Études Germaniques.*
Euph.	*Euphorion.*
DVLG	*Deutsche Vierteljahrsschrift für Literaturwissenschaft und Geistesgeschichte.*
G	*Goethe. Vierteljahresschrift der Goethe-Gesellschaft* (vols. i–iii, 1936–8); *Viermonatsschrift der Goethe-Gesellschaft* (vols. iv–viii, 1939–43); *Neue Folge des Jahrbuchs der Goethe-Gesellschaft* (vols. ix ff., 1944 ff.).
GJb	*Goethe-Jahrbuch* (vols. i–xxxiv, 1880–1913).
GR	*The Germanic Review.*
GLL	*German Life and Letters*, N.S.
JbGG	*Jahrbuch der Goethe-Gesellschaft* (vols. i–xxi, 1914–35).
JbFDH	*Jahrbuch des Freien Deutschen Hochstifts.*
JEGP	*Journal of English and Germanic Philology.*
MLR	*The Modern Language Review.*
PEGS	*Publications of the English Goethe Society*, N.S.
PMLA	*Publications of the Modern Language Association of America.*
Graef.	Graef, Hans Gerhard (ed.), *Goethe über seine Dichtungen.*

Preface

AREN'T there enough books on Goethe? This question tends understandably to be asked each time a new book on Goethe appears. To add to this plethora of publications by offering an English version of an earlier book in German may appear additionally burdensome. Yet there has never been a book on Goethe's novels in English, and the only book in German prior to my own book *Goethes Romane* of 1963 was Robert Riemann's *Goethes Romantechnik*, published in 1902, more than sixty years earlier, a book which deals only with the formal aspects of Goethe's fiction. An assessment of Goethe the novelist in book-form may thus appear permissible. Since Goethe is most easily accessible to the English reader through his novels, a book in English on his novels might fill a gap.

At this stage of Goethe scholarship, revolutionary appraisals are likely to be either mistaken or trivial. Any account of Goethe's major works must rely on earlier writings. I have sought to take account of all that has been written on the subject, but, following common practice, I have cited only those works to which I knew myself to be directly indebted. Considerations of space compelled me to include a select bibliography only. I listed those works actually cited and I added only some which, I think, should be noted, but by no means all which I consulted and found profitable. A lengthy bibliography, in any case, would be only a repetition of such well-known and exhaustive bibliographies as those by Goedeke (3rd ed., iv, 2–5), Hans Pyritz (*Goethe-Bibliographie*, Heidelberg, 1955 ff.) as well as those found in the relevant volumes (6, 7, 8, 14) of the Hamburg edition of Goethe's works (Hamburg, 1948 ff.) and in *Goethe. Neue Folge des Jahrbuchs der Goethe-*

Gesellschaft, xvi ff., Weimar, 1952 ff. I am, indeed, only too conscious of my debt to the whole corpus of Goethe scholarship which cannot be acknowledged in detail.

This book is not a translation of the German version, but has been rewritten for an English reading public. For that purpose, many details have been omitted, especially since the book is intended not only for the student of German, but also for the general reader of European fiction. On the whole, I have avoided quotation in German, except for quotations of poetry, of which a translation in prose is appended. I had, therefore, to omit a detailed discussion of Goethe's language and imagery which was one of the features of the German version. Since *Wilhelm Meisters Wanderjahre* has never made an impact on the English reader, I have particularly pruned the chapter dealing with this novel. But I trust that nothing essential has been lost by this economy. I have also sought to make use of anything that has been written on Goethe's novels since the German edition of my book appeared.

Finally, I should like to thank all those who have helped and encouraged me at various stages. First and foremost I should like to acknowledge my debt to L. A. Willoughby and Elizabeth M. Wilkinson, whose studies of Goethe have been models of what Goethe scholarship can be. Others – Henry Hatfield, Edna Purdie, Fritz Martini, Christopher Middleton, Walter Müller-Seidel, the late William Rose, Friedrich Sengle, Emil Staiger – have given me valuable counsel. Armin Arnold, Alexander Fischer and Max Heinrich Fischer greatly assisted me with the writing of the German book; Irving Massey, H. B. Nisbet, and R. T. K. Symington have helped in the preparation of the English manuscript. Above all I am, however, indebted to Michael and Estelle Morgan, whose counsel and help on matters of style and content have been invaluable. The McGill University Research Fund and the German Academic Exchange Service gave me financial help, for which I am most grateful, to visit European libraries. For all errors I am, of course, myself responsible.

H. S. REISS

Wills Memorial Building
The University
Bristol
December 1966

Introduction

GOETHE is one of the greatest figures in world literature. Like Homer, Dante, and Shakespeare, who are often called his peers, his fame is said not to undergo the rise and fall which the reputations of lesser men experience. In our time, a host of scholars, journalists and mythologists have fostered this belief. It is now one of the truisms of literary opinion that *Faust* is a pinnacle of literary achievement and Goethe one of the most versatile men that ever lived. Changes in literary fashion have never been able to extinguish interest in him, because his achievement presents so many facets – as an imaginative writer he excelled in lyric poetry, in drama, in prose fiction and in autobiography; as a scientist he did work in botany, geology, meteorology, comparative anatomy and zoology as well as physics, and his research in some of these fields was important; he also discoursed with considerable insight on many other subjects. In addition, he was an able administrator in, admittedly, rather a small country, and the managing director of an important theatre. He was, in fact, a universal genius who was able to move many minds deeply both in his own lifetime and after his death. In German-speaking countries his work is, of course, part and parcel of the general cultural tradition, however much Germany at times has moved away from the Goethean spirit. His influence there has indeed grown and deepened.[1]

In the English-speaking world it has been different. While his name is much esteemed, most of his work is not widely read. A few lyrics are well known through the medium of music. *Faust* is probably read by many people, especially since it has become a paperback,[2] but translation fails to convey adequately its matchless poetry. Goethe's other dramas are virtually unknown and hardly ever acted. Of his four novels, two, *Die Wahlverwandtschaften* (*The Elective Affinities*) and *Wilhelm Meisters Wanderjahre* (*Wilhelm Meister's Travels*) have virtually no reading public in the English-speaking world, but then the latter work is scarcely read in Germany itself. *Die Leiden des jungen Werthers* (*The Sorrows of Young Werther*), which once took Europe by storm, is still read, though much less than it was. So is *Wilhelm Meisters Lehrjahre* (*Wilhelm Meister's Apprenticeship*), frequently referred to as *Wilhelm Meister* to the exclusion of the *Wanderjahre*. Yet these novels are not nearly so popular in the Anglo-Saxon world as they were in the heyday of their reputation.[3] *Werther*, in the first decade following its publication in 1774, was a best-seller. The *Lehrjahre* became widely known in the early part of the nineteenth century. While lip-service is frequently paid to Goethe as a great novelist, it must be doubted whether most critics really regard him as one. In those classic works on the novel, Percy Lubbock's *Craft of Fiction*[4] and E. M. Forster's *Aspects of the Novel*,[5] his fiction is not discussed, though here he is in good company with Manzoni and Verga, and even Cervantes, whose novels are not discussed either.

To make out a case for reading Goethe's novels may, therefore, be justifiable, but to champion a writer may not win more readers for his work. Yet if an interpretation is able to show that his novels genuinely offer something to the reader, those who have not read them may perhaps be tempted to read them, if only to test the validity of the argument. And those who have read them, but do not value them, may feel inclined to read them again to dispose of our argument even more conclusively. Moreover, the student of the novel will want to know more precisely what kind of novels Goethe wrote, what he attempted to do in them, what reasons compelled him to resort to the form he chose, what themes he developed in them and what function in each novel he assigned to these themes. There is no other novelist of Goethe's stature for whom the novel was not the principal mode of literary creation. For Goethe, the novel was one literary genre among several in which he wished to excel. Nonetheless, there are not many years during the more than six decades of Goethe's creative life when he was not in some way or other writing fiction.

At the age of twenty-five in 1774 he achieved world-wide fame through *Werther*, written in a few months; of an earlier attempt at novel-writing only a short passage has remained. Only three years before his death, in 1829 – with the publication of the second version of his last novel, the *Wanderjahre* – did he finally cease writing novels.

In all these years, other kinds of prose narrative apart from the novel – the short story, autobiography, even the history of science – engaged his creative energy. Indeed, his prose – whether it be that of his diaries or of his letters, of the autobiographical account or of fiction – has decisively influenced the development of German prose writing.[6]

Goethe, it must be remembered, never claimed for the novel the same status as for lyric poetry or the drama, although he spent so much creative energy and time on the writing of novels. The novel, indeed, makes quite different demands on the reader. Its impact on him is likely to lack the concentrated power of drama and lyric poetry. To analyse it, specific difficulties have therefore to be overcome. Since the form and the material do not appear to be fully integrated,[7] interpretations are often misdirected; it is tempting to look for direct access to the meaning or rather the import (*Gehalt*) of the work without an appreciation of its form (*Gestalt*). If this is done, the import is not properly apprehended and the necessary feeling for the *whole* work is lacking. Individual parts are emphasized and not seen in the context of the work as a whole. As the boundaries of the novel are not so clearly marked as those of drama, it is easy to miss the organic character of a novel, which it must possess if it is to be a work of art. Percy Lubbock has clearly stated the problem at the end of *The Craft of Fiction.*

> The book vanishes as we lay hands on it. Every word we say of it, every phrase . . . is loose, approximate, a little more or a little less than the truth. We cannot exactly hit the mark, or if we do, we cannot be sure of it . . . there are times when a critic of literature feels that if only there were a single tangible and measurable fact about a book – if it could be weighed like a statue, say, or measured like a picture – it would be a support in a world of shadows.[8]

The concept 'novel' in fact includes quite a few heterogeneous types; both the verse epic and the prose narrative can be described by that name, though Goethe clearly distinguished these. Writers tend to disparage this literary genre. Goethe and Schiller called it 'an impure form';[9] in our century E. M. Forster in *Aspects of the Novel* termed it a 'low atavistic form'.[10] Kafka, as always, took an even more extreme stand. He spoke of the shameful depths of novel-writing and instructed his friend Max Brod to burn his novels.[11] Undoubtedly Goethe and Schiller are right; the novel is an impure form. It is capable of containing lyric poetry, dramatic scenes, monologues, letters, diary-entries; even specifically foreign matter, such as documents, pamphlets, essays and philosophical discourses, may become organic parts. The limits of narration are not clearly defined. A biography, an autobiography, even a historical work can be called a novel without necessarily losing its specific quality. For instance, Goethe's autobiography *Dichtung und Wahrheit* (*Poetry and Truth*) may be ranked among his novels. In this study, however, the delimitation of the novel is more conservative. Only the four works are studied which, in accordance with Goethe's own usage, are commonly called novels.

Another difficulty in elaborating a theory of the novel is size. It varies considerably. It is, therefore, hard to discover general structural laws. Often a clearly recognizable plan cannot be detected.

When Goethe began to write, the first serious attempts were made in Germany to explore the character of prose fiction. His beginnings as a novelist coincide with endeavours by German theorists of the novel to accord the novel equality of rank with drama and the verse epic. Drama had, in the eighteenth century, claimed pride of place.[12] Significantly, Gottsched's reform of language and literature centred on drama and on the theatre. Goethe, indeed, inherited a widespread belief when he adjudged prose fiction to be inferior to the verse epic. Schiller echoed these sentiments by calling the novelist a half-brother of the poet. Neither of them elaborated a theory of the novel, perhaps because they did not think highly enough of its claims to literary status. Their comments on the theory of the novel are, indeed, meagre.

Other contemporary writers thought differently. At Easter 1774, six months before the publication of *Werther*, the first substantial German treatise on fiction, Christian Friedrich von Blanckenburg's *Versuch über den Roman* (*Essay on the Novel*) was published. Inspired by Sterne, Fielding and Wieland, Blanckenburg sought to explore and define a literary genre which could no longer be overlooked by serious critics of literature. In the wake of the English experience of Richardson, Sterne and Fielding, the novel of the *Aufklärung* had been capturing the reading public in Germany, as evidenced by the steadily increasing number of German novels published, fewer than twenty in 1740 and almost a hundred in about 1780.[13] Furthermore, Wieland, at that time still the most influential German prose writer, had produced in his *Geschichte des Agathon* (first edition 1766/7, second edition 1773) the first eighteenth-century German philosophical novel of note. Encouraged by Wieland's success,[14] Blanckenburg dared to place the novel on the same level as the verse epic.[15] His approach to these two genres is not altogether dissimilar from the method applied by Herder to his comparison of Greek and Shakespearean drama, for Blanckenburg, too, saw the need to discuss the historical context of works of literature.[16] In his opinion, the verse epic meant to the Greeks what the novel means to modern readers.[17] The epic relates external events and describes public personalities, the novel recounts psychological events and depicts the life of private individuals, of ordinary men and women.[18] In Blanckenburg's theory of fiction, the psychological foundation of events in the novel looms large.[19] The novel is to be a whole nexus of causal events[20] which carry conviction because they are based on or related to an individual's inner life. The story must be concentrated on one individual, the novel's hero, and all other characters exist for his sake. The hero's development – and here *Agathon* is the distinct model – is caused by events which he encounters. The novel is not to end before the action is completed or the hero's character is sufficiently developed,[21] for the reader's curiosity must be satisfied. However much Blanckenburg's treatise is marred by digression and wordiness, its enlightened tone cannot be mistaken. It is a landmark in the German theory of fiction in the age of the *Aufklärung*.[22] It speaks for its author's soundness of judgement and literary taste that his predilection for Sterne, Fielding and Wieland has stood the test of time.[23] If he criticized the epistolary novel, mainly perhaps because he did not care for Richardson, he did not exclude the possibility that a genius might transform this genre. When *Werther* was published six months later, he was quick to recognize the hand of genius; his review in the *Neue Bibliothek der schönen Wissenschaften und der freien*

Künste[24] was by far the most penetrating at the time. Blanckenburg examined *Werther* according to his own principles of fiction, discussed its artistic qualities and praised the psychological necessity of the action.

The *Versuch über den Roman* is symptomatic of a change in the practice of fiction. Blanckenburg's argument is steeped in the rationalistic thought of the *Aufklärung*, but he looks to the future. In 1774, too, his contemporary Johann Jakob Engel also insisted on psychological motivation.[25] Like Blanckenburg, he criticized a mere narrative, but, unlike him, considered the dialogue the best way to convey motives underlying the action in the novel, claiming the authority of Diderot in support of his views. Blanckenburg's and Engel's argument in favour of the psychological foundation of prose fiction could be taken as an unwitting defence of the epistolary novel, for which they evinced little or no enthusiasm.[26] On the whole, their views were ahead of their time. When Johann Karl Wezel, a writer who shared these views, sought to put some of them into practice in his novel *Hermann und Ulrike* (1782) he failed to conquer the reading public.[27]

Yet in time these ideas prevailed. A quarter of a century or so later the German Romantics assigned to the novel equal status with other genres.[28] Indeed, it appeared to them specifically suited to exemplifying Romantic doctrines of the *Gesamtkunstwerk*, the work of art that was to encompass all literary genres and even media. The novelist Jean Paul, although he did not belong to the inner circle of the Romantic school, stated in his *Vorschule der Aesthetik* (1804), a treatise on poetics, that the spaciousness of the novel's form was capable of containing almost all other forms,[29] a feature which he regretted. This idea of totality was certainly echoed by Hegel[30] who, in his *Vorlesungen über die Ästhetik*, refers to the totality of the world represented by the novel.[31] Jean Paul himself preferred the dramatic novel, which he called rather neatly 'a race-course of characters',[32] for he thought that the looseness of prose-fiction needs and profits by formal rigour.[33]

There is, in fact, no conclusive evidence of any direct influence of contemporary theories of fiction on Goethe's practice as a novelist. For instance, he apparently did not read Jean Paul's *Vorschule der Aesthetik*[34] nor did he pay attention to Blanckenburg.[35] He thought little of authors' attempts to justify their novels by prefaces.[36] Only *Werther* has a preface, which is very brief, in fact considerably shorter than the original draft, which was itself not too long. The absence of direct evidence does not, however, mean that he was not affected by the climate of opinion. Blanckenburg's injunction that truth and naturalness should prevail in fiction was obviously heeded in *Wilhelm Meisters Theatralische Sendung* (*Wilhelm Meister's Theatrical Mission*), the first version of *Wilhelm Meisters Lehrjahre*, but then this idea had also been propounded by Merck, one of his closest friends.[37] Lichtenberg,[38] too, had expressed similar views. There is no need to examine the whole body of German theoretical writings on fiction in the late eighteenth and early nineteenth century to accept this hypothesis of indirect influence. It is indeed probable that changing attitudes to fiction affected Goethe's mode of writing. Yet it is his achievement as a novelist which, more than anything else, has altered German thinking about fiction. The gulf in outlook between *Werther* and the *Wanderjahre* is substantial, for when Goethe began to write, the novel was only beginning to emerge from being a form of mere entertainment. When he concluded the *Wanderjahre* almost sixty years later a different attitude prevailed: the novel had become accepted as a vehicle for serious, indeed for philosophical, thought. *Werther* suggests that Goethe never despised the novel as his contemporaries did in his youth; on the other hand, he remained much more conservative in theory, even if not necessarily in practice, towards the end of his life.

It is difficult to classify Goethe's novels, as they certainly do not conform to one individual type. On the contrary, each one of his four novels, despite some common traits, possesses a distinct form of its own. The shortest by far was his first novel *Werther*; it provides a convenient starting-point for our inquiry.

Notes

1. Cf. Wolfgang Leppmann, *The German Image of Goethe*, Oxford, 1961 (*Goethe und die Deutschen*, Stuttgart, 1962).

2. *Goethe's Faust I*, London, 1949; *Faust II*, London, 1959 (both trans. by Philip Wayne and published by Penguin Books); also *Goethe's Faust, The Prologues and Part One*, the Bayard translation (rev. and ed. Stuart Pratt Atkins, Collier Books), New York, 1962.

3. For Goethe's reputation in English-speaking countries cf. William Rose, 'Goethe's Reputation in England during his Lifetime', *Essays on Goethe* (ed. William Rose), London, 1949, pp. 141–85; W. H. Bruford, 'Goethe's Reputation in England since 1832', ibid., pp. 187–206; Edwin H. Zeydel, 'Goethe's Reputation in America', ibid., pp. 207–32.

4. Percy Lubbock, *The Craft of Fiction*, London, 1921.

5. E. M. Forster, *Aspects of the Novel*, London, 1927.

6. See Eric A. Blackall, *The Emergence of German as a Literary Language 1700–1775*, Cambridge, 1959, pp. 482 ff.

7. Schiller, *Über die ästhetische Erziehung des Menschen in einer Reihe von Briefen* (*On the Aesthetic Education of Man in a Series of Letters*), 22nd letter, 'Herein resides the secret of the master in any art: that he makes his form consume his material.' (I owe this translation to Elizabeth M. Wilkinson); cf. also Elizabeth M. Wilkinson, 'Goethe's Conception of Form', in Elizabeth M. Wilkinson and L. A. Willoughby, *Goethe: Poet and Thinker*, London, 1962, pp. 167–84, and ' "Form" and "Content" in the Aesthetics of German Classicism', *Stil- und Formprobleme in der Literatur* (ed. Paul Böckmann), Heidelberg, 1960, pp. 18–27, for a careful and subtle analysis of Goethe's use of the terms *Stoff* (material), *Gehalt* (import) and *Form* (form).

8. Lubbock, p. 273.

9. Goethe, letter to Schiller, 13 December 1797; Schiller, letter to Goethe, 20 October 1797.

10. See Forster, p. 45: 'I wish . . . that it could be something different – melody, or perception of the truth, not this low atavistic form.'

11. See for instance letter to Max Brod, 5 July 1922 (Franz Kafka, *Briefe 1902–1924*, Frankfurt/Main, 1958, pp. 384 ff.).

12. Cf. Eva D. Becker, *Der deutsche Roman um 1780*, Germanistische Abhandlungen, 5, Stuttgart, 1964, p. 5.

13. Cf. ibid.

14. Cf. Friedrich Sengle, 'Der Romanbegriff in der ersten Hälfte des neunzehnten Jahrhunderts', *Arbeiten zur deutschen Literatur 1750–1850*, Stuttgart, 1965, p. 199; Eberhard Lämmert, Postscript to Christian Friedrich von Blanckenburg's *Versuch über den Roman*, Leipzig and Liegnitz, 1774, 2nd *Facsimile* (ed. E. Lämmert), Sammlung Metzler, 39, Stuttgart, 1965, p. 548; see Blanckenburg, p. 9.

15. Cf. Lämmert, p. 542.

16. Cf. ibid.

17. See Blanckenburg, p. 14.

18. Cf. Lämmert, p. 552.

19. Cf. Becker, p. 65; cf. also Blanckenburg, p. 265.

20. Blanckenburg, p. 9.

21. Ibid., p. 254.

22. Martin Somerfeld, 'Romantheorie und Romantypus der Aufklärung', *DVLG*, iv (1926), p. 480.

23. Lämmert, p. 545.

24. Ed. Christian Felix Weisse, vol. xviii, 1, Leipzig, 1775.

25. Johann Jakob Engel, *Fragmente über Handlung, Gespräch und Erzählung*, Leipzig, 1774 (reprinted *Schriften*, iv, pp. 254 ff., Berlin, 1802); *Facsimile* ed. of 1774 (ed. Ernst Theodor Voss), Sammlung Metzler, 37, Stuttgart, 1965.

26. Cf. Becker, p. 8.

27. Ibid., p. 26.

28. Sengle, 'Der Romanbegriff . . .', pp. 176 ff.

29. Jean Paul [Friedrich Richter], *Sämtliche Werke*, i, 11, p. 232 (§ 69), Weimar, 1935.

30. Sengle, 'Der Romanbegriff . . .', p. 189.

31. Hegel, *Ästhetik* (ed. F. Bassenge), Berlin, 1955, p. 983 (cited by Sengle, 'Der Romanbegriff . . .', p. 189).

32. Jean Paul [Friedrich Richter], i, 11, p. 235 (§ 71).

33. Ibid.

34. Eduard Berend (ed.), Introduction to *Vorschule der Aesthetik*, p. xxii.

35. Lämmert, pp. 576 f. Blanckenburg's name, for instance, does not appear in the indices of either the Weimar edition (W.A.) nor in the Artemis edition (G.A.) of his works, although the latter is admirably thorough and includes his conversations. He also may not even have read Blanckenburg's review of *Werther* which came so near to his own point of view; cf. Peter Michelsen, *Laurence Sterne und der deutsche Roman des achtzehnten Jahrhunderts*, Palaestra, 232, Göttingen, 1962, p. 171.

36. W.A., i, 29, pp. 233 f. (*Dichtung und Wahrheit*, xiii).

37. See Johann Heinrich Merck, 'Über den Mangel des epischen Geistes in unserm lieben Vaterland', *Teutscher Merkur*, xxi (1778).

38. See Georg Christoph Lichtenberg, 'Vorschlag zu einem orbis pictus für deutsche dramatische Schriftsteller, Romanen-Dichter und Schauspieler', *Göttingisches Magazin der Wissenschaften und Literatur* (ed. G. C. Lichtenberg and Georg Forster), i, 3 (1780).

Die Leiden des jungen Werthers

GOETHE'S first novel *Werther*, published in 1774, heralded a new conception of love and revealed a new sensibility. We live in an age with very different views on love and with quite a different sensibility. Attention today is therefore focused on other aspects of the novel. It is, however, the touchstone of a great work of literature that it continues to move its readers, although the reading public comes to it with different intellectual and emotional expectations. A closer analysis of the work may perhaps tell us what response may still be expected.

Goethe was only twenty-four when, by a stroke of genius, he became the mouthpiece of his generation as the author of *Werther*. His fame was immediately established. The appearance of *Werther* also ended the provincialism of German literature.[1]

It has often been related how Goethe's own experience, above all his love for Lotte Buff in Wetzlar and his subsequent affection for Maximiliane La Roche in Frankfurt, provided much of the material for the novel. For two years he had carried this material in his mind. According to his own account, the suicide of a Wetzlar attaché, Jerusalem, the son of the most popular preacher of the German Enlightenment, served as a release; the story suddenly took shape in his mind. The letters in which Kestner, who had married Lotte Buff, related the details of Jerusalem's death, revealed to Goethe how close he had been mentally and emotionally to this unfortunate man. In his autobiography *Dichtung und Wahrheit* he described how the novel was then conceived. He writes:

> In my collection of weapons, which was pretty considerable, I possessed a valuable and well-sharpened dagger. I

> always laid it next to my bed, and before I put out the light I tried to see whether I could not sink the sharp point a few inches into my breast. As I was never able to do so, I finally laughed at myself, cast off all my hypochondriac caprices, and decided to continue living. In order to be able to do this calmly, however, I had to fulfil some poetic task, in which everything that I had felt, thought, and imagined about this important matter would find verbal expression. For this purpose I gathered together all the elements which had been fermenting in me for a couple of years, I visualized the situations which had caused me most affliction and anguish – but I could not give them shape, I needed some incident, some plot to embody them.
>
> Suddenly I learned of the death of Jerusalem. Immediately after hearing a report of it, I received the most exact and detailed description of the occurrence – and at that moment the plan for *Werther* came into being. The whole thing crystallized from all sides and became a solid mass, like water in a container which is just at freezing-point and is immediately turned to hard ice by the slightest shake.[2]

Goethe's account is in fact somewhat misleading;[3] for there was a considerable time-lag between Jerusalem's death in November 1772 and the writing of the novel in the spring of 1774. The biographers, however, took their cue from a statement of Goethe's in *Dichtung und Wahrheit*. He had said that he infused the novel of his youth with all that ardour which allows of no distinction between poetry and reality.[4]

A brief incursion into Goethe's biography may make the relationship between fiction and fact clearer. The story is well known.[5] After obtaining a degree in law at Strassburg University in August 1771 and spending a short while in Frankfurt as a practising lawyer, Goethe went in May 1772 to Wetzlar at the bidding of his father, who himself had spent some time there from 1734 to 1735, as had Goethe's grandfather Textor from 1717 to 1727. Wetzlar was – and had been for over a century – the seat of the *Reichskammergericht*, the supreme court of justice of the Holy Roman Empire. The court was as debilitated as the Empire itself. Its procedure was so sluggish that only about 200 cases could be settled in one year, and more than 16,000 cases were awaiting a hearing, some of them going back a long time, one even to the fifteenth century and another to the sixteenth. The cumbersome procedure of the court was even further slowed up by a commission appointed to clear up some of the cases; it was sitting at the time of Goethe's stay in Wetzlar. Goethe arrived in May 1722; he registered with the court on 25 May. There is no further evidence that he participated in its affairs, but this was not expected from a young lawyer studying the work of the court. Since neither the judicial procedure of the *Reichskammergericht* nor the social life surrounding it appealed to Goethe, the prospect of studying this quaint jewel of the Holy Roman Empire had not excited him.

Wetzlar presented a closely stratified society dominated by the court and its attendants who made up almost a quarter of its 5,000 inhabitants. This included not only the court officials, but also the members of the various legations of the German states, so this small town presented something like a microcosm of the Holy Roman Empire. Strict rules of precedence and conduct prevailed. Wetzlar was not at first sight a promising place for a young poet to live in, though, in fact, Goethe fared better than he might have expected. Surprisingly, he found congenial friends at the inn where he took his meals. These young men, mostly legation officials, had formed a group calling themselves the 'Knights of the Round Table'. They established rules of conduct, one of which was that each was known by a pseudonym. Not surprisingly, Goethe was called 'Götz von Berlichingen', for he had let it be known that he had been writing a play about the Knight with the Iron Hand. While Goethe was friendly with several members of this group, such as von Goué, Gotter and von Kielmannsegg, the man he came to know best was Johann Christian Kestner of Hanover, a secretary to the Hanoverian legation. Kestner, a serious-minded and intelligent man, assiduously carried out his duties which, since the Elector of Hanover was still also King of England, were not unimportant, given the context of the fossilized world of the court. Kestner had for four years been unofficially engaged to Lotte Buff, whose father managed the estates of the Teutonic Order near Wetzlar. Goethe met her at a ball in Volpertshausen, a village near Wetzlar, without knowing that she was engaged to Kestner, who arrived late at the ball. By the time he was apprised of the real situation he had fallen in love with her; his love was increased by seeing her not only as a gay companion at a dance, but also, when calling on her at her father's house the next day, as a serious housekeeper, for being in the household of a widower she carried much of the brunt of housekeeping.

Goethe was a frequent visitor to their spacious house and spent much time in Lotte's company. They were joined by Kestner whenever he could free himself from his official duties. While all three of them delighted in each other's company, Kestner was well aware of how precarious the situation was. He realized, as he wrote to a friend, how difficult it was for Goethe entirely to overcome his inclinations, although Goethe had in fact given up all hope of winning Lotte for himself. Lotte appears to have treated him sensibly and firmly, holding him in check and preventing any uncalled-for advances. When, on one occasion, he stole a kiss, he was sternly reprimanded and treated coldly for a while. Lotte, indeed, never gave any indication that she might have preferred Goethe to Kestner. Kestner, however, began to wonder whether he would be able to make Lotte happy, or whether he could bear living without her, but he felt he could not. At the end of August Kestner wrote Lotte a letter declaring that, while he was unable to do without her, he preferred to release her from her engagement. He warned Lotte, however, that Goethe's words might not necessarily mean what they appeared to. Apart from this, however, no slighting remark of Kestner's about Goethe is recorded, nor did he complain, although it cannot have been easy for him, when returning from work, to find his fiancée frequently in the presence of a remarkable young man. Kestner's dignified conduct stood him in good stead, for it only confirmed Lotte's love for him. She may have felt that Goethe's feelings for her, though sincere, were, in the last resort, unstable. Goethe finally felt a compelling need to escape from this unsatisfactory situation. He left without taking leave of his friends. Lotte, as Kestner noted in his diary, was indeed saddened at his departure, but was also glad that he was gone, since she could not grant him what he wished. Kestner too was deeply moved, although he had expected a sudden departure. He even warmly defended Goethe's manner of leaving when a common friend of theirs blamed him for this precipitate action.

From Wetzlar, Goethe went down the river Lahn to pay a visit to Sophie La Roche, the well-known novelist, at Ehrenbreitstein. He quickly became attracted to her daughter, Maximiliane, who was soon afterwards married to the Frankfurt merchant Brentano, an elderly widower with several children. In Frankfurt Goethe was a frequent caller at Brentano's house, until Brentano became jealous and put an end to his visits. This happened about a year and a half after Goethe's departure from Wetzlar. Almost as much time had elapsed since Goethe had, through Kestner, heard of the suicide of their common acquaintance, Karl Wilhelm Jerusalem, only two years older than Goethe, who had known him during his student days in Leipzig. Goethe thus wrote *Werther*, on which he started work soon after his break with the Brentanos, much later than he admitted in his autobiography.

Jerusalem was the son of a distinguished Brunswick theologian and himself a well-known figure in Wetzlar, where he was a secretary in the Brunswick legation. He appears to have been a strange, solitary man. He wrote on philosophical subjects, was interested in literature and liked solitude both in life and as depicted in literature. His tendency to depression was accentuated by a snub administered to him in the house of Count von Bassenheim, one of the senior judges of the *Reichskammergericht*. He had stayed on after lunch instead of leaving, as the rules of eighteenth-century German society required, when the Count's aristocratic *soirée* began. Some of the aristocrats complained. Count von Bassenheim, instead of protecting his young friend, appears to have politely asked him to leave. This snub became the talk of the town and appeared as a severe insult to Jerusalem who, in Brunswick, had frequently been invited to the ducal table, and whose family enjoyed the friendship of the heir to the ducal throne. To crown his misfortunes, Jerusalem fell in love with Frau Herd, a most beautiful and talented woman, the daughter of the Mannheim court sculptor Paul Egell and wife of the secretary of the legation of Pfalz-Lautern. His love was not returned, and disappointment increased his gloom. He was even heard to defend in public the right to suicide. Finally, he declared his love to Frau Herd who, greatly perturbed, rejected his advances, and asked her husband to tell him not to call on her again. Herd did so the next day, whereupon Jerusalem asked for Kestner's pistols with which, after having written farewell letters to his friends, he shot himself between midnight and one o'clock on the morning of 30 October 1772. Kestner sent Goethe a full account of Jerusalem's suicide and the events leading up to it.[6] Many of the incidents quoted by Kestner are mentioned in the novel; indeed, whole sentences were taken over. Even such details as those of *Emilia Galotti* lying open on his desk and no pastor being present at the funeral were taken from Kestner's letter. Evidently Goethe had been greatly affected by Jerusalem's death. When he returned to Wetzlar in November 1772 – Kestner was at that time absent from the city – he reputedly visited Jerusalem's grave.

The plot of *Werther* undoubtedly contains an amalgam of events and experiences from the lives of Goethe and Jerusalem; perhaps even more than we know of, for it may safely be assumed that even the most assiduous biographers have been unable to ferret out all parallels and prototypes, but enough has been discovered to show how deeply Goethe's fiction was related to fact and how much he adapted the facts for the purposes of fiction. The parallels are many; it would be tedious to relate them all. Let it suffice to say that Goethe and Werther share the same birthday, 28 August, and are of the same age, that each of them comes to the city in May; that each meets his Lotte at a ball in the country early in June; that both in the novel and in real life Lotte is the daughter of an *Amtmann*; that Goethe, on the eve of his departure from Wetzlar on 10 September, had a strange conversation with Kestner and Lotte about after-life, which Kestner mentioned in his diary and Goethe in his novel under the same dates; that Lotte Buff left Wetzlar for a short while to look after a sick friend, just as Werther's Lotte does; that Garbenheim, the Wahlheim of the novel, was frequently visited by Goethe and the Kestners; that both Goethe and Werther enjoyed nature and that both read Homer and *Ossian*. Even Werther's favourite lime-tree has been identified. There are also allusions to events in Frankfurt. There is even an explicit reference to a sermon by the Swiss theologian Johann Caspar Lavater, one of Goethe's friends to whom, in fact, he showed the novel before its completion.[7] In the first book, incidents from Goethe's life abound, and in the second book, incidents from the life of Jerusalem are mentioned, but they are not kept apart. The defence of suicide in the first book might have been Goethe's or Jerusalem's. Undoubtedly Goethe experienced the love of nature as well as the vacillating moods so typical of Werther; Werther's tendency to overrate his ability may represent Goethe's fears, but is likely to correspond to the actual conduct of Jerusalem. Yet some incidents, such as the snub administered at the *soirée*, the petty-minded ambassador, the esteem of the Prince in his native state, the growing desperation leading to suicide – all these instances recall Jerusalem's life-story.

Such a wealth of allusion makes it tempting to read the novel as a *roman à clef*. Kestner and Lotte were understandably the first to do so;[8] they saw themselves portrayed, but neither liked the portrait nor found it accurate. Kestner protested, especially since he felt (quite correctly, of course) that the portraits of Albert and Lotte did not do justice to him or to his wife.

To read the novel as a *roman à clef*, to think of it as a portrayal of fact, is to misunderstand the relationship between subject-matter and imaginative literature, between the sources and the finished product, between the material and the form. To read a novel with a view to rediscovering the 'real' happening, and to criticize the author for misrepresenting history or biography, is to misinterpret literature, which consists in the shaping of the material into a pattern, in creating a work of art with ingredients culled from fact; its realism does not rely on closeness to its source, but on internal coherence and, above all, on truthfulness to the spirit of the themes which are depicted. *Werther* is not a realistic novel because a reader discovers incidents which have happened or because Goethe took over sentences from Kestner. For even if these features were capable of making the work realistic, Goethe would still have to be taken to task for altering Kestner's accounts by omitting some scenes and altering others and varying the nature of the incidents. After all he did not give Lotte the personality of Lotte Buff, nor did he give her blue eyes, but the black ones of Maximiliane La Roche. He also let Werther cherish Lotte's silhouette to nurse his despair. Yet the author who had also received a similar gift with delight had by that time transferred his attention to another woman. Surely what makes a work of art realistic is neither reproduction of detail nor documentation; it is an inner truth which may reflect either strands of contemporary life or eternally valid features of human psychology.

An unhappy, unrequited love for a married woman together with the suicide of a high-minded young man given to philosophical enthusiasm thus formed the basic situation. Indeed, Goethe may have understandably believed that Jerusalem took the irrevocable step which a kinder fate, a more resilient character and a more richly endowed nature prevented him from taking himself. Werther is a young man who, as his name indicates (in German it suggests a worth-while person), merits regard. So did Jerusalem, who, as Goethe wrote to Sophie La Roche, was driven to this sad decision 'after anxious striving for truth and moral goodness had undermined his heart, a fate easily suffered by a noble heart and penetrating mind easily moved by extraordinary sentiments'.[9] Goethe may have felt fortunate that 'the qualities and high motives of philosophical speculation and love'[10] did not lead him, like Jerusalem, to disaster.

So much for the biographical background, which tells us much about the gestation of the work and little, if anything at all, about the work itself. The biographical approach has indeed not always been helpful. This trend was possible because so much biographical material was available. Goethe scholarship during the last four decades has taken a different turn; it is now more usual to consider the novel as a work of literature.[11]

Werther is the story of a young man who, through emotional imbalance, accentuated by an unhappy love-affair, finally commits suicide. Suicide is the most extreme action open to anyone in relation to himself. Boris Pasternak defines it in his autobiography:

> But a man who decides to commit suicide puts a full stop to his being, he turns his back on his past, he declares himself bankrupt and his memories to be unreal. They can no longer help or save him, he has put himself beyond their reach. The continuity of his inner life is broken, his personality is at an end. And perhaps what finally makes him kill himself is not the firmness of his resolve but the unbearable quality of this anguish which belongs to no one, of this suffering in the absence of the sufferer, of this waiting which is empty because life has stopped and can no longer fill it. . . .
>
> What is certain is that those who committed suicide all suffered beyond description, to the point where suffering has become a mental sickness. And, as we bow in homage to their gifts and to their bright memory, we should bow compassionately before their suffering.[12]

The novel opens with a preface by the editor, who has collected Werther's letters to his friend Wilhelm and commends the young man to our compassion. We read of Werther's first arrival in the small town, of his state of mind, of his meeting with Lotte (the daughter of a local official) with whom he falls in love. He discovers that she is betrothed to Albert, but this only makes him love her with an increasingly violent passion. Albert returns, and their points of view differ. Werther, for whom Lotte has become the centre of existence, realizes that he must not stay, and leaves. He enters the diplomatic service of a German principality, but he does not like the day-to-day routine. In society, he is snubbed by aristocrats as a mere member of the middle class. His impatience with the minister in charge of the legation leads him to resign from the service. In the meantime, Albert and Lotte have married. Werther decides to return. He does so after a short visit to his home town. His passion for Lotte passes all bounds. He is less and less able to control himself and becomes more and more distraught. Finally, after Lotte and he have read passages from Macpherson's *Ossian* together, he is unable to restrain himself any more and embraces her. They kiss one another passionately, but she immediately realizes that they have to part and asks him to leave her. Unable to do without Lotte, Werther despairs completely and shoots himself.*

To study the novel, we must first decide which of the two versions of the text we shall use; we must choose between the first version of 1774, which made the novel famous, and the second version of 1787, which was thoroughly revised and amended. Goethe had made important changes, which were, however, in the main the result of Goethe's maturity gained through his poetic work and administrative experience during the decade which had elapsed since his arrival in Weimar in 1775. Furthermore, he must

* We must not be misled in taking this account of the plot as a substitute for the novel itself. It can be no more than an attempt to indicate the main trend of the action. Indeed, any account of the plot must be inadequate, for it can never do justice to the form of the novel and may easily, by way of wrong emphasis, mislead the reader. It can, however, serve as a guide for those who have not yet read the novel or who remember it imperfectly, though to remember novels more or less imperfectly is our common lot.

have recognized that, as an author, he had to avoid any possible identification of himself with the hero, for he had been deeply disturbed by the impact of the novel, in which many had found a justification of suicide.[13]

Goethe, it is true, was as amused by some of the reactions to the novel as he was irritated by others. He was, however, bound to take notice of Kestner's, even if he judged it irrelevant. Kestner, who may well have been the first reader of the novel as a whole, thought it contained an inaccurate, indeed untruthful, portrait of himself and his wife. He disapproved of the characterization of Albert and Lotte, and particularly objected, it would appear, to Lotte's emotional response to Werther's passion. Goethe had sent the novel to Kestner who, as his complaints prove, was the first of a long line of readers to approach the work in the wrong way. Goethe answered these protests by seeking to calm his perturbed friend, promising revision at a later stage, and emphasizing the necessity of his writing the novel:

> Believe me, believe me; your worries, your *gravamina*, they will disappear like nocturnal phantoms if you are patient, and then – within one year I promise to cut out everything that a public keen on gossip has retained of suspicion, misinterpretation, etc. I shall do this just as the north wind drives away mists and odours, although the public is like a herd of swine. Werther must – must be. You do not feel *him*. You feel only me and yourselves.[14]

Yet when the public did not eschew the biographical fallacy, he still did not hasten to revise the novel. Only eight years after its appearance, in 1782, did he set out to prepare a second edition. Not until 1787, in a volume of his collected works published by Göschen, did the revised edition appear. The second edition differs from the first on some important points.

The examination of *Werther* in this book is based on the second edition. To do justice to the work and to unfold its implications, it is necessary to outline the principal differences between the two editions, and to establish the principles underlying the alterations.

Firstly, the language differs.[15] The changes are of detail, not of substance, and produce not a wholly altered impression but a somewhat different flavour. In the first edition, Goethe, under the influence of his own local Frankfurt dialect, did not use the standardized eighteenth-century German finally stabilized by Gottsched. In the second edition, he reverted to standard German, and to a large extent erased the traces of dialect and colloquial speech. He replaced unusual prefixes and prepositions by common ones. Above all, he softened the tone of Werther's letters. In 1774 he wrote a powerful, frequently unrestrained language characteristic of the *Sturm und Drang*. In 1787, after the first decade in Weimar, this tempestuous, exuberant tone no longer appealed to him. He struck out the drastic expressions of colloquial usage, which might offend conventional taste, and tidied up the syntactical structure to achieve smoother and more correct reading.

So much for changes in language. They all reveal the desire to be more factual, to be more objective, to let the characters speak simply and forcibly without linguistic frills which might distract attention from what they mean. They may make the work somewhat less spontaneous and its realism a shade less stark, but it is no less forceful. This 'improved' version bears the marks of a greater artistry, consciously employed to heighten the poetic effect of the novel.

Similar principles underlie the changes in content. In both editions, Werther dominates the work, but in the second, the editor's account takes up more space. It comes earlier in the novel, after the letter of 6 December instead of that of 17 December, which itself is re-dated 14 December. Several letters which preceded the editor's account now follow it. This interruption of the flow of Werther's letters, and thus of the crescendo of passion, retards the action by putting it in a slightly more distant perspective: the earlier the editor's voice is heard and the greater the space given to his detached point of view, so much the less is the immediacy of Werther's letters. But detachment implies objectivity. This change is, of course, in line with Goethe's own development, for he revised *Werther* at a time when he no longer cared to portray personal feeling directly in narrative prose, but reserved it for lyric poetry. The early years in Weimar had taken their toll of extreme subjectivity; a more objective attitude made it imperative to criticize unrestrained feeling and to insist on a balanced portrait.

The main changes, however, affect both Werther's relations to the other two main characters, Lotte and Albert, and the relationship between these two characters.[16] In the first version, Lotte's feelings become involved with Werther to a greater degree than in the second. She appears, to some extent, emotionally torn between Werther and Albert. Certainly, in the end, she follows the dictates of duty, but it almost appears as if it were duty rather than love which makes her side with Albert. In the second version, there are a number of additional touches which emphasize Lotte's ignorance of Werther's emotions, as well as her naïveté and innocence. For instance, there is her displeasure at Werther's thinking that a letter which she had written to Albert was addressed to him. Then there is the incident where she plays with the canary which she allows to peck at her mouth. Werther has difficulty in controlling his passion, as he finds this scene so suggestive, but Lotte is totally unaware of the impression it makes on Werther. In addition, in the first version Lotte's distress is much greater after Werther has embraced her. She dreads the return of Albert whose coldness then inhibits every conversation. She feels guiltier than in the second version. Here, indeed, Lotte is never fully conscious of the conflict, nor can it be said that she has fallen passionately in love with Werther. In the first version her relations with Albert become truly strained. She is afraid of the tone of voice in which he might refer to Werther. In turn, he appears suspicious of her; he virtually quarrels with her and leaves his disapproval of Werther's frequent visits in no doubt. Albert is to a much greater extent seen through the eyes of Werther. It is not an attractive portrait, for he appears to him a philistine who does not deserve Lotte. Albert even goes so far as to tell Lotte not to go on seeing Werther, at least for the sake of appearances and so as to avoid arousing comment. Lotte is also much more moved when Werther calls on her towards the end of the novel. In the second version, however, she is to a much greater degree unaware of any impact which Werther may have made on her. Albert too acts in a more kindly manner. He always welcomes Werther. He is much calmer in the final stages of the novel, while in the first version he appears at this juncture expressly hostile to Werther, and even shows impatience with Lotte.[17]

The greatest single addition, apart from the expanded account of the editor, is the story of the young farm labourer who has fallen in love with a widow for whom he works. He is encouraged by her, but is later disappointed because she prefers another servant to him. In his disappointment and despair he kills his rival. Werther feels akin to a man who feels desperate enough to commit murder to achieve his aim, or rather, to prevent someone else enjoying the love of his beloved. In reality, however, the situation is different, because the widow encouraged the boy, who had some reason to believe that his love was returned. His passion is, so to speak, grounded in fact and not in his own imagination. The episode makes the difference between Werther's hopes and Lotte's reaction stand out. It makes it plainer that Lotte does not, in fact, love Werther, but genuinely loves her husband.

There is, however, another deepening of perspective in the second version which results from Werther's greater self-awareness. We learn only in the second version, for instance, that he keeps a diary, the reading of which brings forth the lucidity of his mind and his weakness of will in face of passion.

The first version gives us a more one-sided and passionate account of Werther's sorrows. It should be given prominence if the primacy of feeling and the immediate impact of the novel were under review. In 1824, Goethe summed up its effect in retrospect:

> It was really the first publication of the novel, through its violent, unconditional character, which achieved the great impact; I do not wish to decry the later editions, but they are mellowed and lack the same spontaneous life.[18]

But since this account is concerned with Goethe's achievement as a novelist, the aesthetically more satisfying second version must be discussed, although the earlier version is perhaps somewhat livelier.

Goethe succeeded in carrying out his intention as defined in a letter to Kestner:

> In hours of leisure I again took up my Werther without changing what had aroused the original sensation. I intend to raise it a few steps higher. It was also my intention to characterize Albert in such a way that the passionate youth [Werther], but not the reader, was able to misunderstand him.[19]

In addition, it was the second version to which Goethe gave

authoritative approval by including it in the standard edition of his collected works, published in his lifetime. The second version, therefore, will be the basis of our study.

If we wish to consider the novel as a work of literature, we must first take into account the impression which the work as a whole leaves on us. Concentration on the inner life of one individual in *Werther* makes this task easier than would be the case with a longer novel. The wealth of imagery and the power of the language may be obstacles to a detached consideration because they stir up the reader's emotions, but it is precisely in its imagery and its language that the inner coherence of the novel is found.

Die Leiden des jungen Werthers is an epistolary novel, following a prevailing fashion in fiction.[20] Yet as an epistolary novel it is quite different from its immediate predecessors: Richardson's *Pamela* and Rousseau's *Nouvelle Héloïse*.[21] It is much more compact, and it is the more powerful for its compactness. Confronted with one person's letters, the reader's interest is focused on him alone; Werther, indeed, does not possess a proper antagonist. Concentration on one person alone affords a much deeper insight into his feeling and thinking than into the inner life of the other characters. We gain an impression of Albert, of Lotte and of Wilhelm, but we learn very little about their emotions. According to some critics, the novel is a diary in disguise;[22] yet to be precise, it is neither the one nor the other; for the editor has the last word in the decisive moment of the action. Of course, Werther's letters often resemble diary-entries. Nonetheless, they constitute only one half of a correspondence, the other half of which we are not given. They present replies to letters received, and in turn demand replies. But they are letters which always centre round their author's inner life. Werther soliloquizes;[23] often he speaks not so much to Wilhelm as to his own heart. He is concerned more with his own experience than with the effect of his outpourings on the recipient. His letters resemble a confession.[24] He notes down thoughts at the very moment of experiencing them, and never attains any distance from the occasion that moves him. Since Werther, however, notes only the heights of his experience,[25] the novel gains in power and coherence. It approximates to drama, to tragedy, for in drama, a more economical literary form, the plot is concentrated on what is essential. It moves within narrower confines than the novel.

The most obvious feature of the novel's structure is the division into two parts. This division is significant. The first book spans the period from 4 May to 10 September 1771, from the time of Werther's arrival in the small town to his departure. It takes him from the unsettled mood of his first letters, through the beginning and growth of his passion for Lotte, to his attempt to free himself from his passion by leaving. It prepares the catastrophe, but the crisis is as yet averted. In the second book, Werther has turned his back on the place and on the cause of his sorrows, but this detachment is only an apparent one: distance does not liberate him from his passion. He returns only to become more enslaved. The second book thus spans the period from the months of his self-chosen exile, when he seeks to live the life of an ordinary man, to his death. This division into books clearly reveals two cycles, one ending in an escape to freedom, the other in an escape by death, even if the latter be an escape conceived in a misguided way; for Werther believes that death leads to freedom.

The first impression leaves no doubt at all about the main issue of the novel. The centre of the work is Werther's inner experience, and his experience is determined by his emotions. Werther's own language proves this. He often writes sentences of an explosive nature, following the pattern of *Sturm und Drang* writing. His sentences are frequently ungrammatical, or they are mere exclamations, or only half-completed. Much of the narrative indeed consists of lyrical outbursts, which is certainly appropriate, since their purpose is to reveal the tale of Werther's emotional life.

Parallels in the structure of the two books can be perceived. Each book can conveniently be divided into three parts. In the first book, there are three periods of almost forty days each: firstly, the time before Werther comes to know Lotte (4 May–16 June 1771), secondly, the happy time of his friendship with her from 16 June to 30 July 1771, the day of Albert's arrival, and thirdly, the time before his departure on 10 September 1771.[26] In the second book, a similar tripartite division can be noticed: firstly, the period which Werther spends at the court, secondly, the time covering his return to his home town, and finally, the last months between his return and his death. His farewell to Lotte at the end of the first book and his death at the end of the second book also afford a parallel. Although there are other similarities, there are not enough of them to permit a detailed comparison of the structure of the two books.

Each of them, in fact, corresponds to a phase in Werther's emotional life. The two books do not cover an equal length of time. If, however, we measure time not quantitatively or conceptually – i.e. by the clock – but qualitatively or perceptually – i.e. by duration or intensity (to use either Henri Bergson's or Karl Pearson's term respectively) – we are confronted with two parts of equal emotional import briefly interrupted by an interlude not belonging to either. Each of them corresponds to the seasons which it mainly describes; the first to spring and summer, the second to autumn and winter.[27] The illusion is almost conveyed that the whole action took place within one year. The first part represents the growth and height of Werther's passion, the second its decline and Werther's final isolation and death. It is true that the interlude lasts almost a year, but the reader does not pay much attention to it in terms of the emotional course of the story. A number of events take place during this period between 10 September 1771 and 4 September 1772, but it is passed over lightly without any explicit reference to the seasons; the hero's emotional life is in the doldrums. The time of narration thus appears much shorter than the time which is narrated. Economy of presentation provides a concentrated picture. About the mood of the action there is no doubt. It is intimated by the title, the preface and the first letters. Werther carries within himself the seeds of self-destruction, which can be detected from the very beginning by the careful observer. Werther is thus doomed to death, and Goethe tells his story with irony and detachment. He has to give a psychological explanation for the hero's suicide, to portray Werther's end as a necessary consequence of his life, and to mould the material at his disposal into a work of literature.

Werther's very first words ('How glad I am to be away! My dear friend, what a thing is the human heart![28]) point to his predicament, the cue being given by the word *Herz* (heart), a word the meaning of which differs slightly, however, at times, according to the context.[29] Here is Werther's habit of reflecting on his feelings, of combining his reflections into a definite point of view, and of projecting this personal point of view as a generalization about life.[30] Werther views the world exclusively from his own angle. His own feeling is, for him, the criterion for judging mankind as a whole, but he is incapable of sustaining general reflections for long. His thoughts, as if under compulsion, revert to himself. Repetition of the word 'I' in the first sentences confirms this tendency which runs through the whole work. Werther is egocentric. For him, as for many egocentrics, his own past experiences are much more important than the presence of others. His promises to mend his ways are not convincing. No one is likely to believe him when he writes:

> I will, dear friend, I promise you, I will mend my ways; I will no longer ruminate over what little misfortunes Fate doles out to us, as I have always done. I will enjoy the present and have done with the past. You are quite right, my dearest friend, men's sufferings would be less if they did not occupy their imagination so intensely – God knows why they are made like that – in recalling the memory of bygone ills instead of trying to bear an indifferent present.[31]

Yet later on in the same letter we read of the tears which he sheds for Count M because he is moved when thinking back upon the Count's sensitivity.

Similarly, his proficiency in practical matters must be doubted. He writes with assurance that he will settle a business matter of his mother's most expeditiously, yet no proof is forthcoming that he is really doing so: all we learn is that he finds it tedious to write about it.

He does not wish to discipline his emotions; on the contrary, he wants to surrender to the moment without restraint. Action is not prompted by circumspection or order; his actions and thoughts are motivated by the claims of the heart. Thus he does not want to stay in the town, but wishes to flee into nature. We sense that any environment which would offer him fruitful practical activity would be repugnant to him.

These indications become more prominent in the next letters. Emotion dominates Werther's thought and activity. He is neither able nor willing to master his feelings. He thus begins the letter of 10 May with the following words: 'My whole soul is filled with a wonderful serenity, like the delightful spring mornings which I enjoy with all my heart.'[32] He abandons himself so completely to the feeling of serenity that it is hardly accurate to call his state of mind serene. He holds nothing back; his whole heart is given up to feeling. He is lost in it and never attains that detachment which can be acquired through clarity of mind and emotional stability alone. His enthusiastic attitude towards nature confirms this; he feels that he is an artist, a painter, but forgets that it is not feeling but creative achievement which alone makes a man an artist. He is able to express his emotion only by writing letters. He is an artist as a writer of letters, but certainly not as a painter. He indeed senses the power of nature, but his attitude, whether it be towards religion, nature or the past, is always unrealistic. His language indicates this; the very image which Werther uses in speaking of art, the image of the mirror, betrays the inadequacy of his point of view. Art is not, as he maintains, a mirror of the soul. Just because he is incapable of detaching himself from experience and of recreating God and nature in the mirror of art does he end his confession with the exclamation: 'My friend – but it brings about my ruin, and I am crushed by the power of this glorious vision.'[33]

These themes are further developed in the next letter of 12 May. Although Werther wallows in his feelings, he is able to describe them with powerful intensity. He does not understand them, but he knows how to depict them. The external world appears to him unreal. He must ask himself whether this sense of unreality is brought about through 'delusive spirits' or through 'the divine and ardent fancy of his heart'.[34] Emotion overcomes him when he sees girls fetching water from the well; for him, this scene immediately becomes an image of patriarchal existence. Since he feels deeply, he demands a similar depth of experience from others; this claim is upheld with moral power.

In order to protect his feelings, Werther also desires to protect himself against external interference. He rejects ideas, if they do not guide, encourage or inspire him. He finds criticism disagreeable and hence undesirable. He is aware of the instability of his feelings, for he writes: 'You have not seen anything so restless, so changeable as this heart.'[35] On the one hand, he expects Homer to calm his feelings; on the other, he does not want to cure himself of this inner disquiet, but only wants to lull it for the moment. Frequently it looks as if he actually enjoys his own self-torture (another parallel to Rousseau[36]).

Just as Werther is disinclined to fit into the normal pattern of life, so is he unwilling to see the world in a traditional, accepted manner. His radical views are intelligible as those of a young rebel – but at the same time he loves what is old and admires a patriarchal mode of living. Within him conflicting tendencies, which he is unable to control, struggle with one another. The letters of 13 and 15 May are therefore dictated by various moods. Again, these moods are given the status of universal laws, because for Werther the world of his private emotion is a symbol of the whole cosmos. Each time his mood changes, the change is reflected in a changing view of the world. At times the world appears monotonous and full of constraint and man unworthy of his freedom: in the letter of 22 May, for instance, he emphasizes that concentration on his own emotions cannot be fruitful or creative for him. The world appears dream-like, his vision is impaired. Nonetheless, he asserts that others are mistaken, while he, in all humility, claims to know the purpose of life. Strange humility! For does he not believe that he can look down proudly on others because he has retained inner freedom, the courage to leave the world while all other men cling to life?

In the next letter (of 26 May), however, we find him expressing a different point of view, which though not absolutely incompatible with, is at least completely opposed to, the view upheld in the previous letter. This time, confined existence is welcome. The image of the hut, which, for Goethe, always means restriction in domesticity, in the narrow sphere,[37] symbolizes this view. Yet how far away Werther is from an ordered, placid life! His attitude to nature shows this; he rejects all rules in favour of nature and forgets that nature has its own rules. Similarly, he savagely caricatures the love of the ordinary man who realizes that, in practical life, the pursuit of love cannot be an activity which consumes all his time and energy. He condemns this sensible view as that of a philistine. He is moved by seeing a peasant leading a quiet, simple life, but immediately afterwards passionate feeling, and not tranquillity, arouses his enthusiasm. His lack of detachment becomes even clearer when he mistakenly believes that he is a poet because he merely experiences the desire to describe a poetic scene. He mistakes recognition of the potential raw material of poetry for the act of poetic creation itself. His one-sided vision stems from his desire to retain the emotions caused by sense-impressions. So when he hears of a young farm-labourer's love for a farmer's widow, he immediately espouses his point of view, because it is the point of view of passion.

Such is the portrait of Werther before he meets Lotte. In him are all the tendencies which make it inevitable that his passion will drive him to ruin. They are typified by the confusion and imprecision of his mind, by his indecision and his longing for the absolute. Werther refuses to accept the external world and loses himself in the apparent fullness of his inner life. The contrast between his inner life and external reality eventually becomes greater and greater, until it finally destroys him. Not love, but his unfortunate temperament destroys him. Goethe said as much himself in a letter written at the time when he was writing *Werther*:

> I have done many new things. I have written a story with the title *Die Leiden des jungen Werthers* in which I depicted a man who, endowed with a deep and pure sensibility and genuine lucidity of mind, loses himself in speculation until at last an unhappy passion overwhelms him and he puts a bullet through his head.[38]

The features of Werther's character which render the final disaster inevitable are intimated, but intimated to the careful observer only. For in the eyes of his friends, of whom Wilhelm is the prototype, Werther is perhaps excessively sensitive or passionate, but by no means diseased. Of course, Wilhelm cannot really be expected to have scrutinized Werther's letters as if he were a psychiatrist. Werther himself does not entertain any doubt as to the essential rightness of his mode of living. Wilhelm sees contradictions in his thought, but they do not appear to alarm him. Werther is accepted in middle-class society without any difficulty. Lotte's father, an official (*Amtmann*)* and a man of experience, welcomes him in his home; the minister, a man of wide practical knowledge, invites him to join the diplomatic service; and even the Prince treats him benignly. From the first Werther contains the germs of

* A word difficult to translate exactly. In real life Lotte Buff's father was in charge of the estates of the Teutonic Order near Wetzlar.

the disease, but it is only when his emotions become involved in a situation which denies him all satisfaction that they break out, so that other people slowly begin to suspect his condition, even if they never fully grasp it. The petrifaction of his emotions, his refusal to accept the external world as it is and to learn from it what it can teach him, his unswerving reliance on his inner life – all this destroys him.

To see the difference between *Werther* and earlier novels, it is only necessary to compare Goethe's style with the style of Richardson, Rousseau and Wieland. Although Wieland was the most important German novelist before Goethe, his style in his major novels – *Don Sylvio von Rosalva*, *Agathon*, *Der Goldene Spiegel* and *Die Geschichte der Abderiten* – is much more circumscribed than Goethe's. These novels eschew the tragic or the lyrical. Wieland writes elevated prose, but it always remains within the bounds of rococo classicism. A subtle art has formed it. Its quality is unimpeachable; wit, irony and serious thought are combined in a masterly manner.[39] The heart, however, never prevails over the head. Feeling and thought are evenly balanced; there is no real tension between them. But despite all his skill, Wieland never arouses a spontaneous reaction in the reader, and he speaks to man's reason rather than to his feelings.

It would be unfair to judge Richardson or Rousseau in translation, for the translations of their novels did not make a distinguished contribution to German prose. But even in the original, Richardson's prose does not amount to much. Though capable of freshness in dialogue, he can descend to flatness. He is not a great stylist. Rousseau's style has greater power and influence; at times, in *Les rêveries d'un promeneur solitaire*, he departs from the established rhythm of French classical prose, but this is not so in *La Nouvelle Héloïse*. Although it reads well and is lively, it is not a turning-point in French or European writing, nor is it famed for linguistic innovation.

Werther is a different case. To gain for his work a new reading public and to express the ambitions and hopes of this reading public, Goethe forged a new style. This style was not all of a piece; it was thus able to appeal to different levels of readers. Above all, Werther's own language speaks to all men who feel, and there are very few whose emotions have never been stirred and who have never felt the power of passion.

There are, apart from passages from *Ossian*, two styles in the novel: firstly, that of the editor, who tells his story with objective calm and sovereign superiority, and secondly that of Werther himself, whose tone is passionate. The editor's language is perhaps best described by the words which he applies to the story of Werther. 'It is simple. . . . What can we do except carefully set down what we have been able to collect through persistence.'[40]

The editor's use of words is economical. He concentrates on what is essential to Werther's story, and we are led to believe that he confronts us only with carefully selected documents. Only when he depicts extreme emotions does he heighten his language by the accumulation of sentences containing rhetorical questions and exclamations. Only then does the language instil in us a sense of passion. This is particularly effective, as it frames the action in sober prose which never loses its detachment, even when recounting the climax of Werther's passion and his suicide. Nonetheless, it is never monotonous.

Conveying the immediacy of experience is the foremost function of Werther's own epistolary style. We can, however, detect two distinct modes in his writing: the quasi-lyrical and the epic. The quasi-lyrical predominates. The opening sentences of the first letter set the tone, with alternate exclamatory and interrogative sentences separated by statements which interrupt the flow of lyrical speech and represent an intrusion of the intellect. By combining these three kinds of sentence, a compound is created which brings Werther's increasing unrest into the open. Suppressed feelings explode in an exclamation which interrogative sentences have led up to: repetitions are skilfully used to indicate the intensity of feeling, the unremitting emphasis on emotional experience.

The fourfold repetition of 'I will'[41] in the first sentences of the first letter is a verbal equivalent of Werther's desperate attempt to assert his own ego and to convey the impression that he wants, at all costs, to overcome his inner self-doubt. This mode of writing is employed again and again.

Another device of Werther's style is the interruption of orderly speech. There are more and more incomplete sentences towards the end of the novel which are interrupted by exclamations. They also refute Werther's own contention that he does not like the use of the *Gedankenstrich* (the dash). They reveal a passionate inner movement. Within a single sentence there can be a shift from one type of sentence to another, as if reflecting the changing tensions of a highly-strung mind. The very abruptness of the change indicates that Werther's speech is determined by emotion, not by reason, that it is spontaneous, not reflective, that it bursts into immediate expression without thought. Only after he has spoken does he examine what he has said.

Closely related to this is another sentence structure, revealing yet another side of Werther's character and outlook, of which the letter of 13 May 1771 provides the first complete example (although instances may be found earlier). Here the sentences balance one another like two equal weights in a pair of scales. Their antithesis reveals the contrast between the outer and inner worlds which in the end imposes so great a strain on Werther. For he confronts the outer world with the claims of his own inner being. When Wilhelm reminds him that the external world cannot be ignored, Werther vehemently protests his agreement. Yet he gives in to the urging of his heart at the expense of his reason. He proposes his own solution to his problem: he will protect himself from his dependence on the outward world by excluding himself from it. A precarious balance between the inner life and the outer world is thus created, but it is a balance that does not last.

Yet another sentence is the long period beginning with a large number of subsidiary clauses. The first sentence of this kind is found in the letter of 10 May 1771.

> My whole soul is filled with a wonderful serenity, like the delightful spring mornings which I enjoy with all my heart. I am alone and am completely happy with my life in this spot which was made for souls like mine. I am so happy, my dearest friends, so absorbed in the feeling of tranquillity, that my art is suffering. I could not draw a line at the moment, and yet I have never been more of a painter than I am now. When the mist is rising from the lovely valley and the sun rests upon the impenetrable shade of my forest, so that only now and then a ray steals into the inner sanctuary; when I lie in the tall grass by the rushing brook, and discover a thousand different grasses on the ground, when I feel

nearer my heart the teeming little world among the stalks, the innumerable, unfathomable creatures, the worms and insects, and when I feel the presence of the Almighty Spirit, who created us all in His image, the breath of the All-loving One who sustains us as we float in illimitable bliss – Oh! my friend, when the world then grows dim before my eyes and earth and sky are absorbed into my soul like the form of a beloved, I am consumed with longing and think, ah! would that I could express it, would that I could breathe on to the paper what is wholly alive and warm within me, so that it might be the mirror of my soul as my soul is the mirror of the eternal God. My friend – but it brings about my ruin, and I am crushed by the power of this glorious vision.[42]

This type of sentence too, is imbued with deep feeling, but it gives it a different form. The subordinate clauses overshadow the main clause almost completely; they could hardly 'humiliate' it more.[43] A powerful urge drives the speaker onward, moving at a tremendous pace, which ends in a final explosion with the exclamation: 'Ah, would that I could express it, would that I could breathe on to the paper what is wholly alive and warm within me.' This exclamation, however, is only an interlude; there is a new intensification which, on a sharply rising note, leads to a new exclamation: 'My friend'. Suddenly another note is struck, starting with the word 'But', as if exhaustion makes further speech impossible. The sentence then falls suddenly as if from a great height; after a weary sigh, 'My friend – but it brings about my ruin', it ends in a final brief reflection: 'I am crushed by the power of this glorious vision'. Werther's yearning, the urge of his feeling and the demands of his nature, and his passion to grasp the absolute in this finite world, gain strength as his feelings burst forth.

This celebrated letter presents 'a genuine diagram of passion'.[44] A poetic illusion is created which may serve as a symbol expressive of feeling. Although the style is new in German fiction, it derives from a long tradition going back to the patristic rhetoric of the fourth century, and in particular to Gregory of Nyssa. Goethe may or may not have been conscious of its ancestry, but this type of sentence was known in Herder's circle as a 'homiletic battle-order'.[45] To quote the perceptive description of two eminent critics, it is:

> a sustained, swelling and elaborately incapsulated protasis (actually there are eleven clauses, but the impression is of nine arranged in a group of three) followed by the dying fall of a far briefer apodosis. By this means, Goethe created the very semblance of the Neo-Platonic soaring of the soul towards its creator and its sighing despair of ever being able to express the divine affinity it feels. Embedded as it is here in the language of confession the figure foregoes its 'rhetorical' fervour and becomes a pure analogue of the felt life within. An analogue of its movements and contours – and of its ambivalences, too. For without benefit of narrator, by the sheer rise of the words put into the mouth of this as yet unsuspecting hero (it is the reader's prescience, not his, that makes, the 'Ich gehe zugrunde'* at the end of the letter so ominous) Goethe lays bare the seeds of self-destruction in this particular mode of ecstasy.[46]

Werther's feeling springs from the dark caverns of his subconscious. His ego cannot resist it; for even when he makes an attempt to do so in a main clause, his attempt is overridden by another elemental outburst in the subsequent subsidiary sentences. In the end, Werther is forced to succumb to this power; he becomes a prisoner of his inner life. The power of his emotions is too great; they dominate the outer world, just as the pressure of the subsidiary clauses overwhelms the main clause. His intellect is at the mercy of his feelings; it does not provide a counterweight to them.

Dialogue is, on the whole, sparingly used in the novel. Since it is simple and spontaneous, its effect is natural. The first dialogue, in the letter of 15 May, is typical. Simple sentences tell us how immediate the impact of the outer world is on Werther's mind. Another more abstract kind of dialogue found in Werther's heated controversy with Albert reveals his inability to accept contradiction. His reaction to the objections of others makes him more and more tense as the argument proceeds.

The second style used by Werther is completely different. It is epic. If emotional sentences represent the lyrical part of the novel, showing its closeness to the lyric poetry of Goethe's *Sturm und Drang*, his epic style strikes a different note. The language is not

* 'It brings about my ruin', literally 'I am dying'.

so excited. There are few lengthy subsidiary clauses, but the preponderance of main clauses never becomes awkward or heavy. Short sentences, interrogative sentences without predicates, and dialogue give the language a liveliness of its own. Again this liveliness results from Werther's inner participation in the events, and the language reveals it. Very often Werther's first, balanced sentences reflect an attempt to be objective, but he cannot sustain this mood. His epic descriptions do not last. He is moved, and his language again betrays the rise of passion. Frequently sentences occur where there is an accumulation of subsidiary clauses or where the main clauses burst into exclamation. This epic, or semi-epic, style does not occur towards the end of the second book. By that time Werther is too greatly disturbed to be capable of using a more leisured, objective style of writing. The function of the objective observer is taken over by the editor.

Werther's own words do not suffice to exhaust the whole scope of his vision of the world. To extend the scope of his feeling he alludes to poetry which conveys more than he is able to say. He refers to Homer, to a poem of Klopstock's, and, finally, he and Lotte read from *Ossian*. The function of these passages translated from *Ossian* is to emphasize Werther's spiritual disease for, as Goethe is reported to have said to Henry Crabb Robinson, 'while Werther is in his senses he talks about Homer and only after he grows mad is in love with Ossian'.[47] For him, then, the language of *Ossian* stands for savagery and extravagance of feeling, which he himself delights in. The tragic note of *Ossian*'s poetry prepares for Werther's suicide. The passages from *Ossian* also confront Werther, and even more Lotte, with the latent implications of their relationship; at the same time, they serve as a poetic parallel to Werther's own experience.

The style of the novel is not only expressed in Werther's language, but also in the structure of his letters. If we consider the structure of the individual letters, we see that Werther does not write according to a plan; his letters are too natural for that. Their structure varies, and a consistent principle of composition does not emerge. But structural variation follows a rhythm which gives life to the letters.[48] Description, exploration of feeling, objective statements and reflective generalizations follow one another, though there is no definite, immutable order of the different parts. All combinations and permutations are possible. They vary just as the tempo of some of the letters varies. The latter variety reflects Werther's youthful, emotional unrest. No letter is without feeling. His heart is never silent even when it sounds in a minor key.

Similarly, there is no distinct design in the sequence of letters as a whole. But here, too, are definite rhythmic changes.[49] An impression of strong emotional movement is conveyed by the change from letters describing idyllic scenes to those charged with emotion. At the beginning there is a balance between these two types of letters. Near the end of the first book, Werther's emotions master his pen, though the book ends with a letter which is mainly descriptive. In the second book, there are a number of descriptive passages, corresponding to Werther's absence from Lotte, but towards the end, the upsurge of his feeling prevents his continuing in this manner. The last letters present a pathological intensification of feeling.

Stylistic analysis makes it quite clear that Werther's language reflects his highly emotional inner life, but also leaves no doubt that his inner life is affected by his language. The power and manner of his speech allow him to enslave his reason, to make it a servant of his passion. His language reveals and furthers his confusion of mind and progressive disintegration.

There are some individual words which in themselves illuminate the nature of Werther's suffering. From among them one word – *Einschränkung* (restriction) – may be singled out as revealing Werther's temperament and thought most distinctly.[50] It recurs again and again in a significant context and can thus be termed a key-word. Unlike other expressions which he uses to express his sense of spiritual aridity, this word does not come from the language of Pietism, the great religious movement of the seventeenth and eighteenth centuries in Germany,[51] a movement which emphasized and sought to cultivate the inner life. Pietism also inculcated personal piety and a highly emotional attitude to the scriptures. From its strong inward religiosity, Werther's sensibility is largely derived.

Undoubtedly Werther's emotions are genuine. He does not suffer silently, but delights in pouring out his feelings into his letters. These letters do not help him to regain his composure, but raise his emotional temperature even further, for writing about his feelings corroborates his belief in his approach to life; at times, Werther gives the impression that he is seeking to enslave his mind by his words. He is, after all, a precursor of Romanticism, a movement in which language was frequently no longer the servant, but became the master of the writer.[52] Werther's monomaniac delight in recording his suffering by virtual soliloquy, the emotional flavour of his thought, the lyrical intensity of his passion, all point to an impact of language on his mind and emotion, for it requires more detachment than Werther is capable of to be entirely unaffected by the words which we use, to escape from the interaction between style and thought. Language can be a powerful moulder of minds; it is rarely content to remain an expression of a man's inner life.

This word *Einschränkung* emphasizes the polarity which determines Werther's inner life, the conflict between the limitations imposed upon man and his urge for freedom. Werther sees himself as a wanderer whose striving will not admit of any restraint. Life appears monotonous and intolerable. He does not want to accept the limits imposed by his senses. Yet at the same time he delights in the experience of his senses so unconditionally that he becomes even more limited than is necessary or wise. His inability to reconcile these polar conflicts into a harmonious mode of being is at the root of his misfortune. His vacillating attitude towards this problem is reflected in the various shades of meaning which this word *Einschränkung* possesses in the novel. Sometimes he delights in it and rejoices in the pleasure of a restricted way of life. At the other extreme, the restrictions appear to him an absolutely unbearable imprisonment. Finally, the word is used to condemn his mode of living, as he enmeshes himself in the cocoon of his own narrow, though intense, vision of the world.

Werther's attitude to nature is likewise determined by his feelings which, although powerful, remain indistinct. The new sensibility, greatly indebted to Rousseau, speaks here too, expressing a feeling for the value and the power of nature and rejecting the conventional eighteenth-century view. It brings *Werther* close to Goethe's *Sesenheim* lyrics, where his new sense of nature was triumphantly proclaimed in song, and a new vision of the world emerged. Nature and human emotions are closely intertwined. Spring is, for him, not an abstract image but an immediate experience. Every blossom, every hedge becomes a revelation. Werther enjoys spring in full measure, but this enjoyment corresponds to the feeling that nature is only a projection of his own inner being. He is looking to nature for a confirmation of his own self. When he wallows in his feelings, he looks for satisfaction in the beauties of nature. He believes that nature makes an artist out of him and that it guarantees the existence and depth of his emotions. He also believes that the ardent, sacred, inner life of nature has become accessible to him.

> How often have I longed to be borne on the wings of the crane flying above my head to the shores of the immeasurable ocean, to quaff the swelling rapture of life from the foaming goblet of the infinite, and to feel for but a moment the restricted energy of my soul extended by one drop of the bliss of that Being who brings forth all things in and through Himself.[53]

By regarding nature not as something which exists in its own right, but as dependent for its existence on his feelings, Werther misunderstands it and becomes, in his later moments of despair, estranged from it. He even calls it a monster. This egocentric view of nature reflects his intrinsic one-sidedness; admiration for and rejection of nature each correspond to one of his moods.

The seasons, too, are for him the scenery of his inner life; he notices them only when he can connect them with his feelings. While in moments of joy he delights in nature, it becomes hostile and monstrous in hours of despair. This close interweaving of nature and feeling is a new departure in fiction; it gives the novel a dimension of its own.

Werther's attitude to religion corresponds to his attitude to nature. For him, nature is not God's creation, but the mirror of his soul. For Werther is a man who believes himself to be independent of God, but who, nonetheless, is still dependent on God.

Werther is neither an atheist nor an agnostic; he believes in God, but his God is not the God of Christianity or any other religion. He is completely unorthodox. His views are at times contradictory, but we must not expect the consistency which is mandatory for a theologian. He wants to speak directly to God, and believes that he does not need the mediation of Christ. He believes in a transcendental God, but God is, for him, also the spirit visible in nature, and nature inspires him to think of God and to participate in His activity. His language indicates that he does not clearly distinguish between God and His creation.[54] God, in a sense, appears to him as the creative spirit of the world.

Intensity of feeling also leads him astray in his religious judgements. On the one hand, he believes that when a child bathes its face in water, its action possesses the quality of baptism; on the other, he regards as superstitious a man who claims to be enlightened, and, therefore, ridicules Werther's belief, but permits his child to be baptized. But this proves how far Werther is removed from Christian tradition. Isolated by his feelings, he is incapable of distinguishing between superstition and ecclesiastic tradition, between feeling and custom. He takes an unorthodox view of baptism, one of the two Lutheran sacraments, and later on he thinks of violating the sanctity of marriage. His attitude springs from spiritual pride and over-reliance on his emotions:

> Does not even the Son of God say that those would be about Him whom His Father has given to Him? . . . Supposing our Father wishes to keep me for Himself, as my heart tells me?[55]

Werther claims a special position in relation to religion when he writes to Wilhelm:

> I respect religion, as you know, and I feel it is a staff for many a weary soul, refreshment for many who are faint: but – can it, must it then be this for everyone?[56]

Experience, in the last resort, means more to him than the teaching of the Christian Church. For Werther, man's end is not to be saved, but to suffer fully, to empty his cup to the dregs. Werther turns away from Christianity; for allusions to, and quotations from, the Bible do not mean that his thinking is in accordance with its spirit. But turning away from orthodox Christianity does not mean that he seeks a new religion, for his faith is simply based on feeling, and is incapable of surviving closer examination. So he believes his passion is peculiar to himself. 'Sometimes I say to myself: your fate is unique; I call everyone else happy; no one has been tormented like you.'[57] He compares his suffering with Christ's suffering. His suffering, too, is unique, and yet representative of human suffering as such. This belief allows us to gauge the full measure of his suffering and the intensity of his feeling. Werther raises his own feeling to an unconditional pitch. He takes his love, indeed all his emotions, too seriously. He overestimates his own achievement. Because he does so, he feels an imperative need to assert his own importance, especially the importance of his own emotions. Religious yearning is mingled with this need to receive the respect and admiration due to him.

Werther is steeped in the gospels. He continually uses words from the Bible, especially from St John's Gospel.[58] His familiarity with the Bible betrays the origins of his thinking in the religious tradition of the West. By placing himself in this tradition, by finding parallels between his suffering and that of Christ, he believes his experience acquires universal significance. But to make claims of this kind is a sign of his insufficiency; for these allusions to the Bible underline the limitations and the futility of his suffering. The title of the novel alludes to Christ's sorrows, of which *Werther* may claim to be a modern, profane version. Werther uses a mistaken analogy when he likens his suffering to that of Christ. It indicates the nature and extent of his pretension. Christ died for others, for mankind; Werther dies for himself. He thus stands condemned by restricting his religion to the worship of the self, an attitude contrary to Christian teaching which demands love of God and one's neighbour, for, in the last resort, his arrogant aspiration to suffering like Christ is an attempt to glorify his own feelings. It also indicates the assumption that, just as Christ's suffering was vindicated by His resurrection, so his own sorrows would be justified by his obtaining Lotte in after-life.[59]

Werther's religion is not based on service for others or for God. God remains distant and silent. When Werther believes in a transcendental God and wants to respond to Him, he also interprets his suffering as not being merely of this world. In turn, the way in which he sees his suffering decisively influences his conception of God. His religious yearning first of all results in his attempt to grasp the meaning of the world. His aim is, however, to do so spontaneously without any deep reflection. Although Werther is looking for the satisfaction of his desires in this world alone, and although he commits suicide, he is a religious man. This religiosity is nourished by his feelings and by Pietism. Since his feelings are so strong his religiosity is powerful. We are confronted with a religious temper, a religion based on and fortified by feeling, and here *Werther* anticipates the romantic theology of Schleiermacher.

Love is the core of Werther's experience as it is of the Christian's. But for him, love does not mean love of God or a Platonic relationship embodying the idea of love, but the violent passion of a man for a woman. And as satisfaction is denied him, he must try to find vicarious satisfaction in imagination and suffering, always refusing to recognize the facts of the situation. His love is unconditional, just as the love expressed in Goethe's *Sesenheim* Lyrics. Everything has to be subordinated to it. Werther is incapable of loving with moderation. This would amount to a betrayal of what is most sacred to him. If for him love is all or nothing, he does not always want to admit its unconditional nature. He refuses to accept the fact that, by loving Lotte, he may be confronted with an 'either/or' situation, either having his love reciprocated or having to renounce it. Werther misunderstands the situation. Life, and particularly the life of feeling, does indeed allow of nuances, but a marriage, if it is to remain a genuine marriage, does not permit any serious infringement, a fact which Werther never wants to admit to himself.

Werther is quite unrealistic; he completely loses his bearings. He forgets that, after all, a kiss, however passionate, cannot simply wipe out, at a stroke, Lotte's married life. But Werther, who in his day-dreams has taken possession of Lotte, sees in this one kiss an act which makes her his own. His death becomes a *Liebestod*; he believes that, after death, she will belong to him.

Love and death are parallel themes for Werther. They are so because Werther does not find in love the fulfilment which he desires. His love thus becomes barren. It does not lead him to a fuller life, but to death; for fulfilment in this world is impossible for him.

Death alone brings fulfilment for Werther, but his death does not have any transcendental significance, for his own salvation or for that of others. He likens his death to Christ's, but he has no right to do so. His death brings neither joy nor comfort to others; and he himself knows this. Though his fate might be called tragic, as he recognizes this truth, it cannot be called in any sense redemptive, and it is blasphemous for him to compare his death with Christ's, as when he says: 'But alas! it was granted to but a few noble souls to shed their blood for those they loved and by this to kindle for them a new life enhanced a hundredfold.'[60] Nonetheless, although Werther is sometimes aware of the pointlessness of his death, he generally stifles this awareness. He deceives himself even to the point of believing that he possesses the happiness which God grants only to saints.

The thought of death accompanies Werther everywhere. It consoles him, because it gives him the sweet illusion of being free to leave the prison of the world at any time.

Death has a positive meaning for Werther. It means freedom. His passion for Lotte makes it easy for him to entertain his view of personal immortality, a view regarded by Albert with indulgent scepticism. It is true that, in the last letter, he speaks of the uncertainty which surrounds his existence after death, but he does not hold this view for long. The excessive power of his desire for Lotte makes him believe in a future world which will grant him fulfilment. Yet his conception of immortality is naïve.

Werther's sorrows constitute a passion in the original sense of the word. Love makes him deny life, not affirm it. The whole novel, indeed, presents a cycle of images of disease.[61]

At the beginning of the novel, Werther's disease is not yet at an advanced stage, but the first signs of a pathological tendency can be detected. Sometimes we hear of disease only indirectly, of Leonore who was seized by passion, of the suffering which men cause themselves through their imagination. These are intimations only of an impending psychological crisis. But precisely at this point an important cause of his disease is emphasized: his refusal to accept the world as it is, his inability to forget past sorrows. The signs and symptoms of the disease increase as the action proceeds. After treating his heart as if it were 'a sick child', after giving free rein to his melancholy, there follows the first outbreak of his disease. After first meeting Lotte, he says that he does not know whether it is day or night, and he is quite unconscious of the world around him.

Again and again in the course of the narrative, Werther, to

characterize his state of mind, uses images which also suggest the progress of a neurosis: he is suddenly seized by a contraction of his senses, his mind becomes clouded; he feels as if someone were clutching him by the throat and he must free himself with one wild blow. Eventually, the neurosis becomes all-powerful. 'Nature can find no way out of the labyrinth of confused and contradictory instincts, and the mortal must die.'[62] 'A sickness unto death'[63] – Werther uses this phrase from St John's Gospel – consumes his strength and foils any efforts to restore his health. He becomes incapable of returning to normality. He embraces the image of disease in order to abandon himself to his passion, and defends himself by presenting a death, which is the result of emotional hypertension, as an inevitable process of nature.

Werther's death is convincing. It follows necessarily and consistently from the events. But this does not mean that it need have happened. What makes the course of his disease inevitable is that Werther thinks it is so. Werther dies because he desires to die, because he is no longer willing to resist disintegration. Goethe himself realized this, for he wrote, with reference to Werther: 'Be a man, and do not follow me.'[64]

Werther wants to present his death as a sacrifice, an assertion which is unjustified. He places it in the religious tradition; its impact and significance thus extend far beyond the scope of an ordinary novel. This religious aspect allows us to gauge the extent of Werther's disease, of his error and of his insufficiency, for Christ's death is a sacrifice where the full significance is only seen in its consequences: resurrection, ascension to heaven and the foundation of the Church. Werther's death, however, does not have any positive consequences. It moves us, but it remains a special case. All that we learn is that egocentric feeling is not a safe guide for living.

Werther gains our sympathy because he is sick, and not because he is healthy and condemned by a sick world. Yet we should be mistaken to look for hints as to how Werther might have overcome his state of mind. Goethe wrote a novel, not a treatise. Werther rebels against society as he finds it. Yet he does not win his battle, and society proves to be stronger. Still, we must ask ourselves whether society is also morally right. To answer this question we must look more closely at Werther's relationship to society.

Werther is intimately affected by the events of ordinary life. Not only does he mention them in his letters; he even enjoys the company of common people, who mean much to him. Werther regards society as full of interest and is ready to participate in its life. He is aware of what goes on around him; he can observe sharply and exactly. But his egocentricity makes him view all the events in the external world as symbols of his inner life. His incapacity to sustain an objective vision makes us suspect that he selects events and situations for mention in his letters on a similarly subjective principle.

Werther, however, does not continue to live in harmony with his environment. At the beginning of the novel he is not an outsider, but an accepted member of society. He is a young man who has had the best possible chance of a successful career, even though he loves nature and solitude.[65] But he is also a man who cannot rest content with the routine of social life. His aim is, as he says in the letter of 15 May 1771, to penetrate to man himself. He abominates class differences, which in his view are a consequence of cowardice, of inner weakness. Because he did not belong to the nobility, but was only a bourgeois, he was told to leave the aristocrats' *soirée*. He maintains that this affront did not affect him personally at the time, but only later, when it became widely known. So he avers. Yet we may well ask whether he does not deceive himself, whether he was not mortified by the insult at the time when it was offered, or at least before he had become conscious of other people's reactions. In fact, he is unable to rise above the consequences which class differences entail.

Werther is no revolutionary. He is critical of social abuses, but he is far too preoccupied with himself to espouse actively the cause of reform, let alone of violent change. He is capable of a sudden act of protest, but his protests are merely the result of spontaneous emotional outbursts, as when, in his discussion with Albert, he defends genius against mediocrity, or when he attempts to save the young farm-labourer from punishment. He protests only when his intellectual freedom appears impaired, or when his views are not accepted. This is why he attacks Albert's views; this is why he seeks to save the boy. But his protests are based on arguments which are hardly valid. For they are not rooted in concrete political or social situations, only in himself and his emotional needs and desires. The further his disease advances, the more he is estranged from society. In the great discussion with Albert, he defends a dangerous point of view, but still does so as a fully-fledged member of the society in which he lives. Albert characterizes this view only as extreme, but does not dismiss it contemptuously as pathological or absurd. Werther's demand to leave the diplomatic service, however, amounts to a refusal to find a place in society. When he espouses the cause of the young farm-labourer who has committed a crime of passion he goes further; for he no longer distinguishes between right and wrong, and he steps beyond the pale of accepted social morality. In thus isolating himself from the society of his fellow-men, Werther anticipates the total isolation of death.

A study of the style and the themes of the novel leaves no doubt that it offers an analysis of a neurotic personality,[66] and this feature is particularly modern. A desire to be noticed, the wish to appear more than one really is, to realize the potentiality of one's ego at any price, all these qualities make Werther the model of an ambivalent character. Werther's mode of thinking is poetic rather than philosophical, and he applies this poetic thinking wherever it is appropriate. In this sense he could be termed 'romantic'.[67] He vacillates between asserting and humiliating himself. This explains the continuous change in his basic attitude and mood, and his indulgent regard for moods, which is so characteristic of him. Werther's vacillating attitude towards nature or towards men reflects his inner insecurity, which never allows him to repose. Werther is the prototype of the neurotic in the modern European novel. Goethe's main concern was not to describe a case of abnormal psychology, but his portrayal is so convincing that it has stood the test of time in the light of modern psychological findings.

Werther, however, is not the only character of the novel who carries psychological conviction; he is merely the protagonist dominating the action. Lotte and Albert, although overshadowed by Werther, are equally convincing. Though their characters are not developed to the same extent as that of Werther, they present a clear image. Lotte's spontaneity, her love for her husband, her sympathy for Werther, and her practical sense tempered by sensitivity are features of a 'round character' (in E. M. Forster's terminology).[68] Certainly Werther means something to her. Her sensitivity enables him to play a part in her life which Albert is unable to. How dear he has grown to her through habit and sympathy becomes apparent when Lotte thinks none of her friends good enough to be Werther's wife. At first she likes Werther only as a friend. It is only when Werther's passion for her comes into the open that she realizes it is more than friendship that she feels for him. Nonetheless, this does not mean that in her emotional life he has taken the place of Albert.[69] Not only duty and custom, but also deep feelings bind her to Albert.* She is indeed deeply moved and disturbed. She finds herself in a situation which she must resolve in an unambiguous manner, and not by compromise. Like Werther, Lotte becomes confused. There is, however, a difference. Lotte is deeply disturbed; not however by an urge within her, but as the result of circumstances which she had no wish to create. She sees no way out of this situation which would be satisfactory for all three of them. She knows very well that there is no place for Werther in her life, but she does not suspect the fateful solution of the dilemma. She is helpless. Her inhibitions prevent her from declaring the truth to Albert; so the last opportunity of preventing the catastrophe is missed. Probably any intervention by Albert, indeed, might only have postponed the fatal act. Lotte thus presents a contrast to Werther. She is infected by a psychological disease, but her healthy nature overcomes it.

Albert and Werther are characters opposed to one another. At first sight it appears as if comparison between them would not be helpful. Albert may not be a person whom one would necessarily wish to emulate; yet by comparison with Werther, he impresses the reader by his calm, reasonable behaviour and by his sense of duty and propriety. His quiet seriousness and his deep love for Lotte make him a far from unattractive character, even when placed beside Werther. Furthermore it would be mistaken to think of Albert as lacking in sensitivity, as we may be inclined to, for we see him almost instinctively through the eyes of Werther, and he is far too annoyed by Albert's different views, by his mere presence even, to give an unbiassed account of him.

At first, he is prepared to see in Albert the very best person alive; but it is significant that he begins his praise with the word

* The situation is, of course, as was pointed out above, different in the first version of the novel.

'indeed', thus qualifying the assertion. A deep gulf, in fact, exists between the two, and it is never bridged. Werther is convinced that Albert does not understand him, and from this he concludes that Albert is incapable of understanding Lotte. Nonetheless, Werther expresses this extreme view only in the last stages of his disease. It was not Goethe's intention to show in Albert only negative traits of character. In the second version, indeed, these negative traits were considerably reduced in importance.

Two other characters, the young farm-labourer and the mad young man, illuminate Werther's character by their likeness to his situation and yet by the unlikeness of their personalities. The story of the mad young man greatly disturbs him. Since he believes it to be analogous to his own, Werther thinks that he is threatened by incipient madness, although in fact this is a mistaken view. He may suffer from a neurosis which compels him to see everything in relation to his psyche and to his suffering. Yet he is far from raving madness, for he always retains the use of his mind, even when his imagination is at its most extravagant. Of course, the desire for self-destruction might be thought a form of insanity, but if it is insanity, it does not deprive him of his reason.

Similarly, the episode with the young farm-labourer serves as a contrast, and not as a parallel, as is often mistakenly believed.[70] Werther is given no encouragement by Lotte, whereas the farm-labourer is by the farmer's wife, who raises his hopes. Only when these are disappointed does he become a murderer. Werther feels that subconsciously he, too, would like to take Albert's life, but he deludes himself. As always, he seeks to relate everything to his own love. The farm-labourer seeks to prevent the marriage of the widow whom he loves by murdering another person. Werther chooses to commit suicide: a contrast rather than a parallel. On the other hand, this encounter plays its part in determining Werther's attitude; he sees a way of behaving which he might follow himself. He identifies himself with the farm-labourer. 'You cannot be saved, unhappy man. Indeed, I see that we cannot be saved.'[71] Werther becomes convinced of this aggressive tendency within himself after he has been turned out of the house of Count C. He writes, 'I wished that some one would dare to reproach me for my behaviour so that I could run my sword through his body; if I were to see blood I should feel better.'[72] There is a further allusion to his attitude in the last sentences of the novel. We read that a copy of *Emilia Galotti* lies open on the table when he shoots himself. Like the prince in Lessing's play, it is implied that Werther might be capable of murder, if murder would enable him to get Lotte for himself.[73]

Werther's personality and his relationship to society allow us to understand his attitude towards reality. In this respect, *Werther* belongs to the tradition of the modern European novel which, since Cervantes' *Don Quixote*, can be seen as an attempt to define our view of what is real, to determine the relation between appearance and reality.[74] In *Werther*, we encounter two views of reality – that of Werther and that of the editor. Werther after all cannot tell the story of his suicide – it is the editor's function to alleviate the tragic effect of the story.

It would, however, be a critical fallacy to believe that Goethe's views are those of the editor. Goethe attempted in this novel to attain a satisfactory view of reality. Werther's view is characterized by his refusal to adapt himself to reality. His enthusiasm presages his later failure. His enthusiastic letters, however, have their counterpart in the editor's objective report. The whole story is grasped only by taking both styles into consideration. For if we base our assessment of the import of the novel on one style only, we take a one-sided view. To side with or against Werther is equally mistaken; both modes of speaking are legitimate, and may exist side by side, even if they appear to create an irreconcilable conflict.

Werther believes that what is felt is alone real. He contemptuously rejects other interpretations of the world, whether those of Albert or of Herr Schmidt, as mistaken. Werther's conception of reality is, as the novel implies, unsatisfactory. By interposing the editor, Goethe intimates that he does not share Werther's conception and that another is possible.

The editor's account is to be objective. At first, the reader is merely assured that an event has been accurately reported. It is not suggested that a view of reality is being developed. But this very objectivity contains the whole essence of another view of the world. To describe the sorrows of Werther without any expression of sentiment is to suggest that reality is not what is felt, that feeling has to be subordinated to reason, that external events take precedence over the movement of the inner life.

What view of reality does Goethe himself take in *Werther*? Goethe's own experience was close to the events of the novel, and a later comment of his brings this out:

> It is difficult to imagine how any one could survive for another forty years in a world which appeared so absurd in early youth.[75]

But Goethe speaks with two voices which contradict one another:[76] each demands to be recognized as the only right one. The two versions of the novel are, apart from slight stylistic changes and from the interpolation of the young farm-labourer episode, distinguished from one another above all by the different character of the editor's account. In the second version, the editor interposes his account at an earlier stage, after the letter of 6 December, while in the first version, he does so after the letter of 12 December. His opening remarks (relating to his activity as editor of the letters) which are missing in this first version create a greater detachment.

> How I could have wished that enough evidence of our friend's remarkable last days had survived in his own hand to make it unnecessary for me to interrupt the sequence of the letters he did leave behind!
>
> I have set myself the task of collecting exact accounts from the lips of those who were in a position to know his story: it is a simple one, and all the accounts agree about it down to the smallest details; it is only over the attitude of mind of the leading characters that opinions differ, and judgements diverge.
>
> What remains for us except to relate accurately all we have found out, with a great deal of trouble, to interpolate the letters the dying man left behind, and to pay scrupulous regard to the slightest note which has come to light, especially since it is hard, indeed, to discover the true, individual motives of even a single action which takes place among people of no common sort.[77]

The editor is detached, but he is not hostile. From the beginning of the novel, he enjoins us to regard Werther with understanding and not to deny him admiration, love and sympathy.[78] He does not rebuke him, a view echoed almost forty years later by Goethe when he wrote to Zelter that 'if the *taedium vitae* overwhelms man, he is only to be pitied, not to be reproached.'[79] Indeed, the editor hopes that the book may be a comfort.

The mention of the activity of collecting information serves a double purpose. It diverts the reader's attention from Werther to the problem of editing his papers. It thus makes detachment a factor in the novel, in accordance with Goethe's later classical conception, and secondly it emphasizes the genuine quality of the documentation. On the one hand, it points out that we are reading a novel; on the other, that we are confronted with a most topical action.

Goethe then does not side with any specific view of reality. He was still, at this stage of his life, uncertain of his development. He had not yet come to terms with the world he had to live in. This uncertainty or lack of adjustment is reflected in the novel. The result is conflict, destructive to a man as sensitive as Werther. For Goethe himself, this mode of behaviour appeared the only possible way of looking at the world. Only as he grew older and more mature was this conflict within him resolved and contained in a homogeneous style. In fact, both modes of writing, that of Werther and that of the editor, had their precursors – Brockes, Gessner, Gellert, Klopstock; all these poets had appealed to the sensibility, of which, indeed, a cult had been made.[80] At the same time, the editor's matter-of-fact voice recalls the dominant tradition of the *Aufklärung*. Goethe's vision, even at the time of his youth, was related to the centre of his being. This concentration is reflected in the compactness of his novel and the carefulness of its design. Whatever mastery, whatever careful design the novel reveals, Goethe has nonetheless here described a world in conflict. The conflict appeared to him too real, too immediate for him to be able, at that stage, to resolve it through the medium of a homogeneous style. He was only at the beginning of his search for the mode of expression suited to him. He did not consider it his task to resolve the conflict; it was his aim merely to present it.

A novel usually reveals much that is symptomatic of its age. Novels are more closely related to society than other literary genres, and

Werther is no exception. Werther, of course, belongs to the middle class, as do most of the heroes of European novels in the last two centuries. Class differences appear not only in the background of the action; they intervene directly in the events of the novel. Although a continuous exchange of ideas may prevail between individual members of the various classes, society, in its public relations, has become petrified. Werther himself is not very conscious of class differences: he is friendly to the poor, and at the same time cherishes the company of Fräulein von B. and Count C. because their personalities and outlook appeal to him. Of course, economic independence shelters him from the struggle of everyday life. He does not become involved in political conflict. The struggle for power and the attempt to realize political aspirations do not interest him, nor is he angered by the social or political barriers which beset the path of most of his contemporaries. They do not frustrate his complete surrender to the passion which has become for him a consuming activity. This isolation from society intensifies his concentration on his personal sorrows. To his contemporaries, Werther may have appeared as a promising young man who might have achieved something within the existing social framework, but, in the end, he is an atypical person for whom social life is not essential. He suffers shipwreck, it is true, since he runs counter to the institutions on which Western society has been built, for example, marriage, but he does not break down because he condemns marriage as such or because Lotte did not possess the strength to liberate herself from the shackles of an unwelcome married life. In a different society in which monogamy did not exist, Werther's fate could not have taken this form. On the other hand, the solution of living with two partners, a *mariage à trois*, which Fernando adopted in Goethe's early play *Stella*, would be inconceivable for Lotte. Since it is not the institution of marriage but Werther's own emotional attitude that causes his downfall, he cannot be considered a victim of social circumstances.

Sociological considerations also require us to study the novel's reception, which had a distinct influence on Goethe's revision of 1787.[81] One of the reasons why he changed the characters of Albert and Lotte in the second version was that the novel had been partly misunderstood. *Werther* was a great success, but not entirely for the right reasons. No doubt poetic originality was one of the causes of its remarkable impact, but its topicality was probably at least equally important. If *Werther*, as has been argued,[82] conveys the intellectual situation of the young generation in the 1770s, much of its success is explained. Most contemporary readers were excessively interested in the material of the novel and took it to be a justification of suicide.[83] Only a few were capable of appraising it as a work of art. The enthusiasm with which *Werther* was greeted and with which it was attacked tell us that a vital nerve of the age had been laid bare. Those who saw in *Werther* an appeal for liberation from the yoke of an intolerable rationality, from the control of religious, intellectual and social traditions, read the novel in a one-sided manner. They admired Werther instead of pitying him. They believed him to be a titan,[84] a champion of their own endeavour. For those who looked at the novel critically, indeed in a hostile manner, it was a peril to youth and a glorification of emotional life, not a criticism of excessive emotionalism.

Both kinds of reader did Goethe an injustice, but both recognized in the novel tendencies corresponding to the aspirations of the age. In Germany since Luther, the importance of man's inner life had been emphasized more and more, even to the neglect of outward activities. Pietism and political absolutism had strengthened this tendency even further. The practical side of life was neglected. Only with the criticism of the Enlightenment had religious doctrines become problematic for traditional-minded men. Pietism and the Enlightenment were still the predominant influences in intellectual life about 1770.

Another reason for the novel's appeal is its sentimentality which, as a mode of feeling, was at that time the fashion.[85] It corresponds to a change in sensibility, particularly in the conception of love.

Werther is the work in which Goethe sought to come to terms with the role and function of feeling in life. Werther's insistence on the absolute priority of the emotional side of life may be mistaken. The novel, however, would never have attained its enormous success if it had not expressed a claim that apparently could be justified.

Inevitably, a psychological interpretation of the novel tends to over-emphasize the diseased element in Werther's character. It can easily be seen as an attempt to attack Werther's view, to disparage it as a psychological aberration. But to do so – and, to some extent, our interpretation has tended in that direction – is to do an injustice to *Werther*. It produces a one-sided reading. The warning against the mistaken assumption that one style, one voice in the novel is the only right one, must be repeated. For this would amount to looking at the novel from the lop-sided standpoint of Albert or Herr Schmidt, without the sympathy for Werther insisted on by the editor in his preface. But even the editor's sympathy is not enough, as the dry tone of his narrative betrays. For to appreciate *Werther* fully, we must be able to participate in the fervour with which Werther approaches life, a fervour of an almost religious kind. From one angle, indeed, it is a delusion to read *Werther* as a psychological novel at all. On the contrary, it should be read as a panegyric on the strength of feeling, a very extreme case which typifies an attitude that was felt to be new at the time (though, in fact, it was not new at all): it was the claim of feeling to have precedence over reason. This claim may appear, at first sight, to be quite unbalanced, yet it is based on an inner necessity; for we can only eschew the claim of feeling at our peril. On the other hand, to grant it priority at any price is equally dangerous. But for this praise of feeling, the novel would not have had its stupendous impact. For feeling comes here to the fore much more vehemently and more profoundly than in any earlier German novel. It feeds on a new conception of the value and capacity of man. In this Goethe was a pioneer. The *Sesenheim* lyrics and the great hymns of the *Sturm und Drang* are the first achievement in this vein. These works share with *Werther* a more vital vision, more vital since it penetrates more deeply the inner experience of life. Because *Werther* so fully conveys this vision it can claim a greater artistic worth than previous novels. The title of the novel recalls that there is talk of mental pathology, for there is explicit reference to suffering. This suffering would, however, not be positive if it were not based on the power of feeling which sweeps across the boundaries imposed by normal life, springing, as it does, from the primordial depths of inner life.

On the basis of his feelings, Werther believes that he possesses a right to liberate himself from the burden of tradition. But he does not realize that, in fact, his emphasis on feeling stems from a tradition, namely that of Pietism. Like the Pietists, he makes extreme demands, and is prepared to stake his life on them. He wants to follow his heart even if this course runs counter to the customs of the world. He refuses to accept the restrictions of social life. In this respect, he is to some extent a follower of the social and political tendencies of his time. *Werther*, indeed, is not primarily a social novel; it deals rather with the fate of an individual. For Goethe himself, *Werther* was the story of the individual. Was it not 'a creature which he, like the Pelican, had fed with the blood of his own heart'?[86] Since this individual, however, belongs to the middle class, it is not surprising that middle-class readers welcomed it and believed that their problems and outlook were embodied in the work.

Werther is the champion of feeling. The exalted tone of his speech, the force of his lyrical incantation may make him appear in the right. But this is just as mistaken as to side with the editor or to treat Werther as a medical case. A sound reading of the novel involves a wider view. Both the vitalizing and destructive forces of feeling must be recognized. Emotion is necessary, but it must not step beyond its limits. Werther's emphasis upon feeling is excessive, but this does not mean that feeling itself is invalid. Goethe has, indeed, written a polemic against an over-estimation of feeling,[87] but he would not have done this if he had not also been aware of the creative qualities of emotion.[88] Contemporary readers read *Werther* mainly as a novel of sentiment.[89] They considered Werther a tragic victim of circumstances beyond his control, and believed his attitude and even his action justifiable.

The novel's intensity and range of emotional power are still capable of moving a reader today. The problem of canalizing a primordial force, the claims of emotion to direct our actions, are still with us. They are the problems of civilization itself. Moreover, Werther appears to speak with the voice of genius. The *Sturm und Drang* was, after all, the age of genius. In the field of poetry, Hamann and Herder had laid the foundation of the belief in the primacy of genius in art; Goethe, in his early theoretical writings on art and literature, had expressed the same view, and had provided practical examples. He knew himself to be a genius and, in his *Sturm und Drang* hymns, he had glorified the right and the divine power of genius. At the same time he was conscious of the flaws inherent in this doctrine. The false prophet who wrongly assumes the mantle of genius was hence a favourite theme in the years before *Werther*.[90] For the contemporary reader, Werther appeared to be *the* protagonist of feeling who perishes, and his suffering was glorified. It is hardly likely that Goethe ever shared this view. After leaving Frankfurt in 1775 he certainly did not do so; even in his Frankfurt years his position was different, and it was always complex. His *Künstlergedichte* and his other lyric poetry, especially *Wanderers Sturmlied*, reveal a humorous, even serene attitude towards reality. Even as a young man, Goethe was a man of the world. Werther was different from his creator; unlike Goethe, he was not a genius, but only believed himself to be one. This belief is pretentious, though it was only unconsciously held. The pretension involves an attempt to lay down the laws of conduct and convention for himself and for others. It is closely related to the pretension of Goethe's Prometheus, only Prometheus is cast in a much more positive vein. This attitude, however, springs from a desire for spiritual independence, from the will to accept one's own fate without paying any attention to the conditions of human existence, for it is Werther's aim to enjoy every moment with the full force of his personality. In the background, however, a critical view of Werther's tendency to stress the value of primordial emotional forces can be noticed; this critical note is found, however, in the background only. The foreground is different, as the *Wertherfieber* (Werther fever) exemplifies.[91] It was engendered by the enthusiasm for Werther's attitude. The foreground is dominated by the sense of ecstasy and enthusiasm conveyed by Werther's attitude to nature and religion, love and death. Only gradually did a more critical attitude develop among readers. Yet without the spark of genius, of the genius which youth possesses even when mistaken, the novel could never have had such power to evoke enthusiasm. A new realm of sensibility was made accessible through the medium of literature. But if literature is to possess any lasting aesthetic value, it must display the qualities of critical detachment and understanding.

Werther is one of the few works of world literature in which intrinsic significance and outward acclaim immediately coincided. For many, especially outside Germany, Goethe was the author of *Werther*. This reputation persisted, and Napoleon is typical in his attitude. The popularity of Goethe's first novel was only much later surpassed by other works, above all by *Faust*. Its immediate impact reveals how close Goethe was to the main trend of his age. Enthusiasm or disgust characterized the reactions to the novel, which were almost invariably extreme. The term *Wertherfieber* was appropriately coined to describe the ferment engendered by these violent outbursts, as well as the state of mind of those who wrote the many imitations of the novel. Goethe had succeeded in touching a vital nerve of the literary public. The reviews and pronouncements of the most important critics, of men like Wieland and Lessing, Matthias Claudius and Merck, show that most readers were overpowered by the material, a fact which Goethe himself regretted. The novel was misunderstood, since no one paid attention to its form. Goethe defined the principle of literary creation which guided him by saying: 'The poet transmutes life into an image. The common crowd desires to lower the image again by turning it back into the original material.'[92] Many well-known figures of German literary life, like Garve, Schubart, Claudius, Nicolai and Goeze, intervened in the dispute about the novel. For them, it was a criticism of or an apology for passion and suicide. Enthusiasm for, and polemics against the work and its author created strange constellations of friends and opponents. For instance, while Garve, the man of the Enlightenment, and Schubart the enthusiast, admired the novel, Nicolai, a champion of the Enlightenment, and Goeze, an orthodox theologian, attacked them. The emotions of the intelligent reading public were powerfully aroused:[93] Werther became a model to imitate, or a fate to avoid.

Of all literary genres, the novel has perhaps the widest appeal. The drama must depend, to some extent at least, on the accidents of theatrical production, but the novel speaks directly to the reader. Goethe gave no reasons why he wrote novels or chose the novel to give form to the experience conveyed in *Werther*. External reasons can have played only a small part in his choice; inner reasons are likely to have been more essential: the desire to experiment and to discover a style of his own. Goethe was tossed about by the waves of his experience; he was searching for something to cling to,[94] for a mode of expression, for a style.[95] This quest characterized his pre-Weimar period. He was faced with the challenge of achieving success as a novelist. He did so by transmuting a traditional form, established, as we have seen, by

Richardson and Rousseau. To resort to a traditional form was characteristic of the young Goethe, but it was equally characteristic of him to transmute it completely. He did this by presenting not an exchange of letters, but a set of letters written by a single individual. In his early writing he intended to complete only works on a small scale; it thus apparently suited his natural inclination to choose a more economical means of portrayal than Richardson or Rousseau. Goethe wrote *Werther* because his impulse to form compelled him to find *the* event, *the* story which would embody what he had to express. The impulse to form, 'the inner form which comprises all forms within itself,'[96] forced him to look for the external form of a novel in letters; for only thus was he able to depict the complete isolation of a man who lived not in a mutually fructifying relationship with other men, but in a wholly barren situation. He described this situation in *Dichtung und Wahrheit*:

> If he [Werther] be at all capable of speaking about it this will take place only through letters; for an outpouring of the inner life by way of letters, whether it be gay or disagreeable, is not directly confronted by anyone; but a reply composed of counter-arguments affords an opportunity for solitary people to consolidate their whims, it provides them with an incentive to be even more obstinate.[97]

The experience transmuted by Goethe in *Werther* was not primarily an experience of the world, but one of form; it was 'an *a priori* manner of seeing the world';[98] only by turning this vision into an experience of form could he create a genuine work of art. External form and the experience which he depicted arose simultaneously, to coalesce in a whole which alone can explain the remarkable impact of the work.

The way in which the theme developed in his mind compelled Goethe to give preference to the form of the novel, even though there was a sufficient number of situations suitable to drama. Lessing had successfully portrayed contemporary life in his comedy *Minna von Barnhelm*. Goethe may have wished to rival him in a novel of contemporary life; he may have felt rightly that, so far, leading novelists had not succeeded in doing justice to contemporary life: indeed, Wieland, the leading German novelist of the day, had avoided a contemporary setting when dealing with its problems, and had set his work in antiquity or an imaginary oriental scene.

To do justice to the literary revolution for which *Werther* as a *Sturm und Drang* product stood, the novel must be placed against its literary background. Goethe was not able to draw on a rich tradition of literary masterpieces in German. Indeed, at the time when he started writing, German cultural life trailed behind the French and English achievement. In fact, literary taste was still largely determined by foreign influence. The *Sturm und Drang* movement, which cannot be separated from the creative work of Goethe's youth, marks the point at which German literature finally emerged from foreign tutelage and German writers began to have confidence in a style of their own. Of course, there were forerunners: Gottsched had stabilized the German language; Klopstock had broken with the conventional pattern of metre and rhythm; Lessing had assailed the French classical pre-eminence in a trenchant manner, particularly in the *Hamburgische Dramaturgie*; Hamann and Herder had expounded a new, indeed a revolutionary theory of poetics, based on a novel conception of sensibility.[99] For them, individual genius and not rules, intuition rather than reason, are the springs of literary creation. *Werther* is not a compound, let alone a pastiche, of previous literature, but it does gather together many strands of writing. They are nowhere obtrusive, for Goethe assimilated these ideas and used them for his work without impairing its freshness and originality.

It would be tedious to pursue the various lines of thought and feeling into the distant past. It suffices to draw attention to echoes of English sentimental writers,[100] such as Edward Young, Richardson, Sterne, Gray and Goldsmith; of the religious poetry of Brockes and Klopstock; of the idyllic picture of nature depicted in Albrecht von Haller, Ewald von Kleist and Gessner; and of the peculiar brand of orthodox dogma found in Lavater's sermons.[101] Gottsched's and Gellert's attempts to make the use of epistolary form in German respectable – it had been customary for elegant letters to be written in Latin or French – prepared the ground for *Werther*;[102] and the family scenes which abound in the conventional fiction and drama of the day also left their mark.[103] There are even passages which, surprisingly, hark back to the traditional imagery of the baroque,[104] and the traces of Pietistic vocabulary cannot be overlooked.[105] The quotations from Luther's Bible are, of course, prominently placed.

The transformation of traditional material is, however, complete, for it is fully integrated into the organic structure of the work. It is, indeed, so complete that a new world confronts us. This new world created by Goethe's genius was prepared and explained by the revolution in poetics which, apart from Goethe's creative achievement, is the most distinctive feature of the *Sturm und Drang* movement. Hamann, Herder, and in their wake Goethe, proclaimed a new aesthetics intended to supersede the classical canons of literature. It asserted the right of genius to create its own standards, and it also emphasized the historical character of the forms of imaginative literature and the individuality of each work of art. Feeling and intuition were writ large in this reassessment. A new vision was to replace old dogmas. The artist was to create an autonomous world which set up its own standards both in ethics and aesthetics. Exuberance, indeed ecstasy, accompanied the discovery of uncharted territories of the mind. No wonder that, for Herder, poetry was energy stored up within the inner meaning of words.

Werther speaks for this desire for emotional intensity and imaginative energy, and for the cult of the extraordinary personality who claims to be a law unto himself. At the same time, it reflects Goethe's sense of the inadequacy of the *Sturm und Drang* poetic doctrine, for at an early stage Goethe insisted on the need to harness emotional energy and imaginative power, which, in life as in art, need to be disciplined by a sense of what is possible. In life, we come to grief if we seek to trespass beyond the limits set to human activity. Art, too, cannot be created without a feeling for form.

The rebellion against established standards in religion, morality and art thus provides the background against which Werther's own revolt is set. Like the *Stürmer und Dränger* he seeks strength in nature; for him, in contradistinction to the thinkers and poets of the *Aufklärung*, nature is not ordered and regulated, but it possesses infinite variety and creative power. He also cherishes the simple emotions of the loving and disappointed heart meeting an unhappy death, as celebrated in folk-song. In fact, Werther is a stylised version of the folk-poem, an elaboration of a simple narrative core made necessary by the requirements of epic form. Affinity with Shakespeare, the great model of the *Sturm und Drang*, is remote. Indeed, his impact was only indirect. Liberation from the bondage of classicism, the wealth of imagery, the richness of language, the delight in nature, provide general rather than particular points of contact. Shakespeare may, however, in one instance have inspired *Werther*, for in Hamlet, Goethe may have seen a personality akin to Werther.[106] For him, Hamlet was the story of a man who was out of tune with reality, as his inner life was in conflict with the demands of the external world. Here was another noble soul whose existence was undermined and destroyed by speculation and inner disintegration.

Werther, thus, if set against the literary and intellectual background of its time, appears to be at a point where many lines of thought and feeling converge; yet one of the reasons why the novel is a convincing work of art is that it succeeded in transforming the past in order to express and mould contemporary experience. It heralded a new development in sensibility, and anticipated the Romantic mode of thinking and feeling predominant in nineteenth-century Germany.

Werther stands out among Goethe's *Sturm und Drang* works for two reasons: it was a remarkable literary success, and it gives proof of Goethe's mastery of form, for the majority of the main works which Goethe wrote in his youth remained fragmentary. Lyric poetry apart, he completed only one major work, the historical drama *Götz von Berlichingen*. *Werther* is a much more compact work than *Götz*. The *Urfaust* is more impressive, but it remained a fragment, and was not published by Goethe himself. The tragedy of Gretchen possesses, indeed, unity of style and content, but is only a part of a greater whole. *Götz von Berlichingen*, though effective on the stage, lacks unity of action. *Clavigo* and *Stella*, two plays with a contemporary setting, do not have the compelling form of a true masterpiece. *Satyros*, whose language rivals that of the *Urfaust* in vigour and originality, is too limited, too indistinct to stand comparison.

In contrast to *Werther*, none of these works belongs to world literature (the completed *Faust* drama does, the *Urfaust* does not). *Werther*, however, possesses unity and austerity of composition as well as significance of meaning. The novel reveals perfection of form, even in the first version, and the differences between the two versions are not great enough for us to distinguish them as two distinct, independent works.

Werther takes a position between the lyric poetry of the *Sesenheim* songs, the great hymns and the *Künstlergedichte* (*Artist-Poems*) on the one hand, and the dramas *Götz von Berlichingen*, *Egmont*, which was begun at that time, and the *Urfaust* on the other. *Werther* speaks of the hero's love, of his desire to be liked, to be independent of God, to be creative as an artist – to be able to save himself through a truly creative deed. The power which characterizes Götz, and the daemonic force which characterizes Egmont, are both effectively combined in Faust. Werther, however, must do without these traits. Yet none of the other works portrays a man who is marked by the same single-minded intensity and concentration of feeling.

These features, in the last resort, made it possible for *Die Leiden des jungen Werthers* to become one of the most successful first novels in world literature. Goethe had looked at Werther's story from two points of view, from that of Werther and that of the editor. He had not yet harmonized the conflict between subjective and objective presentation of experience; as a result, the conflict appears more intense. But the greater objectivity of his later novels in language and in description is already intimated in the language of the editor. As Goethe's experience widened, he wished to explore further areas of human life. The inner life of one person no longer offered sufficient scope. The history of the writing of *Wilhelm Meisters Lehrjahre* tells us the story of this development. For in his new novel, Goethe was to create a work which showed a far wider and more balanced vision, though its psychological insight was less intense.

Notes

1. E. L. Stahl (ed.), *Goethe's Die Leiden des jungen Werthers*, Oxford, 1942, p. v.
2. W.A., i, 28, p. 220.
3. Heinrich Düntzer, *Goethes Die Leiden des jungen Werthers*, 6th ed., Leipzig, 1880, p. 24. I owe this point to a review of Hans Reiss, *Goethes*

Romane, Berne and Munich, 1963, by Stuart Pratt Atkins, *German Quarterly*, xxxvii (1964), p. 266.

4. W.A., i, 28, p. 224.

5. Cf. for instance Wilhelm Herbst, *Goethe in Wetzlar*, Gotha, 1889; Heinrich Gloël, *Goethes Wetzlarer Zeit*, Berlin, 1911; Eduard Berend (ed.), *Goethe, Kestner und Lotte*, Munich, 1914; William Rose, 'The Historical Background of Goethe's "Werther" ', *Men, Myths and Movements in German Literature*, London, 1931; Oskar Ulrich, *Charlotte Kestner. Ein Lebensbild*, Bielefeld, 1921.

6. Letter to Goethe, November 1772. Reprinted in *Goethe und Werther* (ed. A. Kestner), 2nd ed., Stuttgart and Tübingen, 1854, pp. 87 ff., and H.A., pp. 518 ff.

7. See Ernst Beutler, 'Wertherfragen', *G*, v (1940), pp. 138 ff.; cf. Stuart Pratt Atkins, 'J. G. Lavater and Goethe: Problems of Psychology and Theology in *Die Leiden des jungen Werthers*, *PMLA*, lxiii (1948) for a discussion of the relations between Goethe and Lavater.

8. See Kestner's letter to August von Hennings, 7 November 1774 (H.A., 6, p. 523); also his letter to Goethe, either end of September or beginning of October 1774.

9. Letter to Sophie La Roche, November 1772; cf. also Wolfgang Kayser, 'Die Enstehung von Goethes "Werther" ', *DVLG*, xix (1941), pp. 430–57.

10. Letter to Sophie La Roche, November 1772.

11. Cf. the following works: Hans Gose, *Goethes 'Werther'*, Bausteine zur Geschichte der Literatur, 18, Halle, 1921; Ernst Feise, 'Goethes Werther als nervöser Charakter', *GR*, i, (1926) (reprinted in *Xenion. Themes, Forms and Ideas in German Literature*, Baltimore, 1950); Erich Trunz, H.A., 6, Hamburg, 1951, pp. 536 ff.; Emil Staiger, *Goethe*, Zürich, 1952–9, i, pp. 147 ff.; Gerhard Storz, 'Der Roman *Die Leiden des jungen Werthers*', *Goethe-Vigilien*, Stuttgart, 1953, pp. 19 ff.; Hans-Egon Hass, 'Werther-Studie', *Gestaltsprobleme in der Dichtung* (ed. Richard Alewyn, Hans-Egon Hass and Clemens Heselhaus), Bonn, 1957, pp. 83 ff.; cf. also Hans Reiss, '*Die Leiden des jungen Werthers.* A Reconsideration', *Modern Language Quarterly*, xx (1959).

12. Boris Pasternak, *An Essay in Autobiography*, Trans. Manya Harari, London, 1959, pp. 91 ff.

13. Gertrud Riess, *Die beiden Fassungen von Goethes 'Die Leiden des jungen Werthers'*, Breslau, 1924, p. 10, emphasizes the view that the public reaction to the novel played an important part in Goethe's decision to rewrite it.

14. See also letter to Johann Christian Kestner, 21 November 1774, and letter to J. C. and Charlotte Kestner, October 1774.

15. Cf. Martin Lauterbach, *Das Verhältnis der zweiten zur ersten*

Ausgabe von Werthers Leiden, Quellen und Forschungen zur Sprach- und Kulturgeschichte der germanischen Völker, 110, Strassburg, 1910; and Riess, op. cit.

16. For a full account cf. Gottfried Fittbogen, 'Die Charaktere in den beiden Fassungen von Werthers Leiden', *Euph.*, xvii (1910).

17. In a rather scurrilous *paralipomenon*, *Hanswursts Hochzeit*, Goethe appears to side with Albert; he even lets him make fun of Werther (W.A., i, 38, p. 448). His detachment from his work is also exemplified by the poem in which he ridicules Nicolai – *Nicolai auf Werthers Grab* (*Nicolai on Werther's Grave*) W.A., i, 5, p. 159; see also his comment in *Dichtung und Wahrheit* (W.A., i, 28, pp. 228 f., ii, 13) where he also asserts that he does not pay any attention to reviews. A further instance is his *Anekdote*, a brief dramatic scene prompted by Friedrich Nicolai's parody *Freuden des jungen Werthers*, Berlin, 1775 (W.A., i, 38, pp. 37 ff.).

18. W.A., iv, 38, p. 356.

19. Letter to Johann Christian Kestner, 2 May 1783.

20. Karl Vietor, *Der junge Goethe*, Munich, 1950, p. 148. Cf. also Eva D. Becker, *Der deutsche Roman um 1780*, Germanistische Abhandlungen, 5, Stuttgart, 1964.

21. Cf. Erich Schmidt, *Richardson, Rousseau und Goethe*, Jena, 1875, who discusses the main differences between these three writers, but restricts his discussion mainly to the themes treated by them.

22. Storz, 'Der Roman . . .', *Goethe-Vigilien*, p. 22 and 'Zwei Beispiele des Tagebuch-Romans', ibid., pp. 42 ff.

23. Vietor, *Der junge Goethe*, p. 149.

24. Storz, *Goethe-Vigilien*, p. 23.

25. Staiger, *Goethe*, p. 150.

26. Storz, *Goethe-Vigilien*, p. 29.

27. Cf. E. M. Butler, 'The Element of Time in Goethe's *Werther* and Kafka's *Prozess*', *GLL*, xii, 1959, p. 250, who writes: 'So that the overriding impression is of an action taking place during a period of eight months – from the beginning of May to the end of December, from an intoxicating spring and glorious summer through a particularly sad and Ossianic autumn to a cold and cruel winter; whereas, in reality, as Goethe was at pains to indicate by dates, the period covered eighteen months'; cf. also Frank G. Ryder, 'Season, Day and Hour – Time as Metaphor in Goethe's *Werther*', *JEGP*, lxiii, p. 389, who points out that Max Hermann in *Goethes Werke*, Jubiläumsausgabe, 16, p. xii had made this point earlier.

28. W.A., i, 19, p. 5 (4 May 1771).

29. William Rose, who published an excellent English translation (*The Sorrows of Young Werther*, London, 1929), mentioned to me the

difficulties of finding an adequate translation of this word; cf. also Detlev W. Schumann, 'Some notes on Werther' *JEGP*, lv, 1956.

30. See Hass, 'Werther-Studie', p. 107.

31. W.A., i, 19, pp. 5 f. (4 May 1771), see Hass, 'Werther-Studie', p. 111, who points out how Werther's indifference to practical questions emphasizes his self-abandonment to his feeling; see also Hildegard Emmel, *Weltklage und Bild der Welt in der Dichtung Goethes*, Weimar, 1957, p. 31, who stresses that Werther neither knows of, nor is unconsciously able to accept the interaction between the inner and outer worlds.

32. W.A., i, 19, p. 7 (10 May 1771).

33. W.A., i, 19, p. 8 (10 May 1771). For a thorough analysis of Werther's incapacity of understanding artistic creation, cf. Ilse Appelbaum-Graham, 'Minds without Medium. Reflections on *Emilia Galotti* and *Werther's Leiden*', *Euph.*, lvi, 1962.

34. W.A., i, 19, p. 9 (12 May 1771).

35. W.A., i, 19, p. 10 (13 May 1771).

36. Cf. Ronald Grimsley, *Rousseau. A Study in Self-awareness*, Cardiff, 1961, p. 49.

37. Cf. L. A. Willoughby, 'The Image of the "Wanderer" and the "Hut" in Goethe's Poetry', *ÉG*, vi (1951).

38. Letter to Friedrich Ernst Schönborn, 1 June 1774.

39. Cf. Eric A. Blackall, *The Emergence of German as a Literary Language 1700–1775*, Cambridge, 1959, pp. 410 ff. for a full appreciation of Wieland's language; cf. also the standard critical biography, Friedrich Sengle, *Wieland*, Stuttgart, 1949.

40. W.A., i, 19, p. 141.

41. W.A., i, 19, p. 5 (4 May 1771).

42. W.A., i, 19, p. 7 (10 May 1771).

43. See Emil Staiger, 'Ein Satz aus der Winckelmannschrift', *Schweizer Monatshefte*, xxxvii (1957), p. 203.

44. Storz, *Goethe-Vigilien*, p. 32.

45. Ernst Beutler, *G.A.*, 8, pp. 976 ff.

46. Elizabeth M. Wilkinson and L. A. Willoughby, 'The Blind Man and the Poet. An Early Stage in Goethe's Quest for Form', *German Studies presented to Walter Horace Bruford*, London, 1962, p. 50.

47. Conversation with Henry Crabb Robinson, 2 August 1829.

48. See Trunz, H.A., 6, p. 550, who points out that Werther's letters strike many different notes.

49. See Trunz, ibid., p. 551, who refers to the rhythm of the letter-sequence.

50. See Trunz, ibid., p. 564, who stresses the significance of these words.

51. See August Langen, *Der Wortschatz des deutschen Pietismus*, Tübingen, 1954, p. 463.

52. Cf. Emil Staiger, *Die Zeit als Einbildungskraft des Dichters*, Zürich, 1939, pp. 25 ff.

53. W.A., i, 19, p. 75 (18 August 1771).

54. Herbert Schöffler, 'Die Leiden des jungen Werthers. Ihr geistesgeschichtlicher Hintergrund', *Deutscher Geist im 18. Jahrhundert*, Göttingen, 1956, p. 172, calls Werther's religion not pantheistic but pantheizing. Schöffler's comments are extremely subtle, but it is difficult to agree with his contention that for Werther nature and the cosmos are God. Cf. also Beutler, p. 151, who disagrees with Schöffler.

55. W.A., i, 19, p. 130 (15 November 1772).

56. W.A., i, 19, p. 130 (15 November 1772).

57. W.A., i, 19, p. 133 (26 November 1772).

58. Trunz, H.A., 6, pp. 578 ff.

59. Cf. J. J. Anstett, 'La crise religieuse de Werther', *ÉG*, iv (1949), p. 127, who states: 'le baiser [which Werther and Lotte exchange] a donné l'accolade par laquelle Werther a été "sacré chevalier de l'éternité".'

60. W.A., i, 19, p. 189 (24 December 1772).

61. Cf. Max Diez, 'The Principle of the Dominant Metaphor in Goethe's *Werther*', *PMLA*, li (1936). Diez, however, goes too far, for he relates far more words to disease than can legitimately be done. It is also mistaken to assess the worsening of Werther's disease by statistical means as Diez does.

62. W.A., i, 19, p. 71 (12 August 1771).

63. W.A., i, 19, p. 69 (12 August 1771): the phrase alludes to St John, xi, 4.

64. W.A., i, 4, p. 162.

65. Butler, p. 255, considers him a promising young man.

66. Cf. Feise, 'Goethes Werther. . . .'

67. Cf. H. S. Reiss (ed.), *The Political Thought of the German Romantics*, Oxford, 1955 (also Hans Reiss, *Politisches Denken in der Deutschen Romantik*, Berne and Munich, 1966) for a fuller discussion.

68. E. M. Forster, *Aspects of the Novel*, London, 1927, pp. 103 ff.

69. Cf. Gose, op. cit. who takes the view that Lotte loves Werther, a view which I cannot share.

70. Most critics took this view, but Barker Fairley, *Goethe as revealed in his poetry*, London, 1932, p. 47, differed and put forward a view similar to mine.

71. W.A., i, 19, p. 148.

72. W.A., i, 19, p. 106 (16 March 1772).

73. Cf. Leonard Forster, 'Werther's reading of *Emilia Galotti*,' *PEGS*, xxvii (1958).

74. Cf. Lionel Trilling, *The Liberal Imagination*, London, 1951, p. 209.

75. Letter to Karl Friedrich Zelter, 26 March 1816.

76. Cf. Hermann Böschenstein, *Deutsche Gefühlskultur I*, Berne, 1954, p. 248; cf. Stahl, *Goethes Die Leiden* . . ., p. xxv, who distinguishes between the 'lyrical, subjective' presentation of Werther and the 'objective, epic' view of the editor.

77. W.A., i, 19, p. 141.

78. W.A., i, 19, p. 3.

79. Letter to Karl Friedrich Zelter, 3 December 1812.

80. Cf. Victor Lange, 'Die Sprache als Erzählform in Goethes "Werther" ', *Formenwandel. Festschrift zum 65. Geburtstag von Paul Böckmann* (ed. W. Müller-Seidel and W. Preisendanz), Hamburg, 1964, pp. 261 ff.

81. Cf. Riess, op. cit.

82. Cf. Karl Vietor, *Goethe*, Berne, 1949, pp. 39 ff.

83. See H.A., 6, p. 527, for instance, for a reprint of an anonymous review in the *Auserlesene Bibliothek der neuesten deutschen Literatur*.

84. See Friedrich Gundolf, *Goethe*, Berlin, 1916, pp. 169 ff.; see also William Rose, *From Goethe to Byron. The Development of Weltschmerz in German Literature*, London, 1924, p. 24, who criticized this view convincingly.

85. Cf. Stuart Pratt Atkins, *The Testament of Werther in Poetry and Drama*, Cambridge, Mass., 1949.

86. Conversation with Johann Peter Eckermann, 2 January 1824.

87. I owe this point to Elizabeth M. Wilkinson.

88. I owe this point to Fritz Martini.

89. Cf. J. W. von Appel, *Werther und seine Zeit*, 4th ed., Oldenburg, 1896.

90. Cf. Victor Lange, 'The Language of the Poet Goethe 1772–1774', *Wächter und Hüter. Festschrift für Hermann J. Weigand*, New Haven, Conn., 1957, pp. 67 ff.

91. Cf. von Appel. op. cit.

92. W.A., i, 26, p. 357.

93. Cf. von Appel, op. cit., who quotes many of the documents.

94. Cf. Barker Fairley, *A Study of Goethe*, Oxford, 1947, who emphasizes this feature.

95. Cf. Staiger, *Goethe I*, *passim*.

96. W.A., i, 37, p. 314.

97. W.A., i, 28, p. 209.

98. Matthijs Jolles, *Goethes Kunstanschauung*, Berne, 1957, p. 182.

99. Cf. R. Pascal, *The German Sturm und Drang*, Manchester, 1953.

100. Cf. W.A., i, 28, pp. 213 ff. (*Dichtung und Wahrheit*, ii, 13), where Goethe himself notes the influence of English writers on *Werther*.

101. Victor Lange, 'Die Sprache als Erzählform . . .', pp. 263 ff.

102. Ibid., p. 266.

103. Ibid., p. 267.

104. Ibid., p. 267.

105. August Langen, *Der Wortschatz des deutschen Pietismus*, pp. 463 f.; cf. Alfred Grosser, 'Le jeune Werther et le Piétisme', *ÉG*, iv (1949), pp. 203 ff.; and O. Huinandeau, 'Les Rapports de Goethe et de Lavater', ibid., pp. 213 ff.

106. Friedrich Gundolf, *Shakespeare und der deutsche Geist*, Berlin, 1911, pp. 244 f.

Wilhelm Meisters Lehrjahre

THE success of *Werther* firmly established Goethe's literary reputation. He became the leading German writer, and was invited to Weimar, first as the Duke's companion and later as a Cabinet Minister in the small duchy. In a new environment, Goethe changed; the impetuosity and changeability of his *Sturm und Drang* period gave way to a firmer, quieter mood. Yet his achievements during his first decade in Weimar were limited. Several longer works were planned but not completed. The most comprehensive work of the period, *Wilhelm Meisters Theatralische Sendung*, remained a fragment. Only six books, one half of the planned novel, were completed; a seventh appears to have been begun, but is lost.

It is highly improbable that the novel was begun before 1775.[1] The six books written in the years 1777–85 only became known in 1910, when a copy made by Barbara Schulthess, a lady-in-waiting at the court of Weimar, was discovered. Shortly before his journey to Italy in 1786, Goethe apparently abandoned work on it. He appears to have considered the fragment unsatisfactory, for he never published it, presumably because the completed novel, *Wilhelm Meisters Lehrjahre*, had rendered the earlier work redundant.

The *Theatralische Sendung* opens in the 1740s. Wilhelm Meister is a young boy, the son of a successful merchant, who has risen to be mayor of his native town but whose origins are lower middle class. Wilhelm's grandmother still lives in a simple house. Her son discovers that she has kept marionettes for her grandson, whose sensitive imagination delights in this first introduction to the theatre. He takes a passionate interest in them, and performs plays at the earliest opportunity. This also serves as a creative outlet for a boy growing up in a restrictive bourgeois world and in an unhappy home, for his parents are emotionally estranged. His early enthusiasm for the puppet-theatre is followed by an attempt to stage plays for children. He thus tastes the first delights of the stage, but is also confronted with its difficulties and drawbacks. When he has grown up, he frequents the theatre, falls in love with a beautiful young actress called Madame de B. or Mariane. His love for her is blind, and certainly she is far from being innocent, as he assumes. She starts an affair with Wilhelm, without having got rid of her last lover who happens to be away on business. She genuinely falls in love with Wilhelm, and is greatly disturbed by the equivocal situation in which she finds herself; she cannot, however, summon up the courage to tell him the truth. In loving Mariane, Wilhelm also indulges his enthusiasm for the theatre. He wants to become an actor. His friend and brother-in-law, Werner, attempts in vain to acquaint him with the real situation. When he finally discovers Mariane's affair with Norberg, his world collapses. He does not even attempt to confront Mariane with his discovery, and stops seeing her. His disappointment is so severe that he at once ceases to believe in her love, and falls seriously ill. On recovering, he has many conversations about literature with Werner. We read of his views on problems of tragedy in general, and on French tragedy in particular, and of his early dramas, from two of which – *Die königliche Einsiedlerin* (*The Hermit Queen*) and *Belsazar* – passages are quoted. Wilhelm travels on business, but is quickly attracted again to the theatre; he becomes familiar in turn with various levels of the stage, he watches the primitive acting of miners, and he encounters a group of acrobats and meets the actor Melina, by whom he is introduced to Mme de Retti's travelling theatre company. He also meets Mignon, a young girl of Italian origin whom he protects against the managers who exploit her. Later on, he decides to look after her. Mme de Retti stages Wilhelm's drama *Belsazar*. Because the main actor Bendel has fallen ill on the opening night, Wilhelm plays the principal part and achieves a great success. Afterwards, however, Mme de Retti refuses to return money which he has lent her. There is a scandal caused by Bendel's inadequate acting. Mme de Retti finally takes flight with Bendel and is succeeded as director by Melina. Wilhelm continues his association with the theatre: he meets Herr von C., a highly cultured officer deeply interested in literature; Philine, the pretty and flirtatious actress who appears to like him; the mysterious Harper whose melancholic songs move him; the Count and the Countess, who are patrons of the theatre, and whose secretary, a dilettante writer himself, invites him and the whole company to the Count's estate. When they arrive they are not, however, well received, though finally they are allowed to perform in the castle. An officer introduces Wilhelm to the works of Shakespeare, which overwhelm him. After leaving the castle, Wilhelm becomes director of the company. Highway robbers attack them on the road. Wilhelm is wounded and nursed by Philine. A surgeon accompanying an aristocrat who is passing by treats his wound. Wilhelm is greatly affected by the appearance of a young woman on horseback who is also with this party. Soon after this attack the company disperses, and Wilhelm travels alone to a city called H., where Serlo, a well-known and successful theatre director, welcomes him. Wilhelm has most interesting discussions with him and his sister Aurelie about the theatre. They urge Wilhelm to join Serlo's theatre, especially as Serlo is taking over Melina's company. Wilhelm, after some hesitation, accepts the offer in the hope of realizing his aspirations for a national theatre. An added inducement arises from his surmise that a beautiful actress, whose impending arrival Serlo had announced, might be the same woman whom he had seen on horseback after he had been wounded.

It is not known how the novel was to end. Ludwig Tieck, the German Romantic poet, reports a conversation with Frau Aja, Goethe's mother, who (so he avers) told him that Wilhelm was to found a national theatre and marry Mariane;[2] it is possible that Goethe had such an end in mind. To have him meet Mariane again and then to marry her would be a dénouement that would agree with the pattern of the *Trivialroman* (novel of entertainment or conventional novel) of the period from which Goethe borrowed many features. This account is, however, in no way corroborated. We cannot be sure how the novel was to progress and whether his plans about its future course had, in fact, matured.

Whatever contemporary material Goethe may have used in *Wilhelm Meisters Theatralische Sendung*, he adapted and changed it for his own purpose more than in his first novel. Just as the story is not as concise as that of *Werther*, so the material is also more heterogeneous. Yet this difference does not mean that he portrayed contemporary life here less realistically than in *Werther*. Indeed, he did not; only the tangible events which inspired *Werther* can, to some extent at least, be singled out from the pattern of the whole work. The story described in the *Sendung* is less personal, although personal elements enter into it. It gives a vivid account of the theatrical life of the period, but the stage experiences depicted cannot be pinned down to one particular theatre. Nor could this be expected. For by contrast to *Werther*, the action is not concentrated on a single experience, but is related to a series of experiences.

Although there are many episodes, there are only two main elements contained in the story, and these are interconnected. The first deals with the personality of the hero, Wilhelm Meister, and his development, the second with the theatre and its world.

The fragmentary character of the novel does not diminish its readability; in order merely to enjoy the story on a superficial first reading, it is not necessary to know anything about the probable turn which events would have taken in the concluding six books, which were never written. A satisfactory interpretation of the *Sendung* is, however, greatly handicapped by the fact that it is incomplete. The difficulties begin with the title.

Did Goethe intend the title *Wilhelm Meisters Theatralische Sendung* to be taken seriously, and did he wish to describe the theatrical mission of Wilhelm Meister in such a way as to end in some form of triumph for the hero, who would by then have become the founder of the national theatre? Or did he wish to criticize the hero's mistaken hopes and his lack of realism? Our interpretation of the author's purpose must determine our view of the hero's personality. Is Wilhelm a great poet from whom a revitalisation of the German theatre, and indeed of German culture, can be expected or is he merely an amiable, though talented, young man who is inclined to indulge in wishful thinking? Does Wilhelm deservedly bear Shakespeare's Christian name, or does this name merely serve to emphasize the incongruity between endeavour and achievement? Is Wilhelm called 'Meister' only because it is ironically implied that he is an eternal learner, or because he is on the way to create masterpieces in the realms of poetry and the theatre? Is Wilhelm a portrait of what Goethe might have become if he had more consistently pursued his theatrical ambitions, or is he merely a foil intended to criticize uncalled-for expectations entertained by his creator? And is the theatre meant to provide a picture of the world, as the baroque emblem of the world as a stage does,[3] is it a moral institution, as Schiller would have it,[4] or is it merely an account of specific history?

These are questions which are raised by any careful reading of the novel. Scholars are divided in their answers.[5] The text must supply the answers to these questions, though in the case of a fragment, any other available evidence of Goethe's intention, including the biographical and historical background, assumes particular importance.

What arguments can be advanced for the view that Wilhelm is a poet? We hear of early attempts at writing poetry as a boy, we learn of several plays based on religious or biblical subjects – *Die Königliche Einsiedlerin* (*The Hermit Queen*), *Jezebel*, *Belsazar* and others – written by him as a young man. From two of them, *Die Königliche Einsiedlerin* and *Belsazar*, a few passages are quoted, some though not all of which are impressive. Not only Amelie and Werner (who, as close relatives, are after all likely to be biased) respond favourably to his work, but even the experienced actors of Mme de Retti's troupe appear to like *Belsazar*. This play is, in fact, a success on the stage, with Wilhelm playing the main part. But even more than that – Wilhelm translates, or rather writes, a poem in imitation of an Italian song recited by Mignon, which is one of the gems of German lyric poetry: *Kennst Du das Land*, written in Goethe's early Weimar period. Anyone capable of writing a poem of that calibre might claim to be a poet of genius. But in addition Wilhelm discourses perceptively on poetics and on French tragedy, and he puts forward interesting interpretations of the origin and theory of tragedy, which to a large extent are in advance of his time. For the novel, unlike *Werther*, is set in an earlier period. It covers the period from Wilhelm's boyhood in the 1740s to his activities as a traveller, an actor and playwright in the 1760s. Wilhelm is, then, a good ten years older than Werther, and the period corresponds to the thirty years before Werther's sorrows began.

Furthermore, Wilhelm is so successful as an actor and theatrical organizer that Serlo, one of the leading theatre directors of the day, goes to great lengths to secure him for his theatre.

These arguments in favour of accepting Wilhelm's theatrical mission may, on the surface, appear so overwhelming as to render further discussion superfluous, but they will not stand the test of closer inspection. From the very beginning, there is an ironic criticism of his hopes and endeavours. Admittedly, this is always friendly and sympathetic, yet it leaves no doubt that he is capable neither of judging his own abilities nor appraising the cultural circumstances of his time soundly.

Irony is, of course, an elusive quality. Frequently it depends on careful listening to the tone of the work, for irony relies on meaning or implying the opposite of what is stated. It springs from the incongruity between what we expect and what can be attained. In the *Sendung*, irony emanates, in the main, from the attitude of the narrator, who more often implicitly than explicitly criticizes the hero, exposing his limited perception.

The hero's lack of realism cannot be overlooked. There are many instances of it: his attitude in the first book to Mariane, whom he loves blindly, without any awareness of the real circumstances of her life, his unbridled enthusiasm for the theatre, his overestimation of his talents, his excessive eulogy of the poet, his praise of aristocrats, and his inability to perceive the true character of the actors, who are more interested in mundane matters than in cultural ideals. Each time, Wilhelm is unrealistic. He is not easily deflected, however, from his enthusiasm. He is prepared to reconsider his views only when something happens that cannot be misunderstood, as, for example, when he discovers a *billet doux* from Mariane's lover or when Mme de Retti steals the theatre's cash-box. Only then does he wake up out of his dreams and recognize the limits which life sets to our imagination. Even his apparent success, on closer consideration, turns out to be of doubtful value. His successful reading of his tragedy *Belsazar* owes much to the punch-drinking of the actors. His performance on the stage is welcomed enthusiastically, but only by a public which can hardly be called sophisticated. Indeed, even his enthusiasm for Shakespeare is suspect, for an experienced practitioner of the theatre such as Serlo reacts to his Hamlet interpretation with some reserve. It is true that, at the end of the novel, he appears to look forward to a renaissance of the German theatre, but here again it is not clear whether it is not a mirage. Do the circumstances really permit Wilhelm to realize his hopes, and is his personality really sufficiently powerful to make the kind of impact on his environment required for an enterprise of this magnitude?

Favourable circumstances would, given the cultural and social situation in eighteenth-century Germany, require the novel to have a utopian ending, of which the penetrating realism of the extant books gives no inkling whatsoever. But is Wilhelm's personality sufficiently impressive to warrant the great hopes placed in him? Hardly, for Wilhelm is too amiable, too receptive a person to be expected to lead a literary or theatrical movement. Only an outstanding personality, a man of genius, could hope to do so. He may appear to claim that stature, but he is far too immature to convince us of the validity of such a claim. After all, a few striking stanzas in a longish play, a remarkable poetic translation of an Italian model, interesting but obscure and almost bizarre views on tragedy, and an original, but one-sided interpretation of *Hamlet* do not add up to much. Certainly they reveal an interesting, perhaps an unusual mind, but they do not portray a personality whose impetus is overwhelming. Indeed, it would be foolish to expect a rejuvenation of the German theatre or even a renaissance of German drama from a young man who, though pleasant, is so clearly limited. How could so ingenuous a man hope to succeed where Lessing failed? His name and his claim to success and perfection are a testimony to persistent irony, later on developed even more fully in the *Lehrjahre*.

Clearly this ironic interpretation cannot be ignored. Yet is it capable of confuting the serious view of Wilhelm's theatrical mission? It does not appear to do so, for in neither case can conclusive evidence be found; it would seem as if two contradictory interpretations were valid; but this is clearly impossible. How can we avoid this dilemma? Since the work is not complete we cannot do this by reference to the text alone. It is therefore essential to examine the novel in relation to Goethe's own development.

Wilhelm Meisters Theatralische Sendung falls between the first and second versions of *Werther*. If the second version shows a greater attempt to be objective, the *Sendung*, written over a lengthy period, portrays stages on the road to objectivity. *Werther*, as we have seen, reveals a world in conflict, a conflict mirrored in the conflicting styles of Werther and of the editor. If in the *Sendung*, in contrast to *Werther*, the narrative style is uniform, this does not mean that the conflict is overcome.

It is, in fact, a conflict which is fought out not in the open, so to speak, but in the realm of stylistic nuances: a conflict between the two tones of the narrative of which one is subjective, emotional and serious, the other detached, objective, and ironic. In *Werther* the emphasis had lain on the individual's emotional and spiritual life. The external world is of interest only in so far as it impinges on Werther's personal fate. In the *Sendung* the world is still seen in relation to its hero, Wilhelm Meister, but what happens in the novel does not necessarily relate to the vacillations of his inner life. On the contrary, his relationship to his environment is in the foreground. If in *Werther* the right appears to be more on Werther's side in the first version than in the second, any one-sided interpretation of his struggle with the external world, siding with him or the world around him, would be mistaken. Only an interpretation embracing both perspectives can do him justice. It is not greatly different in the case of the *Sendung*. It is not clear to what extent Wilhelm's assessment of the external world is correct. In any case, the situation is not so extreme as in *Werther*. Wilhelm is capable of adapting himself to his environment. His claims are not rejected, but warmly welcomed. But this attitude is far from realistic. He is still developing his sense of reality. Two conflicting views prevail. On the one hand, it looks as if Wilhelm's aspirations are realizable. The theatre was the only place from which, in a secular period, culture in Germany could be resuscitated and Wilhelm's talents are of the kind to carry out the campaign necessary to bring about this revival. On the other hand, it appears as if Wilhelm has misjudged his powers which do not suffice to make him realize his aims. Above all, the theatre could never be the rallying point for a cultural renaissance. Only in a period of social and political stagnation, as represented by the later half of the eighteenth century, could an erroneous belief of this kind arise. Wilhelm has to find his way through the maze created by these different points of view. He is not aware of these conflicts, but they provide the background against which his education takes place.

A further complication making it impossible to assess Wilhelm's achievement is created by the character of the theatre itself. Criteria are bound to be elusive in a place where semblance is reality. In addition, the theatre in eighteenth-century Germany could not be certain of an educated audience, which is needed if an agreed standard is to prevail, a standard without which it is even more difficult to judge achievement. It is, of course, possible that the later books of the *Sendung* would have made it clear whether Wilhelm was to realize his ambitions or not. But it is also possible that a definite answer would not have been given. For why should we expect to have an unambiguous account of so complex a matter as the theatre in eighteenth-century Germany? Much could be expected from the theatre in those days: Gottsched's success in reforming the German stage and the German language is proof of what a man with limited talents but a strong determination could achieve. Yet greater men – Lessing, Goethe, Schiller – failed in their attempt to accomplish cultural reforms. Lessing's *Hamburgische Dramaturgie*, Goethe's und Schiller's *Xenien* and Goethe's essay *Literarischer Sansculottismus* bear witness to this impasse. For Lessing's dramatic criticism culminated in his account of the failure of the Hamburg National theatre, and Goethe's and Schiller's polemical epigrams were, like Goethe's essay, directed against the cultural poverty prevailing in the Germany of the day. All these three works tell of the disappointment experienced by the three greatest imaginative writers of the age. Realism can, so we learn from them, be abandoned only at great emotional cost.

Given the failure of the great dramatists of the classical age to realize their ideals, why should the *Sendung* describe a success which life had not provided? Could not the end of the *Sendung* have left the issue in doubt, which would have been in keeping with the actual situation? Only if Goethe himself or someone else had succeeded in creating a German national theatre before the completion of the novel would it have been possible to expect it to end with Wilhelm's bringing his mission to a fruitful close. It is, of course, possible that Goethe changed his mind in the process of composition. The length of time which he spent on the novel, indeed, made a change of plan not unlikely. Nonetheless, we should not conclude that Goethe was not sure of his style and therefore alternated continually from one level of writing to another. For the novel does not convey the impression of uncertainty in the author. Like the majority of the novels of the period, it belongs to the middle style,[6] i.e. neither to the high and lofty reflective style nor to the comic low novel, but among these middle-style novels it stands out for its literary qualities. It also far surpasses the German adventure and travel fiction out of which it emerged, because its power of description, its liveliness of style and its immediacy of presentation are so much greater. Even Wieland, the undoubted master of the German novel before Goethe, cannot compete. One of the qualities which makes the *Sendung* so impressive is its style, which is not in one key only. The subject-matter of the novel – the development of a dramatist and the theatre – demands a differentiated treatment, and not a simple account.

The ambiguity inherent in a poet's existence clearly preoccupied Goethe. If in the *Sendung* he sought to describe the rise of a poet, he had almost inevitably to leave the quality of the poet's work in doubt in the early stages of the novel. *Torquato Tasso*, the first version of which was written at the same time, throws some, though not much, light on the problem. *Tasso* is the drama of an established major poet. Goethe here deals with the complicated reasons for the disproportion between life and poetry. Tasso, in contrast to Wilhelm, is greatly honoured and esteemed by the society of his time, for the court of Ferrara, where he lives, represents all that matters in distinction and taste. Yet Tasso does not succeed in establishing harmonious relations with his environment; his claims, though justified from the standpoint of pure poetry, cannot be met by those concerned with living. The incongruity between the unconditional demands which he makes on life and the necessities imposed by life give rise to his tragedy; from a similar incongruity spring the irony and complexity of Wilhelm Meister. Goethe had called Tasso a Werther on a higher level.[7] It would, however, be wrong to make a similar comparison between him and Wilhelm Meister; for Wilhelm's personality certainly lacks the magic of Werther and Tasso, but he is also more adaptable to life. This very adaptability, however, creates a less clear-cut situation. In addition, Wilhelm's ability to adjust himself, to be at peace with the world in which he lives, means that he does not feel misunderstood. It is left to the narrator to point out Wilhelm's misunderstanding of the world. Thus, in the last resort, the contrast between the narrator and the hero is also crucial for an interpretation of the novel, presenting a variation of the different attitudes revealed by Werther and the editor of his letters.

The problems created by the personality and by the achievement of the hero are not the only central theme of the novel. The theatre itself also occupies much space in the foreground. Of course, its function can be understood only in relation to the hero; its nature is, however, described fully and vividly.

The lively account which Goethe gives of the theatre is in part based on contemporary history, in part on personal knowledge. It has even been maintained that Shakespeare's biography, as recounted by Wieland in his introduction to his translation, may have served as a model; for both Wilhelm and Shakespeare had parents who were merchants, and both were meant to follow in their father's footsteps.[8] Both become involved with theatre companies, write plays and strike up important friendships; yet in fact the parallel is remote. Goethe's own experience may undoubtedly have been a source.[9] His enthusiasm for the theatre was awakened in his youth. His own acting in Weimar and his contact with actors may have given him an insight; indeed, even a carpet on which Wilhelm walks when he plays Belsazar has been identified with one used by Goethe in a performance of *Iphigenie auf Tauris*. We also know that at Ilmenau in the Duchy of Weimar Goethe saw plays performed by miners. It is also possible that the Count is modelled on Prince Henry of Prussia. Further models may have been the dramatist Christian Friedrich Weisse (for the Count's secretary who writes dramas), the poet Ewald von Kleist (for Herr von C.), the poet Gleim (for the Harper), and the actor-manager Friedrich Ludwig Schroeder in Hamburg (for Serlo and his city theatre); the Weimar actress Corona Schröter might well have appeared in a later book as the beautiful actress who was to join Serlo's theatre. These suppositions, however, some of which are very far-fetched, do not help us much in our understanding of the novel. There is no doubt that most of the subject-matter of Wilhelm's plays was well known. Several performances dealing with the story of Saul and Goliath are attested; other plots are taken from Gottsched's *Deutsche Schaubühne*, a collection of well-known eighteenth-century plays. All these features add to the historical flavour of the work; they are not, however, documentation, and do not matter much. The *Sendung* is clearly not a documentary historical novel; it is a form of fiction which is not hostile to fact.

The term 'National Theatre' had acquired a definite meaning by the time that Goethe made Wilhelm Meister aspire to become the founder of an institution of this kind.[10] It was, in the first place, a theatre which (unlike the court theatres or the touring companies) should appeal to the whole national community, and not merely to a section. In the second place, it meant a non-commercial, permanent theatre, subsidized like other institutions which already existed in the German states for educational and cultural purposes. Thirdly, it was to be a focal point where indigenous culture could be promoted to equal and to supplant the French theatre in Germany. It also had a strong pedagogic and moral purpose, for it was to help in raising the educational and cultural level of the country. High hopes had been associated with these ventures that bore the name 'National Theatre'. Not necessarily one single theatre was envisaged; indeed, 'National Theatres' proliferated in the later decades of the eighteenth century. The rise of the National Theatre movement does, however, reflect the dominant trend in the whole history of the German theatre from Gottsched onward. In a Germany divided into many petty states, the German language was the only common cultural bond. Since even the church was subject to the state, the theatre alone promised freedom. The National Theatre was to spell independence from the courts, which were merely gratifying their own tastes by establishing foreign operas and theatres.

At Hamburg, at that time a prosperous port, the first attempt to establish a National Theatre was made at the instigation of an ambitious young man called J. L. Löwen. Although Lessing was its dramatic critic, it was short lived, for the Hamburg merchants who backed it soon found it too expensive, and discontinued their support. The high aims to give the theatre a dignity it had never possessed before and to make it into an institution capable of improving the moral conduct of the public, as set out by Löwen in a grandiloquent pamphlet, were not realized. Despite its failure, it pointed the way for later attempts: in Hamburg itself under the aegis of the actor-manager Friedrich Ludwig Schröder, who opened the theatre to the drama of the *Sturm und Drang* and did much to establish Shakespeare on the German stage; in Gotha, where an enlightened Duke established a theatre of highly professional actors with Ekhof as its director; in Vienna, where the Emperor Joseph II, probably influenced by Klopstock and Lessing, made the *Burgtheater* a national theatre; in Mannheim (1779) with Dalberg, an aristocrat director, and Iffland as its main actor and playwright, the theatre which first staged Schiller's *Sturm und Drang* dramas *Die Räuber*, *Fiesko* and *Kabale und Liebe*; in Berlin (1786), where Iffland, then the leading actor and one of the most successful playwrights, had gone from Mannheim; and Weimar (1791), with Goethe as its director, followed suit. Permanent theatres were established, and the foundations were laid for the pre-eminence of the German theatre in the nineteenth century. In Weimar, mainly through Goethe's influence, a classical style of staging and acting was established. The theatre played an important part in cultural life, perhaps on account of the many cultural centres resulting from the centrifugal force of political division. No other country, indeed, could boast of so many theatres. Yet the high-minded hopes of raising the cultural level of the nation, of bringing about a moral renaissance through the theatre, were not fulfilled. The theatre was incapable of providing an answer to the social and political problems that beset Germany. At the time when Goethe wrote *Wilhelm Meisters Theatralische Sendung* the future of the theatre was still unsettled.

The importance assigned to the theatre in the *Sendung* is enhanced if it is realized that it had an important function in the structure of eighteenth-century life in Germany. Hopes for cultural change, even social reform, and for a different style of life, were then associated with the theatre which, in a period of secularization, had taken over some of the functions of ecclesiastical institutions.

The stagnant social scene did not offer any possibilities of meaningful activity for many gifted men. It is also doubtful whether either Wilhelm or the theatre would be equal to the lofty task assigned to them. Wilhelm's interpretation of Hamlet as a sensitive individual whose fate is to cope with a task for which his powers are inadequate and which consequently crushes him, may well suggest to Wilhelm a feeling of inadequacy which he never admits to himself. Yet Wilhelm is never aware of any dangers that may lurk in his path. His confidence in his own ability and in the theatre is never shaken. Only the reader is invited by the narrator to share doubts which are never unambiguously resolved. Not only Wilhelm's passion for the theatre, but passion and the theatre themselves are critically portrayed. Still, we must remember that Goethe wrote about aspirations which at the time of writing were being translated into practice. The unsuccessful venture of the Hamburg National Theatre precedes the beginning of Goethe's composition of *Wilhelm Meister* by one decade only. In dealing with the gestation of the struggle for a German national theatre, the *Sendung* depicts the rise of German classicism, which was, of course, closely associated with the theatre. In a large measure German classicism and the culture of Weimar itself are the story of Goethe's own endeavour and achievement. To see more clearly the general tendency and implication of the *Sendung*, and the reasons why it was not completed, it may help us if we recall the development of Goethe's life and thought. The *Sendung* was the first major work which Goethe tackled after his arrival in Weimar as a companion of the young Duke Karl August in 1775. It was the only large prose work which he wrote during that period, and its composition extended over almost ten years. Inevitably, Goethe's views developed and changed during so long a period. It is possible, indeed even probable, that these changes were reflected in the novel. It would be a gross over-simplification to suggest that Goethe started out by sharing Wilhelm's enthusiasm but, on reaching the beginning of the seventh book, abandoned the work because he had ceased to believe in the value of the theatre and Wilhelm's creative power. This hypothesis would imply that Goethe had not conceived a definite plan from the beginning. But to suppose that Goethe was continuously modifying his plans, that he vacillated from chapter to chapter, would mean that he was entirely at the mercy of passing moods, and that writing was hardly a serious matter for him. Undoubtedly, changes of mind can be noticed in the novel, as indeed elsewhere in Goethe's work, but all the available evidence does not point to a disorganized mind. What is possible, however, is that Goethe depicted in

Wilhelm Meister, whom he called his 'beloved dramatic self-portrait',[11] some of his own hopes and problems. The *Sendung* may even amount to an ironic commentary on these. He undoubtedly believed that a new culture might be created. The revolution in poetics ushered in by Herder and carried out to a large extent by Goethe himself engendered in other writers a mood of confidence, frequently not matched by their actual achievement. Yet the *Sendung* does not convey the flavour of a programmatic novel. It is far too realistic and subtle for that. But who is to say with certainty what is possible in a sphere so amorphous as culture and what is not, especially if an emerging culture is involved?

In the course of his first years at Weimar under the influence of Frau von Stein (with whom he was in love), and later under the impact of his growing interest in natural science, Goethe became inclined to view the world less from a directly personal angle. His experience as an administrator, admittedly of a petty principality, as well as the secluded though highly civilized atmosphere of a small court, left their mark. His attitude changed; he became increasingly detached and objective. Subjective feeling was no longer the sole criterion. Like Werther, Wilhelm has had a passionate love-affair which ends in his disappointment, but his love, in contrast to Werther's, is returned. His disappointment shatters his world, but it does not spell the end of his zest for life. His emotional strength and independence revive, because his attitude to his environment is different. For him, the world is not so much a mirror of his own soul as material to be moulded; it opens a series of situations with which it was worthwhile becoming involved. This difference illustrates Goethe's own changing attitude as he became increasingly aware of man's possibilities and limitations, and thus felt more and more the need to assess the world realistically. In *Werther*, the world was shown in conflict; in the *Sendung*, this conflict still persists, but no longer openly delineated. It is assimilated into the story that is told. As part of the narrative texture, it becomes a problem to be viewed in some measure from outside, with detachment. Such doubts as Goethe had about the power of feeling and the danger of excessive emotion formed the background to *Werther*. These doubts are transferred to another plane in the *Sendung*. They are the doubts as to the efficacy of his own art and as to the role of the artist in society. Goethe may not have doubted his own specific genius, but he was uncertain about the extent and power of its impact, and the degree to which his work was accepted. Here, hopes and disappointment dwell side by side, for the story of Goethe's uncertainties has been interwoven with the story of Wilhelm Meister. The hero's life draws on incidents of Goethe's own life – his interest in the puppet-theatre, kindled by the French lieutenant during the French occupation of Frankfurt in the Seven Years War, the early plays about shepherds and shepherdesses, the tragedies *David und Goliath* and *Belsazar*, his early preference for French tragedy, succeeded by an enthusiasm for Shakespeare – but these incidents do not turn Wilhelm into a portrait of Goethe. A segment of his versatile personality sufficed to form the basis of Wilhelm Meister's personality.

The drama must have absorbed much of Goethe's creative effort, much more, in fact, than could be explained by his interest in the Weimar court theatre or by his own acting. Goethe and the Duke, for instance, joined professional actors to stage the prose version of *Iphigenie auf Tauris*. The story of Goethe's involvement in the drama cannot be fully fathomed, for the evidence is lacking. We can thus surmise that the attachment was deeper than might be suspected at first sight. We can also presume – and the *Sendung* tells us so implicitly – that it was an involvement not without risks, self-doubts and self-searching, representative of Goethe's poetic task itself. To abandon the theatre, as Wilhelm Meister does in the *Lehrjahre*, thus anticipating Goethe's own resignation from the directorship much later in life, was one possible development, but it need not have happened that way if circumstances had been different for Goethe and the German theatre. Yet perhaps failure was always implicit in the attempt to make an institution based on such hazardous and uncertain foundations the springboard for reform. The *Sendung*, however, does not suggest this conclusion, yet it does depict in a large measure the uncertainties and vacillations accompanying a struggle of that kind. It would therefore be foolish to expect it to be a work capable of a simple interpretation. Its subject-matter, on the contrary, demands on two levels, those of irony and of plain seriousness, the comprehensive treatment which it received.

In the *Lehrjahre*, however, the point of view had shifted. Youthful enthusiasm and the theatre are treated consistently with irony, and accordingly Wilhelm Meister, whose personality in the *Sendung* was depicted as that of a possible genius in the making, was duly deprived of any element of genius. Only his receptivity and amiability remained.

When Goethe returned to the 'Wilhelm Meister' theme in 1793, he created a new work. Although many passages in the first half of the *Lehrjahre* correspond almost exactly to their equivalents in the *Sendung*, the work was so greatly changed that it would be mistaken to consider it merely a new version. It must be regarded as a different work. The problem of the artist, the major theme of the *Sendung*, is seen in quite another light during Goethe's classical period.

As Goethe had grown more mature as a person and as an administrator through his experiences in Weimar and through his travels in Italy, the original plan that Wilhelm was to find fulfilment in the profession of a playwright became less and less attractive to him. Firstly, after his return from Italy, the theatre no longer appeared to him the place in which Wilhelm could be fully educated. His acquaintance with Karl Philipp Moritz, author of the autobiographical novel *Anton Reiser*, only confirmed him in this view.[12] For Anton Reiser, the theatre was an educational force which allowed men to escape from the narrow confines of social class, and Shakespeare was the model whose work was not a mere aesthetic phenomenon. On the contrary, Shakespeare became a symbol of his own longing for glory. The course of Anton Reiser's – and Moritz's – life in some ways resembled Wilhelm's. It revealed the same passion for the theatre, whose pedagogical powers were stressed. Above all, the impact of Shakespeare on both Moritz and Goethe was just as great on their heroes. Appropriately, Goethe gave his hero the same Christian name. Anton Reiser's passion for the theatre became a substitute for religion, a guide for life itself. But Moritz's own experience proves how problematic his passion for the theatre was, how ineffectual it was as an educational force.

For Goethe, recognition of the defects of the theatre was part of an endeavour to develop his whole view of art and nature. Even before he defined, in conjunction with Schiller, his classical theory of art, he recognized that the plan of Wilhelm's theatrical mission involved discussion of a special problem, the problem of genius. Belief in the power of genius was, indeed, one of the main ideas of the poetic theory of the *Sturm und Drang* movement.[13] Even Goethe shared it. His poems about the artist, the so-called *Künstlergedichte*, his great hymns, *Faust*, even his plays *Götz von Berlichingen*, *Egmont* and *Torquato Tasso*, deal with extraordinary, powerful, even titanic personalities. Goethe's rhapsodic praise of Shakespeare in his essay *Zum Shakespeares Tag* tells even more unambiguously of this passionate cult. *Werther*, however, is a criticism of a man who thinks that he is a genius, but is not, and ruins his life by clinging to this mistaken belief. The new atmosphere of Weimar and the more objective tendency of Goethe's thought made him turn away from the view held earlier that the genius might exemplify the problems of man and society. On the contrary, genius was too much of a special case. In art, too, it was Goethe's aim, in accordance with his study of nature, no longer to apprehend the specific, but rather the typical.[14] Another view of life had to be taken. Religion and social activity claimed their due. Wilhelm was to educate himself and find a purpose in life. Goethe's conception of art had become more clearly defined.

While, therefore, much material could be taken over from the *Sendung*, and much had to be revised or cut out, much had to be added. The later parts of the novel, especially the last three, spring from a completely new conception. The first four books, which correspond to the six books of the *Sendung*, also reveal a different picture of Wilhelm's development. Since the *Sendung* was neither completed, nor published with Goethe's approval, the *Lehrjahre* alone can be considered a novel in the full sense of the word. For the purpose of our consideration, the *Sendung* is therefore mainly of interest because of the light it throws on the *Lehrjahre*. While the same characters, with a few exceptions, appear in both novels, and even possess the same names, they are, in fact, different persons; and although events are often similar, their character in each book is moulded by a different way of experiencing them. His study of nature had taught Goethe to look no longer for the isolated instance, but to see each particular phenomenon in its relation to the whole. Stylistic and structural changes became necessary in the *Lehrjahre*, because Goethe's view of the world had changed following his journey to Italy. The first four books of the *Lehrjahre* appear more closely organized than the corresponding six books of the *Sendung*. Many passages, whole scenes were struck out; others are much more convincingly expressed, and some figures and scenes are new. In the *Sendung*, Wilhelm's development is depicted from his childhood onward, while in the *Lehrjahre*, he appears as a young man, whose early years are recaptured only by means of his memories. The *Sendung* is a novel of the theatre: the *Lehrjahre* pursues a completely different aim. As it is avowedly an account of Wilhelm's education, it treats his passion for the theatre with a certain irony.* The *Sendung*, by narrating Wilhelm's childhood directly rather than by the device of subsequent recollection, does not set it at a distance from the reader, and so lacks one of the principal means of irony found in the first book of the *Lehrjahre*. Several episodes in which Wilhelm's theatrical success is described are missing, and characters like Mme de Retti and Bendel, who do not appear in the *Lehrjahre*, no longer confirm his involvement in the theatre. Above all, Mme B. or Mariane in the *Sendung* is a much more experienced woman than Mariane in the *Lehrjahre*. Wilhelm's passion for Mme B. proves that he is much less of a realist than in the *Lehrjahre*, for the later Mariane merits his love much more. These changes and many smaller ones, taken together, cannot fail to make the two heroes very different. The Wilhelm of the *Sendung* is an offspring of an unhappy marriage; the theatre, therefore, represents for him a kind of escape from the compulsions of middle-class life, for its narrow confines and its materialism appalled this idealistic youth. When, finally, he feels destined to become a part of the theatre as a producer and an actor, he is not sufficiently aware of what he is capable of doing and what is beyond his capacity. The Wilhelm of the *Lehrjahre*, on the other hand, attains a state of mind allowing him to be self-critical.

A linguistic comparison of the two novels[15] reveals these differences, and we learn that the Wilhelm of the *Sendung* is a more spontaneous, but less realistic person than his namesake in

* An ironic comment on any hopes which Goethe may have entertained is afforded by his more severe criticism of the stage at a time when he had assumed the directorship of the Weimar court theatre (in 1791).

the *Lehrjahre*,[16] and that he is given to abandoning himself more easily to the mood of the moment.

To understand the origins of a novel has its value, but it by no means obviates the main task of criticism: to review the work as a whole. The plot of the *Lehrjahre* differs considerably from that of the *Sendung*. When we first meet Wilhelm Meister, the son of a well-to-do merchant, he is deeply in love with Mariane, an actress. His love for her is matched by his enthusiasm for the theatre. He tells Mariane how this enthusiasm was first kindled by watching a puppet-play as a child. Discussions with his friend Werner bring out his enthusiasm further; on a business trip he encounters Melina, a travelling actor, and thus sees another side of theatrical life. His love for Mariane knows no bounds, especially since he believes that she may be expecting a child by him. These experiences confirm him in his desire to embark on the career to which he brings such high ideals, regrettably not shared by some of the actors. He suffers a cruel disappointment when Mariane is unfaithful to him (as he mistakenly believes), because Mariane had never told him of her former association with a merchant called Norberg. He stops seeing her.

After a slow recovery from this shock, he eventually sets out on another trip. He falls in with a company of travelling actors. He is attracted by the actress Philine, a delightful, insouciant person, but he also takes care of Mignon, a strange young girl who is without a home, and a Harper who appears half-demented. Only much later does he discover that Mignon is, in fact, the Harper's daughter. The actors are subsequently invited by a Count to his castle, where Jarno, an aristocratic officer, introduces Wilhelm to Shakespeare. Wilhelm falls in love with the Countess. The actors travel on. An attack by highway robbers, together with quarrels among the actors, precipitates the dissolution of the company. Wilhelm gives up his connection with them and travels to a city where he meets Serlo, the director of a famous repertory theatre, and his sister Aurelie, with whom he has many stimulating discussions about *Hamlet*, and about the novel and drama. The climax of Wilhelm's stage career is a performance of *Hamlet* with Wilhelm in the title role. Aurelie, whose personality interests him and whose fate moves him, dies of a chill caught after a performance of Lessing's *Emilia Galotti*, in which she played the Countess Orsina, a role akin to her own experiences, for she herself had been abandoned by a nobleman called Lothario. Her doctor gives him a book to read called *Die Bekenntnisse einer schönen Seele* – (*The confessions of a beautiful soul*). It recounts the life of a woman who is dedicated to religion as conceived in the Pietistic tradition, and renounces worldly life, becoming a *Stiftsdame.** After reading the book, Wilhelm travels to the estate of Lothario who, he suspects, is the father of Felix, a young boy whom Aurelie looked after. He arrives to remonstrate with Lothario for his desertion of Aurelie, but discovers that Felix is in fact his own son by Mariane. He is, however, accepted into the aristocratic society, and is made a member of a mysterious Society of the Tower, whose head is the Abbé, a friend of Lothario's. At a formal ceremony, his apprenticeship is declared at an end. He also learns that this society has a somewhat veiled purpose; to further the education of men like Wilhelm and to plan for the future of its members. Wilhelm then meets Natalie, Lothario's sister. He discovers that she is also a sister of the Countess and a niece of the *Stiftsdame*. He finds her living on an estate of her late uncle, who during his life-time had cherished a deep concern for the aesthetic education of man. The mysterious history of Mignon and the Harper is cleared up; their end, however, is unhappy. Mignon dies of a heart-attack produced by an excess of emotion, the Harper by his own hand. A number of women have played a greater or lesser role in Wilhelm's life – Philine, the Countess, Mignon, Aurelie, and Therese, to whom he was actually engaged, but who became Lothario's wife. It is, however, Natalie who accepts his hand in marriage. This acceptance appears to Wilhelm to symbolize that he has arrived at a point of rest, after much effort and error.

For any one who has read the *Sendung* before the *Lehrjahre*, the most unexpected addition is the sixth book, *Die Bekenntnisse einer schönen Seele*. This spiritual biography unfolds a world totally different from that of the theatre, that of Pietism. Contemporary readers were, indeed, greatly surprised at Goethe's intimate knowledge of this world of extreme religiosity. He himself was never a Pietist, but during and immediately after his serious illness

* This untranslatable term denotes an aristocratic lady who has retired to a religious institution to lead a life remote from the world.

in his late teens, he was deeply interested in Pietism. Pietists judged the world by reference to the inner life; spiritual development and values were more important to them than worldly success. Education was seen as a coming nearer to God, and not as a process leading to a realistic appraisal of the world. Goethe, as he admits himself in *Dichtung und Wahrheit*,[17] modelled the *Stiftsdame* on a cousin and friend of his mother, Susanna von Klettenberg, whose essays and letters,[18] though published only later, were known to him; there is no evidence that she wrote an autobiography which Goethe might have utilized. He wanted to describe the moral experiences which result from self-observation. Like the *Stiftsdame*, Susanna von Klettenberg suffered from illness, which she bore patiently, her manners were excellent, her personality lively; yet Goethe also observes that she did not get on too well with the other women who were seeking to lead a religious life. Goethe had many arguments with her, because she felt that his restlessness and vacillation, his questioning and searching resulted from his not being at peace with God, which Goethe denied, for he thought that what mattered was that he felt at ease with himself.[19] Goethe undoubtedly discerned in Fräulein von Klettenberg's attitude and conduct a way of living which, though he did not follow it himself, commanded respect.

The other noticeable addition is Wilhelm's entry into the sphere of aristocratic landowners and the Society of the Tower. Both represent aspirations of the Weimar years. Goethe, a Frankfurt burgher, felt – and this is not surprising for an eighteenth-century man – that he would improve his social and cultural position if he were accepted by the society of the court at Weimar. It was socially preferable, because court society was socially superior; it was culturally preferable, because Anna Amalia, the Dowager Duchess of Weimar, had during her regency assembled a number of writers at court and introduced a cosmopolitan atmosphere. Aristocratic landowners, of course, were accepted by the court society and generally enjoyed more independence than the courtiers. In making the novel end with Wilhelm's engagement to an aristocrat, Goethe may have been giving vent to his own social aspirations.[20] It may also recall his love for Frau von Stein in the first Weimar decade, but here we step beyond the limits of permissible conjecture.

The Society of the Tower is evidently based on the many Freemasons' lodges which grew up in eighteenth-century Germany, and which played a not unimportant part in its social and cultural life.[21] Goethe was himself a member of the Weimar lodge, named after the Dowager Duchess Anna Amalia. There is, however, no reason to believe that he took his membership very seriously.

The Society of the Tower may also have been inspired by the popular novel of the day, the so-called *Trivialroman*, which included secret societies among its stock-in-trade.[22] This fiction provides prototypes and parallels not only for mysterious figures like Mignon and the Harper, but also for the ending in engagement and marriage as well as for the discovery of family relationships, both of which feature in the last two books of the *Lehrjahre*. Yet in any comparison between Goethe's fiction and its popular counterpart, it is not the closeness of the incidents and themes that matters, but the manner in which they are used for turning the novel into a serious work of art. Only a critical analysis of the novel can bring out its literary values.

Over and above this particular addition, however, neither the action nor the structure of the novel makes it easy for us to see the work as a whole. The many years of work on the novel is one of the reasons, the long duration of the action, the multiplicity of characters and themes are others. The *Lehrjahre*, like *Werther*, has a centre in the hero – but concentration on the experience of one person can be carried out much more rigorously in a shorter work. Unity of action is also far more clearly visible in *Werther*, since a much more limited period of time is described, and by focussing the action on the passions, Goethe is able to give it a remarkable intensity. A much longer period in the life of Wilhelm is depicted. Time plays a central role in *Werther*, but here we are hardly conscious of the length of time traversed, and Goethe did not intend to emphasize the time-element.[23]

There are, in fact, considerable affinities, and particularly the *Sendung* recalls *Werther* on occasion, despite the differences in theme and presentation between *Werther* on the one hand and the *Sendung* and the *Lehrjahre* on the other. An almost direct line leads from the earlier novel to the later. In both works, the story of a young, sensitive man is told. Whereas the life of Werther ends in a catastrophe, the 'Wilhelm Meister' novels, from the very onset, are conceived in a different vein. The mood of the *Sendung* intimates that the hero will at least partly accomplish his aims and make use of his intellectual abilities. In the *Sendung* Wilhelm Meister possesses artistic capacities denied to Werther. He is endowed with some of the gifts which, later on, might have enabled him to become the creator of a German national theatre. Nonetheless, although we hear much of Wilhelm's enthusiasm for, and a certain amount about his successful activity in, the theatre, there is not sufficient evidence of his poetic talent. Wilhelm Meister is, however, far more capable of adapting himself to his environment than Werther. The immediacy of presentation in the *Sendung* emphasizes the creative capacity of this young man, but the work has not the same intense power as *Werther*.

If we compare the titles of the two novels, the basic difference emerges. Werther's passion culminates in death, while Wilhelm Meister's apprenticeship has neither a clear beginning nor end; the end of the novel, of course, does not coincide with the end of the apprenticeship. Werther's path leads to death, Wilhelm's to life, although this path does not follow a clear design, but moves forward, apparently following a random course, by way of detours.[24]

In the *Lehrjahre*, it was not Goethe's aim to describe a special case, but a sensitive individual of his age in the midst of its social pattern. *Werther* is the novel of the individual who sees himself as the centre of his own world, who becomes an eccentric, even an outsider, since he is unable to agree with the traditional conception of nature and society, religion and love. Wilhelm Meister, on the other hand, is seeking to find a place in the world. First of all he suffers shipwreck when he is disappointed in love and in his plans for the theatre. Seeing himself as the creator of a German national theatre is an illusion. He recognizes this, and moves into different spheres. The variety of themes demands a breadth of view and flexibility of character outside Werther's narrow experience. Moreover, Wilhelm's development is from the beginning depicted in an ironic tone which is powerfully distinguished from Werther's lyrical outpourings. *Werther* is too direct, too intensive to leave much room for irony, nor would it go well with the tragic tone of the novel. The *Lehrjahre* is kept far removed from tragedy. The narrator's pervasive irony introduces a mediating note.

Much criticism has been directed against the *Lehrjahre* as a work of art. Even if the length of the novel and the diversity of material do not make it a concentrated work, this does not mean that it ceases to be a work of art. It may not possess the restraint of drama, but however unconnected some of its parts may be, a certain unity exists. To define this unity accurately is not easy, and it must wait for a later discussion. Above all, it has been maintained that what external coherence there may be has been purchased at the expense of inner truth, for to many critics, the dénouement resulting in unravelling a number of mysterious and apparently unrelated happenings appeared unconvincing. It seemed an unnecessary concession or throw-back to the popular taste of the time, as exemplified in the conventional novel (*Trivialroman*).

In the *Lehrjahre*, it is not Wilhelm's psychological and spiritual experience that matters, but his development in the context of such issues as the theatre, social problems and education. In all the books of the novel except the sixth book, attention is focused upon the hero, as in *Werther*: even when something unconnected with him is described, it is by means of stories told in Wilhelm's presence or by way of events which take place not far from him. We do however hear, by contrast with *Werther*, of the lives of many different people; of this the sixth book is the most striking instance. This book also has a completely different form from the other seven, for it is not subdivided into chapters. The story of the *Stiftsdame* has no obvious relationship to Wilhelm, but it connects the first five books with the last two. Indeed, the last two books were considered so different from the first five that critics have spoken of a break in the conception of the whole.[25] A closer study alone is capable of elucidating the impact of the sixth book on the last two, and of thus bringing out the interplay of all the books.

At first sight it looks as if the novel does not present a coherent whole, but falls into disparate parts – the first five books concerned with Wilhelm's life in the world of the theatre, the sixth book relating 'the confessions of a beautiful soul', and the last two books about Wilhelm's life with Lothario and his aristocratic friends. We have to look more closely to discover the novel's deeper, inner unity. If we find it, the truth of Schiller's[26] and Friedrich Schlegel's[27] observations would be substantiated; for they maintained that the last two books constituted a drawing-together of many threads. A study of the images and the language of the novel may help to reveal an organic development.

The language of the novel exhibits a calmness and dignity of style. There is hardly a sentence which is uneven or incomplete; all are carefully balanced,[28] none move along in a tempestuous fashion with interruptions. Sentences such as occur in Werther's letter of 10 May 1771 are not to be found. The main clause is now treated with the greatest respect. The sentence structure is characterized by a complex continuity. Most of them are of moderate length, though sometimes an alternation of shorter and longer sentences takes place, creating an equilibrium between the two. Language never becomes vague, nor is it made awkward through the untoward accumulation of nouns, adjectives and prepositional constructions, or through a badly built sentence structure. It flows along smoothly and does not create an impression of constraint. The various parts of the sentences move at the same level. None dominates. Lengthy sentences are avoided, the short sentence occurs rarely, a striving for clarity prevails. Every sentence is self-contained, presenting a microcosm of its own. Its rhythm is autonomous. Nonetheless, it is never isolated, but is rhythmically related to the sentences which immediately precede or succeed it. All sentences are simultaneously related to the whole. They express a state of affairs representing a criterion for Wilhelm's inner development. The even measure of the language is still more noticeable if it is compared with the language of the *Sendung*.[29] A consideration of the stylistic changes which Goethe made in the *Lehrjahre* reveals the desire to make everything more concentrated and weightier. He struck out not only minor persons, but also insignificant sentences. The number of subsidiary clauses is diminished. Goethe replaced them with an adverbial or adjectival construction, changed them into main clauses, or struck them out altogether. A sentence often shrinks into an apposition and gains in stringency and power. Pronouns are frequently replaced by nouns. Auxiliary verbs are on many occasions deleted. Over-complex sentences are simplified. But concentration is not the only means of making sentences well balanced. The same effect can be attained by extending them or by rounding them off if incomplete. The rhythm is also more balanced in the *Lehrjahre* than in the

Sendung. The various parts are weighed more equally, the smaller number of subsidiary clauses produces a stronger rhythm: the main clauses possess more power. They move along more firmly.[30] The even measure of language is equalled by a similar evenness of tone. Crude expressions are deleted or weakened. The language is purified, and is more classical.

Unity of style requires that no substantial differences in the use of language exist between the various parts of the novel. This demand has been fulfilled in the *Lehrjahre*; the language of the last three books does not differ materially from that of the first five; even when letters of Wilhelm or conversations are reported, the tone hardly differs from that of the narrator. The dialogue cannot be considered as an intensification of the narrative; it does not involve a basic divergence. Goethe avoids the extreme mode of speaking, characteristic of the style of his youth, and also the extreme economical concentration of his old age. It is classical prose. Wieland's language, in contrast, is much more formalistic.[31] There is a certain self-evident rightness about the prose of the classical Goethe which makes the reader take it for granted. We are not conscious of its originality. This is partly because of the simplicity of the language, partly because the modern reader has accepted Goethe's classical style as the model of a solid, yet elegant German prose, with enough nuances not to become monotonous. Objectivity of presentation, economy of energy and conciseness are matched by breadth of narration. These features reflect his classical view of art, for classical use of language meant uniformity of style.

The only distinct interruption of the measured prose of the *Lehrjahre* is provided by its lyric poetry. Here a different world intervenes; the ordinary world is apparently insufficient. At least, the prose of the narrator is not in control of the action which must, therefore, be described in a different, i.e. lyrical manner. In the *Lehrjahre* there are two kinds of lyric poetry: the songs of the Harper and Mignon, which speak with almost primordial force, and occasional poems, as for instance the poem mocking the baron, or Philine's song. The latter poetry is nearer to prose. Nevertheless, the difference between the two is less significant than it may appear. Both the prose of the narration and the verse-form belong to a language which emphasizes what is socially acceptable. The songs of the Harper and Mignon, on the other hand, represent interventions; the elemental world interferes with the world of normal events.[32] The power of song is demonstrated. This penetrating lyric poetry opens a view into another world. Since lyric poetry speaks to us immediately, it has a different task from the more objective, detached narrative. In these well-known lyric poems powerful forces come forth immediately, while in the novel they move below the surface and are pushed aside in the end. Their existence proves clearly that the narrator does not represent the whole of reality; there are spheres indubitably outside his view. The effect of these poems – they are among the most effective and the best known of Goethe's – is powerful. Since they are related to the story of the Harper and Mignon, these two mysterious figures, they suggest a sphere of mystery and irrationality remote from ordinary life. The impact of these poems on Wilhelm permits us to divine the power which this sphere has over him. This kind of lyric poetry occurs only seldom. It can therefore be concluded that this sphere represents a limited aspect of Wilhelm's life. Mignon's and the Harper's lyrics do not, however, have the function of being symbols of poetry itself, as Novalis asserted.[33] Mignon's and the Harper's deaths, therefore, do not mean that Goethe wanted to repudiate poetry in the novel. Lyric poetry has a right to existence, both poetry and prose have a function in the structure of the novel.

To polish the style, nonetheless, was to affect only the surface of the work. The process of producing a uniform style was likely to conceal rather than to avoid or remove deeper inconsistencies. But style as it is expressed by the position or order of a sentence is only one aspect of the novel's form. Imagery is another. Certain keywords and images, by recurrent use at significant places, may allow us to recognize more easily the unity and coherence of the work.

Wilhelm's appreciation of art also develops from inexperience to maturity. At first, he is moved by its content alone. Only after having lived in the company of the Abbé and Natalie, in the house built by her uncle, does he acquire a deeper understanding of the nature of art and appreciate the significance of form.

The mists which surrounded Wilhelm's view in the first part of the novel are gradually lifted, and in the last books, clarity and order prevail. This process implies Wilhelm's inner development. Confusion and chaos are now rejected in favour of order and exactitude, clarity and purity of vision and form. In contrast, Mariane's life is characterized by confusion and untidiness. Even the room in which she is living is untidy. The same is true of Philine. On the other hand, we see the purity of life of the *Stiftsdame*. Similarly, Natalie's uncle wanted to inculcate the impression of purity in art.

A study of the novel's imagery shows Wilhelm's development from illusion to clarity of vision.[34] In order to visualize others, Wilhelm forms in his mind images which are part of the imagery of the novel. The more sharply and clearly they are delineated, the stronger is their relationship to reality. Wilhelm's lack of understanding of the world becomes evident in the inexact mental images which he forms. At first he sees others, especially when he is in love, as if through a mist. Only later, after having lived for some time near Natalie, does he succeed in gaining a distinct image of other people. Another image is the mirror.[35] For the younger Wilhelm the stage, or acting, is the mirror of all that matters. Later on, when he is more mature, his interest is not focussed on the stage, but on his own development; he therefore looks into the mirror to divine more definite characteristics of his own personality.

The group of images of the bird and the wanderer is also revealing, indicating movement and unrestricted expression of the inner self. The nest and the hut, their 'polar opposites', which signify restriction within domesticity, can also be associated with them. As long as Wilhelm uses the images of the bird and the wanderer to illustrate his position in life, he has not yet found a fitting place in this world. These images also reveal how Wilhelm is always subjected to the storms of existence. Yet the final image of the novel, the journey of Saul, the son of Kish, who set out to fetch his father's asses and found a kingdom, illustrates the progress which Wilhelm has made, a progress which, in accordance with the novel's ironic tone, was achieved incidentally rather than by design.

These images point to the path by which Wilhelm is able to acquire an education. At the same time, they intimate that the novel has that kind of unity which must be achieved in a great work of art. No unified pattern emerges, but this continuity, inherent in the imagery, points to a basic consistency of the novel (*Stetigkeit*), which, as Schiller puts it, is more than half of the unity.[36] Concentration on different groups of images to define each direction in Wilhelm's education brings out some very important imaginative connections. They signify the great polar tensions between dynamic self-expression and self-restraint, between lucid vision and illusion, between confusion and order of mind. Images and philosophical views are blended together into a whole, and present an inner coherence which can easily be missed on first reading.

This inner continuity of words and images permits us to penetrate even more deeply into the innermost kernel of the *Lehrjahre*. In this way we can catch a glimpse of the struggles which accompany the partly unconscious growth of Wilhelm's personality, for these images represent vital inner drives. They cast light on his attempt to master conflicting inner forces and reach clarity of mind, to adapt himself to his environment, and on his growing ability to put his mental faculties to good use. They depict the struggle between reason and feeling. They intimate Wilhelm's failure and drifting. We recognize how close he is to destruction.

In Goethe's view, man's development does not consist in an unrestricted, aimless progress, but in the deed – i.e. in the limited purposive conquest of a restricted sphere of life. The study of imagery not only provides us with an introduction to the themes of the novel, but also points to the well-known truth that the novel's main concern is its hero's education.[37] Although his development is of the greatest importance, it would be mistaken to take his own views at any stage too seriously. The narrator's interventions make this clear, for he continuously creates distance and thus sets Wilhelm's personality and experience in relief.

When we consider Wilhelm in relation to the other characters in the novel, we see how much his ambitions have to be seen in the light of a certain irony: his imagination and expectations are at variance with reality. Human beings are only too frequently different from what he believes them to be. His criteria of judgement are often wrong, since they result from a disproportion between his own plans and reality. Irony springs from this incongruity. It may be deep-seated irony inherent in the situation and the development of the story, and which can be detected only by viewing them as a whole. Or it may be of a more obvious kind created by the narrator's interventions. Since the method is so subtle, an ingenuous reader could enjoy the whole work without perceiving its ironic implications. But such a reader would view Wilhelm's experience and feeling with insufficient detachment, would take him too seriously, and thus misread the story. Of course, we must not fall into the opposite error of just finding Wilhelm's aspirations and actions ridiculous. The narrator safeguards detachment. Wilhelm's hopes and deeds appear desirable and intelligible, but are relegated to their true place in the cosmos. In his youthful zeal, Wilhelm overestimates his own powers, and underestimates the difficulties facing him. It is the privilege of youth to abandon its mistaken views in order to strengthen its sense of reality.

The narrator's interventions usually imply irony rather than bringing it forcibly to the reader's attention. In order to avoid jarring on the reader, irony must be implicit rather than explicit. Many passages in the novel thus gain a different significance on re-reading. If we compare the *Lehrjahre* with the novels of Wieland we cannot help noticing how much more subtle Goethe's irony is. There can be no doubt, for example, that Don Sylvio's adventures in Wieland's novel *Don Sylvio von Rosalva* are related with irony. *Don Sylvio* is obviously a satirical novel, but *Agathon*, another novel by Wieland, belongs to the genre of the *Bildungsroman*. Yet we laugh with Wieland about Agathon's consistent idealism which allows him to be deluded only too easily. From the very beginning, the serious problem of man's education, of his learning to accept the world, is treated in the most ironic manner, as the tone of the narrator's commentary clearly indicates.

In the *Lehrjahre*, irony is used differently. Goethe uses the narrator's commentary to achieve detachment from the passion which he describes.[38] The narrator refuses to be explicit. We often have to listen to his tone rather than to the words which he uses to catch the irony. The title itself is ironic, for it is surely incongruous for a young man endowed with the names 'Wilhelm' and 'Meister', the one alluding to Shakespeare, the other to mastery, to undergo an apprenticeship.[39] He would, as Goethe acknowledged in a letter to Schiller, have been more appropriately called *Wilhelm Schüler* (Wilhelm Pupil).[40] He himself becomes aware of the inappropriate character of his name, and changes it. In the *Sendung*, either to indicate his hope of later success, or in a moment of realistic self-appraisal, he assumes the name of *Geselle*[41] (journeyman) when he joins the strolling players. In the *Lehrjahre* the word *Geselle* would perhaps suggest his real status and would thus be out of place in a work more remote from allegory and much more definitely critical of Wilhelm's aspirations.

One passage among many may be illustrative:

> If first love, as I find generally accepted, is the most intense a man can experience in his whole life, then we must count our hero thrice happy, that it was granted him to enjoy the ecstasy of this unique moment in all its fullness. Only a few men are so specially favoured, for most of them are parted from their earlier feelings by a hard school which compels them, after a bitter pleasure, to learn to renounce their noblest wishes and to abandon for ever what they visualized as the highest bliss.[42]

The narrator's commentary here refers to Wilhelm's first love. First of all it is praised, but this praise is immediately qualified. Turns of speech such as 'I find generally accepted', point to a widely recognized truth. Widely known and valid to a certain degree, it does not always correspond to the facts. It is a hypothesis containing a kernel of truth, but it cannot be maintained in this particular formulation, for it is related only to a part of human experience. To experience bliss is an obscure wish, characterized by the words 'to hover before one's eyes' (*vorschweben*), a turn of phrase frequently used by Goethe to indicate vagueness of mind. Yet it would be false to identify the narrator with Goethe, for Goethe uses the narrator to put forth an opinion whose validity is at first neither confirmed nor rejected, but since it contains truth and falsehood, appears ambivalent. By way of this irony, life is characterized in its limitation and relativity.

Later, the narrator writes:

> Wilhelm was still in those happy days when it is impossible to believe that a beloved girl or a venerable writer can have any faults.[43]

By using the word 'happy' (*glücklich*) he implicitly takes an ironic view of Wilhelm's attitude, an attitude which, indeed, is not without justification, but does not withstand critical observation. Similar commentaries are repeated, each time intimating that a naïve reaction to one's first love cannot be generally valid.

At the beginning of the second book, the narrator assumes more openly the role of a commentator. He does so because he wishes himself to carry on the narration. When Wilhelm has discovered the ostensible infidelity of Mariane, direct description breaks off and the first book ends. In the next book, the narrator's commentary mitigates the effect of Wilhelm's unhappiness. It is in fact noticeable that Goethe does not wish to open up tragic perspectives. This differs from his practice in *Werther*. The narrator writes a commentary on what has gone before. He allows us to recognize that this love relationship could not last.

From now on, the narrator's function becomes much clearer. He produces, as various examples show, a general commentary on Wilhelm's situation. This general commentary is by no means haphazard, nor is it mere comment; on the contrary, it furthers the action, since each time it points to the stage which Wilhelm has reached in his way of life. It broadens the reader's horizon, and makes him see the hero in a different light from that in which he sees himself. All the time, Wilhelm's relations to others, e.g. to Mignon, to Philine and to the world of the theatre itself, are delineated more clearly. The narrator's irony relies mainly on the discrepancy between Wilhelm's ideas and his awareness of the situation in which he actually finds himself. This discrepancy is often intimated rather than stated, and implicitly points to the main theme of the novel: the education of the hero not by the mere accumulation of knowledge, but by his acquiring a greater understanding of the external world.

Goethe hardly criticizes Wilhelm's attitude of mind in the way that Wieland criticizes Don Sylvio's. On the contrary, he regards it most sympathetically. Wilhelm may be taking a false direction, but his development is according to his own nature. Goethe's irony intimates that a young man of Wilhelm's character and birth must undergo a one-sided development. The more his individuality is unfolded, the more he recognizes that he is following a law that determines his life, a law that relies on receptivity, enthusiasm and hope, but also on seriousness and zeal. What one individual misses can be made up through contact with others, for as it is maintained in the letter of apprenticeship 'it takes all sorts to make a world'.[44] Even here Wilhelm's encounters with others are seen first of all in the light of irony, although Wilhelm always envisages them seriously. The narrator's irony depends on Wilhelm's overestimation of his importance, for instance, on his taking the theatre too seriously. Yet the irony, though handled lightly, is never casual, and its criticism is always serious. Wilhelm mistakes talent for genius and his interest in the theatre for an ability to create the new German national theatre. Similarly, he ascribes to his love for Mariane a uniqueness which claims far too much for a normal human experience. It is, like all human relations, 'unique' in opening a door to another world, the world of love, but it is not, therefore, comparable to the experiences of others, nor is it without its all too human pitfalls; Wilhelm's blindness and excessive zeal know no limits. He notices Mariane's untidiness, but fails to draw the proper inference. The disorder in Mariane's room and in life is seen in an ironic light, but so is Wilhelm's family: Wilhelm unwittingly lulls Mariane to sleep when he relates his childhood experiences. He does not realize that lack of order and confusion arising from a bad conscience make up a part of Mariane's dubious, yet very real charm. In the end, his disappointment is all the greater since at first he had idealized her. Only much later does he succeed in achieving a more realistic and just appraisal. In his early conversations with the stranger about fate, and with Werner about poetry, similar problems arise.

All these incidents are treated with irony, and so is Wilhelm's relationship to Jarno and Serlo. Both men, like Werner, are cool and sceptical: the easy manner with which Serlo treats the purpose of art, his way of approaching all problems and situations from the standpoint of the moment, his sense of practical reality and his firm conviction, are an ironic foil to Wilhelm's aspirations and endeavours. This does not mean, however, that such an attitude is condoned by the narrator, let alone by the author. At the same time, Wilhelm is seen as a typical representative of the German mentality: he belongs to a nation which, as Aurelie remarks, takes everything seriously (*schwer*),* and thus everything becomes heavy (*schwer*) in its hands.[45] Similarly, it is equally typical of him as a

* The German word '*schwer*' which is used here connotes both 'serious' and 'heavy'.

German that he likes to give an account to himself of everything he does.[46] That this criticism is ironic is symptomatic of the narrator's method.

In the course of Jarno's conversation with Wilhelm the latter's lack of realism becomes equally apparent. His enthusiasm for the theatre is based on limited knowledge: certainly it is meant ironically that Jarno has to criticize his view of the theatre. For Jarno considers that all that is true of the theatre is also true of the world. This does not mean that Jarno's views are right. Jarno's didactic, even mocking attitude is also regarded with irony. Neither when reading the second part of the *Lehrbrief*,* nor when subsequently engaged in conversation about the problems raised in it, is Wilhelm convinced by Jarno's argument; indeed, Jarno even succeeds in annoying him. But the irony is directed mainly against Wilhelm.

There is no need to mention all the occasions when Wilhelm's activity is depicted in an ironic manner. It is a recurrent feature of the novel. The ironic temper of the novel lies also in the structure,[47] for a number of contrasts recur, weaving the texture of the action. They are such contrasts as those between appearance and reality, intention and achievement, life and reason, cause and effect. Wilhelm – and not only Wilhelm – misunderstands many situations. He mistakes appearance for reality; he does not see that intention is not enough. Anxious to achieve much, he overrates his own capacity for achievement in the world of affairs. His commitment to the theatre, indeed, takes him far away from his bourgeois origins, but he travels quite a different road from the one he had envisaged. He enters the Society of the Tower, a world of activity completely opposed to that of the theatre. His relations with Mariane compel him to accept responsibility, but only in a delayed and quite unexpected manner, when he discovers that Felix is his son and realizes that he has to look after him. Wilhelm learns more by teaching Felix than he has learnt by his own efforts.

At a deeper level still, this incongruity is expressed in the contrast between Wilhelm's aspirations and his achievements: the relationship between cause and effect often appears obscure, and planning only too often mistaken. He is admitted into the charmed aristocratic circle, but from the inside, the aristocratic world looks

* The certificate of apprenticeship which here consists of a number of maxims.

different from what it did from without. Again, the Society of the Tower appears to believe in guidance, even if it is of a peculiar kind, for it interferes as little as possible, in the hope that, through trial and error, man will develop for the best. Only occasionally, at critical moments, is it ready to interfere. Yet this mysterious society is, in fact, inadequate for the deepest needs of life. Not the efforts of the Society of the Tower but the thoughtless Friedrich's remarks bring about Wilhelm's engagement to Natalie, which crowns the novel. Life always defeats the best laid plans or brings them to fruition in an unexpected manner.

On this underlying incongruity inherent in the very nature of irony, the ironic temper of the novel is based. To believe in fate is really mistaken; chance rules life. Only in retrospect does a pattern emerge which may be called fate, a plan of life. Goethe had moved far away from the world of the *Aufklärung* where belief in a fixed plan of life was widespread. He is even more remote from the Baroque, where belief in Providence was common.[48] A secular agency, the Society of the Tower, takes the place of Providence, but it is an emaciated force by comparison with the Divine power in which we may believe. Meaning is given to Wilhelm's life rather by the richness of his own experience, by the good fortune rooted in the nature of his personality. His life is like that depicted in *Hamlet*; the hero does not act according to a plan, but the play itself has a meaning. The discrepancies and incongruities which result from these contrasts give rise to irony; for they reveal the disappointments of human expectation and the shortcomings of the imagination when dealing with the multifarious, unpredictable hazards of life. It is here unnecessary to quote many instances of irony, for it would easily become tedious and do injustice to Goethe's lightness of touch. Once the general intention is grasped, they can be detected easily.[49]

Wilhelm is the person on whom attention is focused. The narrator ironically calls him 'our friend'. This epithet is not only ironic; it also invites the reader to view Wilhelm's development with sympathy. This development can best be gauged in Wilhelm's relations with other people. In the first book, his love for Mariane overshadows everything. Wilhelm is inwardly moving away from his home. His retrospective reflections on his childhood and youth make this quite clear. On the whole, he is an immature youth, lacking experience of life. He is therefore blind to the foibles of the actors, and in contrast to Werner, neglects the obligations imposed by middle-class life. His development is devious, owing to the relationships in which he becomes enmeshed. Many of these are false, and at the time he is unaware of this; this is true, for instance, of his relationship with the actors, with Mignon and the Harper, with the Count and the Countess, and with Aurelie and Therese. Attraction and repulsion, attachment and separation characterize his relations with others, and indeed his development as a whole. Wilhelm's relationship to Werner is a very clear example of this.

From the outset, they have different ideas about life and living. By praising the double-entry system of accounting, the nature and aim of trade, Werner's predilection for order and clarity becomes apparent. Wilhelm's more imaginative views of life spring from the strength of inner experience which Werner, a more limited person, lacks.

This contrast is seen throughout the novel as the action unfolds. In their dispute about the nature of poetry and the function and stature of the poet, Werner speaks on equal terms with Wilhelm; each is able to produce many arguments in support of his point of view, even if neither of them can give a really satisfactory definition of the nature of poetry. Wilhelm's travels lead him away from his middle-class origins. Later on in his letter to Wilhelm, Werner appears as a friend who reports on events at home and seeks to persuade Wilhelm to pursue the same aims in life as he does. He depicts the lives of others from a purely bourgeois point of view, and therefore sees in collecting works of art, which Wilhelm's grandfather enjoyed, a sterile and dilettante activity. Werner looks at the world through the eyes of a businessman, though of one who is not attached to possessions. He does not realize that a collection of works of art may be fruitful because it is a product of experience and of creative imagination, and because it may give an insight into the inner experience of man, a view held by Natalie's uncle.

Werner's letter brings about the very opposite of what he wants to achieve, a fate which not infrequently befalls confessions of faith and attempts at persuasion. Wilhelm's ironical answer shows that there are good reasons for the opposite point of view and that it may well be right. Werner's letter has, however, a decisive effect on Wilhelm. He recognizes that he cannot become cultured along the lines prescribed by his friend. The world of commerce, as Werner describes it, appears to be wholly philistine: it imprisons man in a straitjacket and petrifies both his mind and his spirit. To escape from this prison, Wilhelm turns to the theatre. When the two friends meet again, it is clear that, despite all his mistakes and false beginnings, Wilhelm's life has been much richer and more fruitful than Werner's. Whereas Wilhelm has, in Werner's own words, become 'larger, stronger, straighter, more cultivated, and more agreeable in his demeanour',[50] Werner's inner growth has been stultified. Werner, who judges everything, including himself, in purely economic terms – 'if I had not gained enough money in the meantime, I should not amount to anything'[51] – is a prematurely aged person with sunken cheeks: as the narrator remarks, 'a hard-working hypochondriac'.[52] While no causal connection between business and hypochondria is postulated, it is implied that inner attitudes and external appearances are not without connection. His reaction to Wilhelm's fine, healthy appearance emphasizes the limitations of his standpoint. He praises it, but instead of drawing the right conclusion, he insists on imposing his point of view: he tries to use Wilhelm's appearance as a bait for a rich heiress.

Wilhelm feels differently. His conception of the middle class is characterized by his sense of its narrowness. This view is the opposite of Werner's. Werner's world is limited: trade is *the* experience of life. Outbursts of an almost lyrical kind characterize his remarks about trade. To be a merchant is for him not only a means of earning a living, it is life itself. This is a thoroughly uncritical view, although from Werner's standpoint it is not inappropriate. Trade for him is more than merely the activity of sober-minded men; its variety and change captivate him so much that he is fully absorbed by it, and has nothing to spare for art as a representation of life. His plans are therefore perfectly sensible and realizable, but his standpoint is eccentric; for Werner has given himself up so completely to the life of business that in his home there is no place for him except at his desk. He is unwilling to offer others hospitality, but wants to live outside his home himself. It is a utilitarian, indeed egotistical attitude.

So too is the attitude of Wilhelm's bourgeois parents, who suffer from the same mental restrictions which narrow Werner's life. They consider trade the noblest undertaking, and they keep a sharp lookout for any profit which speculation could bring them. Despite his love of splendour, Wilhelm's father follows a monotonous, rigid pattern in his life. He hardly entertains. Werner's father, on the other hand, is hospitable, but he does not care about the setting of his hospitality; the food is good, but the house is dark. Neither of them knows how to combine form and content in his life, how to live in true style; only aristocrats know how to do this.

Wilhelm's criticism of Werner is severe, but incisive. He rebukes his friend for misunderstanding life; by paying attention to commercial and social activities, he ignores what really counts in life. While Goethe does not expressly state his own opinion, the whole development of the novel is an implicit criticism of Werner and his way of life. Business activity is not valueless; on the contrary, this way of life serves as a corrective to a sensitive person like Wilhelm, whose emotions need powerful nourishment and whose active imagination does not readily fit into daily life. The bourgeois world has its place, but it is not capable of satisfying Wilhelm, since it does not offer a sufficiently rich field of experience to a sensitive and imaginative person who desires creative activity.

Apart from the hero, Wilhelm, and the *Stiftsdame*, whose biographies are given in full, the other characters are not treated in depth. Even if we are given a biography, it is succinct, as for example that of the Harper or Serlo. The characters appear individualized enough – they are 'round' rather than 'flat' in E. M. Forster's terminology[53] – but give only a laconic report of their inner life. Most of the characters – Werner, Mariane, the Count, the Countess, Therese, Natalie, her uncle, Jarno, Lothario, Laertes, Melina and his wife, Friedrich, Philine, let alone the Abbé, or the two strangers – are delineated only in so far as their psychological experiences are of relevance to Wilhelm's development. We are given a little background knowledge, but the door to their inner life is never opened wide. Conversations and the progress of the action rather than the narrator's comments enlighten us. This paucity of psychological information does not however make dull reading. Philine, surely, is lively by any standards. Yet most characters do not substantially differ from those of the conventional picaresque novel to which they originally belonged. Mignon is the exception *par excellence*. She too comes from the conventional novel of the day, for a person whose origins are mysterious and whose true identity is discovered only towards the end of the novel is a commonplace feature.[54] Goethe, however, totally transformed this type. He created a subtle study of a young girl growing up, whose hermaphrodite tendencies are unmistakable and whose emotional life is full of complexities. But her life is cut short. We therefore never know what the full range of her personality might have been.

Wilhelm's relations with the other figures of the novel do not show his inner development so clearly; yet they intimate much. In his relationship with Mariane, the impetuosity of his youth breaks forth; later attempts to find her recall the hazards caused by impatience. Inner needs which bring him into the society of Philine, Mignon and the Harper allow one to gauge the dangers which imaginative and sensitive men run. Philine's charm disturbs him and threatens to make him squander his emotional resources. Mignon and the Harper point to emotional instability at an even deeper level, for this unstable pair attract Wilhelm precisely because they appeal to the unstable in him. Here, affinity of mind testifies to an excessively strong sensitivity that imperils inner balance.

Serlo and even Aurelie are never very close to Wilhelm; there is, therefore, no danger that he might stagnate on the level of life which they represent. Much more profound is his relationship with the *Stiftsdame* whom of course he never meets. He has arrived at a new stage of his development; a new world is opened to him and captivates him so thoroughly that he becomes estranged from the theatre. He does not really belong to this world, but it is, nevertheless, an important part of his life. His experience prepares his entry into the aristocratic world, though once inside it he finds that a wide gulf still exists between himself and the noblemen. Only after he has gained enough experience and understanding of life is he accepted in their circle as an equal. Only when he is free, in his maturity, from all trace of the theatre, is his apprenticeship at an end. Outward circumstances mirror his inner development. Lothario chooses him as a friend, the Abbé introduces him into the Society of the Tower, and Natalie accepts his proposal of marriage. Wilhelm has 'arrived' socially. He has moved into the charmed circle of the landed aristocracy. The manner of Wilhelm's rise in social life is an implicit criticism of the society of the day which circumscribed the opportunities available to the upper middle class. The bourgeois was unable to find a healthy basis for the development of personality. In eighteenth-century Germany, only a nobleman could hope to do so. This restriction also affected the German novelist who, by comparison with an English or French one, found himself stultified by the poverty of German social life. Goethe complained bitterly about the social conditions so unpropitious for a German writer:

> Scott's charm . . . rests on the splendour of the three British Kingdoms and the inexhaustible variety of their history, while nowhere in Germany from the Thuringian Woods to the sandy deserts of Mecklenburg is a fruitful field for the novelist to be found; so that in *Wilhelm Meister* I had to choose the most appalling material that can be imagined – travelling actors and poor gentry – only in order to get some movement into my picture.[55]

The nobleman alone, it seems to Wilhelm, can appear as a public person.[56] He alone possesses the independence and strength which permit him to gain a general education, to become cultured. The bourgeois cannot acquire culture or educate his mind. Wilhelm's words are doubtless to some extent determined by personal disappointment; yet they contain a kernel of truth in the German social order in the eighteenth century – i.e. the bourgeois had to live within narrow limits, to which the nobleman was not confined. The bourgeois, however talented he may have been, was unable to exercise an immediate influence in political and cultural affairs.[57] His value does not consist in what he is, but what qualities of social life he is able to acquire. The social order itself should be blamed for this– so at least Wilhelm's remarks imply.

Wilhelm's views do not make him a social revolutionary, even though he talks of the shortcomings of the society in which he lives. It must not be forgotten that he judges the position of a nobleman too much from the standpoint of a discontented member of his class and that of an enthusiastic youth. Furthermore, he is guilty of a certain self-deception. The enthusiasm with which he meets the Countess proves this. Enthusiasm has, in Wilhelm's case, always indicated unreliable thinking, and his views have to be received with scepticism. He is still far removed from a realistic conception of life, and he praises the world of appearance, the theatre; still deeply influenced by his love for the stage, he is deceived by appearances. Only gradually does he see life more clearly. Nonetheless, it is quite clear that the aristocrats have more opportunities to be active. And if – like Natalie's uncle, Lothario and the Abbé – they make use of their opportunities, they can achieve something. Wilhelm's view of the aristocrats is limited, since it represents only his own experience. It is by no means without validity, but it needs to be supplemented and corrected.

What picture of aristocratic society, then, does the novel represent? Not only do many aristocrats have faults; there are also evident disadvantages in the way in which they live. The Count and the Baron, indeed, are men to whose words others listen respectfully. The gulf between them and the others is evident. They follow their wishes and whims. No one dares to contradict even their unreasonable views on the theatre, and so they remain uninformed and prejudiced. When the actors are bidden to the Count's castle, they travel happily thither, thinking it a fairy castle. But this belief is mistaken, and their illusions are destroyed only too quickly. When they arrive, they are led into an empty, old, uncared-for castle where they spend a most disagreeable night: the aristocrats possess power and authority, but their servants do not always obey their orders.

It would be wrong to believe that the houses of these noblemen betray any architectural merit; on the contrary, the old castle at least appears to be a monstrosity, a pointless agglomeration of styles. Aesthetics are subordinated to function. The castle's appearance makes so little impact on Wilhelm that he rides on without thinking about what he has seen. Even if, at this stage, he is not educated enough to distinguish properly between form and content, he is not completely blind to the effect which an important piece of architecture creates. The building is apparently not sufficiently striking to make an impression on Wilhelm, pre-occupied as he is with his thoughts and feelings. Therese's house makes some impression on him, but it is not its aesthetic quality but its solidity which impresses: it is a house not intended to be beautiful, but lasting and convenient. Only in the uncle's house can Wilhelm find an example of the purest and most dignified architecture, which is truly impressive. The house recalls Palladio; it represents the ideal type of an art created in the Greek spirit.[58] True harmony prevails, as Goethe's remarks about Palladio's *La Rotonda* indicate.

> Only in the presence of those works [built by Palladio] can we recognize their great value; for their greatness and physical quality then meet our eyes, and the beautiful harmony of their dimensions satisfies our mind, not only through their abstract plans, but also through their whole perspective movement forward and backward.[59]

Goethe was completely convinced of the value of this neo-classical art. For him, Palladio's villa *La Rotonda* near Vicenza, probably the model of the uncle's house, had a supernatural power. There is something divine in its structure, 'something of the force of a great poet who, out of truth and falsehood, makes a *tertium quid* which enchants us.'[60]

Wilhelm has become receptive to such impressions. At the same time, the personality of Natalie gains in strength for him, on account of her surroundings. Architecture and personality influence one another. True art forces us, in the most agreeable manner, to recognize the pattern of our innermost being. Architecture, like every other art, teaches man to know himself. The impact which it can have can be fully gauged in the Hall of the Past, where Natalie's uncle has been able to realize all his architectural ideas. Here, magnificent ornament is seen in purely architectonic setting: everyone who enters the Hall senses this quality, is raised to a higher level, and is able to discover through this harmonious art what man is and what he can be.

The inscription written above the entrance – 'Remember to live'[61] – conveys the uncle's philosophy. How is this aim to be achieved? Education through art, as Wilhelm receives it in the uncle's house, is aesthetic education in Schiller's sense: the work of art enriches and refines the quality of man's life. It prepares him immediately for the practical tasks of life by educating his feelings and by allowing him to become a better person: Wilhelm acquires the maturity without which Natalie would probably not have accepted his proposal of marriage.

Only after he has acquired the right mental attitude is he capable of appreciating Natalie. Only then does he recognize the significance of a work of art and turn away from the theatre, which appears a dangerous world of illusion. The figurative arts and the drama, it seems, are mutually exclusive. Yet this could easily be a misinterpretation; what in fact is needed is a realistic appreciation of both art-forms.

Is the theatre really a world of illusion fraught with fatal dangers? Or is this merely a view reached by Wilhelm on the basis of his disappointment? From dependence on the theatre, Wilhelm grows to independence of mind. At the beginning of the novel, he is completely under the sway of the theatre. He does indeed love Mariane for her own sake, but his imagination is quickened by his enthusiasm for the stage. When his mother scolds him, he protests vehemently, and rejects her attempt to cry down the puppet-play which excited him so much. The vehemence of his rejection betrays the strength of his early enthusiasm. It was clearly a deep experience. He does not, however, know why his curiosity was roused. When the impact of the first performance has passed, he wants to know how the puppet-play was staged. Wilhelm's early passion for the theatre deeply affects his emotional life. His enthusiasm for, and his faith in, the power of the theatre, his admiration for the actors, all give him indescribable joy, but they are only steps on his path to becoming an actor himself. Furthermore, the reader does not need to share Wilhelm's enthusiasm, for this enthusiasm is treated with irony. What is appropriate to a boy is not appropriate to a man: when Wilhelm tells Mariane of his enthusiasm, she falls asleep, although she is fond of him, and old Barbara goes on enjoying her wine. It is difficult not to feel that Wilhelm's experience as a puppet-player is significant for him, but not for the world in general. And the incongruity between his desire to be a poet and his poetic talent is also revealed, for the puppet-play makes him want to be a playwright, but his attempts at writing plays only reveal his inexperience and lack of creative ability and of critical detachment. He likes those plays which give him an opportunity to please. His judgement is not firmly based;

he chooses parts for which he is not suited. Later on, he believes that he has overcome this weakness, but this is self-deception. He is most clearly mistaken in his judgement when he plays Hamlet. The apparent success of the performance is belied by the Abbé, who possesses a deeper understanding of the theatre and knows that Wilhelm really played himself.

In the long run, the theatre is not a satisfactory form of education for him. Wilhelm grows out of it, just as he grew out of the puppet-play. His love for the theatre was at first adequately sustained by his love for Mariane. This experience was vital, immediate. Mariane represented for him the theatre and life, two experiences in one.

Wilhelm's love for Mariane and his enthusiasm for the theatre fructify one another. Both are passions, both are equally unrealistic. He sees himself as the creator of a national theatre, an excellent actor, but it is a poetic image which he has formed. He lacks the talent to be a poet, for he is unable to detach himself from the material which he ought to fashion, namely his personal experience, and is able to conjure up only vague images in his mind. He thinks only of the impact which his work will have on him, and has no idea of the organic nature of art. It is therefore not surprising that none of his plays matures, and that he tires of them before they are half completed.

This basic lack of aptitude does not weaken Wilhelm's faith in his mission for the theatre. He wants to affect the minds of men, to appeal to their inner thoughts and yearnings. Hence the theatre appears to him moral; the tasks of the stage and the pulpit are similar to one another. In both places, God and nature are to be glorified through men of noble spirit. For him, sentiment is more important than ability. His image of the theatre is idealized; nonetheless, his feelings about it are seen as a necessary prelude to his stage career.

Wilhelm's relationship with the theatre is therefore determined from the very beginning by unreal ideas; like his love for Mariane, it is condemned to failure. At the same time, the worldly view is not necessarily right in all respects. It is not true that the theatre is entirely ruled by intrigues or that it has a purely economic function. It is a mixture of many elements. This is clearer to Wilhelm when, after a long interval occasioned by his disappointment in Mariane, he again watches a play and recognizes that giving pleasure is the beginning of all acting.

The impact of the theatre is not necessarily beneficial. Plays are not always properly understood or appreciated. Only too often, prejudice or personal interest play a part. When Wilhelm reads a play to an audience of actors, each of whom immediately sees himself in a leading part, they are delighted. They are also moved by the German character of the play and by a vague national pride. They leave with a sense of elevation only to douse it in a drinking bout – a distinctly ironical touch.

Quite different from this, however, is Shakespeare's impact on Wilhelm. Not only does their common Christian name hint that Wilhelm's experience is representative of the Shakespeare mania of the age, but Shakespeare, indeed, moves him so deeply that he abandons himself completely to his world. His reaction is highly emotional, even passionate: his grasp of reality is imperilled, yet at the same time Shakespeare gives him the strength to avert disaster and turn to life. Wilhelm has to recognize, slowly, that the theatre is a world of appearance. As an inexperienced spectator, he was incapable of distinguishing appearance in the theatre from reality in life, and was therefore in a false position. Serlo noticed this, and criticized Wilhelm's views. This experienced man of the theatre realized that most people are incapable of quickly grasping the spirit of an author. Since the spirit of the whole work is only rarely fathomed, it is necessary for an actor to know his part well. Serlo truly appreciates the practical needs of the theatre. We thus learn by way of contrast how unrealistic Wilhelm's enthusiasm has in fact been. Illusion is necessary, but the producer and the actor have to know that it *is* illusion. If the relationship between reality and appearance is misunderstood, it may have evil consequences. This happens when Aurelie mistakes the task of the actor and, in Orsina, plays her own part. It is a warning for Wilhelm who, in *Hamlet*, plays himself, not the Hamlet whom he is supposed to play. Aurelie acts in a manner which no poet in the first fire of his enthusiasm could ever have imagined, but the result is not only a storm of applause from the public, but also an emotional storm which actually brings about her own death.

In the end, Wilhelm recognizes the inadequacy of the theatre. He has to reject it as a valid educational force, for it has come to seem to him a world in which everyone pays homage to himself and is a prey to self-love. In a conversation with Jarno, he condemns the theatre in the most extreme terms; everyone in it, he asserts, wants to be not only a principal actor, but the actual protagonist. High hopes are disappointed because the actors insist on having their way. When Wilhelm rejects the theatre, he is surely also influenced by his reading of the *Bekenntnisse einer schönen Seele* as well as by his association with Lothario and his friends. His judgement is still not independent. His rejection of the theatre displays a lack of detachment, and his thinking still proceeds far too much from his immediate experience. Jarno has to correct him. The actor cannot avoid the weaknesses which repel Wilhelm so much. Compelled by the very nature of his art to create illusion, he must rate the applause of the moment higher than anything else. As he belongs to a world of appearance, it must be his aim to impress. His emotions must be ruled by self-deception. He is not to be condemned for this. Jarno is prepared to forgive a man the faults of an actor, but less ready to forgive an actor the faults of a man. He therefore insists, against Wilhelm's protests, that all the faults which Wilhelm had found in the theatre are also found in the world. Yet if the world of the theatre is a world of appearance, it has a close relationship to reality. It offers an analogy – but what kind of analogy?

There is no explicit answer in the novel, but a pretty clear idea is given by the famous criticism of *Hamlet*. The burden of doing a great deed is placed on Hamlet, but he is not adequate to the burden. The impossible is demanded of him. What is demanded may not be impossible for all, but it is impossible for *him*. Hamlet's character allows Wilhelm to get his bearings in life; as a result, he feels he understands life better. Still, his judgement of the character is faulty. He does not see the drama with aesthetic detachment.[62] He views the hero as if he were a man like himself, possessed of the same sensitivity and the same desire for education.[63]

Furthermore, the theatre is analogous to the world in representing a complex in which various stages and levels of existence exist side by side and interact. Similarly, our views of the theatre and of reality change, for our perspective changes. At first the theatre, like the world in which we live, appears self-sufficient; but we later discover that it is threatened by forces from real life, and recognize that its claim to autonomy is not wholly valid. New worlds arise which have also to be taken into account. The stage no longer provides an adequate image of the world.[64]

Wilhelm must above all learn that outward splendour can be considered unimportant. Wilhelm does not lack fullness of experience, but at the end of the novel, the direction which his education has taken is not clear. He is still attached to errors due to a confused view of man and his environment. Yet his various experiences have made their impact.

Wilhelm gains experience through error, above all in his relations with women which play an important part in his life. In a sense, the *Lehrjahre* tells a series of love stories.[65] Love determines much of the action. To read the novel primarily in terms of the love story would at first sight appear plausible; for it begins and ends with one: Wilhelm's passion for Mariane and its unhappy end on the one hand, and his love for Natalie, culminating in his engagement, on the other. Much that happens to Wilhelm between these two points in his life is occasioned by the twists and turns of his emotions. Love stories provide time-honoured plots of fiction, and much of the repertoire of the conventional novel recurs in the *Lehrjahre*.[66] His encounter with Natalie, who appears to him as the beautiful Amazon, their immediate separation, and the complications and detours which precede his final acceptance by Natalie are clearly an instance. But what takes up so much space in a conventional novel and what in fact makes it so trivial, occupies only a fraction of the *Lehrjahre*, and is of relatively little importance. Only towards the end, in the eighth book, do the relations between Wilhelm and Therese and Wilhelm and Natalie come to the fore, and even then they have to compete for the reader's attention with other themes, just as Wilhelm's love affair with Mariane in the first book is put side by side with his passion for the theatre. But although his relations with Philine, Mignon, the Countess, Aurelie and Natalie take up much space in the action in the following books, they do not dominate it. Neither is the *Stiftsdame's* love for Narziss the main issue of the *Bekenntnisse einer schönen Seele*.

Wilhelm's love for Mariane occupies most of the first book of the novel. Its end, which has a tragic quality, coincides with the end of the first book. Except for the conversations with the stranger about fate and chance, this book could be considered a self-contained story of a tragic experience.[67] Wilhelm's love is based on a misapprehension of her personality. Her name is significant, for it 'might – and probably did – come straight out of the pages of Marivaux or Gellert'. It 'evokes by literary association the more light-hearted and ephemeral aspects of love'.[68] This first experience, however, is decisive. The serious illness following Wilhelm's discovery of Mariane's apparent infidelity allows us to gauge the intensity of his passion. It takes a long time before his nature can reassert itself, before he returns to health. It takes much longer before he is deeply affected again by love. He falls in love only when he sees Natalie for the first time; appropriately, he does so when he is about to enter a new stage in his life, a stage which is marked by the dissolution of the company of wandering actors. It takes even longer before he again thinks of marriage. To think of marriage means to seek out the opposite of Mariane, i.e. Therese. For is not Therese characterized as much by order as was Mariane by disorder? Does she not appeal as much to his intellect as Mariane did to his emotions? Does he not, as he recognizes himself, revere her rather than love her?[69]

The interval is characterized by his inner restlessness which finds expression in his half-hearted love affairs with Philine and the Countess, the unavowedly erotic relationship with Mignon, the nature of which he does not become fully aware of, and his friendship with Aurelie. He cannot resist the charms of Philine, but the attraction is primarily physical; her instability is symbolic. Her name, derived from the Greek verb φιλεῖν,[70] points to the ephemeral nature of this love, and furthermore symbolizes the instability of the theatre to which Wilhelm has given allegiance, an allegiance which for so serious-minded a person as Wilhelm can only be temporary.

His love for the Countess is never allowed to blossom fully. It is left uncertain (probably deliberately) to what extent the attraction of her personality is reinforced by the charm of the unattainable and of her higher social status. For Aurelie, to use his own words, he feels esteem, but not love.[71] Her relationship to Lothario, and Lothario's conduct towards her, serve as a foil to his own conduct towards Mariane. By seeing Aurelie's misfortune and by believing Felix to be her son, he is able to view a situation analogous to his own in a detached manner. Since he is not at all aware of this analogy, this detached view allows him to gauge his relationship with Mariane more realistically. Undoubtedly this experience contributes to his inner growth, just as responsibility for Felix furthers his own maturity.

Mignon – and the Harper – exercise a remarkable fascination over Wilhelm. Indeed, it can almost be said that he loves Mignon without being aware of it. His action in taking care of her is certainly unusual, but so is Mignon. A certain ambiguity characterizes her. Both masculine and feminine pronouns are applied to her. Yet as she grows up, her femininity is inevitably more and more emphasized. It is she – and the Harper – who break out into song. They have an aura of poetry about them; indeed, they have been taken to be symbols of poetry itself. To assume this is of course mistaken. They may appear as Romantic figures, but a Wilhelm who learns to be realistic moves away from them.

Wilhelm does not seek clarity in his emotions for Mignon. He is blind to her feelings for him. Although he is not really guilty, he undoubtedly hurts her. It is not accidental that her death follows his engagement to Therese; for Mignon loved him at first instinctively, but after Philine's nocturnal visit consciously, as her changed appearance after that night testifies.

Wilhelm loves Therese because he respects her; it is not instinct but reason that has led him to her. In the sphere of love, reason alone is not enough. A friendly inclination has become love, but it is a love that will be found incapable of withstanding the discovery that Therese is not the daughter of the Baroness with whom Lothario had a love affair, and that Lothario can therefore marry her. Wilhelm's love for Natalie, on the other hand, is a synthesis of his love for Mariane and Therese. He loves her at once without knowing her, but he goes on loving her after he has got to know her. Instinct and knowledge, love and esteem are blended. In this sense, he has at last reached his goal. He finds Natalie while searching for a place and a task in the world. Natalie is right by nature; she is, as her name reveals, 'right by birth, and even by her birthday; she not only embodies the qualities of the other women, but transcends them.'[72]

Critics have always felt, however, that her personality is somewhat shadowy. Her main virtue is unselfishness – a great virtue, of course. Friedrich, her profligate younger brother, told her that she would marry out of sheer good nature if no other bride were to turn up. Friedrich's remark must be taken with a pinch of salt, but Natalie is, in fact, less a woman of flesh and blood than the representative of an idea. By marrying, Wilhelm is able to satisfy his social aspirations, for to marry into the nobility with the concurrence of the bride's relations and friends surely spells full acceptance by that class. So even here, the attraction of goodness and the quest for higher social status, even if this quest is concealed by the desire to round off his education, are subtly mingled. Yet they are not two distinct, separate acts; they are inextricably blended into one act of assent.

The very ethereal refinement and unselfish goodness of Natalie's character prepare for and make possible Wilhelm's prolonged separation from her in the *Wanderjahre*; it anticipates the doctrine that true love must be based on renunciation (*Entsagung*). But this is of the future, it belongs to the *Wanderjahre*. Let it suffice to say that in Natalie, Goethe created less a woman involved in the life of the senses than 'a beautiful soul', for we may agree with Schiller that this term really ought to be applied to her rather than to the *Stiftsdame*.[73] Undoubtedly, the point of view of the novel has shifted as the hero's education has been unfolded. Goethe no longer dwells on immediate sensuous experience; Wilhelm is more detached. Feelings are, to some extent at least, guided and corrected by the intellect. Different qualities now appear attractive. Nonetheless, Wilhelm can still come close to despair. Just before the happy dénouement, he fears that he may lose Natalie; on the other hand, his more detached vision is reflected in the view which he gains of Natalie. His growing maturity can also be gauged by a certain detachment through which the persons around Wilhelm are now depicted, for everyone is seen in relation to him. The loss of spontaneity is inevitable, but it is the tribute exacted by the law of compensation if there is an increase in spiritual maturity.

Thus, in a sense, the novel can be read as a series of love stories culminating in Wilhelm's final good fortune – his finding a suitable partner. It is, however, but one aspect of Wilhelm's development as a man and of his mental and spiritual education.

Another aspect is seen by way of contrast. In *Die Bekenntnisse einer schönen Seele*, Wilhelm is confronted with another way of life and different criteria of judgement. His new knowledge helps him to correct his vision of life, for a new vista is opened to him. This sudden intervention of a transcendental world makes the sixth book different from the previous ones, which are almost completely concentrated on this world with only occasional references to the world beyond. In his youth, Wilhelm had mistaken ideas of fate and life. He thought that there ruled over him a fate to which he could abandon himself, a power which would arrange everything for the best without any regard to his efforts. But this too naïve view is by no means shared by the first stranger whom he meets on his journey. This stranger sees things differently. For him, it is man's task to combine that which is necessary with that which is arbitrary. What the stranger criticizes is a superstitious conception of life, saying that it is wrong to ascribe to chance a kind of reason;[74] for he emphasizes the strength of man's inner nature. Man has the power to fashion his life, just as an artist moulds his own material. He must utilize chance. This point of view is, however, modified by a second stranger whom Wilhelm meets later during a boat-trip. This stranger asserts that outward circumstances can also powerfully affect life, and man cannot always master chance; on the contrary, it may drive him off his course. For the first stranger, inner form matters more, and for the second stranger, outer forces predominate. At these moments, the internal dialectic of the novel is revealed: Wilhelm learns to emancipate himself from a naïve deterministic approach, but he also discovers that it is hazardous to theorize about life, for during the course of the novel, events again and again take on a different meaning and a different importance if viewed at later stages of life. As we discover later, both strangers are members of the Society of the Tower; it therefore appears as if these encounters were not fortuitous, but had been arranged by the leaders of that society. Yet all the reasoning of this society, all its attempts to guide men, even through error, are found wanting. Theory is no match for life, whose course defies all planning.

The sixth book reveals not only a religious development, but an image of the world seen from the standpoint of a religious individual. Its criteria are different from what they appear to be to the man caught up in the welter of social life and its illusions.

Values are not related to man, but to God. The *Stiftsdame* judges life from her own Christian point of view: experiences are good if they bring her nearer to God, evil if they do not. She regards those years as empty in which she allowed herself to be swayed by the world. Her piety and her relationship to God are based on her emotions. Her religion is not meant to be directed against nature. On the contrary, it seems to be in tune with it. Her love for Narziss, so she feels, does not lead her away from God, but brings her nearer to Him. In the end, however, she breaks off her engagement to Narziss, because he is unwilling to grant her the freedom to follow her convictions. She does this not so much because her love for God and her love for Narziss are incompatible, but rather because he is no longer worthy of her love, since he has developed in a different way.

Further emotional disturbances are necessary so that a spiritual life of this kind can develop. Her relationship with Philo, although perfectly proper, gives her a feeling of sin, but again it deepens her religious feeling. She becomes conscious of the true nature of faith. She understands and feels that Christ's blood washes away all sins. The deep current of her inner life makes her turn to the Moravian Community. In it, she finds a deeper religion than in the Church. But she has to recognize that although religion is for her the most important element in life, other spheres exist which demand attention: cultivating one's inner life is not enough. She has to admit that she was mistaken in her enthusiasm for religious images lacking aesthetic value, and that feeling alone is no sound basis for aesthetic judgement; knowledge is necessary as well. Nonetheless, the centre of her life is religion. Nature is not merely of this earth, but also transcendental: regard for what is purely human is not sufficient for education, as love of God is also necessary.

Wilhelm must admit that her feelings are not without effect upon him. The purity of her existence deeply affects his thoughts. He admires her independence of mind and her refusal to accept anything that does not agree with her religious convictions. The *Stiftsdame*'s confessions prepare Wilhelm for his meeting with Natalie, and indirectly help to forge the bond between them.

Nonetheless, the *Stiftsdame* has her faults too. Natalie points out that she is too preoccupied with herself. Her religiosity restricts her impact on the world. She does not know how to be tolerant or accommodating. Such a person is an example we are unable to imitate, but who can inspire us. At least so Natalie suggests.

There are allusions to the transcendental world in other places, but they are rare. In the funeral service for Mignon a religious note is struck, but the exhortation given is different from that made by the *Stiftsdame*. We are asked not to turn away from life, but to face it and prove ourselves in it. And, of course, such allusions occur in the Harper's poetry where a note of anguish is struck.

Indeed, of all the figures that bring out the irrationality of life, the figure of the Harper is undoubtedly the most important. Mysterious, invisible forces are hinted at by his songs. The poetic power which emanates from them gives the words and his whole personality a strength and weight of their own. Only later do we discover that this is the result of an unhappy past. Religion and nature are in conflict. Through this conflict, Sperata, his sister, is driven to madness and death.

The Harper may be seen as a symbol of irrational forces, but he remains on the periphery of events. Wilhelm does not at this stage concern himself at all deeply with religious questions. This happens only when he hears how his own behaviour has affected the Count and the Countess, for both have been hurt by his conduct; here, he has been innocent and guilty alike. But it is only when he has been shaken by Aurelie's despair and death and stirred by reading the *Stiftsdame*'s confessions that he is in a receptive state of mind and likely to be affected in a positive manner.

Religion thus plays a minor part in the novel. So does nature. Whereas in *Werther*, nature and Werther's sensibility are closely interwoven, in the *Lehrjahre*, nature is mentioned only intermittently, as for instance in the second chapter of the second book, at the beginning of the seventh book and in the eighth book, where nature is described as a symbol of Wilhelm's hopes. Nature plays a subordinate part. The hero himself is the main factor in the novel; it is his inner nature, therefore, on which attention is focused.

Wilhelm's intellectual development, however, is a natural one. It is not always directed towards a particular goal, but there definitely is progress. Different stages can be discerned.[75] The same is true of his emotional development (if, indeed, intellect and emotion can usefully be separated). He learns through trial and error, particularly in his love affairs. Wilhelm is tossed to and fro and thus avoids petrifaction.

Do the other characters in the novel undergo a similar development? We do not know enough of many of them, such as the Abbé or Jarno, to consider their whole life. About others we learn more; Lothario, Natalie, and to a lesser degree Therese, Friedrich, Serlo and even the *Stiftsdame*, have furthered their natural talents through trial and error. Other characters make an impact through their limitations, even through their failure to develop. This is true of Werner, whose spiritual talents fail, and of the Count and the Countess who, disturbed by their superstitions, are compelled to change their way of living. Other ways of life lead to catastrophe, for instance those of Mariane, Mignon and the Harper, or of characters whose fate Wilhelm experiences in literature, like Hamlet and Ophelia. They are not strong enough to bear the fate imposed on them.[76]

Wilhelm is found in the centre of the nexus of relations formed by all the characters of the novel; the lives of the others are contrasted to his. A whole complex of figures is formed, a kind of 'beautiful planetary system', to use Schiller's words.[77] These relations bring about the action of the novel. Everything is related to Wilhelm. He possesses a healthy nature, and is able, therefore, to continue his education despite all the dangers that threaten him. Wilhelm overcomes them through his own inner resources and by identifying himself with his friends whose personalities are already harmoniously developed; he succeeds in furthering his own education.

Since Wilhelm's education is apparently continuous, and since it is his declared desire to be educated, the *Lehrjahre* has always been considered a pedagogic novel.[78] In the eighteenth century, education was taken more seriously than ever before; its importance was enhanced by the growing secularization of Christian values; the Christian tradition had enjoined upon the individual the duty of aiming at perfection, but secular culture now made him focus his efforts on improving his mind and personality.[79] Wilhelm and the *Stiftsdame* here afford contrasts, for while Wilhelm is influenced by secular conceptions of education, the

Stiftsdame looks back to a tradition where spiritual perfection was to be the criterion of action. The main plot of the *Lehrjahre*, however, deliberately aims at depicting a young man's education; it shows not only how he grows up, but, both by implication and by discussion, studies the underlying philosophical problems of his education. But does the epithet 'pedagogic' really apply to the novel? A recent German critic, after a thorough investigation, came to the conclusion that Wilhelm was indeed educated, but not in a general way; he was educated rather to perform a special function, which this critic, however, never defined.[80] Originally he appears to have aspired, in the Renaissance tradition, to become a universally educated man, an *uomo universale*, an aspiration which, of course, he never realized.[81]

'Education' (*Bildung*) must be distinguished from inner development. Development is a process in which characters do not substantially change. *Bildung*, on the other hand, is a 'teleological process'[82] capable of changing or influencing a character, of leading him to a specific goal which nature and society have set for him. Wilhelm is unaware of the goal, but it can be seen, when viewing his life in retrospect at the end of the novel, that he has advanced towards a goal. Since Wilhelm's character is changed by his experiences and since his education leads to a goal, the carrying out of a limited activity in a sphere of landowners – though this activity is never defined – it is correct to call the *Lehrjahre* a pedagogic novel; above all, to delimit the concept of '*Bildung*' does not mean that it does not matter to Wilhelm. On the contrary, he is consciously concerned with his education; to become educated was his hope and desire from early youth. Wilhelm learns to recognize that we are able to do only what we are capable of doing, that we can be effective only with those talents which we possess. He recognizes that he is not destined to be an actor or the creator of a national theatre. Indeed, like Lessing, he is neither 'an actor nor a poet',[83] but an ordinary citizen. The positive result of his education, on the other hand, consists in his attaining a more objective assessment of reality. He no longer views the world from the standpoint of feeling; he now knows that it is also determined by experience and reason. Thus he sees it more clearly. His education can be moulded by an inner process which prescribes an external way of life for him and leads him not to an inappropriate activity in the world of trade and commerce, but to an appropriate sphere of activity among noble landowners. However, we learn nothing of a specific activity which he performs or ought to perform in this sphere. Wilhelm would now, in principle, be in a position to lead the life of a nobleman. Through Werner's business acumen, he has the money to purchase an estate. The Marchese assigns to him the estate in Italy which Mignon would have inherited and Natalie is, of course, a rich heiress with substantial landed property. Though outwardly Wilhelm is well equipped to use this new social position to great ends, we learn of no plans which he wishes to carry out. Indeed, his thoughts do not turn to a specific useful activity nor to a continuation of his education – they centre on Natalie, whose love he wishes to gain. She has become for him the criterion of his own worth.[84] Though spiritually impressive, she is anything but colourful. This may not matter, since Wilhelm has sobered down and his enthusiasm has waned. No longer his fancy, but realism informs his mind, and appears to condition his attitude to others and even determines the choice of his company, of his desires and conduct. The novel here, as elsewhere, is ambiguous, intimating the gains and losses incurred by Wilhelm and, indeed, the shortcomings of any conception of *Bildung*. This ambiguity partly derives from Goethe's failure to distinguish clearly and consistently '*Bildung* as self-cultivation from *Bildung* as the shaping of an organic whole through the interplay between its "entelechy", the formative forces within, and its environment, nor this again from the final "shape" it assumes.'[85] Nonetheless, despite its ironic undertones, despite colourlessness of the aristocratic world in the last two books of the novel, despite the uncertainties created by the concept of *Bildung*, Wilhelm has clearly moved on to a higher plane – his companions are more worthwhile. He has improved in appearance, and though appearance is not conclusive, it may, on balance, be taken as a sign of healthy development, especially in a world like that of the eighteenth century which valued outward demeanour and appearance so highly. Wilhelm has been lucky to the point where the dénouement recalls a fairy-tale ending, a fact of which even he himself becomes aware. In this respect, too, the irony of the novel becomes apparent, for Wilhelm's apprenticeship ends in an air of unreality, leaving him in a utopian environment.

So it is all left very vague. All we hear is that he has reached a stage in life where he is able to regard the world calmly and where there are opportunities for practical activity. Does this amount to much? Hardly, yet we are left with the distinct impression that Wilhelm has shed some of his illusions and has become capable of adapting himself to whatever situations he may face. Goethe was thus in tune with the suggestion expressed by Christian Friedrich von Blankenburg in his *Versuch über den Roman*, namely that the 'highbrow' novelist had to have different intentions towards his characters from those customary in adventure and travel books. It was the 'highbrow' novelist's task to train, or rather to write the history of, the forces of thought and feeling.[86] Since, for Goethe, everything is in flux, to describe the formation of a personality is most appropriate. This view stands, of course, in contrast to that of the Enlightenment, where *Bildung* was still seen as a mental process of mind determined by the will.

Imaginative literature can be not only an image, but also a model. Does the novel tell us how we are to educate ourselves? Undoubtedly, there are some didactic rules, such as we find in the *Lehrbrief*. Its maxims are not exhortations for practical use; they are rules which inform us about life and which are to be consulted on account of their reasonableness. We are also confronted with different views on education. The Abbé believes that man is capable of being educated only if he is allowed an opportunity to go astray. Jarno contests this view. He thinks that a man who follows a wrong turn should be warned – but he also admits that the Abbé has a knack of penetrating other people's minds. Wilhelm's life appears to prove the Abbé right.

Bildung is a gift of grace which not everyone is capable of attaining. Wilhelm succeeds in doing so, although the process of his education is not completed. He is a man who enters from 'an empty, indistinct ideal into a practical, active life without losing his power of idealism'.[87] A further direction is intimated, especially since he has reached a point on his path through life where he is able to look back calmly upon past errors. Not all the characters reach a similar level.

If, on the whole, *Bildung* is the goal of the action, it is also a criterion by which man's attitude to the external world can be determined. *Bildung* is possible only if the individual stands in a fruitful relationship to reality. What image of reality does Goethe depict in the *Lehrjahre*? By way of contrast to Werther, Wilhelm is a man who has learnt how to acquire true education from life. The whole tendency of the novel is therefore directed against those who are unable to find a practical attitude to life, but also against those who completely succumb to practical activity. Thought and action, emotional maturity and practical activity combined, create a truly cultured person. Education, however, inevitably makes us one-sided. By developing one particular skill or tendency, we develop one side of our personality at the expense of another. Society at that date, indeed at any time, demands this one-sidedness which does not permit a general education. Wilhelm should not close his eyes to its being one-sided, but he should accept the need for it to be so.

Wilhelm Meister becomes educated to the point where he is capable of undertaking new positive tasks. The world of the *Lehrjahre* is, however, not identical with the process of his education. Other ways of living are indicated. A motley world is described, but it is seen primarily from Wilhelm's point of view. Many aspects appear to him strange, because he feels that much in the life of noblemen is dubious, and hinders them from working out their education. Other aspects are valuable, because they appear to be of use to him. The narrator's irony implies that Wilhelm's criteria are not necessarily right. Later on, as Wilhelm's views about his aim in life change, his perspective changes too. Some obstacles now appear more significant, and some victories only Pyrrhic victories.

Success and failure are assessed differently at different stages of life. Not all stages can serve equally as models, but Wilhelm's whole career may be seen as typical. Wilhelm becomes more realistic through error, for capability and good fortune favour him. He thus learns that the theatre is able to move men so powerfully because it makes us believe that the fragment of life depicted stands for the whole of existence. The belief held by Natalie's uncle and the Abbé in the power which works of art can have over men springs from the same basic conception. Even the books in the uncle's house are chosen with a view to giving those who may read them a sense of a proper order. This sense for the whole is necessary for a consideration of a work of art. Only thus can the form of a work be apprehended; without this awareness of its form, its import cannot be known.[88] The uncle's house, therefore, radiates harmony. Not all spheres of life achieve this.

Many spheres of society form the world of the *Lehrjahre*.[89] In contrast to *Werther*, the point of departure is not a protest against the conditions of life. Wilhelm is, on the whole, not discontented with life, but looks at it in a positive manner. He criticizes the conditions and abuses the forms of life which appear to him restricted and inadequate, but he knows how to adapt himself to circumstances and how to benefit from them in spite of occasional despair and apparent failure. He has moments of dissatisfaction, but not enough to imperil him seriously, let alone destroy him. If he is imperilled, it is less because he is incapable of adaptation, than because he is excessively receptive to the personality of others, such as Mignon or the Harper. Of course, there are flaws in his personality – he has his share of insecurity, but he is able to ward it off in the last resort. The only one who turns away from the world of external reality, if only for a while, during his madness, is the Harper. His fate in the novel could alone be called tragic. Aurelie, who faces existence without compromise, and Laertes, who looks at it misanthropically, do not really reject life. Aurelie's despair is rooted in her disappointed passion. Laertes has a melancholic temperament, but his view of the world appears of little consequence for the novel. Mignon is like Hamlet; neither of them is strong enough for the world. Hamlet is aware of his predicament, Mignon is not.

Reality is not seen in terms of conflict. There are different conceptions of life; but, by way of contrast to *Werther*, no one single conception of life claims to have sole validity.

Since the action of *Werther* is restricted to a limited sphere of experience, it does not impinge on other sectors of life. The *Lehrjahre*, however, goes beyond the experiences and problems of any one person. Although Wilhelm is the character around whose development the action revolves, the novel also describes the lives of several others. Wilhelm, like Werther, speaks for a generation of young men, but others also claim attention. Many events are depicted over a longer period of time; a fuller image of reality is therefore given, though what the novel gains in breadth it loses in intensity.

Although there are plenty of conflicts in this novel between the world of the theatre and the limitations of the bourgeois, these conflicts are not insoluble. This might be gathered from the uniformity of style. The balanced style of the narrator reflects an image of reality which keeps an equilibrium between external and internal experience, between thought and action, between the obligations which the individual owes to society and those which he owes to his own education. It is a harmonious world. Man gathers the results of his experience, so that at a single moment past and future become present through symbolic images. It is a world in which a fruitful mental and spiritual development is possible for an individual if good fortune favours him. A man endowed like Wilhelm is able to prosper without fear of perishing because the community or an inner drive demand it.

The completion of the *Lehrjahre* not only falls within Goethe's classical period as a creative writer, but also within the first important period of his writings on natural science. One of the features of his study of natural science at that time was his morphological method. An attempt to apply morphology to a study of the novel has appropriately been made, but it has not been fully successful.[90] It can, however, be agreed that various human lives are opposed to one another, which describe man not in a static spiritual and physical condition nor in a single phase of his development.

Not only a pedagogic, but a biological process is depicted. Different human beings are educated: characters slowly change during the course of the novel. Metamorphoses follow one another. The analogy of growth, as Goethe depicts it, can be applied here, but must not be pressed too far. The basic relationship should be indisputable, but no specific laws affecting the details of the lives of the individuals can be detected. The relations between Goethe's view of natural science and the *Lehrjahre* are not limited to these aspects only. Connections at a deeper level can be found. An important essay on the methods of natural science, *Der Versuch als Vermittler zwischen Subjekt und Objekt* (*The Experiment as Mediator between Subject and Object*), affording a concise statement of Goethe's scientific method, is revealing in this context; for it shows that Goethe's view of man's education agrees with the results which can be gained from the study of nature. Wilhelm's educational process is natural, since he is not subjected to external constraint, but follows laws which are natural. What kind of laws are these?

> The further we continue these observations, the more we interrelate objects, the more we exercise the gift of observation within ourselves. If we relate this knowledge to ourselves by action, we merit being called intelligent. For a well-organized man who is either moderate by nature or is limited by circumstances, this intelligence is not a difficult matter: for life puts us right at every step. If, however, the observer desires to apply this severe criterion to the examination of the secret relations of nature, if he desires to watch his own steps and moves in a world in which he is, so to speak, alone, if he wants to guard himself against all hastiness, and to have his goal continuously before his eyes without leaving anything useful or harmful unnoticed, if, even where he cannot be easily guided by anyone else, he is to be his own most severe critic, and always distrustful towards himself in his most enthusiastic pursuits; in these circumstances every one can see how severe these demands are and how little we can hope ever to see them properly fulfilled, whether we make them on ourselves or on others. But these difficulties, we may say this hypothetical impossibility, should not stop us from doing all that we can; we shall at least get furthest if we seek in general to picture to ourselves the means by which outstanding men have been able to extend the sciences, and if we mark out the ways in which they have been sidetracked and in which a large number of disciples, sometimes for centuries on end, have followed them until later experiences put the observer on the right path again.[91]

Here Goethe speaks about the experience which we gain from studying the history of the natural sciences, and also from our own experiences in natural science. The intelligent and well-organized man whom Goethe describes is doubtless the man Wilhelm Meister wants to become; a man who is inwardly as well organized as Wilhelm is hardly capable of satisfying the expectations which he has of education. Despite all his concern for education, Wilhelm, like the scientist, goes astray, and the errors unavoidable in experimentation also form part of his life.

It is also possible from another angle to perceive the impact of

Goethe's scientific writings in this novel. He had taken the view that a law of compensation prevails in nature: 'that it was impossible to add anything to any one part without taking something away from another or vice versa.'[92] This conception agrees with Wilhelm's development. He may gain in consistency and stability of action, but at the same time he has lost spontaneity and enthusiasm. Not every advance in intellectual education is profitable. Wilhelm gains a more precise image of life, of his own awareness of reality and of his fellow men, but he loses emotional freshness and intensity. His feeling for Natalie is no less deep than his love for Mariane, for Natalie's image had had a lasting impact on his emotional life from their very first encounter. His love, however, moves along different paths. Wilhelm has become an important member of a community of enlightened landowners. His turning to a more realistic conception of life simultaneously brings about a reduction of his emotional and imaginative strength; this, however, appears to be an appropriate natural development.

Does this view of *Wilhelm Meister* agree with Goethe's conception of the novel? He did not normally expound his works at length; his comments were mainly made at random. This is true of the *Lehrjahre*. The best insight into his mind can be gleaned from his correspondence with Schiller; for Schiller wrote at length about this work in his letters, and Goethe replied to some of the points raised by his friend. The *Lehrjahre* was written at a time when their friendship found expression in continuous and intensive interchange of ideas. Probably the most important piece of literary criticism Schiller ever wrote are his letters to Goethe on this novel. Their discussion affords us an insight into Goethe's artistic intention. In his letters, Schiller's critical acumen, his empathy for the novel is striking. Among German literary critics who wrote on *Wilhelm Meister*, there is no one, not even Friedrich Schlegel, who can rival Schiller in penetration and understanding.

What are the main points which Schiller stresses in his reflections on the *Lehrjahre*? He interprets the novel from the point of view of its characters. He looks at Wilhelm's relationship with Therese and Natalie; he sees points of contrast between the *Stiftsdame*, Therese and Natalie. His analysis of other figures, such as Mignon, the Count, the Countess or the Marchese, is perceptive.

What matters most to Schiller is the form of the work. He is therefore interested in knowing how the characters are connected with the whole and how far their appearance is organically rooted in the context or to what degree they are intertwined with the development of the action. There are events which, he thinks, are not organically connected with this development but appear to be random occurrences; e.g. the appearance of the Countess in the second half of the eighth book. He strongly defends the sixth book, which appears to him necessary for the whole work; this is so not only because it acquaints us with the character of the *Stiftsdame*, but also because we indirectly learn about Natalie's family before we encounter them as a group of people involved in the action.

Above all, Schiller describes the development of the hero; his interpretation represents a fundamental assessment even today. The main development of Wilhelm's inner life, so Schiller argues, leads to a firm grasp of reality. His maturity consists in his ability to find a happy mean between philistinism on the one hand, and indulgence in unrealistic fantasies on the other. For him, Wilhelm fulfils his purpose in the happiest manner. His path lies in the progress of his education, but not in its effect; therefore as soon as he takes account of what he has achieved in life, it must appear unimportant to him.

> Apprenticeship (*Lehrjahre*) involves a concept of proportion: it demands its correlate, mastery (*Meisterschaft*), and furthermore the idea of the latter must clearly explain and establish the former. But this idea, which can only be the result of mature and fulfilled experience, does not itself guide the hero of the novel; it cannot and must not stand before him as his end and goal; for if he were to think of the goal, he would have *eo ipso* attained it: it must stand as a signpost *behind* him. In this way, the whole acquires a beautiful purposiveness without the hero having a purpose; reason finds a task fulfilled while imagination completely maintains its freedom.[93]

According to Schiller, this purpose is the only one which really comes to the fore in the novel. It is presented without heaviness or rigorousness. Schiller wanted Goethe to indicate clearly the novel's aesthetic structure and the poetic necessity of events.[94] Goethe saw it differently. He avoided complying with Schiller's request on this point. If he was evasive, his intention was unmistakable and his answer decisive: he spoke strongly of how much Schiller's attempts to make these requested changes had irked him.[95] He defended himself by emphasizing the touch of realism[96] peculiarly appropriate to him. He was quite willing to follow many of Schiller's counsels, but he was not prepared for the structure of the novel to become too open to analysis. There had to be scope for the readers' imagination! too much clarity of intention would reduce the poetic power and preclude other possible interpretations.

We may agree with the main features of Schiller's argument. The end of the *Lehrjahre* coincides with Wilhelm's more realistic assessment of reality, but his education is by no means over. Dangers threaten again and again to interfere with its course. Since Goethe wanted to emphasize this, the novel did not conclude with the declaration that the hero's apprenticeship was completed. Another aspect of the novel is constituted by the Society of the Tower. The impression which it conveys is deliberately meant to be imprecise and to awaken the reader's speculation. At the same time, the impact of this society was to be given an aesthetic value.[97] In this resides its immediate power, i.e. it was to possess symbolic force and to symbolize the power which a positive view of life can have.

We can gain a further understanding of the novel if we contrast it with drama. Goethe was deeply interested in this comparison. He emphasized in the seventh chapter of the fifth book that the drama and the novel belong to different worlds, and that it is the task of the novelist to depict a world in a wider context. The essay *Über epische und dramatische Kunst* (*On Epic and Dramatic Art*) which he wrote with Schiller again clearly delineates this. If we consider not merely the outer form of the work, but also its inner form, it becomes apparent that the epic poet describes events as belonging to the past while the dramatist depicts them as present. Hence a calm manner and reflective power characterize the epic writer. He appears detached and wise, as is indeed true of the narrator in the *Lehrjahre*. Schiller defined the problem even more sharply:

> It becomes clearer and clearer to me . . . that the independence of its parts constitutes a principal characteristic of the epic poem. Pure truth, taken from the inner life, is the purpose of

the epic poet. He merely describes the calm existence of things. His purpose is already found in every point of this movement.[98]

This definition also agrees with the *Lehrjahre*. The various situations have, in retrospect, their definite share in Wilhelm's education, but on first reading, the various episodes demand attention independently. The course of the novel, thus, is slow. Not fate, as in drama, but chance holds sway.[99]

The agreement between theory and practice which is characteristic of the poetic and aesthetic plan of classicism applies not only to Goethe's theory of the novel, but also to his conception of art in general. Goethe changed the *Lehrjahre* not only because he had come to look at the world of the theatre from a different point of view, but because he had meanwhile crystallized his theory of art.

Goethe completed the *Lehrjahre* in the period when he and Schiller had defined their theory of art. He did not write the *Lehrjahre* to prove this classical theory by a practical example. It is not a piece of epic algebra. The novel may, however, be assessed in accordance with these principles. Goethe had to find an appropriate form to describe social and intellectual problems in a concrete manner. This form was the pedagogic novel. A particular form is convincing only if the import (*Gehalt*) is substantial; this import is much more substantial in the *Lehrjahre* than in the *Sendung*. More scope is given to education and religion. Wilhelm's education is no longer orientated towards the theatre in a one-sided manner. His inner life now has wider dimensions; he has come to know other aspects of social life. At the same time, the aim of education has been limited and intellectual aspirations have been made precise, so that Wilhelm's efforts are no longer pointless.

Goethe describes situations from the life of an individual, but it is important for his classical view of art to note that this specific event represents something general. Just as he did not consider analysis legitimate without synthesis, so the specific instance was only of value if it led to the discovery of what was generally valid. He thus believed he could see the *Urpflanze*, the archetype of all plants, for it contained what was typical of all plants. His scientific interests hence led him to a consideration of the general. He defines this view in a well-known aphorism:

> It is true symbolism where the specific represents the general, not as a dream and shadow, but as a living instantaneous revelation of the unfathomable.[100]

This aphorism can be applied to the *Lehrjahre*, but not to the *Sendung*. In this manner, Wilhelm acquires in the *Lehrjahre* a healthy mental education. This was not the case in the *Sendung*. In the *Lehrjahre*, his education corresponds to the theory of metamorphosis, which says that errors are of the same kind as the disorders of a healthy man, for they can be overcome and even be beneficial. If the specific is healthy, it will also be of general validity:

> The poet must grasp the particular, and provided that it contains something healthy, he will also depict the general by means of the particular.[101]

Strength and health are thus, in Goethe's view, necessary for truth. 'The pure and generally human element which stands above all that is accidental and momentary endows the object with significance and dignity, with inner import.[102]

This universality which is appropriate to the novel as a classical work of art gives it its symbolic power. It thus has a philosophical quality which alone explains its remarkable impact on the contemporary world, shown, for instance, by Friedrich Schlegel's extravagant, but impressive assertion: 'The French Revolution, Fichte's Theory of Knowledge, and Goethe's *Wilhelm Meister* are the greatest tendencies of the age.'[103] This contention has, indeed, subjective rather than objective validity, but it allows us to divine what the novel meant for many intellectuals in Germany at that time. Its philosophical character is also one of the reasons why it has served as a model for so many later German novelists, from the Romantics in the early nineteenth century to Thomas Mann and Hermann Hesse in our time.

Goethe's classical theory of art as evolved at this time helps us further. 'Truth' is one of the essential features of art. 'Beauty' is another. For him, beauty is the inner essence, as well as the outer veil of an organic whole. Motifs and images allow us to infer the existence of an organic continuity. Wilhelm and the other characters are living, highly organized persons. So Goethe fulfils the demand he had made in his essay on Laocoon that only people who were highly organized ought to be represented in literature.

The *Lehrjahre* possesses an order of its own; but clearly its proportions are not of a symmetrical kind. The novel, it cannot be denied, reveals inadequacies on the technical level. Despite the underlying organic connection, the relationship between the first five, the sixth and the last two books is not entirely harmonious. The function of the last three books is clear, but there are differences between the parts which make it difficult to see the work as a whole. They reduce its impact on the reader. External regularity need not be the criterion, but the material must be appropriately ordered,[104] i.e. the division of the novel into three main parts corresponds to the laws which are relevant to the form of this novel. In the first part, above all, the world of the theatre is described: Wilhelm embraces it, but finally withdraws from it. The second part, the sixth book, is almost entirely devoted to the portrayal of religious experience. In the third part, Wilhelm is initiated into meaningful activity in the practical world. According to Goethe, the perfection of a work of art does not necessarily mean regularity, order and decorativeness; it involves the embodiment and realization of a living and natural compliance with law. Art has, for Goethe, to be understood as an organic development, analogous to nature. The *Lehrjahre* was for him a natural product, because it corresponded to the organic conditions of an action which is unfolded in a natural manner. Nonetheless, art is something made and not natural, and this novel can be no exception, but the biography of a young man in the natural stages of his development is analogous to a process of nature. The work thus possesses a characteristic touch, a uniformity of style resulting from the organic relations which all its parts and aspects have with one another. It is, therefore, a classical work of art.

Nonetheless, Goethe found the genre of the novel inadequate. He knew that perfection could not be expected from it. Perfecting the novel technically by smoothness of language, organic relationship of images, consistency of intention and so on, was not enough. The form of the novel itself was 'impure'; it contained foreign elements, so to speak, such as lyrical poetry. It could not therefore stand comparison with dramatic form.

In a letter to Rochlitz he made this point quite clear:

> What you have said of *Meister*, I understand very well: all of it is true and even more. Its imperfection has given me a lot of trouble. A pure form gives help and support, whereas an impure one is a hindrance and disturbance. Whatever may come, it will not so readily happen again that I make a mistake in subject matter and form.[105]

The form of the novel makes greater demands on the reader than drama or lyric poetry. At first it appears more easily accessible, but the more severe form of drama or lyric poetry presents a more immediate challenge, and is thus more easily apprehended. The novel particularly lends itself to misinterpretation. Goethe himself regarded it as a happy accident if poetic communication appealed to the reader directly:

> Form always retains something impure, and we must thank God if we are capable of infusing it with so much import that feeling and thinking men wish to occupy themselves with sifting it out again.[106]

Goethe did not betray any discontent with the import of the novel; his discontent is mainly with the material which contemporary Germany offered a novelist. His aim was to write a novel which was representative of the social reality of his age. But reality in Germany was of such a nature that Wilhelm, his hero, had no real place in life. This fact has, to some extent, hampered the reception of the *Lehrjahre* outside German-speaking countries. Goethe's novels have not become serious rivals to the great French, English and Russian novels. The *Lehrjahre* suffers from the national and political situation in eighteenth-century Germany, which, despite the greatness of German literature, was not conducive to the growth of culture. Lessing pointed out this weakness quite distinctly when he spoke of the ingenious plan of a group of Germans who sought to found a national theatre at a time when Germany was not yet a nation.[107]

Originally, the *Sendung* must have originated from Goethe's desire to depict the development of a young man in eighteenth-century Germany. Emphasis was to be laid on positive aspects of life, and it was no longer a criticism of emotional extravagance, as in *Werther*, but an appreciative appraisal of an attempt to discover a way of education. Wilhelm Meister was to find a promising sphere of activity as a creative individual. Personal interest in drama and the political and social conditions made the theatre an obvious field, but it was not Goethe's aim to write a moral or political tract. The moral purpose of art in general and of poetry in particular had become the main theme of aesthetics in a predominantly non-political society. In a certain sense, the theatre was to take over the task of the pulpit in a secularized world. The theatre was either praised as a moral institution, or attacked as a centre of corruption; writings on this theme by men like Gottsched, Lessing, Rousseau, Diderot and Schiller, to mention only a few important eighteenth-century writers, prove that Goethe once again moved in traditional paths.

The direction of this Wilhelm Meister novel changed as Goethe grew more mature. It was no longer a question of depicting the life of a creative but rather of a sensitive person. Artists appeared much less suited than ordinary men to be representative of the general tendencies of the age. Persons and spheres of activity had to be seen as symbolic, as representatives of the age. It was a question of bringing what is perfect and beautiful into a harmonious equilibrium; this was an ideal which determined the atmosphere and particularly the dénouement of the novel.

The *Lehrjahre* has also its appointed place in Goethe's period of classicism. Since it is of heterogeneous origin, it does not constitute so organically composed a work as *Hermann und Dorothea*, a relatively short epic poem. But this lack is not inappropriate; Wilhelm is still on the road to the zenith of his life. The *Lehrjahre* also covers too large a span of time to be capable of depicting a man only at one moment of life. The road upwards is depicted to a point where, if only for a moment, past and future meet in the present.

Wilhelm Meister's future cannot be clearly discerned, even if his engagement to Natalie and his acceptance into the Society of the Tower and participation in its activities allow him to look with confidence into the future. Unlike *Iphigenie auf Tauris*, *Torquato Tasso* or *Faust*, the novel is not inspired by legend or history, but is set in contemporary society. This topicality, Wilhelm's increasing maturity and insight, and his growing recognition of the multiplicity of life, are all reasons why the sphere of the work became increasingly broad. It was not merely a question of depicting

Wilhelm's experience, but also that of others, for this wider view helps us to understand his life by way of the continuation of the story. The ageing of the poet, the political events of the decade and the severe hostility of the Romantics in turn brought about a changed attitude to life. It was not a radical change, but it betrays a shift in Goethe's vision. This change in turn caused inner disturbances. As a result, a work was created which placed the extraordinary (*Ungeheuere*) at its very centre, thus moving far away from the tenor of the *Lehrjahre*. This theme, accordingly disrupted Goethe's original plans for a series of tales connected with Wilhelm Meister, a series which was intended as a continuation of the *Lehrjahre* and for which the name of the *Wanderjahre* had been chosen. A work actually resulted which had originally been conceived as a tale within a cycle of tales, but soon demanded an independent existence of its own; it became Goethe's third novel: *Die Wahlverwandtschaften*.[108] Begun in 1808, it was expanded, revised and, relatively soon afterwards, published in 1809. Goethe's own words most clearly explain this change of a *novelle* into a novel – for the force of the contents demanded a more important form:

> These brief tales occupied me in leisure hours, and *Die Wahlverwandtschaften* too ought to have been treated quite briefly. But it expanded, the matter was too important and too deeply rooted in me, and I was therefore unable to dispose of it so easily.[109]

Notes

1. See Hans M. Wolff, *Goethes Weg zur Humanität*, Berne, 1951, p. 20, who surmises that Goethe began to write the novel in 1773. His argument is subtle, but does not carry conviction.

2. See R. Köpke, *Ludwig Tieck*, Leipzig, 1885, i, p. 329.

3. See L. A. Willoughby, '"Name ist Schall und Rauch"; On the significance of Namer for Goethe', *GLL*, xvi (1963), p. 302.

4. Cf. Schiller, *Die Schaubühne als moralische Anstalt betrachtet* (1784).

5. The first scholar to pose the question was the first editor of the *Sendung*, Harry Maync, who in his introduction to his edition of *Wilhelm Meisters Theatralische Sendung*, Stuttgart and Berlin, 1911, pp. xxi ff., recognized that more than one interpretation was possible. Among the later interpretations, the view that the title should be taken seriously predominates, though the other view of an ironic interpretation is still held and has never been conclusively refuted. For the former interpretation cf. Hugo von Hofmannsthal, 'Der Urmeister', *Prosa* iii, Frankfurt/Main, 1952, p. 77 (originally published in *Neue Freie Presse*, Vienna, 1911); Albert Koester, 'Wilhelm Meisters Theatralische Sendung', *Zeitschrift für den deutschen Unterricht*, xxvi (1912); Friedrich Gundolf, *Goethe*, Berlin, 1916, pp. 355 ff.; Max Wundt, *Wilhelm Meister und die Entwicklung des modernen Lebensideals*, Berlin & Leipzig, 1913, p. 153; Bernhard Seuffert, *Goethes Theaterroman*, Graz, Vienna, Leipzig, 1924; Georg Brandes, *Goethe*, German trans. Erich Holler and Emilie Stein, 4th ed. Berlin, 1922, p. 239; Benedetto Croce, 'Die beiden Fassungen des Wilhelm Meister', *Goethe*, trans. Werner Ross, Düsseldorf, 1949, p. 76; J. G. Robertson, *The Life and Work of Goethe*, London, 1932, p. 186; Günther Weydt, *Wilhelm Meisters Theatralische Sendung*, Bonner Texte, 7, Bonn, 1949, p. xii; Trunz, H.A., 7, p. 613. The ironic view is held, or at least considered, by Erich Schmidt, 'Der erste Wilhelm Meister. Auszüge und Bemerkungen', *Internationale Monatsschrift für Wissenschaft, Kunst und Technik*, vi (1912), p. 68; Robert Hering, *Wilhelm Meister und Faust und ihre Gestaltung im Zeichen der Gottesidee*, Frankfurt/Main, 1952, pp. 112 f.; Wolfgang Baumgart, G.A., 7, pp. 684 f.: a more differentiated view allowing for possible changes of intention is put forward by Emil Staiger, *Goethe*, Zürich, 1952–9, i, pp. 470 ff., and Jacob Steiner, *Sprache und Stilwandel in Goethes Wilhelm Meister*, Zürcher Beiträge zur deutschen Sprache und Stilgeschichte, 7, Zürich, 1959 (2nd ed. Stuttgart, 1965).

6. Cf. Becker, *Der deutsche Roman um 1780*, Germanistische Abhandlungen, 5, Stuttgart, 1964.

7. The phrase '*gesteigerter Werther*' defies exact translation. The phrase, incidentally, applies both to the play and its hero. Cf. Wilkinson, '"*Tasso – ein gesteigerter Werther*" in the light of Goethe's Principle of *Steigerung*'; 'Goethe's Conception of Form', E. M. Wilkinson and L. A. Willoughby, *Goethe: Poet and Thinker*, London, 1962.

8. See Seuffert, op. cit., *passim*, for a discussion of possible sources.

9. Cf. Hans Knudsen, *Goethes Welt des Theaters*, Berlin, 1949.

10. Cf. Julius Petersen, *Das Deutsche Nationaltheater*, Leipzig, 1919; Hans Kindermann, *Theatergeschichte der Goethezeit*, Vienna, 1948; W. H. Bruford, *Theatre, Drama and Audience in Goethe's Germany*,

London, 1949; Willi Fleming, *Goethes Gestaltung des klassischen Theaters*, Cologne, 1949.

11. Letter to Charlotte von Stein, 24 June 1782.

12. Cf. Eckehard Catholy, 'Karl Philipp Moritz. Ein Beitrag zur Theatromanie der Goethezeit', *Euph.*, xlv (1950); cf. Eckehard Catholy, *Karl Philipp Moritz und die Ursprünge der deutschen Theaterleidenschaft*, Tübingen, 1962.

13. See R. Pascal, *The German Sturm und Drang*, Manchester, 1953, especially, pp. 133 ff. for a consideration of the role of genius.

14. Cf. E. L. Stahl, *Die religiöse und die humanitätsphilosophische Bildungsidee und die Entstehung des deutschen Bildungsromans im 18. Jahrhundert*, Sprache und Dichtung, 56, Berne, 1934, pp. 156 ff.

15. Cf. Albert Fries, *Stilistische Beobachtungen zu Wilhelm Meister*, Berliner Beiträge zur germanischen und romanischen Philologie, 44, Berlin, 1912.

16. Hans Reiss, *Goethes Romane*, Berne and Munich, 1963, pp. 76 ff.

17. W.A., i, 27, p. 199 (*Dichtung und Wahrheit*, ii, 8).

18. Cf. *Die schöne Seele. Bekenntnisse, Schriften und Briefe der Susanna Katharina von Klettenberg* (ed. Heinrich Funck), Leipzig, 1911.

19. W.A., i, 27, p. 201 (*Dichtung und Wahrheit*, ii, 8).

20. Willoughby, 'Name ist Schall und Rauch', p. 302, points out that Natalie's name indicates the fusion of social classes.

21. Cf. Franz Josef Schneider, *Die Freimaurerei und ihr Einfluss auf die geistige Kultur in Deutschland am Ende des 18. Jahrhunderts*, Leipzig, 1909.

22. Cf. Marianne Thalmann, *Der Trivialroman des 18. Jahrhunderts und der romantische Roman.* Germanische Studien, 24, Berlin, 1923; cf. also Marion Beaujean, *Der Trivialroman in der zweiten Hälfte des 18. Jahrhunderts. Der Ursprung des modernen Unterhaltungs romans*, Abhandlungen zur Kunst-, Musik- und Literaturwissenschaft, 22, Bonn, 1964.

23. Cf. Günther Müller, *Gestaltung-Umgestaltung in Wilhelm Meisters Lehrjahren*, Halle, 1948, who studied the time-element; cf. his review of his own book in 'Die Goethe-Forschung seit 1945', *DVLG*, xxii (1952), p. 394, where he admits that his emphasis on the time-element did not carry conviction.

24. See W.A., i, 22, p. 291 (ii, 8); W.A., i, 23, p. 124 (vii, 9).

25. This view was widely held in the nineteenth century; cf. Wilhelm Scherer's important *Geschichte der deutschen Literatur*, 3rd ed. Berlin, 1885, p. 566, as a typical example.

26. Letter to Goethe, 2 July 1796.

27. Friedrich Schlegel, 'Über Goethes Meister', *Athenäum*, i, pt. 2, Berlin, 1798, p. 354.

28. Cf. O. H. Olzien, *Der Satzbau in Wilhelm Meisters Lehrjahren*, Von deutscher Poeterey, 14, Leipzig, 1933.

29. Cf. Fries, op. cit.; cf. also Steiner, op. cit.

30. Cf. Fries, pp. 3 ff.

31. See Blackall, *The Emergence of German as a Literary Language, 1700–1775*, Cambridge, 1959, pp. 410 ff.

32. Cf. Oskar Seidlin, 'Zur Mignon-Ballade', *Euph.*, xlv (1950), p. 86; cf. also Herman Meyer, 'Mignons Italienlied und das Wesen der Verseinlage im "Wilhelm Meister". Versuch einer gegenständlichen Polemik', *Euph.*, xlvi (1952), p. 165 and, for a general consideration of these lyrics, Storz, 'Die Lieder aus Wilhelm Meister', *Goethe-Vigilien*, Stuttgart, 1953, pp. 104 ff.

33. Novalis, *Werke*, ed. Ewald Wasmuth, Berlin, 1943, iii, p. 179.

34. Cf. H. S. Reiss, 'On some Images in *Wilhelm Meisters Lehrjahre*', *PEGS*, xx (1951), pp. 111 f.

35. Cf. L. A. Willoughby, 'The Cross-Fertilization of Literature and Life in the Light of Goethe's Principle of "Wiederholte Spiegelungen" ', *Comparative Literature*, i (1949) (Reprinted as 'Literary Relations in the Light of Goethe's Principle of "Wiederspiegelung" ' in Wilkinson and Willoughby, *Goethe: Poet and Thinker*).

36. Letter to Goethe, 2 July 1796.

37. Cf. Wundt, op. cit., for a full account of this aspect.

38. Cf. H. Baumhof, *Die Funktion des Erzählers in Goethes 'Wilhelm Meisters Lehrjahre'*, Heidelberg (unpublished. Diss. 1958–9); cf. also Arthur Henkel, 'Versuch über den Wilhelm Meister', *Ruperto-Carola*, xlv, Heidelberg, 1962, and Hanno Beriger, *Goethe und der Roman. Studien zu 'Wilhelm Meisters Lehrjahre'* (Diss.), Zürich, 1955.

39. See Willoughby, 'Name ist Schall und Rauch', p. 302.

40. Letter to Schiller, 6 December 1794.

41. W.A., i, 51, p. 207 (iii, 3).

42. W.A., i, 21, p. 12 (i, 3).

43. W.A., i, 22, p. 155 (v, 4). This word 'happy' (*glücklich*) is often employed in an ironical manner (cf. W.A., i, 21, p. 85, (i, 15) for instance).

44. W.A., i, 23, p. 216 (viii, 5).

45. W.A., i, 22, p. 128 (iv, 20).

46. W.A., i, 22, p. 173 (v, 6).

47. Cf. Hans Egon Hass, 'Wilhelm Meisters Lehrjahre', *Der deutsche Roman*, i (ed. Benno von Wiese), Düsseldorf, 1963, pp. 132–210, a most perceptive study to which the following remarks are greatly indebted.

48. Arnold Hirsch, 'Barockroman und Aufklärungsroman', *ÉG*, ix, Paris, 1954; cf. also Hirsch, *Bürgertum und Barock im deutschen Roman*.

Ein Beitrag zur Entstehungsgeschichte. (2nd ed. Herbert Singer) Literatur und Leben, N.F., i, Cologne-Graz, 1957.

49. Cf. Henkel, op. cit.

50. W.A., i, 23, p. 132 (viii, 1).

51. W.A., i, 23, p. 133 (viii, 1).

52. W.A., i, 23, p. 132 (viii, 1).

53. E. M. Forster, *Aspects of the Novel*, London, 1927, p. 103.

54. Cf. Thalmann, *Der Trivialroman. . . .*

55. Conversation with Friedrich von Müller, 17 September 1823.

56. W.A., i, 22, p. 150 (v, 3).

57. Cf. Werner Wittich, 'Der soziale Gehalt von Goethes Roman "Wilhelm Meisters Lehrjahre" ', *Hauptprobleme der Soziologie. Erinnerungsgabe für Max Weber*, ii, Munich and Leipzig, 1923.

58. Cf. Hermann Meyer, 'Kennst Du das Haus? Eine Studie zu Goethes Palladio-Erlebnis', *Euph*, xlvii (1953), pp. 285 f.

59. *Italienische Reise*, 19 September 1786 (W.A., i, 30, p. 77).

60. Diary entry of 19 September 1784 (W.A., iii, 1, p. 214); in the *Italienische Reise* Goethe writes: 'whose borrowed existence charms us'. (W.A., i, 30, p. 77).

61. W.A., i, 23, p. 198 (viii, 5).

62. Cf. Friedrich Gundolf, *Shakespeare und der deutsche Geist*, Berlin, 1914, p. 317.

63. William S. Diamond, 'Wilhelm Meister's Interpretation of Hamlet', *Modern Philology*, xxiii (1925–6), pp. 89 ff.

64. Cf. Willoughby, 'Name ist Schall und Rauch', p. 302.

65. I owe much of the subsequent argument to a perceptive, as yet unpublished paper by Hans Eichner on 'Natalie and Therese: Some remarks on Goethe's Conception of Love and Marriage', read at the 78th meeting of the Modern Language Association of America at Chicago, December 1963.

66. Cf. Thalmann, *Der Trivialroman . . .*; cf. also Becker, op. cit.

67. Cf. Hans Egon Hass, 'Wilhelm Meisters Lehrjahre', *passim.*

68. Willoughby, 'Name ist Schall und Rauch', p. 302.

69. W.A., i, 23, p. 243 (viii, 7).

70. Willoughby, 'Name ist Schall und Rauch', p. 302.

71. W.A., i, 23, p. 243 (viii, 7).

72. Willoughby, 'Name ist Schall und Rauch', p. 302.

73. Letter to Goethe, 3 July 1796.

74. Cf. Eric A. Blackall, 'Sense and Non-Sense in *Wilhelm Meisters Lehrjahre*', *Deutsche Beiträge zur geistigen Überlieferung*, v, Berne and Munich, 1965, pp. 49–72, to which the subsequent argument is indebted.

75. Jürgen Rausch, 'Lebensstufen in Goethe's "Wilhelm Meister" ', *DVLG*, xx (1942), p. 65.

76. W.A., i, 22, p. 76 (iv, 13).

77. Schiller's letter to Goethe, 2 July 1796.

78. Cf. Max Wundt; op. cit.; cf. also Fritz Martini, 'Der Bildungsroman. Zur Geschichte des Wortes und der Theorie', *DVLG*, xxxv (1961), pp. 44 ff., who points out that the term *Bildungsroman* (pedagogic novel) was first coined by Karl Morgenstern, Professor at the University of Dorpat at the beginning of the nineteenth century, who based his argument on a discussion of the *Lehrjahre*.

79. Cf. W. H. Bruford, *Culture and Society in Classical Weimar 1775–1806*, Cambridge, 1962, p. 254.

80. Kurt May, ' "Wilhelm Meisters Lehrjahre". ein Bildungsroman', *DVLG*, xxxi (1957).

81. Cf. Martini, p. 47; cf. also Hans Eichner, 'Zur Deutung von Wilhelm Meisters Lehrjahren', *JbFDH* (1966), p. 168.

82. For a discussion of this problem cf. E. L. Stahl, *Die religiöse und die humanitätsphilosophische Bildungsidee* . . .; cf. also Max Wundt, op. cit. and Melitta Gerhard, *Der deutsche Entwicklungsroman bis zu Goethes 'Wilhelm Meister'*, *DVLG* Buchreihe, 9, Halle/Saale, 1926; and Eichner, 'Zur Deutung . . .'.

83. Lessing, *Hamburgische Dramaturgie*, 100th-104th piece.

84. Cf. Eichner, 'Zur Deutung . . .' to whose subtle analysis the following remarks are indebted.

85. Bruford, *Culture and Society* . . ., p. 258.

86. Cited by Joachim Müller, 'Phasen der Bildungsidee im "Wilhelm Meister" ', *G.*, xxiv (1962), p. 59, to whom I am indebted for the following remarks.

87. Letter to Goethe, 8 July 1796.

88. Wilkinson, ' "Form" and "Content" in the Aesthetics of German Classicism', *Stil- und Formprobleme in der Literatur*, ed. Paul Böckmann, Heidelberg, 1960.

89. Cf. W. H. Bruford, 'Goethe's "Wilhelm Meister" as a picture and as a criticism of Society', *PEGS*, ix (1933) for a description of the various social spheres in the novel.

90. Günther Müller, *Gestaltung-Umgestaltung* . . . and 'Goethe-Forschung seit 1945'.

91. W.A., ii, 11, pp. 22 f.

92. W.A., ii, 8, p. 16.

93. Letter to Goethe, 8 July 1796.

94. Ibid.

95. Conversation with Eckermann, 23 March 1829: 'You are right, he [Schiller] was as hasty as all men who proceed from an idea. He was restless and could not make up his mind, as you can see from his letters about *Wilhelm Meister*, which he wanted to be one thing at one time

and another at another.'

96. Letter to Schiller, 9 July 1796.

97. Ibid.

98. Letter to Goethe, 21 April 1797.

99. Cf. W.A., i, 22, p. 177 (v, 7).

100. H.A., 12, p. 471, No. 752.

101. Conversation with Eckermann, 11 June 1825.

102. Jolles, *Goethes Kunstanschauung*, Berne, 1957, p. 233.

103. Friedrich Schlegel, *Athenäum-Fragmente*, No. 216, Berlin, 1798, i, p. 232.

104. Cf. Jolles, pp. 252 f.

105. Letter to Johann Friedrich Rochlitz, 29 March 1801.

106. Cf. Letter to Schiller, 30 October 1797.

107. Lessing, op. cit.

108. Neither the manuscript of the first version, which was in the form of a *Novelle*, nor that of the final version is extant. Hans M. Wolff sought to reconstruct the *Novelle*: cf. his *Goethes Novelle. Die Wahlverwandtschaften. Ein Rekonstruktionsversuch*, Berne, 1952, and his discussion of the problem in *Goethe in der Periode der Wahlverwandtschaften (1802–1809)*, Berne, 1952. His account remains, however, highly speculative and the verdict, at the very best, must be 'not proven'.

109. *Tag- und Jahreshefte. 1807* (W.A., i, 36, p. 28).

Die Wahlverwandtschaften

Die Wahlverwandtschaften continues the main features of *Werther* and the *Lehrjahre*. On the one hand, the novel – like *Werther* – tells the story of the failure of individual effort; on the other hand, as in the *Lehrjahre*, the impact of society is decisive. The two trends converge, because, by way of contrast to *Werther*, it is not the fate of the individual, but the tragic complications of a group that are depicted. If in *Werther* the lyrical element predominates, *Die Wahlverwandtschaften* inclines towards drama,[1] a consequence of the interplay of the four main characters, Eduard, Charlotte, the Captain and Ottilie, which forms the kernel of the action. This structural aspect distinguishes this novel from its predecessors. The title of the novel defines their relationship: it is also a symbol, for this technical term taken from chemistry – *Wahlverwandtschaften* (*Elective Affinities*) – the meaning of which is fully explained in the novel, stands for the dissolution of the emotional relations which exist between Eduard and Charlotte, and for the subsequent attachment which springs up between Eduard and Ottilie on the one hand, and the Captain and Charlotte on the other. At the same time, however, the title is misleading. This term refers to a law of nature in the world of matter, but in the world of human and social relations, the law of nature does not rule unchallenged, for there morality and free-will are also important. Like the title, the style of the novel is symbolic. Much becomes clear only on closer inspection, for the first reading is deceptive, and the transparency of the style conceals the depth and value of the thought. Goethe himself thought that *Die Wahlverwandtschaften* would not yield much at a first reading. According to Wieland, he maintained that it had to be read three times.[2]

To his friend Zelter, he wrote that he concealed much in the work,[3] and many years later he apparently said to Eckermann that more was to be found in it than anyone would be able to grasp on first reading.[4]

A brief summary of the story can only glide over the surface of this rich work and must necessarily miss much of importance.

Eduard, a rich aristocrat, has married Charlotte, also of noble birth. For both of them, it is a second marriage. They had been in love with one another when they were young, but for social reasons had been compelled to marry someone else, but as soon as their partners were dead, they had married, because Eduard insisted on it. They appear to live happily together, but Eduard's inviting an old friend of his, the Captain, to stay with them interrupts their solitude. The Captain comes, although Charlotte is reluctant to have an outsider in their midst. Soon afterwards Ottilie, Charlotte's foster-daughter, arrives to stay, as she is finding it difficult to fit into her boarding-school. These two arrivals disturb the marital harmony of Eduard and Charlotte; Eduard and Ottilie, and the Captain and Charlotte fall in love with one another, at first unconsciously, but slowly they become aware of their love. A Count and a Baroness pay a visit. They are travelling together, but are unable to marry as their previous marriages cannot be dissolved. Their visit serves as a catalyst to make the two couples fully conscious of their feelings. Before admitting that he loves Ottilie, however, Eduard succumbs to an impulse to spend a night with his wife, a deed which afterwards fills him with abhorrence, for imagination and physical reality had been at odds; he was thinking of Ottilie when making love to his wife. Similarly, his wife was thinking of the Captain when in the arms of her husband. Charlotte, on grounds of principle, does not want her marriage to break up. She controls herself and tacitly agrees to the Captain's departure. Eduard is incapable of self-control. He wants a divorce so as to marry Ottilie, but Charlotte refuses to agree to the divorce: her position is strengthened by the fact that she is expecting a child by Eduard. So Eduard leaves home to fight in a war because, if he stayed, Ottilie would have to return to her boarding-school.

Charlotte and Ottilie are left alone. Their life is reflected in extracts, often about architecture, from Ottilie's diary. Luciane, Charlotte's daughter by her first marriage, comes to spend some time on the estate, whose normal routine goes on. Her visit provides a contrast to Ottilie's deep inner life. There are other visitors: an Assistant who had taught Ottilie at school, and an English peer and his companion who are travelling on the Continent. When Charlotte's child is born, it resembles the Captain and has Ottilie's eyes.

Eduard returns from the war. He meets Ottilie again, and she is deeply moved by this unexpected encounter. This meeting delays her return, and she sets out to row across a lake to save time. An accident occurs, the boat almost capsizes, and the child, Eduard's and Charlotte's son, is drowned. Ottilie collapses and loses consciousness, but, on awakening, recognizes that she has acted against her true self by abandoning herself to her love for Eduard. She refuses to marry Eduard, although Charlotte is now ready to agree to a divorce. She seeks to go away to take up teaching, never to see Eduard again. But Eduard foils her attempt by following her to an inn. She takes a vow never to speak again and keeps it until the very moment of her death. Eduard, Charlotte and Ottilie now live together in the same house. Eduard's and Ottilie's love for one another is unabated. Ottilie starves herself and dies on hearing an infelicitous speech on the sanctity of marriage by Mittler, a moralizing ex-parson. A legend grows up about her, reinforced by her maid's miraculous escape from death on the occasion of her funeral. She is venerated as a saint. Eduard lives on, uncomprehending, entirely devoted to her memory until death overtakes him. Charlotte orders him to be buried at Ottilie's side, so that the two lovers are united in death.

The story does not reveal any obvious connection with Goethe's life. Yet he said about this novel that every instance had been experienced, but none was as he had experienced it.[5] On another occasion he remarked that 'no one will fail to notice a deep passionate wound which is reluctant to heal, a heart which is afraid of recovering.'[6] Inevitably, scholars tried to fathom the personal elements which made up the amalgam of experiences and sought to penetrate the disguise allegedly worn by the characters, but without success.[7] It was possible to identify some of the contents of the box in Ottilie's possession with those of a box owned by Sylvie von Ziegesar, a young girl with whom Goethe had apparently been involved emotionally for some years before he wrote the novel. Her box contained a lock of Goethe's hair and other momentoes of their friendship,[8] but an identification of this kind amounts to little or nothing. Goethe may have been in love with Sylvie, her father's estate at Drakendorf may, in some ways, have been the model for Eduard's estate,[9] but is there any convincing reason why any of the many other estates which Goethe knew might not have inspired him too? The case for considering Minna Herzlieb, another girl whom Goethe knew at that time, as the inspiration of Ottilie, is even weaker.[10]

All that can safely be said is that the story of a middle-aged married man falling in love with a young girl could have been experienced by Goethe personally in the decade before the composition of *Die Wahlverwandtschaften*.

The plot of *Der Mann von funfzig Jahren*, the central story of the *Wanderjahre* – most of which was written at the same time – is a parallel story with a different, i.e. non-tragic ending. The stories were certainly close one to another in Goethe's mind, for in the first extant mention of *Die Wahlverwandtschaften* in his diary on 11 April 1808, both works are bracketed together.[11] In each of them he experimented with a theme which must have mattered greatly to him. It is possible that, just as in the case of *Werther*, he worked out in his mind a course of events which he might have followed if he had given way to his passion; otherwise, the situation of *Die Wahlverwandtschaften* does not at all reflect Goethe's own circumstances. In principle, therefore, the biographical approach here yields even fewer results than it does with *Werther*. He remarked that in this novel, as in his fragmentary drama *Pandora* (written at the same time) he treated the necessity of doing without that which one desires.[12] Yet this observation is again too general to permit any precise biographical inference. Renunciation certainly is likely to be the experience of any ageing man who becomes aware of the effects which the passage of time has on him.

The basic theme of the novel is closely associated with Goethe's studies of natural science. The term *Wahlverwandtschaften* had earlier been given in 1782 by its German translator Heinrich Tabor to his translation of a treatise by Torbern Bergmann, the eminent Swedish chemist, entitled *De attractionibus electivis*

(1775). Goethe knew this work; he may also have been familiar with an article on the same topic in Gehler's *Dictionary of Physics* (1798). He himself talked about such relationships as early as 1796 in his writings on anatomy,[13] and used the same image, though not exactly the same term, in a letter to Schiller in 1799.[14]

Varnhagen von Ense, a German writer closely associated with Romanticism, says that General von Rühle told him that the idea had been transmitted to Goethe by Schelling.[15] Yet it is equally possible that it was Goethe who first communicated the conception of elective affinities to Schelling; for in the late 1790s they were continuously exchanging ideas about the study of nature. The evidence is elusive. It is almost impossible to discern priority, in any case always a hazardous undertaking. It is, however, most probable that the idea of elective affinities had been in his mind for some time before it took shape in a story.

There is another link between Goethe and Romantic natural philosophy.[16] The Romantics were greatly interested in magnetism, as well as in natural forces operating on the level of the subconscious. Ten years before Goethe wrote the novel, he and many of his Weimar friends had been preoccupied with similar problems. They attended scientific lectures, discussed scientific questions and undertook experiments. It was the time when the mechanistic explanation of the universe was called into question and it was widely believed that electricity and magnetism were the basic tendencies of nature.[17] Goethe himself introduces magnetism to illustrate Ottilie's closeness to nature. The whole story, of course, abounds with references to and explorations of subconscious forces, though Goethe was much more critical and selective in his approach than the Romantics. A similar discerning approach can be seen in his use in the novel of *tableaux vivants* taken from stories or legend, a favourite device of the Romantics of which Goethe disapproved, since they pretend to be art when in fact they are not art but life – a confusion which he considered illegitimate.

The novel may also be taken as a commentary on the theories and practices of the Romantics who were searching for a different ethic. Extramarital relationships leading to the break-up of marriages and the creation of new unions and, in the case of Karoline von Günderode, even to suicide, had been the hall-mark of the lives and doctrines of several of the Romantics. Wieland had already treated this attitude with his customary irony in a tale *Freundschaft und Liebe auf Probe* (*Friendship and Love on Trial*), published in 1804. In this story, two couples exchange partners, but find that it does not work out as they had hoped, and restore the *status quo*. Wieland's tale is amusing; *Die Wahlverwandtschaften* is a profound and tragic variation on a similar theme.

We also know that there was an earlier version of the novel which has been lost. It appears to have been considerably shorter. It is, of course, impossible to know what was added in the second version. One scholar has suggested, in a rather foolhardy argument, that the additions consisted largely of episodes of the second book introducing minor characters, such as the architect, the English peer and Luciane.[18] This view is plausible, but must, of course, remain mere speculation. If it were correct, it would mean that the original story revolved about the crisis in Eduard's and Charlotte's marriage and its tragic end, while in the second version the inner development of Ottilie is given much more prominence. Yet as the first version is not extant, it would be mistaken to go further than to state the likelihood that Goethe introduced further perspectives when revising the work. Probably this rewriting amounted to his making it possible for the reader to see the group of characters from different points of view. Such a development from the first version to the second would be entirely in keeping with Goethe's practice when revising the other novels, for it would mean that revision brought about a greater degree of objectivity.

Die Wahlverwandtschaften is a much more closely-knit work than the *Lehrjahre*. Its structure is clear and resembles *Werther*'s much more than that of the more indeterminate *Wilhelm Meister* novels. Since the action, however, is not centred on one single event or person, economy of action rather than tautness of structure would here appear to describe the pattern most appropriately.

The interplay of character gives the novel a dramatic quality. Spatial concentration[19] is one of its most striking features, appropriate to its dramatic essence, for the whole action takes place on Eduard's estate. The narrator tells us very little of what goes on outside this limited sphere, whether it affects major or minor characters. The only important exception is provided by the Assistant's letters about Ottilie's life at school. Significantly, it is not the narrator who reports these events, for his gaze is focused on the world of the main action from which there is, in fact, no considerable departure but for the interpolated tale *Die wunderlichen Nachbarskinder* related by the English peer's companion. As a result, the novel gains in intensity and avoids the dispersion of attention which would result from a plethora of irrelevant information.

Die Wahlverwandtschaften, for a novel, is concentrated not only in space, but also in time,[20] not as extremely as a classical drama, of course, or a modern novel like *Ulysses*, yet it covers nonetheless a limited span of time, possibly even shorter than that of *Werther*. The story begins in April. The action progresses to its end without any break in the chronology. There are no flash-backs, apart from a few relatively unimportant recollections of the past. As in *Werther*, passion is aroused in spring, the appropriate season for germination and growth, but, unlike *Werther*, Ottilie's death takes place in autumn, in September, on the eve of Eduard's birthday. No date is given for Eduard's death nor for his burial next to Ottilie.

Chapter follows chapter with hardly an interval of time. In each book, a quarter is taken up with the events of a three-day period in June of each of the two years. The first of these two periods focuses attention on the crisis which comes about as the characters become fully aware of their passion. In the June of the second year the harvest of passion is reaped.

The strict chronological sequence of the novel makes the temporal concentration stand out even more in relief, for it also brings out the relative importance attributed to various parts of the novel. The days of crisis in the characters' relationships stand out against the events in the castle during the ten months or so of Eduard's absence at the war. The dramatic quality of these brief critical periods makes them more memorable. A paradox is thus explained: that although the shorter period covered in the first book takes up more narrative time than the longer period of the first twelve chapters of the second book, time appears to pass more quickly in the first book. On the other hand, the telescoped narration of events in the longer period of Eduard's absence makes time move slowly. We here feel with the characters, particularly with Ottilie, who remarks:

> Why is the year sometimes so short, sometimes so long, why does it seem now so short and now so long in one's memory?[21]

This is explained by the difference between time measured by the clock or the calendar and time experienced emotionally.*

But if focus on crisis, if the *crescendo* of passion reveals the dramatic qualities of the novel, the *andante* of the first two-thirds of the second book points to epic qualities necessary to unfold the gradual germination of Ottilie's awareness; her spirit does not mature suddenly, but is able to develop over a period of time, only because the action seems to proceed so slowly. Epic retardation is more appropriate to spiritual development than dramatic speed. This quality makes itself felt particularly at the very end of the novel, for the narrator does not tell us how much time elapses between Ottilie's and Eduard's deaths;[22] time has become a matter of no consequence for Eduard once Ottilie has died. It virtually stands still for him; he lives entirely in his memory of her. He seeks to imitate her, only to feel his own sense of inadequacy, his lack of genius, compared with the martyrdom experienced by her. So he does not even become aware, as Ottilie did during his absence, that time drags. His defective sense of time here points to his lack of appreciation, an ironic repetition of an earlier episode when time stood still for him during the rise of his passion.

The closeness of the texture, the symbolic quality of events make careful consideration and re-consideration of many points necessary, for often incidents imply different meanings depending on the standpoint from which they are viewed. In fact, the most perplexing quality of the novel is its ambiguity. In retrospect, events do not appear to mean what they first signified or adumbrated. 'Adumbration is of its nature ambiguous since the eventual actualization usually occurs in totally different and unexpected circumstances and it is thus connected with irony.'[23] Simple statements and clear-cut events appear double-edged. While the development of the action appears to cast light on obscure passages, new problems confront the reader on further reflection. Goethe's statement about *Wilhelm Meisters Wanderjahre* that 'everything

* Henri Bergson defined this difference by the terms of 'temps' and 'durée'; Karl Pearson, the biometrician, by 'conceptual' and 'perceptual' time.

has to be taken as symbolic, and everywhere there is something else concealed as well. Every solution of a problem is a new problem',[24] can be applied *a fortiori* to *Die Wahlverwandtschaften.* What appears to have been clarified in the course of the action again appears uncertain. The meaning which had been located in allusions and statements, in events and symbols, seems once more elusive. Each interpretation falls short of the truth, for it is difficult to disentangle the whole nexus of events. From the very beginning, ambiguity pervades the novel, and it is chiefly created by the structural irony which, with the passage of time, gives events a different colouring in the light of what has gone on before and of what happens afterwards. The detached, sceptical ironic mode of narration leaves much unclear and unsaid. Much remains in doubt, inviting interpretation which, again and again, is proved to be inadequate. The very strength of the novel resides in its obscurity of deeper meaning. However clear the surface of the novel is, the depths cannot be adequately charted. So all interpretation remains tentative. Even where certainty appears to prevail, it may, on further reading, turn out to be mistaken. All interpretation must be hypothetical, but normally at least we can, indeed we must, rule out the irrelevant or the mistaken.[25] In the case of *Die Wahlverwandtschaften*, it is not even easy to sift out demonstrably false interpretations, for even what may have appeared false may, in the end, turn out to be relevant. All interpretations are provisional: some structures are, however, more durable than others, or at least they are based on firmer ground. Yet only too frequently, interpretations of *Die Wahlverwandtschaften* appear to be built on quicksand.[26] The following account is, therefore, not only hypothetical, as it must needs be, but it should also be seen as no more than an attempt to provide points of orientation for the reader's attention: it does not claim to delineate incontrovertibly right paths.

Like *Werther*, the novel is divided into two books (of eighteen chapters each). As in *Werther*, the end of the first book coincides with a deep incision in the action: just as Werther flees from home, so Eduard leaves home out of despair. Both novels end with death, *Werther* with the death of the sole protagonist, *Die Wahlverwandtschaften* with that of Ottilie and Eduard, the most prominent figures. In *Werther*, the change is at first one of location, not of style; the change of style occurs only later. In *Die Wahlverwandtschaften* there is no major change of style, only slight stylistic differences between the first and the second books.[27]

The stylistic differences between the two books in *Die Wahlverwandtschaften* are, however, important. There is a greater preponderance of dialogue in the first book and a corresponding speed of narrative; the action is economical, focused almost entirely on the four main figures. In the second book, the rate is slowed down, minor figures take up attention and two of the main characters, Eduard and the Captain, are absent for a very long time. In *Die Wahlverwandtschaften*, attention is concentrated in the first half of the second book on the experiences of Charlotte and Ottilie, and as a result the perspective is altered. This is emphasized by extracts from Ottilie's diary and the short story *Die wunderlichen Nachbarskinder* which is interpolated.

The consequences of this change are significant. In the first chapter of the second book, the relations between the four main figures, which are almost of a symmetrical character, no longer occupy the foreground. Interest has become focused on one person, Ottilie. In the first book, the four main figures are primarily seen in the light of their reactions to one another; in the second book these relations are no longer in a process of violent change, but are, so to speak, fixed. The crisis brought about by the revolutionary change in their relations has been clearly delineated, and their reaction to the crisis is now the primary concern. The second book, then, does not have the compactness of the first where, within a short span of time, the four main figures are confronted with one another and by an inner logic are compelled to define their relations to one another.

A closer examination of the structure shows quite clearly that the eighteen chapters of each part cannot be distinctly divided into further symmetrical subdivisions; any such attempts are misleading.

In the first book there is more dialogue, which gives it a more dramatic note.[28] It is more direct, even more objective than the second book, for dialogue conveys objectivity, since it portrays directly. Furthermore, the action is tauter since, in dialogue, the time of action virtually coincides with the time which the reader spends in reading it. In the second book, however, a broader picture of society is portrayed and the characters are depicted in greater depth. The first book describes the rise and outbreak of passion and the immediate consequences; the second book the more lasting consequences. Goethe describes how a person like Ottilie is capable of developing strength from her own nature in order to counter her passion; events thus develop her character. Since a major part of the events affects Ottilie's inner life, descriptive narration becomes more appropriate. In addition, the extracts from Ottilie's diary permit us further insight into her thought. They are, by way of contrast to the dialogue, not bound by time, and therefore allow us to get to know her personality in greater depth. The comparatively rare occurrence of dialogue corresponds to the much less concentrated action. But these differences must not be exaggerated. There is dialogue in the second book, just as there are parts in the first book where the narrative speeds along when great tracts of time are quickly covered. In both books, however, the narrator plays an important part. In *Werther* there was no narrator, but the editor who took his place had an important function: to criticize Werther's conception of reality. In the *Lehrjahre* the narrator's task was mainly to expose Wilhelm's naïvety and imprecision of thought, and so to act as a foil to Wilhelm, but his intervention also provided detachment. In *Die Wahlverwandtschaften*, the narrator is more independent. His function is no longer to correct the protagonist's vision, but rather to analyse the experiences of the several characters and their relations to one another. He also comments on events and feelings by prefacing or following them with more general assertions or observations. He is concerned not only with describing the individual case, but with discovering the general in the specific, and with discerning its symbolic value.

At the same time, the commentary involves a detachment from the events, for the narrator regards them from a different standpoint, that of general observation. These reflections stand out from the course of the main action as if they were general laws of life, permitting us to gauge events and experiences.[29] The reader thus sees the action not immediately but, so to speak, through the eyes of another person.[30]

The narrator's reflections betray his awareness of the mode of his narration. We learn that he regards it, if not always self-critically, at least in a manner which is observant and reveals insight. It is significant that he prepares the reader at the end of the first book for the role which Ottilie will assume in the second. The first book ends:

> After Ottilie had learnt of Charlotte's secret, she was taken aback like Eduard, only more so, and she withdrew into herself. She had nothing further to say. She could not hope, and she dared not wish. Her diary, some of which we intend to reproduce, affords us a glimpse into her soul.[31]

The simple matter-of-fact sentences convey more than appears at first sight. They indicate that Ottilie will determine the action more than before and that her conduct will spring from the hidden depths of her inner life. The words which communicate her reaction to this new development are informative, despite her reserve. Eduard's emotional reaction was powerful. Even greater was Ottilie's emotional disturbance, which is indicated by the words 'only more so'. They are, indeed, an extreme understatement, for the words 'taken aback' do not describe Eduard's state of mind at all adequately. Ottilie's silence is anticipated by the following sentences: 'She withdrew into herself. She had nothing further to say'. The tragic quality of her love is intimated by the pointlessness of her hope; her later return to conduct based on the moral law, on the other hand, is foreshadowed. At the same time, we hear that 'she withdrew into herself' – for to read that her diary will give us a glimpse into her inner life makes us realize that we are able to understand her experience only indirectly.

The beginning of the second book is also characteristic; it prepares us for the change of tone in the next chapter, and hints that we must approach the events from another point of view.

> In ordinary life, we often encounter what in epic poetry we usually praise as the poet's artistry; that is to say, when the main characters withdraw, hide, or sink into inactivity, their place is immediately filled by a second or third person, who, scarcely noticed until now, by demonstrating his whole activity, appears to us equally worthy of attention and sympathy, even of commendation and praise.[32]

This explanation of, or rather apology for what takes place afterwards, focuses the reader's attention on the differences between the first and the second book. It intimates that the action – quite differently arranged – is no longer concentrated squarely on the protagonists, and points to a new perspective. The narrator here detaches himself from the events by considering them from a distance and by explaining the different structural arrangement which, from now on, will be appropriate; they give the reader an opportunity to become aware of the change of approach which the narrator has singled out as essential. The narrator's detachment is ironic, but his irony is directed less at ingenuousness or imprecision of thought as in the *Lehrjahre* than at excessive confidence in reason and the will:

> Eduard – this gives a name to a rich nobleman in the prime of life – Eduard had spent the loveliest hour of an April afternoon in his plantation, grafting newly-arrived slips on to young trees. His task was just finished; he replaced the tools in their case and was surveying his work with pleasure when the gardener came up and was delighted with his master's diligence in their common pursuit.[33]

We gather that the narrator is a man who tackles his themes with great care, who does not use a superfluous word, but who intimates much that can be understood only after mature consideration. The first words of the narrative, indeed, contain an implicit suggestion that Eduard's name is not the original one, but has been assumed by him. As we hear later on, he was christened Otto, but preferred the name Eduard because it sounded better. From the very beginning, Eduard's social position is clearly defined. He is a gentleman of leisure who can indulge his fancies. We also sense, too, that the arbour which his wife has built has no deeper meaning for him, for the narrator continues:

> 'Have you seen my wife?' asked Eduard, preparing to move on.
>
> 'Over in the new grounds', the gardener replied. 'The arbour which she has built on the rock opposite the castle will be finished today. Everything has turned out well and is sure to please you, my lord. There is an excellent view: down below the village, a little to the right the church, and you can almost see over its spire into the distance: opposite is the castle and the gardens.'
>
> 'Quite right,' said Eduard, 'a few paces from here I could see the people working.'

'Then,' the gardener continued, 'the valley opens out to the right, and across the rich meadows you have a pleasant view into the distance. The path up the rocks is most prettily laid out. Her ladyship understands that sort of thing; it is a pleasure to work for her.'

'Go to her,' said Eduard, 'and ask her to wait for me. Tell her I want to see her new creation and enjoy it too.'[34]

The narrator reports the events with sovereign calm. He rarely provides an explicit commentary on an event; what he has to say is intimated rather than stated. Only occasionally are events or persons described more closely. When he calls Mittler 'funny'[35] and 'strange'[36] or when he describes Eduard as 'unaccustomed to denying himself anything',[37] he comments on Eduard and Mittler, but so concisely and unobtrusively that we do not think of it as a commentary. This method is quite different from that used by Wieland, for instance, who comments explicitly and profusely.

The narrator's detachment also characterizes his comments on Ottilie's diary. He points briefly to its general function by saying: 'Her diary, some of which we intend to reproduce, affords us a glimpse into her soul.'[38] Later on he speaks of the thread of affection and attachment which, in his opinion, runs right through the diary, like the red thread which is supposed to run through all the ropes of the British Navy.[39] He is here self-critical in considering the value of what he has to give the reader. He thus enhances the value of what he has to say, but also diminishes the immediacy of presentation. The narrator does not know where Ottilie has taken these sayings from; he can only assume that she has copied them. He maintains his detachment to the very end, to the death of Ottilie and Eduard: in his description of the apparent miracle at Ottilie's bier, in his description of Eduard's death:

> And so this heart, too, which a short while ago had been stirred to unending emotion, now lay in undisturbed peace; and as he had gone to rest full of thoughts of the saintly Ottilie, he could indeed be called blessed himself;[40]

and in the last words of the novel, which alleviate the shock that the catastrophe has produced:

> So the lovers rest side by side. Peace hovers over their graves, serene angels, akin to them, look down from the vaulted

ceiling, and what a happy moment it will be when one day they wake up again together.[41]

Even in moments of crisis, the narrator's language never loses its evenness of expression, and is always restrained; only shorter main clauses intimate different shades of meaning. Sometimes the speed of the action is increased by a change from the past to the present tense. When this change coincides with an accumulation of main clauses, as happens in the scene in which the child is drowned, a powerful linguistic force is created which conveys the catastrophe more immediately. A dynamic means of expression is formed by these intensive, immediate sentences which, however, fit completely into the general stream of the narrative.[42]

The narrative style is calmer than that of the dialogue, though there are features common to both. In all parts of the novel, antitheses are found, but the rhythm creates a state of equilibrium which has not yet become petrified. A calm, observant view of life is portrayed. Whoever speaks does so within a coherent linguistic pattern.

Goethe never seeks here to describe a crisis immediately through language. This control of language, this serene, calm, sovereign handling of words, prevents the narrator from identifying himself with the events which he describes; dialogue, therefore, does not belong here to the heights of crisis, but to the moments which lead up to it.

The style, then, hardly betrays the violent and tragic character of the action. To comprehend this, we have to probe more deeply.

The basic characteristic of a living whole: to divide, to reunite, to extend into the general, to remain particular, to be transmuted, to become specific, and, as life may appear under a thousand different conditions, to emerge and to disappear, to solidify and to melt, to petrify and to flow, to expand and to contract. Because all these activities occur in the same moment of time, each and every thing can take place at the same time. Originating and vanishing, creation and destruction, birth and death, joy and sorrow, all operate continuously, in the same sense and to the same degree; hence the most specific occurrence always appears as the image and likeness of the most general.[43]

Encounter, separation and reunion are indeed features of all novels, but in *Die Wahlverwandtschaften* the reader's attention is focused almost exclusively on the relationships of the main characters. From the very beginning when Eduard is alone and then joins, or rather rejoins, Charlotte, to the last moment of the novel when Eduard is once more alone in death, or rather rejoins Ottilie in the grave, there is a continuous alignment and re-alignment of the characters. The reader becomes more and more conscious of the various constellations which arise: for instance, Mittler is quickly compelled to leave; there is no place for him in a house still dominated by the relationship between Eduard and Charlotte. The Captain's arrival disturbs the equilibrium of Eduard's and Charlotte's marriage, while Ottilie's subsequent arrival quickly leads to the complete change in relationships culminating in the virtual break-up of Eduard's and Charlotte's marriage. The departure of Eduard and the Captain each time leaves a gap, which is in turn filled, however inadequately, by the architect, the Assistant, Luciane and the peer until the chief male protagonists return.

The importance of these relationships can be gauged if we study the development of the protagonists within the framework of these relations. At first, the relations between Eduard and Charlotte appear harmonious, but if we listen more carefully to undertones, we can recognize a concealed discontent. Eduard's desire to have a third person around him, and his feeling that the hut, the symbol of domestic contentment, is too narrow, betray latent dangers. The arrival of the Captain changes the relationship between Charlotte and Eduard. Charlotte is isolated. The equilibrium is restored only through Ottilie's arrival, but in a way quite different from what might have been expected. The whole picture changes. The relations between Eduard and Charlotte no longer absorb the reader; instead, it is the relations between Eduard and Ottilie, and the Captain and Charlotte.

Mittler is isolated from others; he is not attached in any intimate manner to anyone else, although he would because of this freedom be well suited for the role of mediator for which his name appears to have destined him, and which he has chosen himself. In fact, his isolation makes it much more difficult, indeed impossible, for him to understand human beings involved in a close relationship.

The task of mediation is, therefore, beyond him. In the course of the novel we become aware of how relations grow and change in the first book. Eduard is the more active partner in determining his relationship with Ottilie, but as Ottilie grows in stature and inwardly matures, the roles are reversed. Eduard has to follow her initiative instead of her following his.

The names of the main characters themselves reveal their latent affinity, for the names Otto – the name of both Eduard and the Captain – Charlotte, and Ottilie contain the same root.[44] Luciane, a name derived from the Latin *lucere*, stands in contrast to Ottilie, for St Odilia[45] becomes blind, but her inner light shines in contrast to the mere outward dazzling of Luciane. Mittler's name is, as is discussed elsewhere, an ironic comment on his self-assumed role of mediator. So the names already presuppose the nature of the relationships between the characters.

The images used in the novel also afford an insight into its structure, for example, the images of the hut, of the house, and of the arbour.[46] The images, like other details and incidents, do not obtrude. They have to be viewed in the context of the work as a whole, for they recur, but they do not recur in the same way or for the same purpose: time has progressed, a different stage of the novel has been reached.[47] But because details can be related to the action, illustrating and emphasizing what has happened in the meantime, they impose on the novel 'the inner consistency'[48] rightly expected of a work of art. By means of the hut, Goethe indicates the attitude of his characters to reality. Eduard's inner discontent becomes visible in his belief that the hut is too narrow for him, but narrowness is only a pretext for a spiritual malaise of which he is not yet conscious. When Charlotte, who wants to preserve this style of living, disagrees with him, insisting that there is enough room for the two of them, Eduard replies, 'Well, of course, there is room for a third person as well'.[49] Here Eduard contradicts his earlier statement, and contradiction, just as in the case of Werther, betrays inner unrest and dissatisfaction. When the hut is mentioned the next time, apparent contentment prevails. Eduard, Charlotte, the Captain – all three go to the hut, which is the scene of a happy meeting. But although Eduard believes himself to be content, he is really still discontented. He points out to

Charlotte that there is still room for a fourth person. He is subconsciously restless until he finds peace in his love for Ottilie. When later on all four of them go for the first time to the hut, it seems right that a new path should be built to it, so that instead of the slow and difficult climb there should be an easy and comfortable one. A new and natural mode of life prevails. It does so, because it springs from their true natures.

When Charlotte has become conscious of her love for the Captain, but fears that she will lose him, she hurries back to the hut and abandons herself entirely to panic, to passion, to despair, of which she had not before had the slightest warning, though at the same time her resolve to save her marriage is implied, for her suffering arises from her love for the Captain whom she must give up if she wishes to go on living with Eduard.[50] At this moment, the hut becomes for the first time a place of pain and suffering, of the pain and suffering which later overshadow the novel. Charlotte is isolated; her later isolation and the destruction of her marriage are here anticipated. After the birth of the child, Charlotte and Ottilie spend some time alone in the hut. Charlotte is conscious of two vacant places and she expresses her hopes for Eduard's return, which have understandably been nourished by the birth of the child. But they are not soundly based. Her plan for a marriage between the Captain and Ottilie is not feasible, for when all four of them had sat together in the hut in apparent contentment, the Captain and Ottilie were not attracted to one another. On the contrary, the seeds of love between Eduard and Ottilie, between the Captain and Charlotte had already been sown. The hut, therefore, allows us to discern the nature of the relations between the main characters at important points of their development.

The house, too, is a symbol.[51] Eduard and Charlotte are planning to build a new house, a *Lustgebäude*, a pleasure pavilion, in addition to the old castle, perhaps an unconscious admission that all is not well with their marriage. Ottilie wants it built on a hill from which the castle is no longer visible, a symbol of the aspiration of her love for Eduard. Her wish is that it should command a view of a wild, uncared-for landscape, instead of the well-ordered world of the castle, the park, the chapel and the village, a suggestion in which Eduard quickly concurs, symbolizing their uncontrolled passion. Ottilie realizes that they would find themselves in another world, though she does not recognize the import of this change of perspective as it affects human emotions.

But the house is also a symbol for the restricted domestic sphere; it stands in a polar relationship to the world. Eduard and Charlotte seek to withdraw from the world into their house. Yet from the very beginning we realize that their withdrawal can only be an interval, not a permanent state. Charlotte is conscious that they must be of one mind to preserve this idyll, itself standing in contrast to the life of the Count and the Baroness, but Eduard is not. He only becomes conscious of it after he has fallen in love with Ottilie, who is domesticated by nature. Eduard intuitively recognizes this feature of her personality. When he is fully aware of his love for Ottilie and sees that Charlotte will not grant him a divorce, he seeks delay by leaving the house and by insisting that Ottilie stays in it. He himself has lost his bearings in his own house.[52] He flees into the world because he is at bay, for his own proper sphere of existence appears no longer accessible to him. His insistence on Ottilie's staying in his own house is an act of desperation, for he hopes to retain what he has, in fact, lost. Ottilie only slowly becomes aware of what has happened. Its full poignancy only strikes her when she sees the life which the English peer leads, wandering round the world without a home to return to. Finally, it is the glaring red colour of roof-tiles which, on Eduard's return from the war, rouse an 'irresistible yearning' within him; he insists that the Major (the Captain has, it would appear, been promoted to this rank during the war) should, on that very evening, persuade Charlotte to agree to a divorce. From this yearning, too, springs his fateful decision to go to the lake, where he encounters Ottilie and delays her return to the house, a delay which, on account of her consequent hurrying back, leads to the child's death.[53]

The lake is a symbol too. At the beginning of the novel it was dammed into three lakes, in order, as the Captain remarks, to reduce the danger which might come from water, 'clearly representing the civilizing forces of society and the moral laws'.[54] A stranger's wish to have the old order restored because it looked more impressive leads to Eduard's decision, later viewed with regret by the Captain, to destroy two of the dams as part of the re-shaping of his estate. If this had not been done, the child would not have been drowned. Water, as the English peer's companion remarks, is a friendly element if we know how to deal with it, but just as order created by man to tame the forces of nature is destroyed, so the moral order breaks down when passion begins to rule. Disaster ensues in either case.[55]

Another symbol is the plane-trees which stand at the edge of the lake.[56] Eduard wishes to preserve them, for he himself as a youth had planted them, and succeeded in saving them when his father wished to destroy them in the process of laying out a new part of the park. Perhaps Eduard was attached to them because he had planted them, but when later on he discovers that they had been planted not only in the same year, but on the very day of Ottilie's birth, this coincidence suffices to strengthen his conviction that Ottilie and he are destined for one another. From the moment of this discovery the trees appear to promise a fulfilment of his love. He alone, however, sees them in that light, and he only does so while he is happy in his new love for Ottilie. This reveals a marked feature of his character – seeing the external world in the light of his desires. Later on, Ottilie's favourite walk leads to the plane-trees which recall to her Eduard's absence even more vividly. After the death of the child Ottilie's boat drifts to the shore with its plane-trees, which suggest Eduard's mistaken presumption; for as they recall his fond hopes, they serve only to emphasize how presumptuous it is to attach human desires to inanimate objects, thus enhancing the tragic aspect of the catastrophe that has just occurred.

Another image closely associated with the four is the lay-out of the park. This shows what the characters can do, thus intimating their relationship to the outer world. At the very beginning, we learn that Eduard is fond of gardening in a dilettante way:[57] he has spent a beautiful April afternoon grafting shoots on to young trees. He enjoys this activity and does it well, but it is no more than the diversion of a rich nobleman, the refinement of what is already refined.[58] A valley and a hill virtually separate him from his wife, who, at the same time, though he does not know it,[59] is planning to lay out the park. But she too is an amateur, and her plans are faulty. The Captain, who is knowledgeable in these matters, sees this at once and explains it; but it is left to Eduard to point it out to Charlotte. Thus the business increases the inner estrangement, and strengthens the attachment of Eduard to Ottilie, and the Captain to Charlotte.

The next description of the lay-out of the park and of the plans for building gives us further insight into the characters of Eduard and the Captain. Eduard's belief in being right in what he does is based on intuition, while the Captain's views are based on knowledge. Carrying out these plans further separates Eduard from Charlotte, and brings her closer to the Captain. For Eduard it creates a vacuum which is filled by his attachment to Ottilie. His interest in these plans is, in the last resort, a form of self-gratification reflecting his moods, in complete contrast to Ottilie, who wants the new building to be on a hill away from the castle, as a vantage-point of independence, indicating her genuine inner growth.

Both Charlotte and the Captain are further characterized by their attitude to the lay-out of the park. The Captain gladly leaves the work at the lake to the architect, since whether he is there or not does not matter to him. For him, the work is more important than the development of his own personality. After Eduard's departure, Charlotte allows the work to go on. It becomes a symbol of her hope that Eduard will return and that their marriage can be restored. But her hope is based on misunderstanding: Eduard's interest in her plans had always been limited and superficial; their ways have diverged, and he will not turn back.

The lay-out of the park does indeed give pleasure. This is symbolized by the circular path, which stands in contrast to the labyrinth with its power to confuse.[60] The image of the labyrinth is powerfully used at the two climaxes of the novel: the first when Eduard goes to Charlotte's bedroom, the second when he hurries after Ottilie into the inn where she finally refuses to marry him.

For Ottilie, it is the garden which gives secret joy, a joy which has its origin in her love for Eduard. We notice it when she tells the gardener of Eduard's interest in the garden. It deepens her interest in nature: she comes to love all plants through her relationship to Eduard; they form a bridge between her and her memory of him. Nature speaks to her of him, filling her with hope, but also with fear: will it be granted to her once more to celebrate Eduard's birthday? When asters from the garden decorate her corpse and her bier, they establish yet another link; for her love, of which they were a symbol, inevitably leads to her death.[61]

External nature, the landscape, thus illuminates essential aspects of the relations between the main figures. The changing background is important; we are able to gauge the state of their feelings by seeing whether they still walk in the park or whether they have gone into the wider open landscape. In the latter case, the desire to flee from the severe limits of social obligation becomes visible. Man is estranged from nature, and nature appears indifferent to his fate.

If man acts contrary to his own inner nature he may be even more alienated from external nature. After the night which Eduard had spent with his wife, but during which he was thinking of Ottilie, it appears to him as if the sun were shining upon a crime.

It is virtually impossible to catalogue all the symbolic relationships of this novel; despite the novel's comparative brevity, such a list would almost inevitably be incomplete, for new relationships emerge on repeated readings. It would in any case be a long list involving overlapping, for many objects and incidents which in themselves appear neutral suddenly acquire a symbolic significance; furthermore, there are interrelations between many of them which endow them with a different significance according to the perspective in which they are placed. The relational pattern of the novel is, in fact, inexhaustible. A few further relations which become themes might, however, be explored in some detail.

An important group of words and images refers to the grave and death. Eduard does not like to go past the churchyard. At first this seems a mere idiosyncrasy; only later does its significance become apparent. On Mittler's arrival, because Eduard is in a hurry, he uses the path across the churchyard. Normally he avoids it because of its melancholy associations. So he is glad when Charlotte redesigns the churchyard to please the eye and the imagination. Another hint in this context is Charlotte's putting out the rescue equipment which, however, is not quickly available when the child is drowned. There are also allusions to an earlier death by drowning in the life of the Captain. Eduard would like to discuss it, but the Captain is silent and Charlotte avoids discussion. This reveals the character of each of them: Eduard's lack of restraint, the Captain's reticence, and Charlotte's self-control.

Later the Captain rescues a boy from drowning during festivities celebrating the erection of the pleasure pavilion and Ottilie's birthday. This throws an entirely different light on the action. Eduard and Charlotte do not understand each other any more; they have become too estranged. For Eduard, the episode is another extraordinary event like his falling in love with Ottilie. Because one remarkable event has taken place, he feels it to be right to persevere in his love for Ottilie. For Charlotte, it is imperative to behave in a fitting manner; it is therefore her desire to put an end to the festivities and cancel the planned fireworks, but she has to yield to Eduard's determination to carry on with the celebration, for his need to give expression to his love for Ottilie by this public festivity overrides everything.[62] In the tale *Die wunderlichen Nachbarskinder*, this motif is repeated. Death comes very close here, too; but this time, in the fairy-tale world, the accident appears to lead to happiness.

The death motif makes plain the difference between the two books.[63] In the first book, it is only briefly alluded to, for the characters are still deeply attached to life and its hopes. The allusions acquire significance only in retrospect; for instance, the walk to the lake on the day after the child was conceived later becomes significant in the light of its drowning in the same lake. In the second book, the death motif comes into the open, first of all when the architect is decorating the chapel. Ottilie is taken out of herself and the daily round of life; her final resting place, and by implication her attitude to death, is anticipated.[64] Ottilie's reflections and actions betray how intensively she is preoccupied with death. Luciane appears in the masquerade as Artemisia, the widow of King Mausolus. She persuades the architect to draw the tomb of Mausolus. We also hear of the story of a girl who has unintentionally caused the death of a relation. Later on, death takes place even within the action of the novel itself – the parson dies during the baptism of the child, a distinctly evil omen. The parson, in fact, dies in the midst of a speech by Mittler, anticipating a later event when his words hasten Ottilie's death. Her death is also anticipated by her own behaviour. Physical life appears to her superfluous; to anticipate death, she denies verbal expression to her love for Eduard. Death is for her an answer to Eduard's erotic desires. When the foundation-stone of the house is laid, it is a hint of the grave; a well-known stone is placed in the narrow hole which has been dug. The architect, too, can be interpreted as a messenger of death when he builds the chapel or draws the mausoleum for Luciane's charade. Even Luciane seems to become a harbinger of death, for she almost abandons her role as Artemisia and appears to be playing that of the widow of Ephesus who, after the death of her husband, is bent on her own death by starvation.[65] Similarly, the marriage scene in the interposed tale, *Die wunderlichen Nachbarskinder*, which results in the almost fatal drowning of the bride, anticipates Ottilie's death. Ottilie discerns the need to change the *Stirb und werde* implicit in living things, by remarking in her diary 'everything that is complete in its own way must develop beyond itself and become something else, something incomparable'.[66]

Eduard, however, is unable to accept this view. He desires satisfaction in this world, but his wishes are thwarted. If Ottilie prepares herself for death, the thought of Eduard offers an antidote. Only when this last consolation is taken away from her, when she sees Eduard in the flesh and when the death of the child proves beyond contradiction that she has to renounce him, does she turn away from life. The death of the child by drowning thus reveals the differences between the main figures. The Major (the Captain has by then been promoted) and Eduard are at first not affected by it. The Major's pity and interest are focused upon Charlotte: Eduard considers the impact upon his relations with Ottilie. For him, it is a hint of destiny which has now removed all obstacles to his marrying Ottilie. Eduard has no paternal feeling for the child, only love for Ottilie. Charlotte as the mother is much more deeply moved, yet she preserves her self-control because she believes she must protect Ottilie. Charlotte is bound by her obligation to others. Death forces her to reconsider her attitude towards divorce: now she is prepared to agree to it, for she feels guilty of the death of her child. Both times she misunderstands the situation. At first she believes that she must preserve her marriage on grounds of principle. Then she thinks she must agree to a divorce because her refusal has led to the death of the child, but there is no ground for this belief. Charlotte's self-control is exemplary. She faces death calmly.[67] She seeks to fortify herself against the fear of death by taking up a specific activity, a reaction which once again shows her kinship with the Major. Bound to life, she seeks to control herself in self-defence against nature and irrational forces to which she does not wish to succumb. She does not expect anything for herself; although she does not refuse the Major unconditionally, she rejects the thought of marrying him in the near future. She is prepared to agree to a divorce, not for her own sake, but to let Eduard and Ottilie marry, a solution rejected by Ottilie whose sense of guilt is aroused by the death of the child. This death, indeed, affects Ottilie more closely than anyone else, not only because she spent more time with the child than anyone else, but also because her earlier thinking had made her aware of the prospect of her own death. Death thus leads her to the firm decision to renounce Eduard for ever. She sticks to it with a consistency which does not even allow her to be frightened by her own death.

Eduard's attitude is ambiguous. He seeks death 'like someone who hopes to live'.[68] What drives him to seek it is his love for Ottilie. He does not want to abandon his love for her and he is thus not able to accept Ottilie's death. He wants to die, but at the same time he promises to live on. His death is a symbol of his character. It is not for him an act of renunciation as it is for Ottilie. He never comes to terms with her death. Only Ottilie accepts death; her readiness to do so endows her death with a personal note of voluntary renunciation, even if the form it takes is morally unacceptable.

Mittler does not show any particular understanding of the child's death. He does not feel directly for the child and its parents; he is affected only in so far as his plans for restoring Eduard's and Charlotte's marriage are concerned. His poverty of feeling and his egotism are exposed. His rationalist thought may communicate the correct theoretical view, but he lacks true humanity. The death motif, important for the novel's plot, casts a clear, revealing light on the characters.

Die Wahlverwandtschaften is not only a novel of death, but also to a much greater degree a novel of love. But the two are closely interlinked; for love, which is the product of life, leads here to death. The novel begins with the relationship between Eduard and Charlotte. The German dramatist Hebbel has called it 'a basically void, indeed immoral marriage'[69] and these words have had a powerful echo. It has been maintained that it is not true love, since it is merely based on a memory of a love that is past. This view appears to betray a one-sided attitude. It can also be argued that their love was not entirely an illusion, but that it lacked real depth and thus was incapable of satisfying them permanently. This is particularly true of Eduard. Different shades in the emotion of love are depicted. The love between Eduard and Charlotte is not as deeply anchored in the centre of their being as the later love between Eduard and Ottilie. Earlier attachments must give way to this new feeling. Their relationship lacks the irresistible attraction, the powerful force of nature, which links two people unconditionally to one another leaving them no choice. Eduard and Charlotte were therefore unable to overcome obstacles which, in their youth, had foiled their marriage, even though these obstacles were only rooted in their parents' wishes and not in social custom. So Eduard can lull himself into the illusion that he will recapture the love of his youth by marrying Charlotte; he succeeds in persuading her to overcome her reluctance. She gives way. Eduard really believes that he loves his wife, and for him she is everything. But he deceives himself, just as he does later when he believes that his first meeting with Ottilie has not had a deep effect on him. Its effect is, however, fundamental. Their love is from the first without sense of proportion or limitation, and runs quite counter to the pattern designed by reason and custom.

The love of Charlotte and the Captain is, on the other hand, controlled, for both are people whose lives are determined by reason and custom. The love of the Count and the Baroness also defies convention, but they are indifferent to this and in a state of complete contentment. Quite different is the love between the young neighbours in the interposed tale. This love does not conflict with convention and comes naturally to a happy ending.

Love is described not only in many of its possibilities, but also in many stages. The narrator's remark may be applied to all of them. 'For love is so constituted that it believes it alone has rights and that all other rights vanish before it.'[70] From its earliest beginnings to the outbreak of passion, the course of love is traced with a subtlety that recalls the best *rococo* literature, for instance the comedies of Marivaux.

The development of the love of the two couples is further pursued. Apart from the common preoccupation of the Captain and Charlotte with the lay-out of the park, an unconscious attachment arises between them. Ottilie's feeling for Eduard can be seen in her willingness to help him – indeed, in trifling gestures and deeds that betray her feelings before she is aware of them. A certain childishness in thought allows Eduard to encounter Ottilie on the same level.

The strength of their feelings can be gauged by the fact that they create unrest. Eduard and the Captain are unable to carry out their work, and Eduard falls more and more a victim to his passion, by far the more completely of the two men. As passion gradually takes hold of them, they lose their sense of time. During their walks, Eduard and Ottilie hurry impulsively ahead, reflecting the headlong and conscious onrush of their passion, while the Captain and Charlotte follow, absorbed in serious conversation. On one occasion, while Charlotte and the Captain walk on easy paths, Eduard and Ottilie climb across rocks and through bushes, until Eduard begins to understand his feelings; he hopes that she will fall when they are walking so he can catch her in his arms and press her to his heart, though he would not have dared do this before for fear of insulting her and of hurting her. He begins to break down the wall that separates one human being from another when he asks her for the medallion that contains a portrait of her father. It is, on the surface, fear which prompts him to make this request, as he says himself; fear that she might hurt herself with it if she stumbled during the walk. But his request has a deeper, symbolic meaning, of which Eduard himself is unaware. The image of her father must be effaced, and Ottilie must become free before her love for Eduard can develop without restraint.[71] There are other signs of his love. When Ottilie explains her ideas about the building of the house, Eduard immediately gives his assent. He does so although he has not investigated her proposal at all. The narrator's commentary is revealing, for he notices that Eduard drew in bold outline a rectangle representing his new house, and anticipates the silent disapproval of the Captain who does not like his plans to be spoiled. The passions between Eduard and Ottilie, Charlotte and the Captain grow further. When they play music, this growth of passion comes out clearly. Eduard and Charlotte do not play well together; they are truly out of tune. But Eduard and Ottilie, though not so professional as Charlotte and the Captain, play intuitively together.

Eduard is quite uncritical where his love for Ottilie is concerned, and not only when they are playing, for 'hatred is partisan, but love is even more so'.[72] He continually finds circumstances which show that his love has been commanded by fate. He takes it for a good augury that the plane-trees were planted in the same year in which Ottilie was born, or when he discovers the initials E and O on the glass which does not break into pieces when it is thrown into the air by the mason. Yet later on when the glass is broken, his superstitious belief is stultified in an ironic manner, for it turns out that long ago another glass had been substituted for the original one. Charlotte's love for the Captain becomes apparent through her pleasure at the Count's praise of the Captain; the full measure of her passion only becomes clear when she is faced with the possibility of losing him. Eduard and Charlotte, by continuing their marital relations, sin not against marriage but against love; this act of spiritual self-injury in turn only makes them fully aware of the nature of their love. It prepares the first climax of passion which culminates in the two couples confessing their love. From then onward their passion becomes clear, even if they still try to conceal it. Eduard and Ottilie live in a happy, dreamlike state while Charlotte and the Captain seek to control their feelings. The closer Eduard and Ottilie come to one another, the more they are estranged from the others; in the end, they are quite isolated.

The crisis can no longer be averted. At first the inevitable discussion between Eduard and Charlotte occurs. Charlotte gains the day by her refusal of a divorce. Her belief in the rightness of this decision is confirmed when she becomes aware that she is expecting a child by Eduard.

We thus learn to what extent each one of the four is ready to separate from his or her beloved and how separation affects each one of them. Charlotte and the Captain try to renounce each other and succeed in doing so. Eduard's and Ottilie's love for one another remains unaffected. Whereas Eduard's love remains unchanged and finds expression in the same unconditional, immoderate manner, Ottilie's undergoes an inner development which, in the end, changes the whole of their love relationship. We see, indeed, how she relates everything to Eduard, but how at the same time she grows more mature and how her intellectual horizon is broadened. So she is prepared to act with determination and independence when events finally force her to recognize that it is wrong to love Eduard and thus to estrange him from his wife. She decides to renounce her hope of living with Eduard or of becoming his wife. Of Eduard's inner life we learn comparatively little; we are, of course, aware of his belief that he and Ottilie are inseparable. When he has to recognize that Ottilie cannot be his immediately, life seems no longer worthwhile to him.

Ottilie, whose feelings are more delicate and probably more naïve, experiences the pain even more intensely. Eduard is always present to her mind; he becomes an indelible part of her experience. Even her thoughts about life after death are attached to him. She notes in her diary: 'To rest next to those whom one loves is the most agreeable thought which man can have if he thinks at all beyond life'.[73] The narrator perspicaciously defines her total commitment to her love, indicating that in the last resort, unlike Werther, she would not take a stand against traditional Christian morality. 'Only the Divine, which is all-pervading, could possess her heart together with him.'[74] Nonetheless, life continues and regains Ottilie's attention. She likes to look at pictures of places where Eduard had been. But the remarks of the English nobleman about his life away from home affect Ottilie even more profoundly. She recognizes how deserted, in fact, Eduard's estate is since he has been away. A life away from home seems to her lamentable and appalling. She infuses her love into her feeling and care for the child.

In the moment when Ottilie and Eduard see each other again, their passion knows no limits. Yet Ottilie very quickly becomes conscious of her duties again. She feels responsible for the child she is looking after. Her innate respect for moral obligations comes out. Having spent so much time in the park because of her passion for Eduard, and having neglected her duty, she is now moved by remorse; she impatiently sets out to row across the lake, in a hurry to return to the house. The catastrophe then becomes possible. The child dies.

Ottilie decides she must renounce Eduard, but she does not stop loving him. The love which rules over them as if it were a power of nature has not ceased. But Ottilie succeeds in controlling herself, and foregoes consummation of her love in expiation of having violated the moral law. Her love becomes unselfish and thus perfected. It rises to an 'incomparable' quality. So at least Ottilie appears to think, for she notes in her diary: 'Everything perfect of its kind must go beyond its kind; it must become something else, something incomparable. In some sounds the nightingale is still a bird, but it transcends its class and wishes, so it seems, to indicate to all birds what true singing really is.'[75] It becomes an image of the Divine, thus, in a sense, deserving the epithet 'holy' or 'sacred'. Eduard's love is, however, unaffected by her sacrifice and her death. He goes on loving her just as before. The love between Charlotte and the Captain (by now promoted to Major) on the other hand, after having been controlled, is relegated to the background. It appears as if their love does not possess the strong unconditional force of Ottilie's and Eduard's love for one another. The Major has not abandoned all hope after the death of the child. On the contrary, he dreams of a future at the side of Charlotte. Yet we do not hear any more of this hope; for it seems as if her love for the Major has subsided and no longer matters most to her.

Love affects men and women in different ways. Love is both a natural and symbolic power; it changes the course of people's lives and is capable of imperilling their very existence. 'Custom, inclination, friendship' are capable of becoming 'intensified to love and passion, which, like everything absolute that enters our limited world, threaten to become dangerous to many.'[76]

The relationship between the characters, the force of their love itself, is determined by their inner nature; for inner nature determines the course of one's life and therefore matters greatly in the novel. Its function is summarized by Goethe's comments on his *Urworte Orphisch*:

> for the daemon signifies the necessary limited individuality, expressed directly at birth, by which every individual differs from all others, however much he may resemble them.[77]

This daemon can be fully understood only in love – for

> he, the independent egoistical being who seized the world with an unconditional will and felt only vexation if fortune now and again barred his path, now feels that he is determined and stamped not by nature alone; he becomes aware that *he*

> can determine himself, that he can not only forcibly seize anything fate offers him, but also appropriate it, and, what is more, can embrace a second being like himself in an eternal, indestructible inclination.[78]

When meeting Ottilie, Eduard realizes this truth. He follows the voice of his own nature but, in doing so, he runs counter to the laws of society. But does he not also oppose nature in a wider sense? And is his own nature not in conflict with the social pattern created by nature? Nature requires the union of man and woman. In doing so it creates the family, the kernel of society. To violate marriage means to threaten the foundation of society. As a member of society, the individual is not free. He cannot follow his own desires heedlessly, but must subordinate them to the social pattern. Eduard experiences it, though, contrary to Charlotte and Ottilie, he never learns to recognize its necessity. In his commentary on *Urworte Orphisch* Goethe states this experience in terms of a general law of nature:

> Hardly is this step [to embrace another being] taken when by free decision freedom is abandoned: two souls are to accept that they belong to one body, two bodies to accept that they belong to one soul, and by starting an agreement of such a kind, a third agreement in mutual necessity arises – parents and children must form a whole; great is the common contentment, but even greater the need. The body which consists of so many parts is sick according to the earthly fate of one part or another: instead of taking pleasure in the whole, it suffers on account of the particular, but nonetheless a relationship of that kind is found as desirable as it is necessary. Its advantages attract every one, and one is pleased to accept the disadvantages. Family is linked to family, tribe to tribe; a people has developed and realizes that the whole benefits from what the individual has decided; it makes the decision immutable by law; all that loving inclination voluntarily grants now becomes duty, which develops a thousand duties, and thereby everything is settled for all time and eternity, and state and church and tradition see that there is no lack of ceremonies. All the parts, by means of the most binding contracts, of the most public declarations, take care that the whole, even in its smallest part, be not endangered by fickleness and arbitrariness.[79]

Goethe's account of the working of nature and its impact on society strikingly resembles what emerges from a study of the relationship between nature and society in *Die Wahlverwandtschaften.*

Nature attaches Eduard to Ottilie, Charlotte to the Captain; it is a natural urge opposed to social institutions. In nature, as chemistry teaches us, it is customary for relationships to be severed and new ones formed. The chemical formulae of the 'elective affinities' reveal in their concise manner what forces are effective in nature and what relationships possess all-powerful strength. To formulate a truth of this kind effectively is characteristic of the natural sciences, for 'the remarkable discoveries of chemistry forcefully utter the magical power of nature'.[80] But atoms do not feel, nor have they moral obligations. Eduard is not conscious of such differences between man and nature, and hence he misapplies the analogy used by the Captain when he speaks here of 'couples'.* Charlotte is displeased, and points out that the analogy is mistaken, unconsciously reacting against Eduard's wilful interpretation: she is protecting herself against the dangers inherent in Eduard's character. Man is able to react differently to nature, provided he becomes aware in time and is capable of detachment. Character is more than just nature; it is a combination of nature and social morality.

Eduard and Ottilie, who are closer to nature than Charlotte and the Captain, are more endangered by daemonic forces, for Charlotte and the Captain are able to restrain their natural inclinations, since they are more highly organized people with a greater degree of awareness. As Ottilie's awareness grows, a development denied to Eduard, she too is able to control her actions, though not her feeling for Eduard. In denying herself to Eduard, she may seem to be acting against nature, but this is not so; she has become conscious of the higher aspects of her own nature, an attitude which remains unintelligible to Eduard. It would be mistaken to equate 'nature' and 'natural impulse'. Nature is too rich a concept to allow of one single interpretation, for Ottilie becomes aware

* Eduard, of course doubly misapplies the analogy; for he also speaks of two 'couples' in real life when, in fact, there is only one, Eduard and Charlotte, while the Captain and Ottilie do not constitute a 'couple' at all.

that to follow the dictates of duty is as much (if not more) a part of her nature as her love for Eduard. Human nature cannot be explained by chemical formulae. Man's moral and social attitudes can affect the action: the analogy of the compound composed of elements resembling human relations is misleading.

Ottilie's love for Eduard corresponds to only a part of her nature. Respect for the laws of religion and of society, for the sacred quality of marriage, belongs to her nature in the same manner as her passion for Eduard. An inner contradiction appears to be at work in nature.[81] The natural attraction of Eduard is in contrast to the respect for what is permanent and sacred. It violates the traditional forms of conduct.[82] Out of this contradiction, the tragic element of the novel is born; here, a deeper irony is conceived, to which the title too alludes. The law of elective affinity cannot be applied to the human sphere without creating confusion. Since it does not help man to reach clear recognition, it harms those who come into touch with it. The most important overt sign of this tragic contradiction is the act of 'adultery in the marriage-bed'.[83] Here a deed is done which is fully legitimate according to the recognized laws and customs of society, but which is in contrast to the true feelings of the partners in marriage, since Eduard and Charlotte do not love one another any longer. Although they observe the outward propriety of marital fidelity, they deceive one another in the imagination. What law and custom approve of and declare to be right appears to be a crime. This deed violates the basis of marriage, it violates the integrity of life, even if it does not violate the law. External and internal rights are thus in sharp contradiction. Respect for society and regard for others on the one hand are opposed by natural appetites and passion on the other.

Of all the characters, Ottilie's inner nature is most fully revealed, for her diary recounts the growth of her awareness of herself and of the world.[84] She writes down her thoughts, the thoughts of a person whose life is turned inward and who does not wish to shine in the world. Her diary is a mirror of herself. The spoken word, the direct communication with the external world, concerns her less.

Ottilie's diary-entries fall into two groups, as the narrator himself indicates. Each of them indicates a trend. On the one hand, there are entries which explicitly or implicitly concern

Eduard or other characters; on the other hand, there are maxims. Ottilie adopted for her use only those maxims which she had heard from others, as the narrator himself maintains. The maxims had not, of course, remained unintelligible to her, but she could not think of them on her own. They correspond to general laws which the narrator and other persons pronounce. They represent an expansion of the novel by which abstract thought is presented to the reader.

Ottilie's entries can be arranged according to their content. Some of them obviously refer to Eduard or Luciane, and the context is then quite clear; in the case of others, the relationship to the action is indicated only indirectly. The following main groups can be distinguished, but must not, however, be separated too abruptly, since they overlap. There are remarks about death, the ephemeral nature of life, and the laws which result from the social and spiritual life of men. The more extracts from Ottilie's diary there are quoted, the further the entries, as the narrator indicates, move away from immediate personal experience and signify a development from ingenuousness to maturity through abstraction and reflection on experience. On the one hand, they are general reflections and resemble the maxims of the narrator, but on the other hand, they say something about the nature and direction of Ottilie's inner development. Ottilie is in many ways shrouded in mystery; the critics have made this point again and again. Goethe himself said so, too. As Sulpiz Boisserée recounted:

> During our journey we happened to speak about the *Wahlverwandtschaften*. He [Goethe] stressed how he had brought about the catastrophe quickly and necessarily. The stars had risen; he spoke of his relationship to Ottilie, how he had loved her and how she made him happy. In the end, his speech became almost full of enigmatic forebodings.[85]

Ottilie plays a special part in Goethe's world. Many references to her are enigmatic, even if the diary entries illuminate the darkness a little.

Her reflections on art must first of all be explained as a result of her association with the architect and his collection of pictures. The absence of Eduard awakens a need to visualize him, whether by means of his portrait (which is, presumably, hanging in the castle), or by the image which she has formed of him in her mind. The remarks about death are evoked by the cemetery and the changes there. They throw light on her yearning for death, but also on the manner of her death. Reflections on social life spring from her encounter with Luciane, and they are a sign that Ottilie wishes to find a more satisfactory attitude to it. These preoccupations run parallel to her yearning for death and her love for Eduard.

Her first entry already speaks of death:

> To be buried one day by the side of those whom one loves is the most pleasant thought that we may imagine, if we once think beyond this life. 'To be gathered to one's fathers' is such a heartfelt expression.[86]

This also reflects her hope of being reunited with Eduard after death. Another entry from the diary returns to this theme, for it emphasizes how, for her, life is incoherent without him:

> A life without love, without the presence of one's beloved, is only a *comédie à tiroir*, a poor routine play. One pulls open one drawer after another and shuts them again, and hurries on to the next one. Everything good and important hangs together only in a haphazard manner. One must everywhere begin anew and would like everywhere to make an end.[87]

His absence, indeed, is for Ottilie a kind of death, so that these thoughts are natural to her. She wants to feel him near to her. The impact on Eduard of her later silence is anticipated when she says that a relationship with a human being can exist, or even grow, by his mere presence, 'without his doing anything about it or having the feeling that he stands only in the same relationship as does a portrait.'[88] The more spiritual Ottilie's vision becomes, the more she achieves inward detachment from art and life; for she knows that everything, even art, is transitory:

> But even this picture, this second existence, is extinguished sooner or later. Time will not be deprived of its rights over memorials any more than over people.[89]

For Ottilie, then, the image loses in value. The encounter with the architect is the external reason why the second group of diary entries contains so many remarks about art. She esteems art and the artist highly:

> One cannot evade the world more effectively than by art, nor can one link oneself to the world more effectively than by art.[90]

Many entries afford a genuine insight into her real nature. Ottilie recognizes how little a work of art can be a practical aid to living. This reflection leads her to the thought that she is hardly able to imagine human beings without seeing them.

> Say what you will, but we always think of ourselves as having sight.[91]

Such a view is significant for a person like Ottilie, for whom, as for Goethe, the eye is the symbol of life.[92] But she adds that her inner vision matters to her as much, if not more:

> I believe man only dreams in order not to stop seeing. It might well be that the inner light would one day step outside us so that we should need no other.[93]

But this series of diary entries ends in a thought on the ephemeral nature of life, a recurrent theme of her diary: what dies contains things which are alive and which continue to live. She therefore uses the image of the ear of corn, which, although it has been cut, is still alive and full of nourishment.

Her spiritual life is here alluded to. Ottilie recognizes her failure in this sphere. She is also perceptive enough to relate spiritual experience to society. A number of aphorisms distinguish between spiritual and social life. At first, however, she is unable to recognize her own situation. Her love for Eduard blinds her. General reflections prepare us for her later renunciation:

> Great passions are diseases with no hope of recovery. What might heal them makes them really dangerous.[94]

She will not admit to herself how much she sins against herself by her passion. The remark 'people say he will die soon if he acts contrary to his usual habits'[95] anticipates her later conduct. The entry 'Passions are either faults or virtues, but they are so in an intensified form',[96] however, raises the question whether Ottilie could believe her passion to be a virtue.[97]

As the narrator intimates, her thought is not embedded deeply in the personal sphere, but turns again to the general. Nonetheless, she is often one-sided. This becomes apparent when she writes, obviously thinking of Eduard, that 'a soldier of breeding enjoys the greatest advantages in society in particular and in life generally'.[98] Her love for Eduard may here cloud her vision, but when she apparently refers to Mittler, she is clear-sighted:

> Nobody is more boring than an awkward civilian. One is entitled to expect refinement from such a man, as he does not have to occupy himself with what is gross.[99]

On the whole, she seeks to understand social life, or at least to observe it. Two characteristics, sensibility and moral seriousness, predominate and colour her attitude. Inner depth and goodness of nature emerge from many of her remarks, features without which the force of her love for Eduard would be unthinkable.

> There is no salvation from the great advantages of another person except love.[100]

These extracts from her diary do not allow the reader to learn about her spiritual life directly, but the trend of her thinking emerges. She does not solve her spiritual and emotional problems, nor even look for solutions. Practical activity, but certainly not the formulation of abstract rules, is her destiny. Although Ottilie's mind is not brilliant and it does not impress others immediately, her impact upon them is, in fact, greater than it seems at first.

Ottilie's inner life undergoes a revolution, and she emerges the stronger for it. Personal resilience may withstand the storms if it can muster powerful spiritual reserves. The impact of daemonic forces on society is even more forceful, since destruction of its weaker members or links can easily wreak havoc on all, for society may find it more difficult to grow and adapt itself. Ottilie's diary bears witness to the close links between individual life and the social pattern. The threat to the individual's inner stability is considerably increased if it affects the relationships between several individuals; the danger to marriage from natural forces can be a symbol for similar menaces to society that may arise from irrational forces. Marriage and society must collapse if permanence is imposed when change is necessary, for society needs continuity and stability. If an institution is not able to adapt itself to the continuously changing pattern of life by calling on its own resources, it is in danger of being harmed, if not destroyed, by a new force that arises suddenly. It may appear as if the new marriages which would arise from the union of Eduard and Ottilie, and Charlotte and the Captain could be more fruitful than the situation in which they are all involved. This cannot be disputed; but almost every situation contains an element of stability which resists any change and is often supported by an appeal to supernatural sanction, to a moral command. This can be interpreted to mean that the individual perishes because social institutions are stronger than he is himself. It can also be a criticism of the structure of the social life of the time.

Ottilie withdraws further from the world; she appears to be least affected by her environment. But as her comments on art imply, no one can escape the impact of the external world. Indeed, she remarks in a diary entry:

> No one can walk unpunished among palm-trees, and one's opinions must surely change in a country where elephants and tigers are at home.[101]

The novel takes place in a world of aristocrats and the characters may be seen, if not in all cases, at least in some, as symbols revealing the shortcomings of the nobility. Eduard is undoubtedly a rich nobleman to whom life has not assigned a real activity and who does not know how to find one. Whatever he does, on his estate or in war, lacks a deeper meaning. His work in the garden and his music are the outcome of aesthetic playfulness. He finds the administration of his estate burdensome; so he welcomes the Captain, from whom he expects advice and help. Yet he does not invite him primarily because he feels that the estate needs a manager, but rather because of his friendship for him; furthermore, though he does not dare to admit it to himself, he invites him because he is bored when alone on his estate with Charlotte.

Eduard is a representative figure: a nobleman who, in social questions, acts without deeper convictions, who enjoys a privileged social status without assuming its duties. When he is happy, he does not rebuff the beggar as he did at an earlier stage when he was preoccupied, but gives him presents because he rejoices in his love for Ottilie, not from any real sympathy with him. As he treats him, so he treats himself. He goes to the war, not because this war appears to him a just cause or from any sense of loyalty, but merely to distract himself from his sadness.

Charlotte, by way of contrast to Eduard, is less volatile and possesses more self-knowledge and self-control. It is her aim to preserve order. Hence the leisured activities of an aristocrat appeal to her. To plan the lay-out of her park, to look after her estate – these appear more important to her than to Eduard. For her, the task of a country squire's wife still appears meaningful; hence she considers it natural to stay on the estate.

Goethe does not tell us whether the Captain is a nobleman or not.[102] His meticulous and determined approach to life befits a man who stands on his own feet. It recalls the bourgeois wanting to get on in the world rather than the privileged aristocrat. Undoubtedly, he is closely associated with the nobility, but he lacks the financial independence which Eduard so obviously enjoys. Other insights into the life of the nobility are imparted through Luciane, whose gay, sparkling life shows a complete lack of concern for other people's needs. By way of contrast to her, Ottilie wants to become a teacher, and her relationship to the Assistant and the architect emphasizes this intent. From the presence of these two, we can infer that the nobility contains among its members or its friends at least some people interested in practical life.

The English peer who visits Eduard's estate belongs to a group of people who, like Eduard, live without any definite task, and have freed themselves from any activity in the sphere in which they were born. We do not know what kind of life the Count and the Baroness lead, except that they live at court. The aristocratic society we are shown is on the whole a society of dilettantes,[103] and we witness its privileged position being slowly undermined, but the feudal order is not openly criticized or considered an anachronism.

Apart from the architect and the Assistant, the middle class is represented only by Mittler, a *bourgeois déraciné*. He has acquired a fortune and given up his profession. He is not capable of coping with the freedom acquired by sudden independence, for he lacks the necessary originality and force of personality. Members of other classes are barely mentioned; they play a minor role. We thus learn very little about German social life in the eighteenth century.

In a wider perspective, however, the novel may intimate more; for the family is, of course, the core of Western society, and marriage, the foundation of the family and of society, can provide a symbol for social institutions in general and the impact of society upon human life.[104]

Whether this novel can be called a tragedy of marriage,[105] is open to dispute. Some of Goethe's own observations emphasize the significance of marriage and find the tragic guilt in the violation of the moral order. Undoubtedly, Goethe did not think lightly of marriage, as is proved by his words to Eckermann when they were talking about the novel:

> The late Reinhard in Dresden wondered very frequently that my principles about marriage were so strict while my views on everything else were so indifferent.[106]

In the novel, no marriage is depicted as happy.[107] The first marriages of Eduard and Charlotte, of which we learn by hearsay, though not disturbed by a catastrophe, did not grant any deep satisfaction, and ended with death. We do not meet any other married couples in the novel. Luciane, Charlotte's daughter from her first marriage, is only engaged. Her fiancé is not at all jealous when she flirts with others; he is pleased to see her hold the stage. Her relations with others are superficial. It can hardly be forecast whether she will have such deep feelings for her husband that a lasting and exemplary marriage will ensue. It must never be forgotten that, although Luciane may be provocative, she never offends the rules of the strictest morality. Her conduct only seems offensive, but is, in fact, moral.

Among the minor characters there is only one other couple: the Count and the Baroness. They love one another, but are unable to marry since, for reasons of social propriety, they cannot obtain divorces. Only towards the end of the novel, when they are liberated by death from these bonds, do they look forward to marriage, the goal of their aspirations. The views of the Count, however, are those of a man of the world. He quotes approvingly a friend's opinion. Marriages, the latter argued (half in earnest) should be 'for five years at a time'.[108] If they are unhappy, they should be dissolved. This safeguard would serve as a spur for the partners to keep their marriage a happy one. Marriage as the happy end belongs to comedy, not to life. Why should one expect something permanent from this institution alone, when the world is continuously in a process of change? Still, the Count's action in waiting until he can finally marry the Baroness ironically refutes his own views. It is ironical, too, that their relationship appears to be permanent and happy, even if, or perhaps because, it has no legal sanction. The hope of a later marriage, however, exists; furthermore, their relationship has stood the test of time on human grounds before it is to receive legal and social approval through marriage.

Mittler, the man for whom marriage is the most sacred of all institutions and every attack on it a sin, who considers it his task to preserve the union of others and to prevent marital disputes, is himself unmarried and remains so. He is a tragicomic figure.[109] His views on marriage, although praiseworthy, are not necessarily valid since he does not speak from experience. The irony, of course, is not directed against the validity of his views, which are the ideals of Christian teaching, the established social tradition of the West. What is treated ironically is Mittler's belief that it is possible to counter the primordial forces of life by preaching, by exhortation, by words. Mittler is judged as an over-zealous champion of an important and valid institution. It is significant in this context that he is no longer a clergyman. His presumption consists in seeking to help others through his own striving and teaching in a difficult situation which he sees only from without. His own efforts are thus condemned to be fruitless: his attempts to save the marriage of Eduard and Charlotte are of no avail. He must, however, have been successful in other cases, for while he was a clergyman there were fewer divorces in his parish. It may be permissible to infer that Mittler was successful as long as he was not confronted with primordial natural forces, with genuine passions. In this particular case, he is certainly mistaken to intervene in the lives of others. Since he acts without understanding or self-criticism, his restlessness conveys the impression that he himself lacks inner strength; all his efforts concern external questions. It is wrong to take Mittler for a mere fool; he knows that advice alone is useless, and he wants to deal with concrete questions which he believes capable of solution. The problem of Eduard's and Ottilie's passion lies beyond the limits of his comprehension, just as he is unable to understand the true nature of the relationship between the Count and the Baroness. He thinks too rationally about marriage. He has made into a dogma, into a guide to action, that which over centuries had been developed out of experience and tradition. That is why he fails completely.[110] Incapable of deeper insight, he states only truisms, though they may sound impressive:

> Anyone who attacks marriage, anyone who by word or deed undermines this foundation of all moral society, must reckon with me; and if I can't get the better of him I shall have nothing more to do with him. Marriage is the beginning and the culmination of all civilization. It makes a brutish man humane, and the most educated man can have no better opportunity of demonstrating his humanity. It must be indissoluble; for it brings so much happiness that the individual instances of unhappiness cannot be taken into account. And what is this talk about unhappiness? From time to time man is overcome by impatience and then he is pleased to consider himself unhappy. Once the moment is past, one will think oneself lucky that what has lasted so long still lasts. There are really no sufficient grounds for separating. The human condition involves so much pain and joy, that it is quite impossible to reckon what the partners in marriage owe each other. It is an infinite debt, which can only be paid off in eternity. Marriage can be uncomfortable at times, I can well believe, and that's as it should be. Are we not also wedded to our conscience, which we should often like to get rid of because it is more disturbing than any husband or wife could ever be?[111]

Mittler is a preacher by training and inclination; he would have continued to speak for a long time if the coachman had not announced the arrival of the Count and the Baroness, which prompts him to depart quickly, since he disapproves of their conduct, not realizing that their conduct in fact presents an ironic refutation of his own apodictic assertion. Ironic remarks on the part of the narrator expose Mittler's lack of understanding for others. He is a preacher, but not a spiritual adviser or physician of the mind. He is not able to live up to his self-imposed task of cementing the marriage of Eduard and Charlotte; he overestimates the power of words. His intelligence is as penetrating as his temperament is restless and uncontrolled. What he has to say about marriage is perfectly reasonable, but it is no more than a rationalization, nor is his wordiness an improvement on the decalogue. He is unaware of the irrational element in human thought and action.

Charlotte at first appears, even more than Mittler, to be an advocate of marriage.[112] For he speaks of what he knows only by observation and from tradition; she, however, is able to judge things from her own experience and does not rely merely on abstract theory. Prompted by respect for the moral value of marriage, she is prepared to sacrifice her love for the Captain, although she knows about Eduard's feelings for Ottilie. Charlotte demands much from herself, but also from others. She wants to preserve her marriage artificially after it has collapsed. This would be possible for her, but not for her husband. She misreads his character completely. Temperament and education make self-control impossible for him. Charlotte was not able to prevent him from inviting the Captain when their marriage was still intact. It is as if she had recognized unconsciously, but only unconsciously, that her relationship to Eduard was endangered, and that the arrival of the Captain and Ottilie would be likely to undermine it. Later on, her own self-abnegation does not at all affect her husband and certainly fails to keep his violent passion in check. She believes that she was mistaken in seeking to preserve her marriage at any price. This is a complete reversal of her views; she is now prepared to abandon long-cherished principles. Her readiness to do so shows how deeply the events affect her for if her view of marriage is based on absolutely and universally valid principles, it should not be changed by events, however disturbing. But it does show that her views, by way of contrast to Mittler's, spring from her way of living. When life undermines her whole outlook, she is willing to reconsider her attitude.

Ottilie acts much more unconditionally and consistently than Charlotte. At first she appears to believe either that Eduard and Charlotte will become divorced or that somehow their marriage will not stand in the way of Eduard's and her love. When, however, she has at last understood that, in her case, fulfilment in love is incompatible with the sacredness of marriage, her decision to renounce Eduard, even if her love continues, becomes intelligible. It is Ottilie's desire to bring Eduard and Charlotte together again. Her gesture on returning to the castle after her attempt to leave makes this quite plain; for she puts the hands of Eduard and Charlotte together, recognizing that her love for Eduard is immoral. She is prepared to accept the consequences: the moral power of marriage must prevail over extramarital love. Her decision to renounce her unlawful love for Eduard is quite unshakeable. She knows that he will never be able to renounce her in a similar way. Yet her renunciation destroys her life and Eduard's. By following her feelings, she has erred – 'I have strayed from my path, I have broken my laws, I have lost my sense of them.'[113] As soon as she recognizes her error,[114] she wishes to expiate the wrong that she has done. The institution of marriage now appears to her to be more important than personal desires. Disaster occurs because Eduard is incapable of recognizing the moral character of marriage in which she believes. Neither he nor the Captain looks at marriage from the same standpoint as Ottilie and Charlotte. It is significant that it is not the men but the women who seek to uphold marriage by their action.

Although the ideal preached by Mittler is not realized in the novel, it is nonetheless the guiding force. Still, no views about marriage appear absolutely valid. Only one thing is certain: it must be treated with absolute seriousness.

A social institution, such as marriage, is a criterion by which the development and nature of the characters is revealed. This development is, however, not a straightforward, conscious one; on the contrary, it is affected by the conflict between reason and passion, between the irrational inner forces and man's urge to understand his thought and action. Reason alone is insufficient. Mittler, for instance, who speaks with the voice of reason, is seen consistently in an ironic vein. Charlotte wants to act rationally, since she seeks to restrain passion by insisting on custom and tradition and desires to rescue her marriage. The marriages of convenience or of reason which both Eduard and Charlotte concluded early in life did not satisfy them; the same is true of their own late marriage. The Captain, too, is prompted by reason when he leaves Charlotte and later when he again hopes that she will become his wife. He does not grasp the full significance of events. Similarly, Eduard is mistaken in assuming that the death of the child will remove the obstacle which obstructs his marriage to Ottilie. These errors spring from a misunderstanding of other people's characters, from the mistaken belief that others will act in the same way as one would act oneself, or rather as reasonable people would act. Ottilie, too, is mistaken. Each time rational arguments are put forward; yet they miss the point, because they grasp reality only in part and do not grasp the irrationality of life. Reason has only limited scope. As Charlotte says to Eduard: 'Awareness . . . is no adequate weapon; in fact, it is often a dangerous one for the man who makes use of it.'[115]

Irrational events move below the surface of consciousness. Images and signs alone indicate the development of a situation of which the protagonists are not conscious.[116] For instance, at the beginning of the novel, Eduard's ignorance of where his wife is and of what she is doing is countered by his wish to see her, reflecting a latent contradiction in his mind. Eduard's letter inviting the Captain to stay is blotted by Charlotte when she hastily adds a postscript, thus unconsciously betraying her resistance. Eduard and Charlotte play music badly together, but he is at once *en rapport* with Ottilie. Eduard's feelings are also revealed by his attitude to the use of language. At times he is at a loss what to say to Charlotte, but he finds Ottilie's conversation entertaining when, as Charlotte tells him with a smile, she has barely spoken a word. Wieland singled out this remark as a master-stroke.[117] Similarly, Eduard resents Charlotte's looking over his shoulder to read the book which he is reading himself, while if Ottilie does it, he is delighted. During the discussion of the chemical elements Eduard and Charlotte foreshadow their later views on divorce. He contemplates the separation of the elements with equanimity, but Charlotte reacts violently against it, fearing unconsciously that a parallel will be drawn with their own marriage. Eduard's attitude is superficial. He does not realize how much more Charlotte, as a woman, is bound to her marriage. Later on, Eduard's concealed emotional unrest is delineated when he speaks to the Captain of the relations between A, B, C and D. As soon as he applies the formulae to his own world, he provokes Charlotte's disapproval. Yet the future development has been foreshadowed.

From a letter written by the Assistant who taught Ottilie in the boarding school in which she was a pupil, it emerges that Ottilie's thoughts and actions take place much more on a subconscious level than do those of others. This makes her later growth of awareness more intelligible. Her headache on the left side, and her gestures, permit an insight into her inner life. The forms of expression of her unconscious life gain deeper significance as she gradually uses them consciously. This headache later recalls Ottilie to Eduard's mind since he has a headache, too, only his is on the right side. It appears to him as a complementary fulfilment of destiny. It is first of all mentioned as a joke, but becomes a serious matter. A further instance is Ottilie's gesture of refusal, of which we first hear in the Assistant's letter. He describes how she puts the palms of her hands together, raises them towards her breast, bending a little forward at the same time and looking at him who has made the request in such a way that he only too gladly desists from what he has demanded. This gesture is repeated when Ottilie rejects Eduard; thus the characteristic feature of her being becomes an essential feature of the action. This gesture reveals a trait in Ottilie's nature which determines the end of the novel; on the other hand her adaptability, which is mentioned in the sixth chapter of the novel, permits her to follow Eduard's impetuous temperament. Ottilie's naïveté is also mentioned early. It prevents her from becoming as guilty as Eduard, for he sins in thought when he declares that she is his and when in his imagination he anticipates marriage to her.[118] Ottilie's reaction is different when she gives her medallion to Eduard. She turns more towards heaven than towards Eduard: she retains the image of her father which she has given Eduard, for she accepts the nobler side of Eduard's desires.[119]

Charlotte, at an early stage, betrays a feature of her character which is in contrast to Eduard. She says she would be able to control her emotions better than her husband, anticipating her later decisions, which are prompted by morality. She believes she can demand the same attitude from others.

Without being aware of it, Ottilie is more attentive to Eduard than she need be, clearly showing her affection. On the other hand, Charlotte's love for the Captain comes to the fore when she gladly allows him to alter her plans. Even the Captain, an extremely self-conscious man, does things which reflect subconscious changes; he forgets to wind up his watch for the first time in many years. In the case of Eduard and Ottilie, these signs of unconscious origin are much more pronounced. The Captain's remarks about Eduard's flute-playing annoy Eduard beyond all measure, because for him music has become associated with Ottilie. He believes that nothing has annoyed him more and, characteristically, he feels estranged from Charlotte who had taken the same view. He therefore refuses, after the accident when the boy had fallen into the lake, to break off the festive celebration and the accompanying fireworks, for it would be interrupting his own celebration of his love for Ottilie, and no one must disturb that. His love permeates his subconscious, even his dreams. The same is true of Ottilie, who dreams of Eduard.

In the second part of the novel, the subconscious does not play so important a part as in the first book, even if part of the action moves on an inner and subconscious plane. This is not surprising, for the development of the action leads from a more gentle inclination to an overwhelming passion. A crisis of human relations is followed by a catastrophe.

The narrator describes the power which the subconscious wields in the novel with the following words:

> Whatever usually happens to an individual happens more repeatedly than we think, because his nature directly determines it. Character, personality, inclination, direction, milieu, surroundings and habit together form a whole in which everyone swims as if in an element, in an atmosphere where he is alone comfortable and at ease.[120]

According to this, whatever occurs is part of a chain of events. The external event expresses inner experiences; indeed, an interchange between the inward and outward life takes place. Awareness of the subconscious differs from person to person.

To live and to act fruitfully in this uncharted world depends to a large extent on one's awareness of one's nature and that of others. The human conflicts in the novel arise from the sterility of human relationships occasioned by misunderstanding of human nature and by neglect of social obligations. Indeed, a theme of the novel hidden beneath the surface is the criteria of fruitfulness or sterility, which allow one to judge the thought and conduct of the characters. Sentences like: 'Sowing is not so troublesome as reaping,'[121] or: 'To communicate one's thoughts and feelings is natural, accepting communication of the thoughts and feelings in the sense originally intended is culture (*Bildung*)' point in this direction.[122] Both say how much more difficult it is to complete a mental process than to begin one. The grafting of shoots on trees may be taken as a symbol for Eduard's unconscious concern with this problem. The task which he has set himself is to attain a higher quality in living. But Eduard lacks the patience or the talent to create a field of practical action for himself. His activities are unproductive.[123] The words applied by Ottilie to the fate of an architect can be applied to him: 'How often he [the architect] makes use of his whole mind and heart in order to produce rooms from which he himself has to be excluded.'[124] Eduard's planning is of a similar kind. He cannot enjoy its fruits if there are any. Only in love does Eduard find his true profession. He is conscious of this; he replies to the reproach of dilettantism by saying:

> People haven't actually said so to my face, but I know they've criticized me behind my back, saying that in most things I'm only a dabbler and a bungler. It may be, but then I had not found a sphere where I could prove myself a master. I'd like to see the man who can surpass me in the talent of loving.[125]

Here Eduard finds a field of activity that could be fruitful, but since fulfilment is denied to his love, nothing fruitful emerges. He does not understand others, not even Ottilie. He possesses neither the experience nor the spiritual capacity to follow her to the same level of spiritual experience. His failure was anticipated by his earlier decision to leave home, the natural centre of his activities, to go aimlessly into the world – not at all thinking of any purposeful activity, but simply because he feels that he can do nothing else.[126] Thus, despite his apparent failure he makes an impact which is, so to speak, indirectly fruitful, for by inspiring love in Ottilie he shows others what love really is.'

For Charlotte, fruitful activity is a necessary task in life, and the symbol of the hut intimates that her striving is contained within a limited sphere, but is secure in its effect. She therefore seeks to rescue her marriage; she protects herself from her love for the Captain. All her efforts are aimed at preservation, not change. The plans of the two men, therefore, interfere much more forcefully with the landscape than hers do. The ponds are changed into a single lake, which makes the death of the child possible. Charlotte always seeks to be effective by her moral action. Conscious deeds have limited use and validity. She has to recognize this fact when she faces a catastrophe, the death of the child; the principles which underlie her actions cannot be applied to all situations. At the end of the novel, nothing appears left for her to do except to tend the grave of Eduard and Ottilie, although she has little understanding for the cult which has grown up around Ottilie and little liking for such places. But she respects the memory of Ottilie. She closes the chapel which contains her grave, permitting only Eduard to be buried there later.

For the Captain, too, fruitful activity is the essence of life; it is one of the reasons for his affinity with Charlotte. His main interests also appear limited in scope: they are concerned with practical problems; he seems less attuned to spiritual and emotional ones. Yet this eminently practical man's achievement is only partially successful. He does not succeed in completing his work for Eduard nor is his advice in the last stages of the novel helpful.

Ottilie is born to teach, and the very aim of education, as the word implies, is to be fruitful. Her desire to teach is thwarted, she has to abandon her attempt to escape to the boarding-school to take up teaching. She who is motherly by nature – much more so than Charlotte, who is, or rather becomes, a mother – is denied motherhood, and even Charlotte's and Eduard's child, whom she looks after with motherly care, dies, a result of her own inadvertence. Even when she adorns an especially fine dress with asters, presumably to celebrate Eduard's birthday, she only wears the dress on her bier and the asters picked by her own hand only then adorn her head. Ottilie cannot claim any direct achievement. From a worldly point of view her life would even be called a failure, just as she fails to acquit herself well in examinations. But her impact is indirect, for it is spiritual and aesthetic. So her worth cannot be measured quantitatively by school-examinations, but only qualitatively. She does affect others strongly and positively, though by her beauty in the first place rather than by her character. She lives on in art, for she is the model for the architect when he decorates the chapel with images of the angels. The circumstances surrounding her death give rise to veneration. Above all, she becomes for Eduard, this apparently selfish and superficial man (and perhaps not only for him) an example of perfect love. Yet the two lovers can be united only in another world, and Ottilie's 'incomparable' love brings about her death and Eduard's in turn; her fruitfulness, in the last resort, is ambiguous, as is so much in the novel.

Usefulness is also a criterion for the life of the minor figures. Mittler is the tragicomic example of the man who wants to be useful, but does not succeed. He sows without reaping; he communicates, but is unable to receive communication. The life of the Englishman is similarly unfruitful. His companion's existence can at least be justified by his ability to tell good stories. The architect and the Assistant want to be immediately effective. A definite sphere of activity is prescribed for them, but they go beyond it. The Count and the Baroness appear, like Charlotte, to guarantee a continuity of social life through their existence and activity. The Count's fatherly interest in Ottilie, and the kindly attitude of the Baroness towards Charlotte betray an interest in others. It is therefore wrong to consider them merely as the worldly cynics which they believe themselves to be. Luciane's life, too, is unfruitful. She has an excessive liking for externals, but her strict observance of morality is in contrast to Ottilie's conduct.[127] She indeed errs and does harm by some of her remarks and acts foolishly, but she has a beneficial effect on the young man with the crippled hand. His life takes a turn for the better. Luciane is critical and likes to ridicule what she dislikes, but Goethe does not take sides; it may well be that her criticism, though harsh, is justified. Her personality is ambivalent, but in a different way from that of Ottilie.

Fruitful activity is attained not only directly, but also indirectly. This becomes clear in the case of Ottilie. Ottilie lives on in art. The architect presents her as a Madonna; she becomes a saint for the people. Her life and death become a legend.

The importance of art is openly acknowledged, as one of Ottilie's diary entries betrays:

> One cannot evade the world more effectively than through art, nor can one link oneself to the world more effectively than by art.[128]

Art is thus capable of giving to life an added dimension: by making the individual aware of himself, it allows him to understand reality more adequately. At the same time, it can be a way of escape from the demands of life. The narrator's irony therefore does not spare even art,[129] although its significance is not in dispute. As in the *Lehrjahre*, figurative art plays an important part, but there is no mention of literature or drama and little of music. In the *tableaux vivants* which are acted at Luciane's suggestion, paternal admonition and authority form an important theme.[130] Belisarius, although innocent, is found guilty and is forced to leave society. Similarly, Ottilie must appear guilty, although she is not conscious of her crime. Her belief in her ability to choose a new way of life turns out to be mistaken. The picture in which Ottilie is portrayed as the Madonna prepares the way for the people's later veneration of her. Similarly, the angels that look down on the grave resemble her. The distinctions between figurative art and life are blurred. This tendency, though not criticized in the novel, does not agree with Goethe's own view. It may be doubted whether he, who sharply separated art and reality, approved of *tableaux vivants*,[131] or of the attitude of the architect who thinks of Ottilie as a celestial being.[132] Eduard, however, loves her differently. Presumably, Goethe approved of his commitment to love, for he wrote that he valued Eduard highly because he loved unconditionally.[133] The Assistant, too, is not at all content that the architect paints images of saints and that Ottilie sits for him. Luciane visits the chapel, but her reaction could also be interpreted as a criticism of the architect's views on art. Luciane's delight in the pictures of the monkeys might be read as a mocking criticism of portrait painting.

Luciane ridicules everything and lacks Ottilie's depth and intensity of passion; nonetheless, she is able to control her feelings and keep her life on an even keel while Ottilie fails to do so.

The approach to art indicates the dangers of sterile human relations. Emotional and intellectual immaturity, of which thwarted aspirations are often a sure sign, can drive us to the verge of a tragic situation. A situation of this kind is found in *Die Wahlver-*

wandtschaften. Abeken,[134] the first important reviewer of the novel, and Solger[135] championed this view, which earned Goethe's approval. It has only rarely been challenged.[136] Tragedy is generally seen as arising from a conflict between passion and reason, nature and custom. Merciless necessity, as in Greek tragedy, must prevail. Human relations are uncertain. Good confronts evil, good confronts good. The people involved are at first unaware of their situation.

These tragic features, indeed, exist in the novel, but their existence does not make the novel a tragic one. Nonetheless, these features should not be disregarded. In the novel, as in tragedy, the action is concentrated on persons. A drama deserves the name of tragedy only in so far as it depicts the failure of human striving. The same can be said of a novel. An action is tragic only if the persons, consciously or unconsciously, commit actions which make them incur guilt. Their attempts, however, to extricate themselves from this situation, which they have brought upon themselves by an error of judgement or a mishap, succeed only in further enmeshing them in this pattern. They appear unable to escape their destiny.

Which of the principal characters of *Die Wahlverwandtschaften* are, then, tragic figures? To answer this question, we must first of all consider each of them more closely.[137] In the first chapter, only the essential features of each character are depicted; later on, little is added. Eduard is a man who is almost forty years old. His character consists in not having a character at all. If we assume that character is created only by reflection, personal experience, education and environment, Eduard is a completely unformed nature. His nature is unlimited egotism, which is not mitigated in any way.[138] His egotism furthers his pleasure, and, later on, his passion becomes immoderate too. It does not stand in a rational relationship to his environment. Presumably because of this lack of measure Goethe himself said that he could not stand Eduard:

> I cannot bear a grudge against him [Solger] . . . for not liking Eduard; I don't like him myself, I had to make him in such a way so as to produce this foil. There is incidentally much truth in him, for we find among the higher nobility many people in whom, just as in him, obstinacy takes the place of character.[139]

Eduard is like a child; he is equally obstinate and self-indulgent, though he is capable of patience and cunning if it is a question of carrying through his plans. He thinks and acts as if the world were centred on him. From this egocentricity, his superstition arises. He interprets events as symbolic; they become signs revealing or confirming the course which he believes – or rather wants – his life to take; they always tally with his wishes. His preoccupations are whims; his projects remain projects. He is, as we saw, a dilettante who does not wish to subordinate himself to any compulsion.[140] He possesses an amiability which makes him sympathetic and charming. He intuitively chooses the appropriate means to further his pleasure. His passion, however, overshadows this amiability. He loves deeply, indeed unconditionally, thus everything is made subservient to his passion. He lacks detachment; he is not aware of what he does. His intelligence is completely ruled by his subconscious, and he thus does not understand himself. Nor does he understand others, not even Ottilie, so that all his attempts to bring about his marriage to her appear only destined to foil his plans, thus resembling 'tragic errors', although he does not recognize these errors. The course of his life is prescribed by nature. Because he is so close to nature, he is immature, yet also possesses that child-like 'innocence of the heart'[141] which may help to explain why someone as sensitive as Ottilie is capable of loving him.[142] Her love guarantees his worth despite all his obvious faults. Yet this apparent paradox does not create a conflict since he never becomes conscious of it. For only if action and wish, deed and thought, impulse and reason are in conflict does tragedy occur. Eduard is too one-sided, his instinct rules him too much; he therefore cannot be considered a tragic character.

Nor can the Captain be called a tragic character, though for different reasons. He is, in contrast to Eduard, a man who does not allow natural impulses to rule his life, but runs his life on rational lines. He is an active man with a practical bent. His views are sharp and clear, his actions quick and determined. He appears to control his feelings fully; he is free from any sentimentality, and occasionally even lacks sensibility. Perhaps it was for this reason that Goethe implicitly linked the story *Die wunderlichen Nachbarskinder* with an incident which had taken place in the Captain's youth. This incident shows that the Captain is a man who has been deeply wounded at an earlier stage in his life, and perhaps even suffered a similar fate to the disappointed bridegroom in the tale,[143] which may explain his urge to activity. He knows what he is about, but his behaviour is too self-possessed. He is too far removed from the centre of the novel to affect the action very deeply, to bring about the catastrophe or to accelerate it. He does not involve himself in tragic guilt, nor does he lose self-control for long. This explains why the catastrophic events do not shatter him and why he goes on hoping that, in the end, he may marry Charlotte.

Neither of the male protagonists can be considered a tragic hero. The women are different. Charlotte may be considered a tragic character. Her actions, prompted by a sense of moral responsibility, produce consequences which are precisely the opposite of what she had intended. Her principles, derived from reason and tradition, are of no avail against the forces of nature and love. They offer no bulwark against the irrationality of life; on the contrary, they prepare the way for destructive forces. Charlotte, like the Captain, is a person of moderation. She knows how to control herself and to keep her passion in check. Above all, she is a woman who knows life,[144] who has observed much and has reflected on what she has observed. She is a woman of character, and thus the very opposite of Eduard. She is calm by nature; her thinking is always clear and logical. All the more tragic is her involvement in guilt. Eduard is guilty, too, but he is not aware of his guilt. Charlotte is mistaken because, in a one-sided manner, she follows the voice of reason, but not the voice of her heart. By wishing and seeking the best, she becomes a tragic character; she misunderstands what is essential. She over-simplifies life,[145] and forgets that serenity, balance and inner harmony are required to deal with this situation. Not only does she misunderstand the character of her husband – she loves him, or rather she believes she loves him,[146] but she does not realize that her love is no longer deeply anchored in her being. She agrees to marry him even though reason and instinct warn her against doing so. She marries Eduard partly because of her youthful love for him, partly because she hopes for a quiet, later happiness at his side. What makes her strong are her determined, clear-minded firmness towards herself and others, her loyal attachment to her marriage even when this marriage exists only on paper, and her attempts to lead Ottilie back to another healthier way of life, and to lead Eduard back to himself. All these attempts are in themselves extremely praiseworthy, yet they lead to catastrophe.

Ottilie, too, is a tragic character, though her grief arises from different reasons. She is a tragic figure, not because, like Charlotte, she causes unhappiness through actions based on principle, but because, in acting from deep and sincere feelings, she produces in herself a sense of guilt.[147] She becomes aware of this, and feels that she is violating the rules she has imposed on herself, rules in conformity with the moral law. For Ottilie, the laws of her inner life are commands,[148] so she seeks to expiate her guilt.

Her inner life, not the world without, governs her actions. Feeling, not reason, rules her inner life. The powerful spiritual strength of her life becomes apparent at school, in a foreign environment; her sensitivity, however, is attractive to many people. Artists find her stimulating; the common people consider her a symbol of what is sacred. The intensity of her inner life brings her very close to nature.[149] Her actions are intuitive; she is – like Eduard – a natural person, but she has given herself moral laws. She recognizes that she has violated them because her love for Eduard is sinful. Because she seeks to run away from Eduard, the disaster becomes only more certain. Because she loves the child, she takes it out for walks. Because she loves nature, she wanders to the lake. Because she is attached to Charlotte and because she has a sense of what is proper, she hurries back; so it comes about that the boat almost capsizes and the child is drowned. She becomes a tragic figure when she recognizes that she has gone astray. She comprehends that a valuable, deep feeling involved her in error and guilt, even led her to the death of another being. She begins to understand that her attempts to escape from this hopeless situation have only led her deeper into guilt. Her recognition reveals tragic awareness. She repents and seeks to expiate her guilt. This conduct reveals 'active sublimity', to use Schiller's term. She refuses to accept a happiness based on a violation of the laws that she has given herself; like Eduard, she is too deeply attached to her passion to look for a way out. She therefore chooses death, a truly tragic outcome.

The designation 'tragic' can hardly be applied to the other characters of the novel. Some, like the peer or the architect or the

Assistant, appear too seldom to be fully involved in the action, or for us to know enough about them. Others, like the Count, the Baroness or Luciane, are not tragic figures at all. Only Mittler could possibly qualify for this designation, for he does harm through action prompted by good intentions, but he is ridiculous rather than tragic. His characterization is almost excessively ironic: he is almost a pathetic figure.

Die Wahlverwandtschaften must in this context also be considered as a novel about a group of persons. In this group, all constellations which existed in the beginning or which arise in the course of the action break down. Of course, groups cannot be conscious of their actions, but all their members may desire a happy interaction. In the novel, the deeds of the principal characters frustrate these hopes. According to the degree of their insight, they agree that they have failed because of their own fault. This sense of guilt and inadequacy is very strong in the case of the two women; it hardly exists in the case of the two men. But if this conception of what is tragic can at all be applied to the breaking apart of a group, *Die Wahlverwandtschaften* presents a striking example of this form of tragedy.

Die Wahlverwandtschaften ends in reconciliation; after the death of the main protagonists 'the peace that passeth all understanding' is evoked. This end embodies Goethe's conception of tragedy. For him as for the Greeks, the catastrophe was not the end. Reconciliation follows the catastrophe, a reconciliation with religious implications.

Die Wahlverwandtschaften should be called a tragic novel, for two of the protagonists possess tragic features. As Ottilie dominates the last part of the novel almost completely, this term 'tragic novel' is particularly appropriate, even if the two male protagonists do not possess truly tragic features. The word 'tragic', which belongs to the genre of drama, can, however, be applied to the novel only by way of analogy. It is not mistaken to call the novel 'tragic', especially since the comparatively closed form affords a certain parallel to drama. This analogy to tragedy agrees with Goethe's own view. It springs from 'the contrast of character', from 'the conflict of physical and moral forces'.[150] Goethe also thought that catharsis which, since the time of Aristotle, had been held to be an essential feature of tragedy was to be found in *Die Wahlverwandt-*

schaften. He wrote to Zelter that he hoped, in this novel, to bring about as pure and perfect a catharsis as possible.[151] In order to produce catharsis, according to Aristotle, fear is also necessary, and fear is excited in *Die Wahlverwandtschaften* – at least such was Goethe's interpretation – 'when we see how a moral evil advances towards the protagonists and how it affects them'.[152] This evil could be 'the boundless striving that expels one out of human society, out of the world, viz. unconditional passion'[153] which, if confronted with insurmountable obstacles, is capable of finding satisfaction only in despair, and peace only in death, which comes into conflict with the forces of morality and destroys man.

The tragic is closely connected with the supernatural, for both demand an interpretation of life which goes beyond the particular event, even beyond the limits of physical reality. The origin of tragedy in religious celebration is, of course, well known. Religion may be termed conscious acceptance of the transcendental. *Die Wahlverwandtschaften* does not say much about this. Religion is never directly the theme of the novel; it could be argued that the whole foreground of the action is determined by secular events and that religion is relegated to the background. There are no discussions about religion, nor is the life of any of the protagonists interpreted in a religious manner. Not even the death of the child produces a turning to religion. Only indirectly, through Ottilie, does it play a part. The Assistant rejects the sacred pictures in which Ottilie is portrayed because he feels that religion should be experienced directly and not through images. Yet the novel culminates in the legend which Ottilie's death creates,[154] so religion is shown to be a powerful factor. To ask whether she is really a saint is pointless.[155] This question cannot be answered from the knowledge afforded by the action. There is no talk of any impending canonization by the Roman Catholic Church, the orthodox mark of sainthood. It is indeed doubtful whether she could be called a saint, for the manner of her death hardly stems from a saintly life. What is described is an inner maturity not tied to a particular religion, a maturity which springs from a profound capacity for love. What Goethe himself thought about the process is not clear: his words to Boisserée quoted above remain obscure.[156] Love, of course, was sacred for Goethe, and a love as pure and profound as Ottilie's must have appeared to him doubly so. On one occasion, in fact, he did call her 'St Ottilie' (*die heilige Ottilie*) in a letter to Heinrich Meyer[157] which may, however, as its context appears to suggest, have been meant just as ironically as his remark that his Christianity could not be called in question because he let Gretchen be executed and Ottilie perish of hunger.[158]

Religion, thus, plays a somewhat greater part in the novel than may at first be expected, proving once more that Goethe wanted to express his views only indirectly. In fact, he depicted a very complex cosmos. Yet we notice the power of the irrational only gradually. In the first part, only the discussions about the elective affinities state explicitly that irrational forces are at work in life. In the second part – as attention is focused on Ottilie – we become more and more aware that a different view of the world is being propounded. The purely secular – the world of the Count, of the Baroness and of Luciane, for instance – appears outwardly satisfactory, but inwardly without real power. Their views of reality represent only an extremely limited view of human experience, but this does not mean that these persons are condemned. On the contrary, they are described as happy people who manage their lives successfully – and surely this is no mean thing.

It is different for Eduard. His image of reality is limited. Narcissism characterizes him. His love-making to his wife, where 'imagination prevails over reality'[159] corresponds to his disposition.[160] 'Reality is considered as something imaginary.'[161] These words of Goethe's describe Eduard's mode of thought and action. He views the world as a toy or as a stage for his feelings.[162] Immature as he is, he expects from the world unconditional satisfaction.[163] He regards the world only from the standpoint of feeling. In this respect, his character resembles that of Werther. He, too, believes that he has to insist on the right of nature. By way of contrast to the novel of Goethe's youth, *Die Wahlverwandtschaften* does not, however, contain a protest against the fact that it was impossible for Eduard to impose his view of reality upon the world. Since he does not grow more mature, his unsatisfactory attitude to reality does not change.

The Captain, too, is unable to attain a satisfactory view of reality. His practical sense finds expression and satisfaction in achievement. But he fails properly to appreciate the feelings of others. Since neither he nor Eduard succeeds in determining the course of events, since they are not able to forecast or anticipate it, they later face terrible events completely without understanding. It is not very different for Charlotte, although in many ways she is a more mature person than the two men. If Eduard is moved too little by moral will, she is moved too much. Only towards the end of the novel does she attain a deeper grasp of reality. She recognizes that it is not enough to rely on the will alone, but that she has also to develop her inner resources and to learn to keep in tune with nature. Ottilie recognizes these necessities, but lacks the strength to make her sense of reality effective in the world. This incapacity also betrays a certain weakness, for Ottilie demands too much from herself and thus turns away from life, undoubtedly believing that her example will be effective after death. The principal women characters thus appear more mature than their male counterparts. Charlotte is aware of this tendency, for she remarks to Eduard: 'Men turn their attention more to the individual, to the present . . . Women, on the other hand, more to that which is coherent in life.'[164]

Of the minor figures, Mittler obviously has a false view of reality, for the world cannot be contained by maxims; of the architect and the Assistant we do not know enough, though they lack depth of feeling and maturity by comparison to Charlotte or Ottilie.

Finally, what is the relation between the narrator and reality? Does he know how to distinguish between reality and appearance? Are his views realistic? Does he really grasp life as it is? He does not lack understanding and breadth of mind. He knows the irrational forces which are concealed beneath the surface; he knows the nature of Ottilie's inner life. He seeks carefully to depict the growth of love. If he leaves much unsaid it is because he is conscious of the limits of linguistic expression; symbols and images often tell us more than precise analysis and are more suited to depicting the subconscious. It also appears as if he knows that no single person is capable of depicting reality comprehensively. Goethe's views had developed since *Werther* and the *Lehrjahre*. He no longer found it possible to restrict life to the imaginative experience of one person. It is too manifold; it can be grasped only by the interaction of the imaginative experiences of several people.

The *Lehrjahre* had on occasion pointed to this view; *Die Wahlverwandtschaften*, however, makes it clear that only a subtle view which is aware of the diversity and differentiation of life can be satisfactory. *Die Wahlverwandtschaften*, in fact, falls within a period in which Goethe changed his views on art and life. The hey-day of classicism was over.[165] He developed a new style. It is not yet the style of his old age, found in some chapters in the *Wanderjahre*, but the change from his classical style is sufficiently striking. A different world arises, quite different from the world of the *Lehrjahre*, in which threats, mystery and failure do not predominate. Goethe himself was aware of this change. Two remarks of his explain it, though from a rather different standpoint:

> The only large-scale production where I consciously worked from the standpoint of a comprehensive idea is my *Wahlverwandtschaften.*[166]

The second observation:

> No one can fail to notice in this novel a deep passionate wound which is reluctant to heal, a heart which is afraid of recovering. Many years ago the main idea was seized upon, only the execution was delayed, but it multiplied continuously and threatened to go beyond the limits of everything.[167]

An all-too-literal interpretation of either remark might easily lead us astray. A biographical explanation would, as we have seen, produce only difficulties,[168] and the comprehensive idea referred to defies unambiguous identification.

His sonnet *Mächtiges Überraschen*, however, succinctly conveys the problem facing him:

Mächtiges Überraschen

Ein Strom entrauscht umwölktem Felsensaale
  Dem Ozean sich eilig zu verbinden;
  Was auch sich spiegeln mag von Grund zu Gründen,
  Er wandelt unaufhaltsam fort zu Tale.

Dämonisch aber stürzt mit einem Male –
  Ihr folgen Berg und Wand in Wirbelwinden –
  Sich Oreas, Behagen dort zu finden,
  Und hemmt den Lauf, begrenzt die weite Schale.

Die Welle sprüht und staunt zurück und weichet,
Und schwillt bergan, sich immer selbst zu trinken;
Gehemmt ist nun zum Vater hin das Streben.

Sie schwankt und ruht, zum See zurückgedeichet;
Gestirne, spiegelnd sich, beschaun das Blinken
Des Wellenschlags am Fels, ein neues Leben.[169]

In this poem, Goethe created an impressive image of the course of life suddenly interrupted. The daemonic element here interrupts the normal course of life, just as Goethe described it in the twentieth book of *Dichtung und Wahrheit*:

> Although this daemonic element can manifest itself in all corporeal and incorporeal things, and even expresses itself most distinctly in animals, yet with man especially, it stands in a most wonderful connection, forming in him a power which, if it be not opposed to the moral order of the world, nevertheless does often so cross it that one may be regarded as the warp, and the other as the woof.
>
> For the phenomena which it gives rise to, there are innumerable names: all philosophies and religions have sought in prose and poetry to solve this enigma and to read once and for all the riddle which, nevertheless, remains still unravelled.
>
> But the most fearful manifestation of the Daemonic is when it is seen predominating in some individual character. During my life I have observed several instances of this, either more closely or remotely. Such persons are not always the most eminent, either morally or intellectually, and it is seldom that they recommend themselves to our affections by goodness of heart. A tremendous energy seems to be seated in them, and they exercise a wonderful power over all creatures, and even over the elements; and indeed, who shall say how much farther such influence may extend? All the moral powers combined are of no avail against them; in vain does the more enlightened portion of mankind attempt to throw suspicion upon them as deceived if not deceivers – the mass is still drawn on by them. Seldom if ever do the great men of an age find their equals among their contemporaries, and they can be overcome by nothing but by the universe itself; and it is from observation of this fact that the strange, but most striking, proverb must have risen: *Nemo contra Deum nisi Deus ipse.*[170]

Neither Eduard nor Ottilie are pure embodiments of the Daemonic. Undoubtedly, however, it arises within them; since the characters themselves are incapable of effectively countering the daemonic forces, the catastrophe is inevitable. Similarly, daemonic forces had found expression in the *Sonette*, in *Pandora* and in *Die Natürliche Tochter*, all written in the same period of Goethe's life. They had also been active in Goethe's life or at least in his imagination. In the political and social sphere, the French Revolution revealed the rise of forces of this kind. In France, a similar upheaval had taken place in the political and social sphere as occurred in the sphere of personal relations in *Die Wahlverwandtschaften*. Goethe was undoubtedly worried about the impact of the revolution on human affairs; he was aware that the revolution, and later Napoleon, had transformed social and political life. The connection between these political events and the novel may appear far-fetched, but it is not impossible that, for Goethe, the family could by way of analogy illustrate the problems raised by these upheavals, especially in so far as they affected individuals. There is no evidence for such an interpretation, though it would be consonant with Goethe's custom of describing wider issues in symbolic guise as he did in *Die Natürliche Tochter*. Terrible things can happen if men do not follow the laws of change and the natural rhythm of life. In other works, such as in the revolutionary dramas – *Der Bürgergeneral*, *Der Grosskophta*, *Die Aufgeregten* – Goethe sought to deal directly with these problems. The most mature attempt to come to terms with this problem is in *Die Wahlverwandtschaften*. It is his first large-scale completed work since *Hermann und Dorothea*. *Die Natürliche Tochter* was only the first part of a planned trilogy, and its basic tendency was different, since it described an attempt to restore inner equilibrium and protect the individual against the forces of the external world.

Goethe's starting point is not easy to discover. But we may find a hint in his emphasis on Christ's words:

> The very simple text of this extensive work is the words of Christ: Whoever looks at a woman to lust after her. . . . I don't know whether anyone has recognized them again in this paraphrase.[171]

Another remark recorded by Varnhagen von Ense also speaks for this interpretation. Varnhagen writes:

> ... Goethe once said to [General von] Rühle: I am a pagan? Now, did I not let Gretchen be executed and Ottilie die of hunger? Is this not Christian enough for them? Could they demand anything more Christian? That remark recalls the angry answer which he gave to Knebel, who entertained moral misgivings about *Die Wahlverwandtschaften.* I have written it for you, not for young girls.[172]

To view *Die Wahlverwandtschaften* as a Christian novel about marriage would certainly be mistaken. This does not take account of Goethe's irony. A more subtle interpretation of the biblical quotation signifies that to have committed a sinful act in thought means already to have sinned, so that there is no need to wait for the actual deed. Eduard and Charlotte sin when they commit adultery in imagination. But it would be wrong to impose this interpretation as the idea of the novel. Another remark of Goethe's recorded by Riemer is probably closer to the heart of the matter. He apparently said:

> His idea in the new novel *Die Wahlverwandtschaften* is to present social relationships and the conflicts caused by them in a symbolic manner.[173]

This conception of 'the idea' is of a more general nature; it is the thought that the chemical formulae of *Die Wahlverwandtschaften* can be transferred to human relations. Goethe wrote *Die Wahlverwandtschaften*, indeed, in the same period as *The Theory of Colours* (*Zur Farbenlehre*). Goethe himself, when he announced the publication of the novel, adumbrated this implicit connection:

> The continuation of his work in physics made the author produce this strange title. He must have noticed that natural science often uses moral analogies in order to bring experiences which are very remote from the sphere of human knowledge closer to our understanding, and he has thus wanted, in a moral case, to bring a chemical analogy back to its intellectual origins, especially since there is only *one* nature and since the traces of dark, passionate necessity, which can be obliterated only by the divine, and perhaps not even in this life, are found even in the realm of the serene freedom of man.[174]

However great the influence of *The Theory of Colours* had been, it must not be assumed that Goethe wanted to understand society from the point of view of pure natural science. He thought rather of stressing symbolic relations and of explaining the general nature of society and the relations between people within a community. While in *Werther* and the *Lehrjahre* he was preoccupied with the education of the individual, the whole structure of *Die Wahlverwandtschaften* focuses attention on the development of various individuals in the context of their relations with others.

Goethe had formulated the laws of nature in the most striking fashion when he spoke of the two main wheels of nature:

> of polarity and intensification. The former belonging to matter in so far as we see it in terms of matter, the latter in so far as we consider it from the standpoint of mind. Polarity is in a process of continuous attraction and repulsion; intensification, on the other hand, is in a process of continuous ascension. But just as matter can never exist without mind, so mind cannot exist or be effective without matter, so matter is able to achieve intensification just as mind cannot stop being attracted and repelled.[175]

This basic natural law of polarity and intensification can be applied to social life. The contrast between the characters in the novel produces tensions which can be considered from the point of view of attraction and repulsion, inclination and dislike. A sentence from a diary entry entitled 'Chromatic Reflections and Analogies' throws further light on this issue:[176]

> To love and to hate, to hope and to fear are only different states of our inner life, through which our mind either looks to the light or to the shade. If we look through this dense organic environment to the light we love and hope, if we look to darkness we hate and fear.[177]

There is, in the novel, much talk of love and hope, less of fear, none of hate.[178] This attitude is characteristic of Goethe, whose outlook on life was positive; the basic thought of a distribution of light and darkness in the novel can be ascertained by separating the constructive and destructive forces. Polarity need not necessarily be fruitful: here it even destroys life. Goethe hoped that this kinship with society and nature, poetry and science which characterizes the novel would help the appreciation of his work on natural science.

In a letter to Count Reinhard he wrote:

> Since you consider my Ottilie in so noble, so good, and so sensitive a manner, and also do justice to Eduard, who at least appears inestimable to me because he loves unconditionally, you will probably also appreciate the second part of the theory of colours and like it as much as the first part which found favour.[179]

Intensification is at work, too;* particularly Ottilie, and to a lesser extent Charlotte, experience spiritual intensification, while Eduard stagnates and is incapable of undergoing this process.

Goethe discerns the operation of laws in *Die Wahlverwandtschaften*, for this belief in the existence of laws underlies the novel: he utters this in *Euphrosyne*:

> Ach Natur, wie sicher und gross in allem erscheinst du!
> Himmel und Erde befolgt ewiges, festes Gesetz:
> Alles entsteht und vergeht nach Gesetz: doch über des Menschen
> Leben, dem köstlichen Schatz, herrschet ein schwankendes Los.[181]

In *Die Wahlverwandtschaften* man is subject to nature, but also possesses freedom.[182] The operation of law consists in the fact that in every literature, just as in life, men appear who are to some degree or other akin to one another. All these sympathies and connections are affinities, even elective affinities. Despite the unique, terrible action a general picture emerges.

* The concept of *Steigerung* (intensification) can be used here, for Goethe used this concept in relation to the development or control of a love which has gone beyond the mere natural impulse: 'The formula of *Steigerung* can be applied in the sphere of that which is aesthetic and moral.

Love, as it appears in modern life, is something intensified. It is no longer the single need and expression of nature, but also a being which is in itself refined, compact so to speak, and thus intensified.

It is foolish to reject this kind merely because it exists and can exist in a simple manner.'[180]

Law cannot be separated from the individual, for character contains law; action depends on the repetition of the same features of character and events which, only through repetition and through the attitudes of the persons, become subject to a universal law.[183]

This pattern of law, especially the law of polarity and intensification, forms the basis of *Die Wahlverwandtschaften.* The insight that life is developed according to natural laws determines Goethe's later thought. Even beauty if based on laws; such is the belief of German classicism:

> Beauty is a manifestation of the sacred laws of nature without which this phenomenon would be forever hidden.[184]

It is now a question of finding which laws underlie Goethe's last work. In *Wilhelm Meisters Wanderjahre*, an intensification of the more positive rather than the negative aspects continues the idea of the *Lehrjahre* that a man favoured by fortune is capable of pursuing his life successfully.

Notes

1. E. L. Stahl, 'Die Wahlverwandtschaften', *PEGS*, xv (1946), p. 88, calls it a dramatic novel, basing this appellation on the terminology used by Edwin Muir (*The Structure of the Novel*, London, 1938, p. 57).

2. Letter from Wieland to Charlotte Gessner, 21 November 1809 (G.A., 22, p. 579).

3. Letter to Karl Friedrich Zelter, 1 June 1809.

4. Conversation with Eckermann, 9 February 1829.

5. Conversation with Eckermann, 17 February 1830.

6. *Tag- und Jahreshefte 1809* (W.A., i, 36, p. 43).

7. Cf. André François-Poncet, *Les Affinités Électives de Goethe*, Paris, 1910, pp. 7 ff., for an account of this problem; cf. also Hans M. Wolff, *Goethe in der Periode der Wahlverwandtschaften, 1801–9*, Berne, 1952.

8. See ibid., p. 179.

9. See ibid., p. 180.

10. Cf. François-Poncet, pp. 37 ff.

11. W.A., iii, 3, p. 327.

12. *Tag- und Jahreshefte 1807* (W.A., i, 36, p. 28).

13. See W.A., ii, 8, p. 79; also Benno von Wiese, H.A., 6, pp. 680 ff., who lists several examples, many of which were written after the publication of the novel; Ewald Boucke, *Goethes Weltanschauung auf historischer Grundlage*, Stuttgart, 1907, pp. 361 f., quotes Goethe's diary of 15 June 1797 (W.A., iii, 2, p. 74).

14. Letter to Schiller, 23 October 1799.

15. Varnhagen von Ense, Diary entry 28 June 1843 (H.A., 6, p. 623).

16. Oskar Walzel, 'Goethes "Wahlverwandtschaften" im Rahmen ihrer Zeit', *GJB*, xxvii (1906), and François-Poncet, pp. 26 ff.

17. Ibid., pp. 29 ff.

18. Cf. Hans M. Wolff, *Goethe . . . der Wahlverwandtschaften*, pp. 179 f.

19. Keith Dickson, 'Spatial Concentration and Themes in *Die Wahlverwandtschaften*', *Forum for Modern Language Studies*, i (1965), p. 168.

20. Keith Dickson, 'The Temporal Structure of *Die Wahlverwandtschaften*', *GR*, xli (1966).

21. W.A., i, 20, p. 310 (ii, 9).

22. Dickson, in his perspicacious article 'The Temporal Structure . . .' erroneously assumes that it ends at the time of Ottilie's death, in autumn (cf. p. 172 and p. 178).

23. H. G. Barnes, 'Ambiguity in *Die Wahlverwandtschaften*', *The Era of Goethe*, Oxford, 1959, p. 12.

24. Conversation with Friedrich von Müller, 8 June 1821.

25. Karl R. Popper, *Logik der Forschung*, Vienna, 1935 (Engl. trans. *The Logic of Scientific Discovery*, London, 1959).

26. F. J. Stopp 'Ottilie und das "innere Licht" ', *German Studies presented to W. H. Bruford*, London, 1962, p. 117, writes: 'It is unlikely that critical discussion of Goethe's *Wahlverwandtschaften* will ever lead to a substantial degree of settled doctrine. For this the poet himself must largely be held responsible.'

27. H. G. Barnes, *Die Wahlverwandtschaften. A Literary Interpretation*, Oxford, 1967, an important book, reached me only after my manuscript had gone to press, so that I could make use of, and comment on, his findings only by reference in additional notes (see, however, my forthcoming review in *The Modern Language Review*). Barnes points out that there are, in fact, variations in the language. In his view, the customary narrative style is marked 'by a sparing use of epithets, by brevity and concreteness. Contrasting with this concreteness is the generalizing and abstract quality of his reflective style which becomes almost mannered in its tendency to amplification and reflection' (p. 8). He also notes that by the increasing use of adjectives and nouns, the

narration becomes more solemn in the second part (p. 12). In addition, there are lyrical descriptions in the novel which are placed in the mouths of the characters.

28. Cf. Lubbock, *The Craft of Fiction*, London, 1921, for an authoritative discussion of the relationship between the dialogue and narrative in fiction.

29. There are a large number of them in the novel, not necessarily spoken by the narrator; for a tentative list cf. Reiss, *Goethes Romane*, Berne and Munich, 1963, pp. 304–7.

30. Barnes (*Die Wahlverwandtschaften*, pp. 7 ff.) following Paul Stöcklein, *Wege zum späten Goethe*, Hamburg, 1949 (pp. 10 ff.) appears to believe that the narrator is telling a real story, but for the sake of the narration colours the narrative and adds heightening touches, and that he rearranges the historical order of events for more striking effect and for concealment. He considers the narrator to be a moralist (p. 13), and believes that 'those readers who unreservedly accept [his] point of view . . . find it necessary, when they come to interpret the novel, to have recourse to extrinsic criteria' (p. 26). Indeed 'one of the structural principles of the narrative lies in the contrast between the attitude of the narrator and the tendency of the fable' (p. 4). In Barnes' view, the narrator partially rationalizes what is, for Goethe, the ultimately mysterious process of nature. Barnes thinks that 'his worldly outlook and his conventional judgement do not always seem equal to the task of exploring and illuminating the mysteries of individuality' (p. 100). In fact, Barnes suggests that the narrator, as a result of his moralistic outlook, falsifies the story and provides, to some extent, misleading, tendentious accounts of the characters (cf. p. 27). I cannot accept this ingenious, though extreme view. Barnes is, of course, quite right in pointing out that the narrator is not in sympathy with Eduard's conduct. This is not surprising, for the narrator takes a detached view of life, judiciously appraising human conduct according to principles of sense and regard for others, while Eduard's actions are prompted by the desire to satisfy emotional needs. But Eduard cannot claim either Werther's youth or Tasso's genius as an excuse for his single-minded pursuit of emotional satisfaction. To suggest, as Barnes does, in the wake of Nietzsche, that Eduard possesses a profundity approaching that of Goethe, is misleading (p. 127). While his unconditional devotion to love admittedly indicates profundity, his inability to understand others, even Ottilie, reveals a limitation of mind which cannot be ignored. Barnes is, to some extent, aware of this aspect of Eduard's personality, for he writes: 'as a man of feeling Eduard can be compared to Werther and Tasso; but whereas these have an indubitably personal style Eduard in moments of deep feeling is made to express himself in

borrowed phrases.' This cannot fail to cast doubt on the quality of his feeling and the sincerity of his emotion towards Charlotte (p. 105). But Barnes soon rallies again to Eduard's defence, belittling the relevance of these characteristics and claiming that the narrator jeopardizes Eduard's authenticity (p. 106).

31. W.A., i, 20, p. 196 (i, 18).

32. W.A., i, 20, p. 199 (ii, 1).

33. W.A., i, 20, p. 3 (i, 1).

34. W.A., i, 20, p. 3 (i, 1).

35. W.A., i, 20, p. 22 (i, 2).

36. W.A., i, 20, p. 23 (i, 2).

37. W.A., i, 20, p. 14 (i, 2).

38. W.A., i, 20, p. 196 (i, 18).

39. W.A., i, 20, p. 212 (ii, 2).

40. W.A., i, 20, p. 416 (ii, 18).

41. W.A., i, 20, p. 416 (ii, 18).

42. I cannot agree with the view of Kurt May who, in 'Goethes "Wahlverwandtschaften" als tragischer Roman', *Form und Bedeutung. Interpretationen zur Deutschen Dichtung des 18. und 19. Jahrhunderts*, Stuttgart, 1957, p. 110, speaks of a second type or of a style of language of a second kind. These groups of sentences mentioned by him appear to be merely variations, though significant variations, within the same style.

43. H.A., 12, p. 367, No. 21.

44. J. M. Ellis, 'Names in *Faust* und *Die Wahlverwandtschaften*', *Seminar. A Journal of Germanic Studies*, i (1965), p. 29; L. A. Willoughby, 'Name ist Schall und Rauch', *GLL*, xvi (1963), p. 304; Paul Stöcklein, *Wege zum späten Goethe*, Hamburg, 1949, pp. 73 ff.

45. Goethe states in *Dichtung und Wahrheit* (iii, 11) that, as a result of a visit to the shrine of St Odilia in the Vosges mountains from Strassburg during his student days (1770–1), the image which he formed of this saint and her name imprinted themselves so deeply on his mind that he kept them in his memory until he gave both image and name to 'one of his later, but not for this reason less beloved daughters who was received so favourably by pious and pure hearts.' (W.A., i, 28, p. 79) cf. also Stopp, 'Ottilie . . .' for a discussion of the parallels between St Odilia and the heroine.

46. Cf. Willoughby, 'The image of the "Wanderer" and the "Hut" in Goethe's Poetry', *ÉG*, vi (1951); Emmel, *Weltklage und Bild der Welt in der Dichtung Goethes*, Weimar, 1957, pp. 271 ff.; Barnes, 'Ambiguity in *Die Wahlverwandtschaften*', pp. 6 f. also mentions the image of inclination; cf. also Walther Killy, 'Wirklichkeit und Kunstcharakter. Goethe: Die Wahlverwandtschaften', *Wirklichkeit und Kunstcharakter.*

Neun Romane des 19. Jahrhunderts, Munich, 1963, pp. 19 ff.; this problem is also discussed in a somewhat different manner by Wolfgang Staroste, 'Raumgestaltung und Raumsymbolik in Goethes *Wahlverwandtschaften*', *ÉG*, xvi (1961).

47. See Killy, *Wirklichkeit und Kunstcharakter*, p. 32.

48. W.A., i, 42, p. 91.

49. W.A., i, 20, p. 5 (i, 1).

50. Dickson, 'Spatial Concentration and Themes . . .'.

51. Cf. Emmel, p. 271, whose emphasis on this point, though essentially right, goes sometimes a little too far.

52. Cf. Dickson, 'Spatial Concentration and Themes . . .'.

53. See F. J. Stopp, ' "Ein wahrer Narziss". Reflections on the Eduard–Ottilie relations in Goethe's *Wahlverwandtschaften*', *PEGS*, xxix (1960), p. 72.

54. Cf. Staroste, 'Raumgestaltung . . .', p. 220; see also Dickson 'Spatial Concentration and Themes . . .', p. 167.

55. See Dickson, 'Spatial Concentration and Themes . . .', p. 168.

56. Cf. ibid., p. 169; Staroste, 'Raumgestaltung . . .', p. 215; see von Wiese, H.A., 6, p. 679.

57. Cf. the remarks on gardening in Goethe's and Schiller's joint draft *Über den Dilettantismus*: 'The love of gardening goes on to something endless. . . . It perpetuates the ruling misdemeanour of the age, of wishing to be unconditional and lawless in the aesthetic sphere and to indulge in arbitrary imagination, since, unlike other arts, it does not agree with correction or discipline.' (W.A., i, 47, p. 310); cf. also von Wiese, H.A., 6, p. 687.

58. Cf. Hans Jürgen Geerdts, *Goethes Wahlverwandtschaften*, Weimar, 1958, pp. 39 f.

59. Cf. Paul Stöcklein, *Wege zum späten Goethe*.

60. See Stopp, 'Ein wahrer Narziss . . .', p. 59.

61. See Theodor Lockemann, 'Der Tod in Goethes "Wahlverwandtschaften" ', *JbGG*, xix (1933), pp. 37 ff., for a thorough discussion of this subject.

62. See Dickson, 'Spatial Concentration and Themes . . .', p. 170.

63. See T. Lockemann, p. 46; cf. also von Wiese, H.A., 6, p. 678.

64. See Stopp, 'Ein wahrer Narziss . . .' ed. cit., p. 78.

65. Ibid.

66. W.A., i, 20, p. 310 (ii, 9).

67. Cf. T. Lockemann, p. 54.

68. W.A., i, 20, p. 345 (ii, 12).

69. Friedrich Hebbel, 'Vorwort zu Maria Magdalena', *Sämtliche Werke* (ed. R. M. Werner) xi, Berlin, 1904, p. 42.

70. W.A., i, 20, p. 133 (ii, 12).

71. Cf. J. Havuck, 'Psychoanalytisches aus und über Goethes "Wahlverwandtschaften"', *Imago* i, Vienna, 1913, p. 508; also Staiger, *Goethe*, Zurich, 1952–9, ii, p. 494.

72. W.A., i, 20, p. 145 (i, 13).

73. W.A., i, 20, p. 213 (ii, 2).

74. W.A., i, 20, p. 249 (ii, 5).

75. W.A., i, 20, pp. 310 f. (ii, 9).

76. W.A., i, 36, p. 391.

77. W.A., i, 41, 1, pp. 216.

78. W.A., i, 41, 1, pp. 219 f.

79. W.A., i, 41, 1, pp. 220 f.

80. Letter to Windischmann, 28 December 1812.

81. Cf. Kurt May, 'Die Wahlverwandtschaften als tragischer Roman', *JbFDH* (1936–40), pp. 150 ff.

82. Cf. Grete Schaeder, *Gott und Welt. Drei Kapitel Goethescher Weltanschauung*, Hameln, 1947, p. 301.

83. Stöcklein, *Wege zum späten Goethe*, p. 13.

84. The entries in Ottilie's diary can, so Barnes (*Die Wahlverwandtschaften*, pp. 135 ff.) argues, be linked to the action. They do, however, reveal a consistent inner development in Ottilie.

85. Conversation with Sulpiz Boisserée on the journey from Karlsruhe to Heidelberg, 5 October 1815.

86. W.A., i, 20, p. 213 (ii, 2).

87. W.A., i, 20, p. 311 (ii, 9).

88. W.A., i, 20, p. 213 (ii, 2).

89. W.A., i, 20, p. 215 (ii, 2).

90. W.A., i, 20, p. 224 (ii, 3).

91. W.A., i, 20, p. 262 (ii, 5).

92. Cf. H. G. Barnes, 'Bildhafte Darstellung in den Wahlverwandtschaften', *DVLG*, xxx (1956), p. 47.

93. W.A., i, 20, p. 224 (ii, 3); cf. also Stopp, 'Ottilie und das "innere Licht"'.

94. W.A., i, 20, p. 241 (ii, 4).

95. W.A., i, 20, p. 241 (ii, 4).

96. W.A., i, 20, p. 241 (ii, 4).

97. Staiger, *Goethe*, ii, p. 491, considers Ottilie to be someone who at first has not recognized the difference between good and evil and whose eyes are opened only later on, and who undergoes a metamorphosis analogous to the one depicted by Goethe in his essay on the *Die Metamorphose der Pflanzen*.

98. W.A., i, 20, p. 260 (ii, 5).

99. W.A., i, 20, p. 260 (ii, 5).

100. W.A., i, 20, p. 262 (ii, 5).

101. W.A., i, 20, p. 292 (ii, 7).

102. See Geerdts, p. 50.

103. Cf. W. H. Bruford, *Germany in the Eighteenth Century*, Cambridge, 1935, who describes the general situation of the nobility in a very striking manner.

104. Cf. Alfred G. Steer, *Goethe's Social Philosophy as revealed in Campagne in Frankreich and Belagerung von Mainz*, University of North Carolina Studies in Germanic Languages and Literatures, 15, Chapel Hill, 1955, who stresses the importance of the family in Goethe's social thought.

105. Heinrich Theodor Rötscher, *Die Wahlverwandtschaften von Goethe in ihrer weltgeschichtlichen Bedeutung, ihrem sittlichen und künstlerischen Werte nach entwickelt. Abhandlungen zur Philosophie der Kunst*, ii, Berlin, 1838, pp. 16 ff., specifically took this view.

106. Conversation with Eckermann, 30 March 1824.

107. Cf. May, 'Die Wahlverwandtschaften . . .', p. 146, who states that nowhere in the action is the ideal marriage represented.

108. W.A., i, 20, p. 112 (i, 10).

109. Cf. Edith Aulhorn, 'Der Aufbau von Goethes "Wahlverwandtschaften" ', *Zeitschrift für den Deutschen Unterricht*, xxxii (1918), p. 351.

110. Cf. Michael Oakeshott, 'Rational Conduct', *Rationalism in Politics and Other Essays*, London, 1962, for a criticism of the mistaken belief that we can apply general rational principles to life without possessing the necessary experience.

111. W.A., i, 20, p. 107 (ii, 9).

112. Barnes believes that Charlotte is not opposed in principle to divorce, since she lives in a society which tolerates it (pp. 179 ff.). I cannot agree with this view that by tolerating the worldly conduct of others she implicitly agrees to follow a similar course herself.

113. W.A., i, 20, p. 370 (ii, 14).

114. Barnes (*Die Wahlverwandtschaften*) thinks that Ottilie comes for a while at least to accept the Count's worldly views on marriage and divorce.

115. W.A., i, 20, p. 12 (i, 1).

116. Barnes (*Die Wahlverwandtschaften*) appropriately calls prefiguration the method of adumbrating events before they happen. He points out that prefiguration is also a means of irony, because when events actually happen, they occur in a different context. In his view, they mainly foreshadow the last stages of Ottilie's life, for instance, her inclination to abstain from food; similarly, the girl unwittingly dragged into society by Luciane forecasts Ottilie's own position at the end of the novel. Another example is provided by Ottilie's reference in her diary to the vain attempts of hermits to escape from the world when

a task awaits them there. Prefiguration, and its corollary, recapitulation, in fact afford insights into that which would otherwise have remained hidden.

117. Cf. *Graef*, p. 453, 'For this one phrase "entertaining . . . she hasn't opened her mouth yet" (W.A., i, 20, p. 65, ii, 6) I [Wieland], if I were the Duke of Weimar, would give Goethe an estate as a present.' (Reported by B. R. Abeken, see H.A., 6, p. 652).

118. Paul Stöcklein, 'Stil und Geist der "Wahlverwandtschaften" ', *Zeitschrift für Deutsche Philologie*, lxxxi (1951), pp. 56 f.

119. Stopp, 'Ein wahrer Narziss . . .', pp. 89 f.

120. W.A., i, 20, p. 397 (ii, 17).

121. W.A., i, 20, p. 263 (ii, 5).

122. W.A., i, 20, p. 239 (ii, 4).

123. Cf. Staroste, 'Raumgestaltung'.

124. W.A., i, 20, p. 223 (ii, 3). Stopp, 'Ein wahrer Narziss . . .', points out that this applies also to the love which he has inspired.

125. W.A., i, 20, p. 189 (i, 18).

126. Emmel, p. 301; Stopp, 'Ein wahrer Narziss . . .', p. 83.

127. Barnes, 'Bildhafte Darstellung . . .', pp. 54 ff., has convincingly shown this aspect of Luciane's character. He ascribes to her an ironic function.

128. W.A., i, 20, p. 262 (ii, 5).

129. Cf. Barnes, 'Bildhafte Darstellung . . .', pp. 67 f.

130. Cf. ibid., pp. 57 ff.

131. Cf. *Goethes Werke*, ed. Oskar Walzel, 13, Festausgabe, Leipzig, 1926, p. 23; cf. also Barnes, 'Bildhafte Darstellung . . .', p. 41.

132. Ibid., p. 52 f.

133. Letter to Karl Friedrich von Reinhard, 21 February 1810.

134. Rudolf Abeken, 'Über Goethes Wahlverwandtschaften', *Morgenblatt für gebildete Stände*, 22, 23 and 24 January, 1810, quoted by *Graef*, op. cit., i, 1, pp. 438–47.

135. Karl Friedrich Wilhelm Solger, 'Über die Wahlverwandtschaften', quoted by *Graef*, i, 1, pp. 474–80.

136. The most important treatise in which a different view is expressed is Walter Benjamin's 'Goethes Wahlverwandtschaften', *Neue Deutsche Beiträge*, ii, 1 (1924), pp. 38 ff. (reprinted in *Schriften*, i, Frankfurt/Main, 1955, pp. 112 ff.). On the whole, most critics followed Abeken and Solger, cf., for instance, particularly Karl Vietor, *Goethe*, Berne, 1949, p. 207, May, 'Goethes Wahlverwandtschaften . . .' and 'Die Wahlverwandtschaften . . .'; and von Wiese H.A., 6. Goethe himself called Johanna Schopenhauer's *Gabriele* (1820) a 'tragic novel' (W.A., i, 41, 2, p. 7), and his comments on this novel recall *Die Wahlverwandtschaften*.

137. Cf. François-Poncet. The critical writings on *Die Wahlverwandtschaften* contain many analyses of the characters, but André François-Poncet's account still remains the most important, although more than half a century has elapsed since its appearance and although its author was only twenty-two at the time of publication. In detail, his views require modification, but in broad outline they command assent. I am greatly indebted to this book for the following comments.

138. Ibid., p. 59. Barnes (*Die Wahlverwandtschaften*), is the first to challenge this view on fundamental grounds and request a basic reappraisal.

139. Conversation with Eckermann, 21 January 1827.

140. François-Poncet, p. 64, who considers him, by way of contrast to Werther, to be a superficial person.

141. W.A., i, 20, p. 122 (i, 10).

142. Barnes (*Die Wahlverwandtschaften*, p. 108) is right in pointing out that one of Eduard's main characteristics is an 'innocence of the heart' which is, in fact, corroborated by his apparent principal defect, impatience. For his impatience reveals that his emotions are not ruled by calculation. It is, however, difficult to agree with the suggestion that, in the closing stages of the novel, Eduard's impatience is a functional device used by the narrator for the purpose of showing how Eduard's character becomes ennobled by Ottilie's holy love (p. 119); for Ottilie, who is born to teach, teaches Eduard perfect love. Surely at the end of the novel Eduard and Ottilie remain mentally apart, although their love never abates and they are at peace only in each other's presence. But Ottilie's silence, in my view, precludes communion of mind and Eduard never understands the reason for her silence, let alone her death. Emotionally, they remain as close as ever, but spiritually they move on different levels. While Ottilie achieves perfection, Eduard's love remains an imitation thereof; like an artist he remains 'in the antechamber of what he has created true love' (cf. Stopp, 'Ein wahrer Narziss . . .', p. 85).

143. Walter Weber, 'Zum Hauptmann in Goethes "Wahlverwandtschaften" ', *G*, xxi (1959), p. 291; Barnes perspicaciously points out that the narrator's reluctance to supply a coherent account of the Captain's antecedents (p. 189) makes it impossible for us to be absolutely sure whether the Captain is the disappointed bridegroom in the tale *Die wunderlichen Nachbarskinder*, and we are left to conjecture why such a deserving and competent person should, in the prime of life, be more or less dependent on the charity of his friends (p. 190). The Captain appears to be laconic and yet apparently, in the pursuits of his own interests, betrays confidences to Eduard and Charlotte without showing signs of remorse. Even the significance of the narrator's persistent use of his title, appropriately and perhaps ironically changed after

his promotion, is not clear, though it might well mean much (p. 195).

144. See François-Poncet, p. 67, for these observations.

145. Barnes points out that Charlotte's character is more complex than might appear at first sight. While she possesses intelligence and reason, strength of purpose and great social gifts (p. 161), she lacks spontaneity and tends to apply general principles, often with disastrous results (p. 162). At times convention matters too much to her and she does not appear to evince any profound feelings as a mother (p. 175). On the other hand, I cannot agree with Barnes' contention that Charlotte's central defect is 'lack of true love' (p. 186). To suggest this is to argue that Eduard's and Ottilie's love is the only kind of true love instead of maintaining the more convincing view that there are many different kinds of love portrayed in the novel. Nor can I agree with Barnes' other contention that the narrator does less than justice to 'Charlotte's philanthropic intentions and tireless well-doing' (p. 187). The narrator's portrait of Charlotte appears to me sympathetic, as, indeed, Barnes suggests elsewhere.

146. Ibid., p. 69.

147. See E. L. Stahl, 'Die Wahlverwandtschaften', p. 84. 'In Ottilie . . . and in her alone tragic suffering necessarily ends in death.' Stahl's argument is most perceptive. He also states: 'Ottilie unwittingly transgresses and then atones first by an attitude that reveals, as Schiller called it *Erhabenheit der Fassung* (passive sublimity) and then by an act displaying *Erhabenheit der Handlung* (active sublimity).'

148. François-Poncet, p. 78 f.

149. Ibid., p. 84.

150. Review of Johanna Schopenhauer, *Gabriele* (W.A., i, 41, 2, p. 6).

151. Letter to Karl Friedrich Zelter, 29 January 1830.

152. Conversation with Eckermann, 21 July 1827.

153. W.A., i, 41, 2, p. 7.

154. Cf. von Wiese, H.A., 6, p. 669.

155. Barnes (*Die Wahlverwandtschaften*, p. 64, p. 159 f., p. 206) considers Ottilie a saint, although he has to admit that the narrator only once uses this appellation at the end of the novel. Yet the passage referred to, like the whole conclusion, may well be ambiguous, given the narrator's customary ironic manner. Her love, indeed, is 'incomparable', 'as the nightingale seems to transcend her class' (p. 64) yet it is difficult unambiguously to consider her love as saintly in the orthodox use of the term; it could, however, be called sacred or holy in so far as genuine love reflects the Divine. Goethe, in fact, frequently described love in this way most probably for that reason. So Barnes appears to adopt an extreme position when he suggests that Ottilie 'reveals the meaning of

this seemingly inscrutable novel' by prefiguring her holy love and Eduard's perfect response when she expresses her hopes of the *Gehülfe* [Assistant] (p. 206).

156. Conversation with Sulpiz Boisserée, 5 October 1815. Cf. note 85. Admittedly the narrator also calls her '*die Heilige*' (the holy one) (ii, 18) and 'celestial' child (ii, 18), but his remarks are frequently ambiguous.

157. Letter to Heinrich Meyer, 27 April 1810.

158. Varnhagen von Ense, op. cit.

159. W.A., i, 20, p. 131 (i, 11).

160. Cf. Stopp, 'Ein wahrer Narziss . . .', p. 56 f.

161. W.A., i, 47, p. 310.

162. Cf. Stopp, 'Ein wahrer Narziss . . .', p. 56.

163. Cf. idem.

164. W.A., i, 20, p. 8 (i, 1).

165. Staiger, *Goethe*, ii, pp. 520 ff.

166. Conversation with Eckermann, 6 May 1827.

167. *Aus den Tag- und Jahresheften 1819*, Weimar, 1822 or January 1823 (W.A., i, 36, pp. 43 f.).

168. Cf. Hans M. Wolff, *Goethe in der Periode der Wahlverwandtschaften*, and *Goethes Novelle 'Die Wahlverwandtschaften'* . . . , who provides the most glaring instance of such errors.

169. W.A., i, 2, p. 3: '*Powerful Surprise*. A stream rustles away from the hall of rocks enveloped in clouds in haste to join the ocean. Despite the diverse reflections as it drops from abyss to abyss, it moves on irresistibly to the valley. But the nymph Oreas, whirling mountains and woods in her train, plunges in, daemonic, for her pleasure and bars its course, forming a wide basin. The wave breaks into spray and starts back and loses momentum, drinking its own water. Its striving towards Father Ocean is now arrested. The wave trembles and rests, dyked back into a lake; stars, reflected in the water, look at the flickering of the waves breaking against the rock: a new Life.'

170. W.A., i, 29, p. 176 f. (*The Autobiography of Goethe*, ii, Trans. the Rev. A. S. W. Morrison, London, 1849, p. 158 f.); cf. also Walter Muschg, 'Goethes Glaube an das Dämonische', *DVLG*, xxxii, 1958, pp. 321 ff.

171. Letter to Johann Stanislaus Zauper, 7 September 1821.

172. Varnhagen von Ense, op. cit.

173. Friedrich Riemer, diary entry, 28 August 1808.

174. W.A., i, 41, i, p. 34.

175. W.A., ii, 11, p. 11.

176. Cf. Grete Schaeder, p. 294.

177. Diary entry, 25 May 1807 (W.A., iii, 3, pp. 213 f.).

178. Henry Hatfield 'Towards the Interpretation of *Die Wahlver-*

wandtschaften', *GR*, xxiii, 1948, points out that 'Goethe's attitude towards the love between Eduard and Ottilie becomes increasingly sympathetic as the end approaches' (p. 113).

179. Letter to Karl Friedrich von Reinhard, 21 February 1810.

180. Conversation with Riemer, 24 March 1807; cf. Elizabeth M. Wilkinson, '*Tasso — ein gesteigerter Werther* in the Light of Goethe's Principle of *Steigerung*', ed. cit.

181. W.A., i, 1, pp. 283 f.: 'Nature, how steadfast and great you are in all your manifestations. Heaven and earth obey a fixed eternal law. Everything emerges and perishes according to law, but a vacillating fate rules over man's life; life, that precious treasure.'

182. Cf. Martin Sommerfeld, 'Goethes Wahlverwandtschaften im neunzehnten Jahrhundert', *Goethe in Umwelt und Folge. Gesammelte Studien*, Leiden, 1935, p. 211.

183. Gundolf, *Goethe*, pp. 554 ff.

184. H.A., 12, p. 467, No. 719.

Wilhelm Meisters Wanderjahre

THIS late work is completely different from Goethe's earlier novels. It does not look like a work of art at all, but like a rag-bag of stories, reports and aphorisms, only loosely connected with Wilhelm Meister. Many of Goethe's own references to the *Wanderjahre* confirm this view: 'a strange work',[1] 'a collective undertaking, so to speak',[2] 'only put together for the purpose of linking disparate entities',[3] 'a hazardous enterprise',[4] 'a mere aggregate',[5] 'a mélange'[6] and so does its language, which is as varied as the contents.

Problems different from those of the earlier novels arise. The question can be asked whether the *Wanderjahre* can be called a novel at all. Perhaps it is merely a collection of short stories and fragments linked together only by the fact that it was written, during the last three decades of his life by the same author, who had rather wilfully decided to put them together under the same title. Are the different parts only accidentally put together? Goethe himself described the work as a novel, even if only in the version of 1821,[7] but need we, or can we, agree with this view? Is it an artistic failure? Goethe thought not, but most critics have disagreed.[8] As there is no strictly organized unity of action, it is not surprising that the novel was not enthusiastically received.[9] Pustkuchen's unfortunate imitation follows upon the first, shorter version of 1821 in two volumes.[10] But that work did not have the powerful effect of Nicolai's parody *Freuden des jungen Werthers*[11] (*The Joys of young Werther*), because the *Wanderjahre* did not have the same impact as *Werther*.

It is not surprising that it was received without enthusiasm and then neglected. Only recently has interest in it arisen,[12] because the modern experimental novel has led to great interest in this art form.[13]

The *Wanderjahre* is divided into three books. The second and the third are each followed by a number of aphorisms and by an important poem, the former by *Betrachtungen im Sinne der Wanderer* (*Reflections in the Spirit of the Wanderers*) and *Vermächtnis*, and the latter by *Aus Makariens Archiv* (*From Makarie's Archive*) and *Im ernsten Beinhaus*. Wilhelm appears in all three books: the main action concerns him and his relations with a number of the characters, and provides a framework for a series of short stories which often overlap, and for interjected letters, maxims and comments by the narrator. It is difficult, at times even tedious to read, because there are no outstanding characters and the narrative does not progress quickly and flowingly: it is like a stream which the onlooker can only see from time to time, and in between is hidden by hills and rocks.

Half the novel is devoted to the experiences of Wilhelm, Felix and Hersilie,[14] whose lives, however, are not nearly so closely intertwined as are those of the four main characters in *Die Wahlverwandtschaften*. Other characters step into the foreground from time to time.

Much of the action is compressed into a few pages and there are then many pages of reflection on the action. It is perhaps no accident that several of the aphorisms are devoted to *Tristram Shandy*, that most idiosyncratic of eighteenth-century novels.

At the beginning of the novel, we meet Wilhelm Meister as a wanderer with his son Felix. He has taken a vow never to spend more than three nights in any one place. On his travels, he meets first of all a carpenter whose life resembles that of St Joseph, and who is therefore called St Joseph the Second. He then encounters Jarno, now called 'Montan' because he lives in the mountains devoting himself to the study of nature, and hears his views on nature and education. His next visit is to the house of a man called the uncle, where Felix, now an adolescent, falls in love with Hersilie, the uncle's niece. He observes the uncle's philanthropic way of life. Hersilie tells a story, *Die Pilgernde Törin* (*The Foolish Woman on Pilgrimage*), about a girl who revenges herself for her experiences at the hands of a man by arousing the desires of a father and his son without any intention of showing them any affection. On leaving the uncle's estate, Wilhelm is given the story *Wer ist der Verräter?* (*Who is the Traitor?*) to read, a love-story which, after some confusion, ends happily. Wilhelm goes on to the estate of Makarie, an elderly woman of impressive spiritual power. We hear the story of how Lenardo, a young nephew of Makarie's and of the uncle's, is looking for the daughter of a tenant whom he thinks he has wronged by acting on his uncle's instructions. Wilhelm promises to look for her, but here this tale [*Das nussbraune Mädchen* (*The Nut-brown Maid*)] breaks off. In the last chapter of the first book, Wilhelm calls on a wise old man called the collector, who lives alone but knows all kinds of people and tells him of the Pedagogic Province.

In this province, the first chapters of the second book are set. They describe a utopian world where life is organized according to an educational theory based on reverence. A long short story *Der Mann von funfzig Jahren* (*The Man of Fifty*) is interpolated. This story tells of the love of a young girl, Hilarie, for a man of fifty, the Major, and the love of the Major's son, Flavio, for a beautiful widow older than himself. But nature asserts her rights: Flavio and Hilarie discover their love for one another, the Major has to accept that youth prevails over age, but is perhaps consoled by a hint that the beautiful widow and he will finally come together.

Wilhelm now decides to take up medicine, and for this purpose is allowed to give up his vow to wander. After a visit to Lake Maggiore, where problems of art are discussed, he is joined by Flavio and Hilarie, the Major and the beautiful widow, who now appear no longer to be characters of a story but also belong to the world of the main action. Wilhelm learns that the Society of the Tower is planning an emigration to America. On a second visit to the Pedagogic Province, Wilhelm finds Felix considerably matured, witnesses a festival, and explains to Jarno-Montan that, as a boy, he had made friends with a fisherman's son who was subsequently drowned, and that his interest in medicine had grown out of this accident. A collection of aphorisms and a poem follow.

In the third book Wilhelm decides to join the emigrants, whose leader is Lenardo, as a surgeon. There follow excerpts from Lenardo's diary and two stories, *Die neue Melusine* (*The New*

Melusine) and *Die gefährliche Wette* (*The Dangerous Wager*). Lenardo finds the nutbrown maid, who has become a mature, capable woman. Wilhelm meets *Odoard*, a governor of a province, who has organized a group of people who do not wish to emigrate, but want to find a new way of life in their homeland, in Europe. In the fragmentary story *Nicht zu weit* (*Not too far*) we hear about Odoard's unhappy marriage and his love for a princess. The emigrants pay a visit to Makarie and learn more about her spiritual power. Felix is rebuffed by Hersilie. He rides off madly in search of his father, and falls from his horse into a river on which Wilhelm is sailing. He is saved by Wilhelm, who puts his knowledge of medicine to good use. The story ends here, except for a collection of aphorisms and a poem. This disjointed, fragmentary account of Wilhelm's life and education constitutes the plot, such as it is, of which an inevitably rather summary account has to be given.

The plot, not uncharacteristic of Goethe, took a long time to evolve; for soon after the completion of the *Lehrjahre*, Goethe began to toy with the writing of the *Wanderjahre*,[15] but he did not set about his task seriously for some time. In 1807, he wrote a number of stories which were to feature in the novel: *St Joseph der Zweite*, *Die neue Melusine*, *Die gefährliche Wette*, and *Die pilgernde Törin*, which was, in fact, a translation from a French tale published anonymously; he also wrote parts of *Der Mann von funfzig Jahren* and *Das nussbraune Mädchen* and much of the account given in Lenardo's diary. *Die Wahlverwandtschaften* also belonged to this period. Almost all these stories in some way or other illustrate the problem of passion.[16]

Although Goethe expanded and completed *Die Wahlverwandtschaften*, he did not carry on with the writing of *Die Wanderjahre* for another ten years. In 1820 he took up his task again and fairly quickly published a volume called *Die Wanderjahre, Teil I* (Part I) in 1821.[17] This first version is hardly read today. It has since been published only once, in 1921 on the occasion of the centenary of its first publication,[18] and is now out of print again. It is clearly a fragment, for only the first part of the novel was published; the second part never appeared, for when Goethe started to revise the novel for publication in 1825, he decided to alter it considerably. The first version differs greatly from the second;[19] indeed so greatly that it is almost possible to speak of two different novels.[20]

In the first version, the *Wilhelm Meister* plot is not only less extensive, but two of the major tales, *Der Mann von funfzig Jahren* and *Das nussbraune Mädchen*, are not completed, nor is there a word of the Felix–Hersilie sub-plot, and Lenardo, as a result, plays a much less significant role. Wilhelm has fewer conversations with Montan. We hear less of Lenardo's (and Hersilie's) uncle and virtually nothing of Makarie. Above all, the novel tells the story of men who wander, but do so without a goal in sight. So Wilhelm has not come to a destination in wandering; he has not settled in a profession, nor does any decision loom in sight. He does not think yet of foregoing other activities in order to be able to carry out a definite fruitful task which suits men and which he has deliberately chosen. Nor does he emigrate or even contemplate emigration. In fact, emigration is denounced as a whim undertaken in the deceptive expectation of a better life, for wherever we go, we still have to live in a limited world. It is, so we learn, better to give up the idea of emigrating and merely to wander in the hope of returning to the starting place as a better and wiser man. There is no suggestion that renunciation is a specific activity to be carried on within the framework of a special association. Nor is there any mention of the opposite movement, constituted by a league of settlers who form an association in their native country under the leadership of Odoard to carry out fruitful activity at home, nor of the technological world adumbrated in Lenardo's report. The second version is also greatly enriched by its account of the lives of two old people, Lenardo's uncle and Makarie, so that the world is also seen from the angle of old people. Science and technology are given more space: Lenardo and Wilhelm are interested in them; Jarno-Montan and the astronomer expound scientific principles; Makarie provides a forum for scientific discussion. The two collections of aphorisms added to the second version indicate the level of thought on which this discussion is conducted. The two important poems added, *Vermächtnis* and *Im ernsten Beinhaus*, suggest a symbolic vision of life and thus extend the scope of the novel. A more diversified stylistic spectrum corresponds to the richer content, while in the first version there are only two stylistic modes, the vivid narrative style of the interpolated tale and the more matter-of-fact prose of the main action.

To sum up, the second version is significantly richer, more diversified and more complete than the first version. It affords more ways of looking at the world, it reveals greater detachment, greater awareness of the complexity of life and thus greater objectivity.

The biographical element is remote. Undoubtedly, Goethe's interest in science is reflected in Wilhelm's decision to become a surgeon and in various conversations and aphorisms. The account of the spinners and weavers is closely based on a report given to Goethe at his request by his friend Meyer, the art historian, from which he quotes some passages *verbatim*. The Pedagogic Province owes much to Pestalozzi and von Fellenberg, the two Swiss educationists,[21] but its philosophical and religious ideas go back to a tradition of thought derived from Cicero[22] and St Augustine.[23] Goethe's deepening philosophical approach to life unmistakably leaves its mark on the aphorisms intercalated in the novel, some of which are translations from Hippocrates and Plotinus, from Richard Griffith and Lawrence Sterne.[24] Several times the story of an ageing man who falls in love with a young girl is told; this situation obviously occupied Goethe's imagination in his late fifties and in his sixties and is closely related to his own experience. His scientific interests and his wide reading have inevitably left their mark, too; there are also allusions to the Apocrypha.[25] Visual impressions gained in Italy may also have been models, for the landscape of the Pedagogic Province recalls the scenery around Vicenza,[26] while some of the sacred buildings of the Pedagogic Province resemble the Lateran.[27] But apart from these instances, the novel does not appear to reveal definite points of contact with his life.

The style of the novel no less than its structure shows that Goethe no longer aimed at creating an outwardly coherent work, but rather at doing justice to various aspects of life which confronted him. It is true that the novel was not all written at the same time. The short stories were mostly written at an earlier date than the Makarie chapters, and in a much more sensuous language. These later chapters are reflective in character, and the style is correspondingly less concrete and immediate.

Much, indeed the greater part, of the novel is written in a careful, balanced prose which differs from Goethe's classical prose, but is very close to it.[28] Main clauses predominate. However complex the subsidiary clauses, they are strictly subordinated to the main clause. The style is weighty, but not awkward. In contrast, the narrative prose is lighter, smoother, livelier and moves at a faster speed.

This development of classical prose is one of the stylistic features of the *Wanderjahre*. Another is the return, on a higher plane, to the language of the *Sturm und Drang* period. Goethe, for instance, describes Flavio's sudden return home, when he is greatly perturbed at being repulsed by the beautiful widow, with an immediacy of language which recalls his youthful manner; yet it is different. It reflects the detachment of a mature vision, and is thus closely akin to other prose forms of his old age. Passion is veiled by contemplation. In a similar manner, he handles subtle psychological events through the medium of delicate lyric poetry. But these spurts do not last. Just as Flavio is quickly restored to health, so the language returns to normal in the matter-of-fact speech of the narrator, who is satisfied merely to report. At times he does so very concisely, in his brevity recalling the language of Goethe's *Annalen* (also called *Tag- und Jahreshefte*), the concentrated continuation of his autobiography, where he compresses the events of each year into a few sentences.

The culmination of prose writing, however, is found in the Makarie chapters. The language is lucid but abstract and subtle. It conveys scientific knowledge in a most concise form, but it can also hint at the most profound themes without attempting to plumb their depths. It shows Makarie as belonging to the most spiritual beings of the cosmos. It uses antithesis to great effect to describe the contrast between the outer and inner world, between light and darkness, between practice and thought. It is a language which Goethe had never used before in his imaginative writings and becomes yet more concise in the two collections of aphorisms. The complex relationship referred to by Makarie, and the complex views of the later Goethe, could not be expressed in a simple language capable of being understood immediately. Thus they demanded a language of equal subtlety to express them.

This variety of language recalls *Werther*, where two voices were heard, but in the *Wanderjahre* Goethe speaks not with two, but with several voices. He needs them to convey the various spheres of life and how they are linked with one another. The variety of language, which at first sight appears to bear witness to Goethe's carelessness, proves on examination how careful and sensitive to language he was.

What is true of the language of the novel is also true of its structure. The main action thus develops slowly and its connection with the stories and the aphorisms is complex. Goethe's indifference to the detailed structural arrangement is revealed by his attitude to the place which his collection of sayings *Aus Makariens Archiv* should occupy. At first it had been planned to place it, together with the poem *Im ernsten Beinhaus*, at the end of the first book so that between each of the books there would have been a collection of aphorisms and a poem, thus giving the work a comparatively symmetrical appearance. As the relevant volume had, however, already been set up by the printer, they were placed at the end of the third book.[29] The form had to be capable of permitting such changes as Goethe finally made when he concluded the novel with a series of short, allusive reports. It was not his aim to create a finished work in the ordinary sense of the word, in which each part had a particular place. He wanted rather to design a many-coloured kaleidoscope of life, including everything from the simplest description of events to the most complicated thought-processes. Everything, however, was inter-connected. The images Goethe uses point to this. They allow us to infer that the novel forms a much more closely integrated pattern than could be gathered on first reading.[30] It is, of course, not surprising, since all parts are rooted in Goethe's mind and belong to later phases of his mental development.

One of the central images in the *Lehrjahre* was the *Bild* (*image*), to indicate the view which men take of one another. It allows us to gauge to what extent Wilhelm had developed into a more mature person. In the *Wanderjahre* another function of this image becomes apparent. Some of the persons of the novel, notably Wilhelm, have already attained a higher level of development and reached clarity about their feelings. Only occasionally, therefore, as in Lenardo's relations with the nutbrown maid, is the actual process from confusion to clarity depicted. At first, Lenardo is incapable of remembering her but in the end, after much confusion, he has a clear mental picture of her.

Not only mental images, but also the figurative arts are capable of having a definite influence on the inner life of man. St Joseph the Second experiences how portraits can mould the life of a person; they determine his attitude and the actions of the carpenter. Lenardo's uncle uses pictures to educate the emotions and the imagination.

Another motif which belongs here is the image of the mirror. It is used both literally and metaphorically and expresses aesthetic and spiritual consciousness. It frequently recurs in the novel.[31] The personality of Lenardo's uncle, we read, is 'mirrored' in the proverbs which he orders to be inscribed above the door of his house; they are meant to shock the reader into thought, as for example 'Attention is life'.[32] Lenardo's letter is a mirror which gives a clear view of his own development. Similarly, biography can be a mirror of the mind by focusing attention on the object portrayed. The scholar or collector can capture a person's life from the objects which surround him. Art is a mirror, too; it concentrates human experience and vision.

The mirror not only excites the attention, but intensifies it. We see this particularly when a mirror skilfully imitates the detachment which the observer has to use and compels him to pay more attention to nature. Art allows us to experience this; it concentrates the vision and thus stimulates the imagination more strongly than nature itself.

The mirror also has a moral function, which Goethe depicts when he describes Makarie's gifts and their influence on the life of others. She succeeds in presenting a 'moral-magic mirror'[33] to someone who has lost his way in life; by pointing to the beautiful core of his nature she encourages him to lead a new life. Makarie's words and personality have both moral and magic power: moral power because they make us conscious of hidden problems and exhort us to put them right; magic power because they channel our feelings and produce a definite mood. The mirror succeeds in changing moral chaos into order. It intensifies the power of the imagination and refines sensibility; it allows us to recognize our limitations and mistakes, but deepens our insight by concentrating our experience. It protects us from needless détours and dangers, but it also contains the possibility of distortion against which Goethe expressly warns us.

> Nothing is easily reproduced quite impartially. It could be argued that the mirror is an exception, and yet we never see our face properly in it; the mirror changes our figure and turns our right hand into our left hand. This can be an image for all considerations about ourselves.[34]

The mirror image is a key image because it symbolizes various possibilities of interrelation and interaction of experience, thus adding further dimensions to the world in which Wilhelm originally lives. It widens, distorts and corrects his vision and that of other characters, and it is also a means of linking inner experiences. Another significant image is that of the wanderer, which depicts the impulse to realize and develop one's potentialities.[35] It is not surprising that this image plays an essential part in the *Wanderjahre* where it appears in the title. It occurs for the first time when St Joseph the Second and his son are called 'strange wanderers'.[36] The carpenter, so we learn, was capable of renunciation, since he was prepared to adapt himself to the needs of life. The true wanderer is a person who moves towards a goal because the path itself has become a goal. He gains external experience and relives it inwardly. Travelling means not only roaming about the world but growing spiritually.

The family's wanderings typify its character and show that it is prepared for change. The image throws light on Wilhelm's development too. He feels a sense of kinship with the carpenter, but there is still a gulf between them. If Wilhelm renounces some of his desires, he does so because he has been told to, not because he has grasped the real reason for doing so. That is why he still envies the carpenter.

Wilhelm meets several people who have become true wanderers. Their imagination is neither distracted nor unrestrained. When he gets to know Makarie he can express this experience only in a dream, not consciously. In his dream, Makarie moves like a bird capable of the highest flight. In the Pedagogic Province this movement can also be recognized at the beginning of each account of the life in the Province. But if man wishes to become conscious of movement, of change, he has to limit his sphere of activity.

Another related image is that of the box and key.[37] Felix takes a box and key, which have an air of mystery about them, out of the granite castle. He hands the box thoughtfully to Wilhelm and falls into a deep sleep which, with Goethe, denotes a change to a different level of consciousness.[38] Soon afterwards, he falls in love with Hersilie, but he is not mature enough for her to take him seriously. His passion for her, however, makes him hasty and careless and he inadvertently breaks the key in two. This 'box–key' motif expresses the disharmony between the two lovers. Only when Felix has learnt to control his impulses and Hersilie feels a genuine affection for him, can they find one another. Then the key to the box is found. The motif has other meanings too. Key and box may be thought of as sexual symbols, or as symbols linking two spheres of life, or as in some way related to the stone found in the castle. The box points to a mystery inherent in the stone, the original fount of life. The box's own mystery is a reflection of the mystery of life itself.

Another image related to the wanderer is that of the horse.[39] Education consists in disciplining the impulses. The teachers of the Pedagogic Province consider it their task to teach the disciples the wild, rough skill of horsemanship but, by way of compensation, the most delicate occupation in the world, the use of language.[40] Felix has not only learnt to ride a horse, he has learnt how to read and write. He corresponds with Hersilie, but when he sees her, his hastiness spoils their relationship. He twice falls from his horse; he has not yet mastered his impulsive nature. In Makarie's world accidents of that kind do not occur; impulses are controlled by reason. In contrast, St Joseph the Second lives quietly; he does not ride a horse, but an ass.

It is unnecessary to examine all the images of the novel. It can, however, be argued that the coherence of the vital images points to a deep underlying unity and to the basic principle of the structure: antithesis and parallelism. Goethe defined this method in a letter to Iken:

> Since many aspects of our experience cannot be pronounced unambiguously and communicated directly, I have, for a long time, chosen the method of revealing the more secret meaning to the perceptive reader through works opposed to one another and reflecting one another.[41]

The connection between the main plot and the sub-plots is much closer than it looks at first sight. The stories can be described as parallel tales (*Parallelgeschichten*),[42] a term adopted from a sentence from Goethe's collection of stories *Unterhaltungen deutscher Ausgewanderter* (*Conversations of German Emigrants*).

'I love parallel tales. One points to the other and explains its meaning better than dry words.'[43] The last aphorism in *Aus Makariens Archiv* confirms this intention of making analogy the structural principle of the novel:

> Whoever lives for a long time in important circumstances of course does not encounter all that a man is able to encounter, but at least that which is analogous, and perhaps a few things which are without example.[44]

The characters in the novel are faced not only with their own experience but with analogous experiences which are described in the 'parallel tales'. Wilhelm extends his spiritual horizon. This would not have been possible if he had merely undergone certain experiences. But he has also learned a technique for examining his experience. The complicated form of presentation also makes us recognize the essential role of the narrator. He is reserved and inconspicuous. At first we hardly notice him. Gradually we notice his interventions.

His reticence does not obscure events, but reveals to the reader levels of which he might otherwise have been unaware. The more the action advances, the more the narrator stands out, and the more he directs the reader's attention to the significance of apparently trivial episodes, such as the conversation between Wilhelm and Jarno, of which he sketches the outlines.[45]

Irony is a means which enables the narrator to communicate what he has to say in a manner which is socially appropriate. There is never any breach of decorum. This ironic tone produces detachment, so that the narrator is able to place events in another perspective. The reader becomes more and more aware that he is communicating only a part of the events. The narrator even assumes the mantle of an editor who allows only certain passages to appear and has apparently left others out. As he reports the main points he is ready to discuss only what is really important.

As in *Die Wahlverwandtschaften*, the narrator often speaks in sentences which sound like maxims and which appear to possess the significance of general laws. But in many respects his irony differs greatly from that of the *Lehrjahre*. There it was a criticism of Wilhelm's deficient sense of reality, but here it is directed less against Wilhelm himself than at other characters. The reader's interest is not concentrated so exclusively on Wilhelm. And he has grown up: only occasionally does he need to be treated with irony, for example after his enthusiastic speech on anatomy. The narrator reserves his irony for the immature, for von Revanne, Lucidor, Lucinde, the Major and Flavio,[46] even for immature traits resulting from rigidity of mind in Lenardo's uncle, but not for Makarie, who is truly mature. He even criticizes himself, a most modern trait of narration. This is particularly noticeable in the so-called *Zwischenrede* (*The Narrator's Interpolation*), where he indicates the passage of time and prepares the reader for Wilhelm's return to the Pedagogic Province. The narrator thus aims at detachment from his own mode of narration.

Nature also plays an important role in the *Wanderjahre*. Its landscapes are symbolic. Jarno, like Wilhelm at the beginning of the novel, lives on the summit of a mountain because he is trying to fathom the essential in life. St Joseph the Second, who is contented with his life, inhabits a pleasant valley, but the monastery is in ruins enabling us to see the original plans which the complete edifice would have hidden, suggesting an analogy to institutionalized religion which may conceal the original religious truth. The giant castle is on a rock looking like a work of art but really being a work of nature, an obscure symbol of the history of the world and of Christendom. Lenardo's uncle lives in an ordered landscape on his estate, for he likes to plan his life; this landscape also symbolizes a philosophical attitude to religion. Makarie's estate lies on an agreeable plain, as befits the peace of mind so characteristic of her. Indeed, these last landscapes represent stages preparing us for the Pedagogic Province, since each of them corresponds to one of the four religions.[47]

Landscape also serves the function of reflecting the characters' inner life. When Lucidor, in the story '*Wer ist Verräter?*', believes he has lost Lucinde, the palace and even the park confine him and he has to escape into the open fields to relax the intensity of his emotions. Nature is still magnificent, but he cannot enjoy it. Only when he is reconciled to Lucinde is he again happy in his contemplation of nature. The fecund landscape through which the pilgrims pass after crossing the frontiers of the Pedagogic Province reflects the richness and fruitfulness of its ideas. Wilhelm becomes aware of his separation from Natalie when he reaches the mountain watershed.

The landscape can be an image of love: the spring blossoms in the Major's garden appear as a symbol of his love for Hilarie, while Mignon's exotic character finds an appropriate environment in the luxuriant landscape of Lake Maggiore.

Wilhelm and Felix take up different positions in relation to nature. Differences in character and age become apparent: Wilhelm contemplates, but does not act, while Felix wants to approach nature not by contemplation but by action.[48]

Nature also leads to death. The boy's love of water suddenly changes on learning that his friend and his friend's brothers were drowned. At the end of the novel, Felix is nearly drowned, but Wilhelm's medical knowledge restores him to life, a symbol of man's co-operation with nature. This recalls the central question of *Die Wahlverwandtschaften*. How far can man adapt himself to nature or control it? To what extent is he capable of exercising a dominion over it? Is he capable of acting fruitfully? Goethe did not hesitate to answer these questions in the affirmative:

> The longer I live, the more vexed I am when I see man, who really holds the highest position in order to command nature and to free himself and his fellows from iron necessity, out of some preconceived and false notion doing exactly the opposite of what he wants to do; and as a result, because the situation in general is vitiated, he wretchedly messes around with particulars.[49]

Man must try to develop himself fully as an individual. In himself, he is raw material to be moulded. 'By nature man does not have any defect which cannot become a virtue, and does not have a virtue which cannot become a vice.'[50] A virtue which has turned into a defect is particularly dangerous, for instance with Lenardo, whose extremely sensitive consciousness turns into whimsical weakness. He believes he has hurt the bailiff's daughter and refuses to return home. But this belief is without foundation. His natural disposition has overreached itself; its effect is therefore disturbing and harmful.

In the long run, nothing which is against nature can be effective. Man is able to master nature by following her, but not by acting against her. This view corresponds to Goethe's conviction that nature is an extremely active force, which does not plan according to fixed laws. A permanent movement is presupposed:

> Nature does nothing in vain, a saying to which philistines traditionally resort. She is eternally active, superfluous and wasteful, so that the infinite is continually effective because nothing is permanent.[51]

Man has to understand this law of nature as well as other laws. One of these laws is that man, by nature, has the gift of imitation. It is natural that he wishes to achieve all he is capable of achieving; similarly the most natural thing would be for a son to take up the occupation of his father.

Man's natural disposition directs his energies towards what is possible and appropriate for him. Both Lenardo and Wilhelm learn to act in consonance with nature: Lenardo becomes the leader of the association, Wilhelm a surgeon. Similarly with Jarno; his analytical gifts make him a scientist, an adviser. His scepticism does not develop into cynicism, but enables him to acquire a sober, intelligent attitude to the world. He is thus able to understand the most important law of nature on which all other laws are based:

> Thinking and doing, doing and thinking, that is the sum of all wisdom, accepted from time out of mind, acted on from time out of mind, though not recognized by everyone. Both must, like breathing in and breathing out, interact in life to all eternity; like question and answer, the one should not take place without the other. Whoever makes a law of what the genius of human understanding whispers secretly into the ear of every new-born child, namely to test doing by thinking, thinking by doing, cannot err, and if he does, he will soon find his way back to the right path.[52]

Later on, Jarno is accepted into Makarie's circle, for experience of nature and the power to put it to practical use can be fruitful in this environment. For St Joseph the Second the same is true; his work corresponds to the capacity given to him by nature. By arranging his estate in an orderly manner, Lenardo's uncle tries to lead an exemplary life. The collector has a similar relationship with nature; it is essential to know what forces slumber in man. It is the task of education to guide man in the direction in which nature leads him. The collector, too, knows that man's life is subjected to the rhythm of nature. We must expect change:

> We see the flowers fade away and the leaves fall, but we also see the fruits mature and the buds grow. Life belongs to the living, and he who is living must be prepared for change.[53]

Not only must action match thought, but it must be in tune with nature.

Felix, too, begins to follow the course of nature. Just as he has to learn to tame horses, so he must also learn to discipline his appetites and curb his impatience. But education presupposes maturity. He has not acquired it at the end of the novel; his impetuous activity, which brings him again and again into danger, betrays this. To act against nature is pernicious. The Major thus tries to rejuvenate himself by falling in love with a young girl, and she believes herself in love with him. But her love disappears when she meets a boy of her own age. Each is disillusioned and suffers for it. Flavio's experience is similar. All of them have violated nature. So has Odoard in the story *Nicht zu weit*. He has acted against it because he married for social and political reasons. The hero in the story *Die neue Melusine* has married a woman from another sphere of life and sins not only against morality, but also against nature. Only those who act in harmony with nature are successful: Lucidor and Lucinde, Flavio and Hilarie, St Joseph and his wife.

In the *Wanderjahre*, the role of society is as varied as nature's. The life of the artisan, represented by St Joseph the Second, is one of limited but fruitful activity supported by the specific ethos of a profession. He is not only a craftsman, but is sensitive to art and allows it to affect his imagination.

Another form of existence is that of the scientist. Either he dwells in solitude, alone in the mountains, like Jarno-Montan, or he pursues his research in a friendly circle where he finds the interchange of thought stimulating. In either case, he deliberately limits himself to what he thinks essential: the pursuit of truth.

As in the *Lehrjahre* there are a number of aristocrats – Lenardo's uncle, Makarie and von Revanne, whose independent, enlightened life is based on financial independence.

Very different is the life of the weavers, a life of drudgery determined by their machines and their need to earn their living. Goethe worried whether his minute description of the technique of weaving could be justified from the standpoint of aesthetics. He wrote to Göttling:

> I am particularly pleased that you have become favourably disposed to my weavers and spinners by direct contemplation of reality. I was particularly worried whether this connection of the strictly, but drily technical with the aesthetically-sentimental events is capable of having a good effect or not.[54]

But Goethe included this section because what was 'strictly, but drily technical' was for him a necessary part of life.

More important for the novel than the description of different forms of society is Goethe's vision of social life seen in the perspective of change. Society must change, and only through change can necessary reforms be achieved. On a small scale, St Joseph the Second is an example of this. He brings back what has been lost by restoring a monastic building; he builds his life on tradition and ensures that change does not destroy continuity.

On a larger scale, the league of emigrants is confronted with the problem of change in a new world, the world dominated by the machine. This revolutionary change must be faced. Mechanization is an irrational force which threatens the way of life of a rural community:

> What, however, oppresses me is an economic problem; alas, not for the moment, but for the whole of the future. Mechanization, which is getting the upper hand, torments and frightens me; it whirls around like a thunder-storm, slowly, slowly, but it has been moving in a definite direction; it will come and do harm. My husband was already stricken by this sad feeling. We think of it, we speak of it and neither thinking

> nor speaking can help. And who would like to imagine such fears? Who would like to imagine terrors of this kind? Think how many valleys meander through the mountains like this one you have just come through; there still floats in your mind's eye the pleasant merry way of living you have just seen and of which the crowds swarming in every direction in their Sunday best yesterday gave you the most enjoyable example; just think that it will slowly collapse and die, and the desert, after it has been inhabited and peopled for centuries, will relapse into its pristine loneliness.[55]

A threat of this kind disturbs everyone's way of life. Only two alternatives are open: to grasp what is new, and forestall its destructive powers, or to emigrate. Neither alternative is easy, each has its advantages and its drawbacks.

Under Lenardo's guidance, many people come together, first for the purpose of travelling, later for that of emigrating. The 'League of Emigrants' is governed by the principle 'everyone must be perfect in some sphere or other'.[56] A society of men who are educated or desire to be educated is to be formed. The League is to found and maintain a Utopia,[57] something like the 'Pedagogic Province'. As Lenardo says:

> When I last saw him [the collector], years ago, he told me a lot about a pedagogic province which I could only take for a kind of utopia; it appeared to me as if, behind this appearance of reality, a series of ideas, thoughts, propositions and plans were meant, which were indeed connected, but would hardly come together in the normal course of events.[58]

This view was Goethe's too, for he used the same words when speaking to Riemer about the 'Pedagogic Province'.[59] Patience and moderation are to govern the League, as it aims to create social and political conditions in which the individual can prosper. These must spring from co-operation and freedom of thought. There is to be no central government, no written constitution, no formal jurisdiction, no government programme. It is more important to make men aware of a particular goal than to subject them to the state by force. It is a mistake to be strongly attached to any particular form of government or political attitude, for 'all forms of government become inadequate in time.'[60] Communal spirit achieves continuity and stability within the pattern of society much more effectively.

The League of Wanderers is an example of the most strongly developed form of social life, since its members are mostly in a position to adapt themselves to inevitable changes. It becomes eventually a league of emigrants, for there is a limit set to wandering. It cannot be carried on indefinitely. So the members of the League emigrate in order to settle down on another continent, America. But not everyone is able to emigrate, hence a different mode of existence, almost in polar opposition to the previous one, is prescribed by Odoard and his friends,[61] who stay behind. As was customary in the European society of the day, its political life is organized on patriarchal principles. Authority rules; commands, not persuasion, prevail. Yet each one, as Odoard demands, must find a satisfactory task in life. He must devote himself fully to his task. For Odoard, the governor of this particular province, as for Lenardo, the leader of the emigrants, the purpose of living is to be useful. As Lenardo says: 'Wherever I am useful, there is my country.'[62]

The section dealing with the Pedagogic Province describes a utopian society with social and political principles similar to those in Odoard's province. Although there are strict rules of conduct, it is not a rigidly coercive society, for there is plenty of choice and everyone can choose the kind of work in which he wants to be educated. Above all work does not isolate anyone; through common work, and through participating in common festivities each becomes a member of an active community. Because industrialization appears to threaten the social equilibrium, attempts are undertaken to create new kinds of communal life, such as the Pedagogic Province, the League of Emigrants and Odoard's League of Immigrants. It is the individual's task to find an activity in which he can be useful to the community. The individual must learn to consider himself a member of society, not an independent entity. Only in this way can a catastrophe be avoided. The individual must be aware of the forces which are capable of preserving, restoring and changing society and, through this knowledge, be induced to participate in its life. The *Lehrjahre* culminates in the question: how can the individual find an active place in society? In the *Wanderjahre* the question is:

how can several groups adapt themselves to changes in social life? The answer is: through education. It is not surprising that education plays so important a role in the *Wanderjahre*.

In the *Lehrjahre*, the education of Wilhelm Meister is the central problem, but nothing is said about the specific activity which Wilhelm is to take up: presumably it resembles that of Lothario. Only in the *Wanderjahre* is it determined, and the necessary steps to reach it depicted. Not everyone sees the process clearly; Wilhelm himself does so only after a certain period when he recognizes the effect of his childhood on his inner life. Most people continue in the way of life into which they are born, but Wilhelm is able to shape his life according to his nature. In order to do so he must leave the stable conditions of life which were his by birth, just as he must later leave the estate of Lothario and the company of his friends to become a wanderer. His capacities mature. Yet 'the affairs of life follow a mysterious course that cannot be calculated'.[63] The death of the fisherman's son affected Wilhelm more deeply than he ever knew. The bag of instruments which the surgeon produces when Wilhelm lies wounded becomes a pointer to his inclination to heal others. Outward experience confirms a natural disposition.

Only those images which are appropriate to us are significant for us. We do not, as Jarno says, understand anything to which our minds are not attuned. He believes it to be his duty only to say to others that which they can accept. Jarno knows how important it is to limit the activities of a scholar. He wants to create something useful: this is possible only when a man does not work against nature. Wilhelm seeks to realize these ideas in the case of Felix. Man becomes one-sided, but this one-sidedness is valuable; for 'if an outstanding man does one thing, he does everything. To be less paradoxical: in the *one* thing which he does, he sees the image of *all* that is done rightly.'[64] To find this centre may not be easy, but if his activity is fruitful he will know that he has done so. The astronomer communicates this insight to Wilhelm.

Wilhelm seeks to put these ideas into practice in his son's education. He sends him to the 'Pedagogic Province'. What are the principles of education in this province, the significance of which is emphasized by its central position in the novel? Once again, no exact description is given. The main object of education, which is here imparted only to a chosen few, is a sense of reverence. The boys learn certain physical attitudes and gestures in order to revere what is in them and above them. Reverence alone allows us to become men; it distinguishes us from other beings. The essence of education is, therefore, religious. But reverence is not innate in man; it has to be instilled. The boys must also learn by strict obedience to the rules of the Province. It is the most sacred principle not to neglect any disposition and not to distort any talent. Only then can mediocrity be avoided. The value of this education is proved by the example of Felix, who has grown inwardly and outwardly when Wilhelm returns to the Pedagogic Province.

In the Pedagogic Province, education towards reverence has a religious slant. A religious experience rather than a dogmatic attitude is stressed. This attitude is only one of the many possible forms of a religious life. St Joseph the Second is still deeply indebted to religious tradition, as his name indicates, and the traditional images taken from the life of the Holy Family have a powerful effect on him. His thought and conduct are Christian, though we do not hear anything about his religious views; he lives in the restored ruin of a former monastery but, significantly, in order to be able to live there he had to restore this monastery, abandoned by the abbot and the monks, a task for which his trade (carpentry) was eminently suited. The chapel is not used for divine service. Jarno-Montan reveres nature, in spite of his scientific scepticism, but he does not adhere to a specific religion. Lenardo's uncle is too enlightened to give much weight to religion; he has brought back from America the conception of tolerance for all religions; on his estate, freedom of religion prevails. Makarie appears like a saint but, by way of contrast to the *Stiftsdame* in the *Lehrjahre*, she is attached neither to dogma nor to a definite religion.

Only in the Pedagogic Province is a definite attitude to religion demanded. There is indirect religious teaching by appeal to tradition through images and symbols. It differs sharply, however, from Christian practice, so the sorrows of Christ are not given prominence; on the contrary, His suffering is too much respected to be shown to the world at large, and remains veiled, only to be revealed once a year to the initiated. Attention is focused on His life and teaching, not on the crucifix.

There is also definite religious instruction. The boys learn attitudes; they are to revere what is above, below and at the same level as themselves; reverence is the basis of religion. All the members of the Province must accept religion based on reverence, which is sharply distinguished from the religions based on fear. Fear is a natural emotion; reverence must be learned. There are three kinds of valid religion: ethical religion, which is based on reverence for what is above us; philosophical religion, which is founded on reverence for what is equal to us; and the Christian religion, which is founded on reverence of what is below us. Poverty, mockery and contempt, shame and misery, suffering and crime are not obstacles, but means to grace. These attitudes combine to bring about true religion – reverence for man himself, a *Steigerung*, a raising to a higher level of the other three.[65] This will elevate man to the highest peak: he will realize himself as a work of God and nature; he will dwell on the heights without being dragged down through presumption and egotism.

Goethe, here as elsewhere, departs from Christian tradition. These ideas, indeed, amount to a reversal of the medieval order, of the *ordo caritatis* as propounded by St Augustine and widely accepted since, an order in which God, and not man, was the centre of human regard. 'They may be summed up as *Weltfrömmigkeit*[67] (secular piety), to use a Goethean expression. It demands activity and ability, and men are judged according to this criterion. Authority can, as in the case of Makarie, be of a practical and spiritual nature. A community of saints means, for Goethe, a community of able men.

> As things are nowadays in the world it must be said and repeated again and again: there have been and will be capable men, and to them must be vouchsafed, pronounced and committed to paper a lapidary word. That is the communion of saints which we have espoused.[68]
>
> Useful activity is indeed the best answer to useless suffering.[69]

Fruitful activity is possible only if we give up everything that prevents us from achieving it. So the problem of *Entsagung* (renunciation) assumes a central place in the novel whose sub-title is *Die Entsagenden* (*Those who renounce*). Wilhelm's travels lead him to the League of Emigrants who have renounced their previous lives to found a new state.

Renunciation is a recurrent theme of the novel. Goethe does not define it, but clearly it is renunciation of a special kind. It is a peculiarly Goethean doctrine; indeed, it is at the very core of the thought of his later period. It is a religious attitude which springs from a particular conception of the nature of the world. It is a form of reverence both for what exists and for what will and must necessarily come about.[70] *Entsagung*, as the word indicates, involves foregoing many worthwhile pursuits of which an individual might be capable. It is easy, as Werther does, to lament the restrictions which renunciation inevitably imposes, for at every turn of our life we are faced with a choice which can be made only by the exclusion of other possibilities. But the older Goethe grew, the more he wished to emphasize the positive aspects of choice. *Entsagung* can also be a worthwhile process; it need not only mean foregoing one's desires; it can also mean limitation to what is possible and appropriate for the individual concerned. For Goethe it is a sign of maturity to become conscious of the need to limit oneself to what matters and to act accordingly. In writing about those who renounce, Goethe does not therefore discuss what they have to renounce, but focuses attention on what they have decided to do. He judges characters in so far as they are capable of concentrating on what they can successfully do without frittering away their talents on pursuits outside their reach.

Entsagung alone is, in fact, the basis of culture, for culture can be created only if our efforts are harnessed and directed to a definite goal. It alone enables man to come to terms with himself. It springs not from an attitude of resignation but of affirmation of life:

> To act thoughtfully is the counterpart in the field of the practical to 'know thyself'. Both injunctions must be considered neither as a law nor as a demand; they are like a target at which we must always aim, even if we do not always hit it. Men would be more sensible and happier if they knew how to distinguish between the infinite goal and the limited purpose, and if they gradually discovered what their capacities were.[71]

A practical sense is not to be interpreted as a facile glossing over of difficulties which only produces mediocrity.[72] It has to be inspired by a sense of piety (*Piëtas*). *Entsagung* indeed represents a tribute to a sense of order; to violate it is to disturb order and leads to self-destruction. *Entsagung*, then, attempts to supply an answer to the ills of the world.[73] Renunciation is above all necessary in the sphere of 'Eros'.[74] This does not mean, however, a rejection of passion, for passion is an essential element of life, but passion must not be destructive, it must constructively meet the demands of society.

Renunciation is indispensable, but the different characters have their own manner of renunciation. Wilhelm must go on his travels; separation from Natalie appears necessary for him if he is to be a husband worthy of her,[75] but he does not yet know what his field of activity is to be. He knows that he will have to renounce many possible fields in favour of a single one, and he must keep on until he finds it. Eventually, he chooses the profession of a surgeon. This choice of profession means considerable renunciation in another way, for the surgeon in contemporary Germany had no social prestige. The positive quality of this renunciation is confirmed by Wilhelm's rescue of Felix. It allows us to gauge what impact renunciation has had on his character. Renunciation is a sign of inner maturity. It is not restricted to any particular age; but it is more appropriate to age than to youth. As it demands concentration on a specific activity, it also involves the need to persist in adversity. Goethe's words to Zelter written after the death of his son August confirm this view:

> *Nemo ante obitum beatus* is a saying which circulates in world history, but does not really amount to anything. If it were to be uttered with more circumspection it would mean: You must expect trials to the very last.[76]

Jarno-Montan practises renunciation by withdrawing from society.[77] This is one-sided and not of much value, but by joining the League of Immigrants he finds a place in Makarie's world. He gains Lydia's love and enters into an exchange of ideas about science with the astronomer. Here his thought becomes socially valuable, as he has not insisted on sticking to his one-sided attitude. His withdrawal from society becomes beneficial and his renunciation through limitation to a specific activity, namely science, becomes positive and thus worthwhile.

In Lenardo's life signs of renunciation can be found.[78] His passion prompted by conscience is a kind of renunciation. Since he is urged to act by his inner voice, he has reached a higher level where rules have become a way of life. What, however, brings him into touch with Wilhelm is his attitude to the 'beautiful-good' woman, whose love rules out uncontrolled passion. It is left uncertain whether she will follow him after he has emigrated, although the possibility of a later marriage is not excluded. In the course of the novel Lenardo learns the truth which Goethe summed up in a quatrain:

> Nichts taugt Ungeduld,
> Noch weniger Reue;
> Jene vermehrt die Schuld,
> Diese schafft Neue.[79]

Lenardo has to leave his family; he follows his own inclination and finally becomes the leader of the League of Immigrants.

Odoard is seen from two perspectives.[80] On the one hand, in the fragmentary tale *Nicht zu weit*, he is a tragic figure, a prey to inner anxiety; on the other, he is a man who has saved himself through his work. He has renounced his personal ambitions for work to which he is suited. He is active and useful, though we do not know whether he is happy.

Natalie, though she is described only indirectly, is yet another example of renunciation, as she has to part from Wilhelm. Fortunately for her, renunciation does not mean separation for ever. Eventually, she will join Wilhelm.

But the most important character in this regard is Makarie. For her renunciation is not temporary, but a lifelong, all-embracing state: she must live her life paralysed in a chair. But her personality radiates spiritual power. To her friends she is a saint, though not in the traditional sense. Nature and duty are one in her. What is natural is at the same time a pattern of morality. Renunciation appears to have attained perfection.

By no means all the characters in the novel practise renunciation. Whether the collector does is doubtful. Although he has concentrated his life on a single activity, although he shows Wilhelm the road to the Pedagogic Province and the mystery of the box is entrusted to him, although collecting is in some sort a counterpart to travelling, his activity as a collector is still to a great extent self-centred and ossifies his spiritual life, and it is not clear whether he has learnt anything specific, or whether his collecting merely flows from diversity of interest.

Lenardo's uncle clearly does not.[81] He knows, indeed, that it is necessary to be considerate and patient, but there is no sign that he is prepared to forego the many varieties of experience. His activity on his estate is not professional, it is not a limitation to a specific craft or calling which he has learnt; it is therefore not renunciation. Indeed, renunciation is not a part of the ideas of the Enlightenment to which he belongs and for which the many-sided dilettante was the ideal.

In the short stories, cases are described where renunciation was unsuccessful or not even considered.[82] An exception is, of course the story of St Joseph the Second, for by waiting patiently for his beloved and by being inspired by the example of a saint, he undoubtedly belongs to the sphere of renunciation.

Hersilie is too proud to be capable of renunciation. The story she tells – *Die pilgernde Törin* – betrays this. The heroine of that story does not renounce: she allows her feeling to die, for she wilfully hurts others. Wandering is there an act of foolishness.[83] The characters in *Der Mann von funfzig Jahren* to a great extent, in *Die gefährliche Wette* and *Die neue Melusine*, as their unhappy fate shows, of Lucidor in *Wer ist der Verräter* and Odoard and his wife in *Nicht zu weit* have all failed to adjust their point of view to life, and are therefore unable to renounce.

Renunciation and love are closely connected. For love is exclusive and believes that it alone is right.[84] It is therefore not surprising that many of the examples of renunciation in the *Wanderjahre* are in the sphere of love. Natalie's renunciation by agreeing to Wilhelm's absence for a time alone makes possible his travels and medical studies.

Equally important is the relationship between Felix and Hersilie. The first impression which Hersilie makes upon Felix is decisive and is registered in his fiery glances. She is surprised and flattered and she hands him the most exquisite pieces of an apple which he receives with joy and gratitude. He is so fascinated that he cannot take his eyes off her and cuts his finger peeling the apple. In this image the impetuous and uncontrolled quality of his temperament is conjured up.

The impact of Felix on Hersilie too is obvious; even the apples which lie between them appear to her unwelcome as they compete for Felix's attention. Yet she seeks to remain detached and does not wish to take her interest in Felix and his passion for her very seriously. The story *Die pilgernde Törin* throws light on her character; she believes that father and son are both interested in her, but that she herself can remain detached. Apparently Felix has not yet made a deep impression on her, but he has in fact done so, as the later course of the action indicates. Felix's message of love leads her into difficulties; she is discontented with her answer as she is not clear about her feelings and does not know whether to take Felix's love seriously. Hersilie's letter shows that her love is strengthened rather than weakened by absence, although meanwhile several years have elapsed. How much Felix thought about her during the time he spent in the Pedagogic Province is not made clear, but his attitude to Hersilie when he comes back, his wooing of her, are quite unambiguous. Hersilie, however, is still unsure. She feels isolated and does not know where she stands. When she writes, she gives a broad hint that she is interested in Wilhelm just as much as in Felix. Without ever fully admitting it, she hopes that Wilhelm will respond to her overtures with a like emotion; yet she does not really believe he will, and excuses him in advance by referring to his complete lack of curiosity. It is, of course, not surprising that she finds Wilhelm, and not only Felix, interesting; after all, Wilhelm is older than Felix. Age and emotional maturity place her between father and son. But she does not dare to face this situation. Her attitude is unrealistic, and the narrator rightly calls her letter 'strange'.[85] Wilhelm replies in a friendly manner, yet by evasion foils her hopes. The next letter reveals even greater excitement, as she has found the key to the box. She does not open the box. She holds herself back, but her wishes become apparent as her thoughts are revealed. She imagines that Felix and Wilhelm are coming, that they have come already. She feels confused and hopes that the situation will be clarified. Presumably, the key and the box are here symbols of love.

Hersilie is excited, but so is Felix. His excitement finds different forms of expression. His youthful impetuosity is seen in his impatient demand that the horse's hoof be shod. He hurries off in such haste that even the bailiff is disturbed. He lacks a sense of proportion, and he pays his court too violently, thus recalling Flavio's courtship of the beautiful widow. His impetuousness only makes Hersilie repel him more vehemently than she would otherwise have done, which in turn precipitates Felix's even more hurried departure.

The box is finally opened, but only after a goldsmith has repaired the broken key. Hersilie and Felix are both victims of their own attitude. Felix rides off impetuously, in despair, while Hersilie remains at home confused. But just as the key is finally joined together by an expert, so Felix is healed by a specialist, by his father, who is a surgeon.

In the short stories, too, with the single exception of *Die gefährliche Wette*, love is the power that determines the action. *Wer ist der Verräter?* presents love almost in terms of comedy. It describes in a masterly manner the origin of the love between Lucidor and Lucinde, the course of their love and its misadventures and happy ending. *Der Mann von funfzig Jahren* describes the course of love in another, more serious manner. It unfolds in considerable detail the origins of the love of the Major for Hilarie and his son's love for the beautiful widow. The Major's attempts at rejuvenation and his own misgivings arouse doubts about the possibility of a favourable outcome. At the beginning of the short story, he is in a crisis; he knows that he is ageing yet he does not wish to abandon his youthful way of living. His wish to appear younger does not allow him to act in a ruthless or inconsiderate manner. Hilarie's love for the Major is genuine, but is not based on reason and experience.[86] The sudden, noisy arrival of the distraught Flavio after his hectic courtship of the beautiful widow is the turning point. Hilarie falls in love with him and their love is traced up to its passionate recognition and declaration. Hilarie, however, will not agree to marry Flavio immediately, out of consideration for the Major. Makarie's intervention allows the beautiful widow to recognize that she has misused her charm.

Another short story in which love plays a main part is *Nicht zu weit*. Odoard's fragmentary autobiographical tale again depicts a marriage threatened by both partners; but only the outward situation is similar to that of *Der Mann von funfzig Jahren*. For the emotional relations are quite dissimilar. Odoard is a man of the world, yet he has deep feelings, a strong moral sense, and a concern for social and political affairs. He therefore restrains his feelings for Princess Sophronie, who, for political reasons, had to become the bride of the hereditary prince. Sophronie, though obviously affected by Odoard's feelings, keeps her thoughts to herself. Odoard is in a difficult situation, as it is generally believed that he had written a poem in praise of Sophronie under the name of Aurora. Odoard's marriage with the minister's daughter silences the talk for a while, but his enemies revive it, and he is sent away as governor to a distant province, which he rules benevolently. The futility of his marriage becomes apparent when he tolerates his wife's amour, but her shamelessness finally outrages him. He encounters the Princess by chance at an inn. The story breaks off at this point, though its title indicates both that the characters know the limits imposed upon their feelings by duty and convention, and that it would be going too far to relate any transgression of the moral code. Odoard's wife, too, had to learn by experience, for she discovers that her lover is unfaithful to her and really loves her friend Florine.

Das nussbraune Mädchen shows love from a different point of view: passion prompted by conscience. Lenardo is at first not sure of his feelings, but he searches for the maiden when a less sensitive person would have abandoned the search long before. *Die pilgernde Törin* reveals confusion of mind in love. Father and son woo a woman whose character they do not really know and who apparently acts out of spite. The two men act impetuously, the woman with calculation. All three lack consideration, and thus they have been unable to renounce their own desires. In *Die neue Melusine* the lovers come from different spheres of life, and therefore cannot live in harmony for long.

The power of love is all-pervasive. It challenges men and women, and only a mature personality can hope to avoid the destruction which it can wreak. One of the group of poems *Urworte Orphisch*, called *Ἔρως* concisely sums up how love affects life:

Ἔρως, Liebe

Die bleibt nicht aus! – Er stürzt vom Himmel nieder,
Wohin er sich aus alter Öde schwang,
Er schwebt heran auf luftigem Gefieder
Um Stirn und Brust den Frühlingstag entlang,
Scheint jetzt zu fliehn, vom Fliehen kehrt er wieder,
Da wird ein Wohl im Weh, so süss und bang.
Gar manches Herz verschwebt im Allgemeinen,
Doch widmet sich das edelste dem Einen.[87]

In his commentary on this poem he summarizes what is conveyed in greater detail in the *Wanderjahre*:

> Everything is included here that can be thought of from the slightest inclination to the most passionate ecstasy; here the individual *Daemon* and seductive *Tyche* are joined. Man appears to obey himself, to let his own will prevail, to indulge in its impulse, and yet there are chance occurrences which interpolate strange events making people deviate from their paths; man seeks to catch and is caught, he believes himself to have won, and is already lost. *Tyche* here plays her game, she entices the lost one into new labyrinths; there is no limit to error, for the way itself is error. Now we run the danger of getting lost in the reflection that what appears to be intended for the particular fades away into the general. The rapid entry of the last two lines will give us a decisive hint how we can escape this misfortune and gain life-long security.[88]

Art and craft too demand discipline and renunciation and can lead the practitioner to maturity. But the circumstances must be suitable. The spinners and weavers do not experience the satisfaction which the restoration of the images and the building of the church give the carpenter, Joseph. His work and the integrity of his craftsmanship raise the quality of his life. Respect for the laws of an art or craft enable a man to use his talents and find happiness.

> The sooner man becomes aware that there is a craft, that there is an art which is capable of helping him in a regular intensification (*Steigerung*) of his natural disposition, the happier he is; whatever he receives from the outside will not damage his innate individuality.[89]

Mature men respect genuine art and genuine craftsmanship, but abhor dilettantism:

> The dilettantes, when they have done all they can, usually say by way of apology that their work has not yet been completed. It can, actually, never be completed, because it has never been properly begun. The master puts down his work with a few strokes; finished or not, it is clearly completed. The cleverest dilettante gropes uncertainly, and as his work progresses, the unsureness of his first conception comes more and more to the fore. Right at the end it is discovered that what has gone wrong cannot be put right; and thus the work indeed cannot be completed.[90]

In rather the same way, they exclude actors from the Pedagogic Province, for there is something spurious about them, and about acting. After all, it can only exist if the actors play before an idle, not to say vulgar, crowd.

Figurative art does not play such an obvious role as in the *Lehrjahre*, but there is one episode which stresses its importance. An encounter with an artist who had painted Mignon in the landscape of her birthplace helps Wilhelm to correct his visions of the world. He has gone on a pilgrimage to Lake Maggiore where Mignon was born and grew up, an act of piety to her memory[91] and to the vision she had kindled within him. There he learns from the painter to see nature through art. Mignon, originally a symbol of unfulfilled longing, of lyric poetry which lacks a realistic basis, becomes the starting-point of a realistic understanding of nature and art. This cross-fertilization is enhanced by the merging of fact and fiction; for in this chapter Hilarie and the beautiful widow, characters from the story *Der Mann von funfzig Jahren*, join Wilhelm and the painter in the magic landscape of the North Italian lake. Not only Mignon, but also Hilarie and the beautiful widow cast a spell. Wilhelm has to escape from this spell and continue his journey, but his distress at having to abandon the magnificent scenery and their delightful company is mitigated, and indeed offset, by the realization that renunciation is necessary for his development and that art can preserve the memory of ephemeral experience.

What is true of art is also true of science and scholarship. Here, too, the feeling for the whole is essential. Theory is only useful if it passes beyond analysis to synthesis. Art and science and scholarship are interdependent. The artist or scholar must know his craft, must indeed possess scientific knowledge of, for example geometry, anatomy, calligraphy or grammar.

Scholarship is subject to laws as severe as those of art. Scholars must find out whether tradition is still living and fruitful, and scrutinize the new for genuine inner worth as opposed to surface glitter. Science and scholarship must be combined with living itself, as is done in Makarie's house.

A wide diversity is also revealed in the stages of life which are depicted.[92] The point of view of almost all actions is seen from a twofold perspective: for instance, the mature Wilhelm is set against the boy Felix, or there is Lenardo, a young man who grows mature.

The conflict between the mature man and the youth is a situation which recurs in the novel,[93] as in *Die pilgernde Törin*, *Der Mann von funfzig Jahren* and *Die gefährliche Wette*. Only in *Der Mann von funfzig Jahren*, however, is this conflict of real consequence.

In the *Wanderjahre*, Goethe's aim was not to write a psychological novel. The characters are seen more from without even than in the *Lehrjahre*, let alone in *Werther* or in *Die Wahlverwandtschaften*. Many of them were taken over from the *Lehrjahre* and did not need to be portrayed anew. It was rather a question of depicting their development towards maturity and their personal experiences. So we do not learn much about Wilhelm's or Jarno's emotional life. Jarno is sceptical, but appears more interested in acquiring knowledge. In the case of Lenardo, it is not very different. His search for the nut-brown maiden proves that he has a rich inner life, but details are not revealed. The impact of his personality is strong. He is a leader; he has the capacity to adapt himself to others, as his clarity of observation, his description of the weavers and his speech about wandering show.

We do not learn much about Odoard's inner life in the main action, but in the narrative *Nicht zu weit*, we see him to be a man divided within himself, a man whose fate makes him suffer deeply. A sense of what is proper to his social standing duly determines his life; he is unable to solve the problem of a loveless marriage – the fulfilment of a true love is denied to him. In the main action, only in the case of Felix and Hersilie is a fuller image of inner life given.

The impetuous Felix is unable to control his passion; he hastily follows his impulses wherever they might lead. With Felix, many things happen involuntarily; in this respect, he is contrasted with his father. He does not know how to renounce, for renunciation presupposes awareness, and awareness was, for Goethe, a condition of maturity. He was therefore pleased when he believed that his own son was acquiring this quality on his journey to Italy.[94] Similarly, Faust's development can be called a growth of awareness. Goethe described his own development in his last letter to Wilhelm von Humboldt of 17 March 1832, less than a week before his death, in a similar way.[95]

Hersilie's character, as the vacillation of her feelings between father and son proves, is much more complicated than that of Felix. If she is not at all aware of her feelings, she nonetheless possesses a shrewd appreciation of her environment. Her criticism of the uncle shows this. She combines amiability and freshness of appearance with sensibility and intelligence. We hear very little of the uncle, at least in so far as his external activity is concerned. It corresponds to his personality; his thought is directed to what is practical, not towards the cultivation of feelings. The more egotistical features of his character result from the unfavourable influence of power.

Makarie's character is recognized by its effect on others. She remains enigmatic. We hear of her peculiar relationship to the solar system. She succeeds in combining mind and love, science and morality.[96] Her name itself is symbolic – for it comes from the Greek *μακάριος* ('blessed'). She has a noble presence, a spiritual adaptability which enhances her dignity. But she is not egotistical; her influence is thus widely effective through her goodness, knowledge of people and insight. From the exceptional quality and force of her personality springs her central function in the structure of the events of the novel. She has reached the highest spiritual and moral level.

Lenardo's uncle, the other older character, does not reach this level. Although a man of good qualities, he is too whimsical and intellectually too rigid to make a similar impact on others.[97]

Among the characters of the short stories, there are several of whose inner life we learn something. We hear more about the characters of the most prominent short story *Der Mann von funfzig*

Jahren, which, despite the passion depicted, almost completely retains its tone of serene sociability. The Major is amiable and calm, his behaviour is courteous, he possesses a fatherly understanding for others and is skilful in conversation with his son, the beautiful widow, his sister and Hilarie. He is more than an average country squire; he is something of a poet, and has a fine knowledge of Latin poetry. He is endowed with a sense of what is natural and appropriate, so he instinctively reacts to the news that Hilarie loves him by saying: 'I should not have believed her natural character to be capable of so unnatural an attitude.'[98] He could, in fact, be called altruistic, an attitude which makes his later renunciation of Hilarie much easier. His son Flavio, is, of course, much more impetuous than his father. He lacks insight into the subtleties of personal relations; he therefore has to break completely with the beautiful widow. On the other hand, he is a lyric poet; the verses in which he expresses his love for Hilarie are full of tenderness. She, however, lacks knowledge of the world; this is one reason why she falls in love with a much older man. But her love for the Major springs mainly from her sensitivity, which also allows her to find the right words to encourage Flavio in answering his poem with another one. But her new love for Flavio does not blind her to the obligations which her feelings for the Major have created, and she retires to her room until all is clarified.

The beautiful widow, on the other hand, has sufficient charm to win every man; her social adaptability is extraordinary. But a quality of this kind has its perils; she provokes Flavio more than she intended, thereby causes his impetuous conduct, which only ends in deeply disturbing him. Despite her ability to attract men into her orbit, she is not immoral. Her developing interest in, if not love for, the Major, which she expresses in an instinctive friendliness, could lead to a relationship satisfactory for both.

Nachodine-Susanne first of all appears in the short story *Das nussbraune Mädchen*. We see her indirectly through the memory of Lenardo, who remembers her as someone asking for something. When he meets her again later on, not as a character in the novel, but in life, he finds her a kind, understanding woman, whose nature is well summarized as 'the good-beautiful'. The story of her life, her description of the weavers, and her apprehension concerning future developments, show her to be an understanding, practical woman who also possesses great sensitivity. Here, too, only an outline of her personality is given. The same applies to other characters.

In the *Wanderjahre* there are some generally valid types, who yet have individual features. St Joseph is the prototype of the faithful, useful artisan, with staying power, understanding, and a sense of propriety, while he also has a feeling for tradition, qualities which permit him to win Elizabeth successfully. Lucidor is not remarkable because of his sensitivity, but because his legal training give this sensitivity a peculiar flavour. In *Die pilgernde Törin* we see how a courageous woman is capable of commanding respect. Other figures, like Lenardo, or the two Squires von Revanne, the hero of *Die neue Melusine*, the characters in the story *Die gefährliche Wette* or Odoard's wife, her lover and Flavio are conventionally designed. Nonetheless, we remember them; what strikes us as a feature common to all these characters is that none of them reveals malice or can be called evil, even if some of them, like Odoard's wife and her lover, appear to be without a profound inner life. In the novel, we continuously meet good people who are occupied with meaningful tasks and who approach life in a positive manner. It was Goethe's aim to draw attention to fruitful striving. Interference with the good life by daemonic forces is mentioned only incidentally, for it was his object to indicate their power, but not to describe it fully.[99]

The *Wanderjahre* is in a sense a utopian novel. Though not unrealistic in the sense that its aims could never be fully realized, it describes the characters striving for the good. Order and harmony reign. Goethe believes in the possibility of a serene and moral society, which need not be destroyed by the daemonic if it breaks into it. Major characters like Makarie, Lenardo, St Joseph, and even Lenardo's uncle and the collector, are significant for their positive views and their fruitful deeds. None of them is driven by a daemonic force.

In the course of the main action, almost all the characters come to see that thought and action must agree. But achieving this identity involves limitation and one-sidedness. No one on this earth can have a constant and perfect vision of reality. We are all limited by time and place, and can only strive for perfection.

After this consideration of the language and themes of the *Wander-*

jahre, it is easier to decide whether this is a novel or not.

The world appeared to Goethe to be a complicated structure. In the *Zwischenrede* published only in the 1821 version, but later cut out, he writes:

> And we therefore offer a few chapters, whose presentation is desirable only in an ephemeral form, so that the reader may not only feel that something is lacking here, but be better informed as to what is lacking and may himself develop that which, partly from the nature of the subject, partly from the circumstances involved, cannot be fully developed or put before him with all the supporting evidence.[100]

This evidence reveals that it was not Goethe's intention to create a rounded work, but rather to achieve an effect by a multiplicity of impressions and perspectives, by reports and sayings, however allusive and brief. Goethe abandoned a conventional narrative to take advantage of the almost infinite possibilities offered by fiction.[101] But this abandonment also springs from a sovereign indifference to his work in his old age, as evidenced by his attitude to the place which the collections of aphorisms and the two great poems attached to the novel were to occupy.

Before the *Wanderjahre* was published, no one envisaged a novel in these terms. Goethe created new possibilities for the novel by writing a symbolic work which the Romantics had sought in vain to accomplish in their novels,[102] a work in which prose and poetry, thought and imagination are brought together on several levels and yet fused into a unity. The novel in this respect anticipates modern writing; it demands highly educated readers, for only they can appreciate the subtle mixture. In other respects, of course, he is adapting the picaresque novel to new purposes, though, in contradistinction to modern novelists, he does not entirely abandon the easy ways of the picaresque novels where fortuitousness rather than design rules.

Everything is arranged in such a way that the reader is not immediately affected by the form of the whole work; he is led on from one part which appeals to him to another. Once he has found a firm vantage point, he can penetrate more deeply into the structure by following up suggestions which concern one part or another.

It is imperative to separate the *Wanderjahre* as a work of art from the *Lehrjahre*, for each is a world of its own. It is not possible to speak of a work in two parts as in the case of *Faust*, where the first part would be incomplete without the second. In the *Wilhelm Meister* novels, however, the *Lehrjahre* can be considered an independent work, not requiring a continuation; the *Wanderjahre*, on the other hand, can hardly be thought of without being preceded by the *Lehrjahre*. It is significant that Goethe speaks of parts in *Faust*, whereas he distinguishes these novels by two different titles. Whether Goethe was seriously contemplating the writing of a third novel, the *Meisterjahre*, is highly doubtful.

More useful analogies may be provided by composite works, such as a *roman fleuve* like Romain Rolland's *Jean Christophe* or Trollope's political fiction about Phineas Finn. Each individual work is independent, yet they are connected. In the *Wilhelm Meister* novels, a particularly strong connection can be found in images, symbols, persons and themes. Images, such as those of the *Bild* (image or picture), mirror and wanderer, play a significant part in both works. The motif of the ailing prince corresponds to a basic situation that is repeated: the woman in love with two men or, as a counterpart, the man in love with two women. At the same time, the motif is related to the theme of cure through awareness and love, another basic theme. People from the world of the theatre have not been admitted to the *Wanderjahre*. Mignon lives on only in the imagination. On the other hand, several characters play a major part in both novels – Wilhelm, Natalie, Jarno (Wilhelm's intellectual and spiritual counterpart), and Felix, his son. The foreground theme of education to a communal life is, in the last resort, perhaps the decisive difference demarcating the *Wilhelm Meister* novels from other composite fiction.

The *Wanderjahre*, in the last resort, is a highly diversified whole. The deeper we become involved, the more inexhaustible it appears. Only the main features stand out clearly, and many relations are not visible. In particular, most of the aphorisms in the *Betrachtungen im Sinne der Wanderer* and *Aus Makariens Archiv* appear to lack an obvious connection with the plot and sub-plots. Yet a general affinity exists. Goethe remarked on this issue:

> I do not want the sayings from Makarie's archive to be published prior to the appearance of the whole work. At the

> end of the work and in connection with the whole, they can be understood properly; individually, some of them might cause offence.[103]

The relation of the aphorisms to the events of the action can be perceived only with difficulty. The sayings are not woven into the fabric of the novel, though some sentences, like the well-known 'What is your duty? – The demand of the hour',[104] comment closely on events in the novel. Many others, for instance,

> The Germans, but not only the Germans, have the gift of making scholarship and science (*die Wissenschaften*) inaccessible.[105]

do not show any connection at all, though this can easily be related to the next aphorism, which is an indirect exhortation to be practical:

> The Englishman is a master of the art of using a discovery until it leads again to a new discovery and a new deed. We may then wonder why they are ahead of us everywhere.[106]

Some other sayings are analogous to events in the novel,[107] but most of them are very remote from it and are, in fact, translations from other thinkers. They belong to the same intellectual atmosphere and convey much the same spiritual experience as Makarie and the wanderer.

Many features of the novel are left intentionally unclear in order to strengthen the symbolic effect. This corresponds to Goethe's mode of presentation in his old age:

> I understand very well that my readers have considered many things enigmatic. . . . Everything must be considered symbolic – and everywhere there is a problem concealed. Every solution of a problem is a new problem.[108]

But though enigmatic and symbolic, these things are not meaningless and unrelated.

> Coherence, aim and purpose lie within the book itself. If it is not of one piece, it is of one meaning, and this was precisely the task: to bring strange external events together so that we may feel they belong together.[109]

In this sense, the two poems *Vermächtnis* and *Im ernsten Bein haus* (often also called *Terzinen* or *Gedicht auf Schillers Schädel*) are an integral part of the *Wanderjahre*.

In *Vermächtnis*, which follows *Betrachtungen im Sinne der Wanderer* (the first collection of sayings), Goethe speaks of laws which govern the world. The external and the inner world, nature and mind, correspond to one another. Understanding and imagination are necessary to gain power over life. For 'what is fruitful is alone true'.[110] This principle underlying the poem sums up the views of Goethe in his old age. As he wrote to Zelter: 'I have noticed that I consider true that thought which is fruitful for me, which is akin to my general manner of thinking and which furthers this thinking.'[111] This principle governs the thought and action of those who practise renunciation in the *Wanderjahre*. Only if we follow it will restraint be effective:

> Geniesse mässig Füll' und Segen,
> Vernunft sei überall zugegen
> Wo Leben sich des Lebens freut.
> Dann ist Vergangenheit beständig,
> Das Künftige voraus lebendig,
> Der Augenblick ist Ewigkeit.[112]

The novel culminates in Wilhelm's act of saving his son; this is not the zenith of his life, which is reached at the end of the *Lehrjahre*, but it is the zenith of his medical career. By saving and curing his son, he accomplishes his masterpiece. In this scene the moment has become eternity, for this act recalls the past – the death by drowning of his young friends, and his studies and early experiences in medicine; it also points towards later cures. By anticipating them, it has become a living symbol of the future. It is a fruitful action which associates Wilhelm with the smallest group, composed of those who wander and cure. He can thus become, as he writes to Natalie, a 'useful, necessary member of the community'.[113]

Felix is saved according to law, i.e. the laws of nature discovered by medical science. To use the words of the poem, 'the moment is eternity' since it links father and son again with life itself. The close kinship of the poem with the last scene of the novel reveals how every fact and feature was conceived in the same spirit.

The second poem, *Im ernsten Beinhaus*, condenses the themes of the novel once more by embracing the whole course of man's life. This *memento mori*, in the end, becomes a *memento vivere*. 'Remember to live'[114] – these words of Goethe correspond to the mood which ends the poem. Even death must be looked upon from the vantage point of life. The bones are like *vestigia Dei*, thoughts which have been realized.[115] Every individual life reveals a trace of the divine, and even in the most unusual life, the experienced observer is able to read the secret laws according to which all organisms grow and pass away:

> Was kann der Mensch im Leben mehr gewinnen,
> Als dass sich Gott-Natur ihm offenbare?
> Wie sie das Feste lässt zu Geist zerrinnen
> Wie sie das Geisterzeugte fest bewahre.[116]

These powerful final lines bring these ideas together. Wilhelm has, as a student of anatomy and as a surgeon, discovered the unity of God and nature, and makes practical use of this theoretical knowledge which he had also experienced at Makarie's home and in the Pedagogic Province.

These two poems, like the collection of sayings, recall other works of Goethe's old age: *West-östlicher Diwan*, *Dichtung und Wahrheit* and *Faust II*. *West-östlicher Diwan*, like most of the stories of the *Wanderjahre*, is about love. This cycle of poetry, too, is a book whose parts are only loosely connected, though its themes are much less universal. *Dichtung und Wahrheit* depicts a life within a distinct, historical epoch. Goethe as an autobiographer may have reached the same stage of detachment as the narrator of the *Wanderjahre*, but the young Goethe whose life he was describing had certainly not reached the same stage of renunciation as Wilhelm. It is doubtful whether it is possible ever to have quite the same detachment from one's own life as one can have from a character of one's creation. Nonetheless, the continuation of the autobiography, *Tag- und Jahreshefte* or *Annalen*, recalls some parts of the *Wanderjahre*, for there, too, much that is important is described in a laconic manner. *Dichtung und Wahrheit* itself could be more appropriately compared with the *Lehrjahre*. In *Dichtung und Wahrheit*, Goethe finally reached a point where life appeared to him full of promise, but Goethe's story stops at an earlier stage of his development than Wilhelm's.

The *Wilhelm Meister* novels, like *Faust*, accompanied Goethe throughout his life. Both the drama and the novels show unmistakable signs of the length of their gestation. In the novels, Goethe deals with social institutions and tendencies and reveals a complex multi-dimensional view of the world. Both are symbolic and give us insight into a rich world. The beginning may not be easy, but what we gather is not only the wisdom of Goethe's old age conveyed in a didactic manner, but also his quest for new forms which are outside the range of classicism.[117] The modern way of seeing the world is anticipated. Although in his theory of art Goethe never went beyond classicism, in his practice as a writer and by implication in some of his aphorisms, he suggests new possibilities. A twentieth-century novelist of note, Hermann Broch, believed that the *Wanderjahre* was a forerunner of the modern novel.[118] This view, however, is hardly tenable. The *Wanderjahre* may have inspired Broch; it has not, however, been a model for experimental novelists, but in retrospect, it may appear that Goethe attempted to compose a novel whose structural mode came into its own only a century or so later. To have done so is no mean achievement. If the impact of the *Wanderjahre*, unlike that of the *Lehrjahre*, on literary history has been negligible, it does not mean that the work cannot interest a modern reader; for in fact, its situations can sufficiently compel our attention to make us believe it to be a work of art.

Notes

1. Letter to Sulpiz Boisserée, 30 December 1826.
2. Letter to Johann Friedrich Rochlitz, 28 July 1829.
3. Ibid.
4. Letter to Sulpiz Boisserée, 2 September 1829.
5. Conversation with Friedrich von Müller, 18 February 1830.
6. Letter to Karl Friedrich Zelter, 5 June 1829.

7. W.A., i, 25, ii, p. 1; apparently he thought it unnecessary to spell out this appellation; cf. also letter to W. Reichel, 9 January 1829, in which he wrote 'those words' [novel by Goethe] are 'superfluous here' and should on Reichel's suggestion be 'struck out'; cf. also Hans Reiss, 'Wilhelm Meisters Wanderjahre. Der Weg von der ersten zur zweiten Fassung', *DVLG*, xxxix (1965).

8. Cf. Staiger, *Goethe*, Zurich, 1952–9, iii, pp. 129 ff. for a representative view.

9. Cf. Ludwig Geiger, 'Goethe und Pustkuchen', in J. F. W. Pustkuchen, *Wilhelm Meisters Wanderjahre*, i, New Impression, Berlin, 1913, p. 27; cf. also Gustav Dichler, ' "Wilhelm Meisters Wanderjahre" im Urteil deutscher Zeitgenossen', *Archiv für das Studium der neueren Sprachen*, 87 Jg, 162 Bd. (1932), pp. 23 ff.

10. J. F. W. Pustkuchen, *Wilhelm Meisters Wanderjahre*, Quedlinburg and Leipzig, 1821–8.

11. Friedrich Nicolai, *Freuden des jungen Werthers*, Berlin, 1775.

12. Cf. Eberhard Sarter, *Zur Technik von Wilhelm Meisters Wanderjahren*, Bonner Forschungen, N.F., 7, Berlin, 1914, pp. vii ff. for a review of secondary literature before 1914, and Hans Joachim Schrimpf, *Das Weltbild des späten Goethe*, Stuttgart, 1956, pp. 10 ff. for recent secondary literature.

13. The rise of stylistic analysis appears mainly responsible for seeing the novel in a different perspective; cf. Erich Trunz, H.A., 8, pp. 579 ff.; Deli Fischer-Hartmann, *Goethes Altersroman. Studien über die innere Einheit von Wilhelm Meisters Wanderjahren*, Halle, 1941; R. Lissau, *Wilhelm Meisters Wanderjahre. A critical re-examination and revaluation.* (M.A. Diss. London, 1943, unpublished); Ernst Friedrich von Monroy, 'Zur Form der Novelle in "Wilhelm Meisters Wanderjahre" ', *Germanisch-Romanische Monatsschrift*, xxxi (1943); André Gilg, *Wilhelm Meisters Wanderjahre und ihre Symbole*, Zürcher Beiträge zur Deutschen Literatur und Geistesgeschichte, 9, Zürich, 1954; Wilhelm Emrich, 'Das Problem der Symbolinterpretation im Hinblick auf Goethes "Wanderjahre", *DVLG*, xxxvi (1952), pp. 331 ff. and Schrimpf, op. cit., who all see the novel in a different perspective. An earlier essay in a similar vein is Eduard Spranger, 'Der psychologische Perspektivismus im Roman', *JbFDH* (1930).

14. H. M. Waidson, 'Death by Water or the Childhood of Wilhelm Meister', *MLR*, lvi (1961), pp. 45 ff.

15. Cf. Eugen Wolff, 'Die ursprüngliche Gestalt von Wilhelm Meisters Wanderjahrer', *GJb.*, xxxiv (1913).

16. Cf. Trunz, H.A., 8, p. 600.

17. Stuttgart, 1821.

18. *Wilhelm Meister oder die Entsagenden. Ein Roman von Goethe* (ed. Max Hecker) Der Domschatz, 4, Berlin, 1921.

19. Cf. Kurt Bimler, *Die erste und die zweite Fassung von Wilhelm Meisters Wanderjahren*, Beuthen, 1907 (Diss., Breslau, 1907).

20. Cf. Hans Reiss, 'Wilhelm Meisters Wanderjahre'.

21. Karl Jungmann, 'Die pädagogische Provinz. Eine Quellenstudie', *Euph.*, xiv (1907); cf. also Küntzel, G.A., 8, pp. 892 ff.

22. Harold Jantz, 'Die Ehrfurchten in Goethes "Wilhelm Meister" ', *Euph.*, xlviii (1954).

23. See Friedrich Ohly, 'Goethes *Ehrfurchten* – ein *ordo caritatis*', *Euph.*, lv (1961), a most informative and learned article (see particularly p. 116).

24. Trunz, H.A., 8, p. 718.

25. See Ohly, 'Goethes *Ehrfurchten* . . .', p. 419, who points out that Goethe had been reading August Kestner, *Die Agape oder der geheime Weltbund der Christen*, Jena, 1819. From this book he probably took the name 'Montan' which he gave Jarno and perhaps even the key-word '*Ehrfurcht*' (reverence), but above all, Kestner discusses *Hermae Pastor*, the apocalypse of the early Christians, an important post-apostolic text.

26. See Ohly, 'Goethes *Ehrfurchten* . . .', pp. 435 ff.

27. See ibid., pp. 425 ff.

28. For a full discussion of the language of Goethe's later period cf. Friedrich Maurer, *Die Sprache Goethes im Rahmen seiner menschlichen und künstlerischen Entwicklung*, Erlanger Universitäts-Reden, 14, Erlangen, 1932; cf. also Paul Knauth, *Goethes Sprache und Stil im Alter*, Leipzig, 1898, for a close analysis of Goethe's language in his old age, especially pp. 77 ff.; cf. also Bimler, op. cit. Ernst Lewy, *Zur Sprache des alten Goethe. Ein Versuch über die Sprache des Einzelnen*, Berlin, 1913, p. 15, speaks of a 'tendency towards participial periods' in the prose of Goethe's old age.

29. Cf. the letters to W. Reichel, 4 March 1829 and 19 March 1829, W.A., iv, 45, p. 399; cf. also the following essays on the discussion which took place: Karl Vietor, 'Goethes Gedicht auf Schillers Schädel', *PMLA*, lix (1944) (Reprinted in *Geist und Form*, Berne, 1952); Franz H. Mautner, Ernst Feise and Karl Vietor, 'Ist fortzusetzen . . .', *PMLA*, lix (1944); A. R. Hohlfeld, 'Zur Frage einer Fortsetzung von "Wilhelm Meisters Wanderjahre" ', *PMLA*, lx (1945); Karl Vietor, 'Zur Frage einer Fortsetzung . . . (Antwort)', *PMLA*, lx (1945); cf. also Reiss, 'Wilhelm Meisters Wanderjahre'.

30. Cf. H. S. Reiss, 'Bild und Symbol in "Wilhelm Meisters Wanderjahren" ', *Studium Generale*, vi, 1953, for a more extensive discussion of the problem.

31. Cf. Willoughby, 'The Cross-Fertilization of Literature and Life

in the Light of Goethe's Theory of "Widerspiegelung" ', *Comparative Literature*, i (1949).

32. W.A., i, 24, p. 94 (i, 6).

33. W.A., i, 24, p. 347 (ii, 5).

34. H.A., 8, p. 486, No. 179.

35. Cf. Willoughby, 'The Image of the "Wanderer" and the "Hut" ', *ÉG*, vi (1951), p. 207.

36. W.A., i, 24, p. 6 (i, 1).

37. Emrich, op. cit. has studied the function of this image and has even considered it to be the key of the novel. This symbol is undoubtedly significant, but Emrich's formulation overstates his case; Wolfgang Staroste, 'Zur Ding-Symbolik in Goethes "Wilhelm Meister" ', *Orbis Litterarum*, xv (1960), is more cautious; for him this object is a chiffre linking together disparate parts of the novel (p. 47); cf. also Friedrich Ohly, 'Zum *Kästchen* in Goethes "Wanderjahren" ', *Zeitschrift für Deutsches Altertum*, 1961–2, who discusses the origins of this object.

38. See Barker Fairley, *Goethe's Faust. Six Essays*, Oxford, 1953, p. 74: 'What emerges clearly in all cases of losing consciousness is that in some sense a shift of consciousness is involved; the poem moves from one plane to another.'

39. Cf. Willoughby, 'The image of the Horse and the Charioteer in Goethe's Poetry', *PEGS*, xv (1946), for a fuller consideration of the function of this image.

40. W.A., i, 25, i, p. 3 (ii, 8).

41. Letter to Karl Jakob Ludwig Iken, 27 September 1827.

42. Eugen Wolff, 'Die ursprüngliche Gestalt . . .', p. 169.

43. W.A., i, 18, p. 190.

44. H.A., 8, p. 486, No. 182.

45. W.A., i, 24, p. 51 (i, 4).

46. Cf. Benno von Wiese, 'Der Mann von funfzig Jahren', *Die Deutsche Novelle von Goethe bis Kafka*, ii, Düsseldorf, 1962, gives a subtle appreciation of the narrator's role in this story.

47. Cf. Ohly, 'Goethes *Ehrfurchten* . . .', pp. 411 ff.

48. See Trunz, H.A., 8, p. 607.

49. H.A., 8, p. 283, No. 5.

50. W.A., i, 24, p. 193.

51. Letter to Karl Friedrich Zelter, 13 August 1831.

52. W.A., i, 25, i, p. 30 (ii, 9).

53. W.A., i, 24, p. 34 f. (i, 2).

54. Letter to C. W. Göttling, 17 January 1829.

55. W.A., i, 25, i, p. 249 (iii, 13); the *Wanderjahre* has on occasion been interpreted as a novel with a social message – cf. here above all Ferdinand Gregorovius, *Goethes Wilhelm Meister in seinen sozialistischen*

Elementen entwickelt, Königsberg, 1849; Gustav Radbruch, 'Wilhelm Meisters sozialpolitische Sendung', *Logos*, viii, 1919/20, and 'Wilhelm Meisters sozialistische Sendung', *Gestalten und Gedanken*, Leipzig, 1944, pp. 100 ff.; Pierre-Paul Sagave, 'L'Economie et l'homme dans les "Années de Voyage de Wilhelm Meister" ', *ÉG*, vii (1952) and 'Les "Années de Voyage de Wilhelm Meister" et la critique socialiste 1830–1848'. *ÉG*, viii (1953). (Both articles reprinted in *Recherches sur le roman social en Allemagne*, Aix-en-Provence, 1960, pp. 11 ff.)

56. W.A., i, 25, i, p. 101 (iii, 4).
57. Cf. Trunz, H.A., 8, pp. 650 f.
58. W.A., i, 24, p. 215 (i, 11).
59. Conversation with Riemer, 1823 (G.A., 23, p. 292).
60. Conversation with Riemer, 20 February 1828.
61. Cf. Trunz, H.A., 8, p. 702 f.
62. W.A., i, 25, i, p. 181, (iii, 9).
63. W.A., i, 25, i, p. 56 f. (ii, 11).
64. W.A., i, 24, p. 51 (i, 4).
65. Cf. Ohly, 'Goethes *Ehrfurchten* . . .', pp. 406 ff.
66. Cf. ibid., p. 410.
67. Trunz, H.A., 8, p. 595, cf. also W.A., i, 24, p. 378 (ii, 7).
68. Letter to Karl Friedrich Zelter, 18 June 1831.
69. Cf. Letter from Eckermann to Thomas Carlyle: 'Goethe's high-minded activity is never interrupted, not even for a day, indeed his example compels us to revere the maxim that all useless suffering is to be overcome by useful activity', 6 December 1830 (W.A., iv, 48, p. 32).
70. Cf. Ohly, 'Goethes *Ehrfurchten* . . .', p. 442.
71. Letter to Friedrich Johann Rochlitz, 23 November 1829.
72. Cf. for instance, letter to Zelter, 6 June 1825.
73. Cf. Ohly, 'Goethes *Ehrfurchten* . . .', pp. 444 ff.
74. Cf. Arthur Henkel, *Entsagung*. *Eine Studie zu Goethes Altersroman*, Hermea, Germanistische Forschungen, N.F. 3, Tübingen, 1954, p. 36, a most helpful study to which my argument is greatly indebted.
75. Ibid., p. 132.
76. Letter to Karl Friedrich Zelter, 21 November 1830.
77. Cf. Henkel, *Entsagung*, pp. 42 f.
78. Ibid., pp. 51 f.
79. W.A., i, 2, p. 249: 'Impatience is of no use and repentance even less; the one increases guilt, the other creates new guilt.'
80. Cf. Henkel, *Entsagung*, p. 58.
81. Cf. ibid., p. 48.
82. Cf. Trunz, H.A., 8, p. 600.
83. Cf. Henkel, *Entsagung*, p. 82.
84. Cf. W.A., i, 20, p. 133 (*Die Wahlverwandtschaften*, i, 12).

85. W.A., i, 25, i, p. 82 (iii, 3).
86. Cf. Trunz, H.A., 8, p. 664.
87. W.A., i, 41, 1, p. 218: 'Eros – Love. It does not tarry – Eros rushes down from heaven whither he had blown from the ancient chaos. On a spring day he hovers down with his wings fluttering about his brow and breast. He seems now to flee, but turns back in his flight, there is joy in grief, so sweet and fearful. Many a heart loses itself in the universe, but the most noble devotes itself to one.'
88. Ibid., pp. 218 f.
89. Letter to Wilhelm von Humboldt, 17 March 1832.
90. H.A., 8, p. 284, No. 7.
91. W.A., i, 24, p. 352 (ii, 6); cf. Eric A. Blackall, 'Wilhelm Meister's Pious Pilgrimage', *GLL*, xviii (1965), a stimulating article to which the following observations are indebted.
92. Cf. Eduard Spranger, 'Goethe über die menschlichen Lebensalter', *Goethes Weltanschauung*, Wiesbaden, 1949, pp. 88 ff.
93. Christoph Schweitzer, 'Wilhelm Meister und das Bild vom kranken Königssohn', *PMLA*, lxxii, 1957, p. 432.
94. Letter to Karl Friedrich Zelter, 8 July 1830, 'The great advantage for him and for us will arise from his becoming aware of himself, from his experiencing that which is within him and which he could not become in our simple-limited (*einfach-beschränkten*) circumstances.'
95. Cf. Barker Fairley, 'Goethe's Last Letter', *University of Toronto Quarterly*, xxvii (1957).
96. Cf. Eduard Spranger, 'Die sittliche Astrologie der Makarie in "Wilhelm Meisters Wanderjahren" ', *Goethes Weltanschauung*, Wiesbaden (1949), pp. 197 ff.
97. Cf. Radbruch, 'Wilhelm Meisters sozialpolitische Sendung', 'Wilhelm Meisters sozialistische Sendung'.
98. W.A., i, 24, p. 263 (ii, 3).
99. I cannot share the views of August Raabe, 'Das Dämonische in den "Wanderjahren" '. *G*, i (1936), pp. 119 ff., who maintains that these elements occupy the foreground.
100. W.A., i, 25, ii, p. 109.
101. Cf. Claude David, 'Goethes "Wanderjahre" als symbolische Dichtung', *Sinn und Form*, viii (1956); Victor Lange, 'Goethe's Craft of Fiction', *PEGS*, xxii (1953).
102. Cf. David, op. cit.
103. Letter to W. Reichel, 2 May 1829.
104. H.A., 8, p. 283, No. 3.
105. H.A., 8, p. 305, No. 150.
106. H.A., 8, p. 305, No. 151.
107. Cf. Wilhelm Flitner, 'Aus Makariens Archiv. Ein Beispiel

Goethescher Spruchkomposition', *Goethe-Kalender auf das Jahr 1943*, xxxvi, Leipzig, 1943, pp. 116 ff., for a study of the relations between the aphorisms or groups of aphorisms. He does not succeed in establishing a convincing order, but he is able to show how some of the aphorisms can be related to ideas mentioned in the narrative. Cf. also Trunz, H.A., 8, pp. 681 ff. and pp. 717 ff., who is less inclined to find an order in the aphorisms than Flitner.

108. Conversation with Friedrich von Müller, 8 June 1821.

109. Letter to Joseph Stanislaus Zauper, 7 September 1821.

110. W.A., i, 3, i, p. 83.

111. Letter to Karl Friedrich Zelter, 31 December 1829.

112. W.A., i, 3, p. 83: 'Enjoy plenty and blessing with moderation. Let reason be present in all places where life is happy at the sight of life; then the past is constant, the future is alive in advance and the moment is eternity.'

113. W.A., i, 25, i, p. 60 (ii, 11).

114. W.A., i, 23, p. 198 (*Lehrjahre* viii, 5).

115. Vietor, 'Goethes Gedicht . . .', p. 200.

116. W.A., i, 3, p. 94: 'What can man gain more in life than that God-Nature be revealed to him? How Nature allows matter to dissolve into spirit and how she preserves what mind has produced.'

117. Cf. David, op. cit; Walter Höllerer, *Zwischen Klassik und Moderne*, Stuttgart, 1958; Walther Killy, *Wandlungen des lyrischen Bildes*, Göttingen, 1956.

118. Cf. Hermann Broch, 'James Joyce und die Gegenwart', *Dichten und Erkennen. Essays*, i, Zürich, 1955, pp. 204 ff.; 'Das Weltbild des Romans. Ein Vortrag', ibid., pp. 236 ff.

Conclusion

GOETHE'S novels are only one part of his literary work, but they are as significant as his dramas and his lyric poetry. No other writer of similar stature created important works in all these genres. In all three fields, Goethe was a pioneer. His dramas point to the future; he changed traditional forms.[1] In the novel, too, he was original and unconventional and created a new style for each of his four novels. This style always corresponds to the themes and content of the work and is appropriate to them. The form is determined each time by the specific way in which the individual encounters society, and the action of the novel results from this encounter. In contrast to the drama, however, the events are not taken from history, legend or myth; the individual is confronted with the social problems of his age. Goethe's novels are novels of the period; they not only depict his own time, but also the attempt of an individual to come to terms with it. For the treatment of such questions Goethe considered the novel most suitable.[2] Both external and inner reasons made him take this view. External considerations were a factor because, undoubtedly, the novel's reading public was much larger. Goethe hoped that themes from art and concerned with society would find a large number of readers. The novel was also the rising literary form, even if Goethe himself never accorded it equal status with drama. Inner reasons were also at work: Goethe was anxious to prove his worth in every literary genre and to raise the level of the novel was a challenge. For the description of particular social problems the novel was also especially suitable; to depict the life of an individual who, inwardly isolated, is unable to find satisfaction in society, the form of the epistolary novel was most appropriate. To depict the rich life of the theatre and the development of a young man, the pedagogic novel was necessary, for only this form produced sufficient breadth of description and a corresponding extension in time. As Goethe turned away from the practice of the classical period, it seemed no longer fitting to depict the life of an individual who was attempting to find a place in the community. Since different ways of living had to co-exist, an open form allowing for a series of stories loosely tied together with the main plot seemed more suitable. The dynamic events of *Die Wahlverwandtschaften*, which resulted from the conflict between man, nature and society, demanded a form of their own whose structural law was based on the implicit separation and reunion of characters.

Werther is mainly the story of an individual who breaks down because he makes absolute demands on life, and society does not afford him an outlet for his intellectual capacity. Werther becomes a symbol of political and social deficiencies; his sorrows reveal the inevitability of our social involvement. The *Lehrjahre* depicts a utopian sphere of activity common to both aristocrats and the middle classes, such as existed in England, where the aristocracy was continuously strengthened by recruits from the middle classes. The *Lehrjahre* implies that in a revolutionary period catastrophes should be avoided, though crises cannot. In *Die Wahlverwandtschaften*, social forms have become petrified. It looks as if, in the end, the choice exists only between the breakdown of the institution of marriage and the destruction of individuals. The *Wanderjahre* points to the danger of disintegration in a society threatened by industrialization. Utopian solutions are proposed in order to protect men from complete dehumanization.

Goethe's novels were written when it had become clear that feudalism was doomed and the triumph of capitalism had become inevitable. In the *Wilhelm Meister* novels, ways are delineated by which this transition can take place peacefully, while in *Werther* and in *Die Wahlverwandtschaften* the individual is destroyed because social institutions prove stronger and are incapable of adaptation. *Werther*, close to Rousseau's world, contains implicit criticism of an antiquated social environment; in *Die Wahlverwandtschaften*, the breakdown of married life is a symbol of the social institution of marriage itself and of contemporary society.

There is interchange in the novels between didactic and

descriptive elements. There is no description or analysis of the social structure as such, but some situations can serve as models of social conduct; others may serve as a warning, suggesting the need for social reform.

In Goethe's novels, emphasis is, on the whole, laid on the reaction of the individual to society,[3] reflecting a problem which confronted Goethe himself. From the autobiographical elements in *Werther* resulted the lyrical impulse which, in turn, endowed it with its powerful dynamic quality. *Werther* appeared to Goethe as a work threatening his equilibrium; to think of it still disturbed him half a century later:

> Wer mit XXII den Werther schrieb
> Wie kann der mit LXXII leben![4]

In 1774, when he composed the first version, Goethe had not yet achieved detachment, so that his problems were still more immediately transposed into his epic writings. The autobiographical element still remained in the foreground, but it slowly receded. The more Goethe was capable of seeing himself objectively, of affirming a standpoint from which he was able to consider as historical everything that he encountered,[5] the less autobiographical his fiction becomes.

He therefore restricted the direct discussion of his own life to his autobiographical writings: *Dichtung und Wahrheit*, *Campagne in Frankreich*, *Belagerung von Mainz* and *Die italienische Reise*. These four works belong to narrative prose, but are not novels; yet their structure is in accordance with the principles of fiction, even if they treat autobiographical events.[6] In Goethe's narrative prose, the autobiographical work must be distinguished from the novels; both, it is true, describe the individual in his age, but from a different point of view. To turn to overt autobiography and away from autobiographical – or semi-autobiographical – fiction, means to turn to objectivity and towards a complex vision of life. Both tendencies become more noticeable in each successive stage of life. This development is seen in the language and in the function of the narrator. The unprecedented, powerful rhythm and lyrical manner of speech of Werther contrasts with the calm objective speech of the narrator. In the *Lehrjahre*, the objective tone prevails; only in the lyric poems is the other voice heard. The last trace of an inharmonious manner of narration which still existed in the *Sendung* has been extinguished in the *Lehrjahre*. In *Die Wahlverwandtschaften* there are no lyric poems; the language is evenly balanced, but more reflective and symbolic. In Ottilie's diary, reflection has been granted a sphere of its own. This sphere is further extended in the *Wanderjahre*, but at the same time many modes of style reveal a complex vision of the world corresponding to the reflective, the lyrical or the purely objective descriptive element. In *Die Wahlverwandtschaften*, and in those chapters of the *Wanderjahre* which were written late, a tendency towards a concentrated manner of expression grows; there is more to be apprehended, since more has become capable of being apprehended. In *Werther*, the editor has one essential function. He is critically ironical, but his speech is overshadowed by Werther's emotional outbursts. In the *Lehrjahre*, the ironic narrator plays a much more important role than the editor of Werther's letters, showing how much stronger the tendency to objectivity has become. In *Die Wahlverwandtschaften*, the narrator is also objective; he reveals a deep insight into psychology. His formulations of general laws demonstrate a more intensive objectivity. In the *Wanderjahre*, this comes to the fore even more strongly. He sees himself as an ironic observer who edits the work and makes his objectivity known in an almost scientific manner. He knows that many things can be presented only by intimation, in a concentrated form through a series of images which reflect one another.

The images which occur in the novels are mainly links holding ideas and experiences together. Both the images, and the themes which they illustrate – nature, society, religion, love, death and reality – are seen in different perspectives in each novel.

Man is closely attached to nature; indeed, he is part of it. For Werther it mirrors his inner life; he is incapable of regarding the rhythmic change in nature with detachment, of abandoning himself to its rhythm. As long as he is hopeful, he is in tune with it; if he is in despair, he is estranged from it and lives without any hope of new growth. In the *Lehrjahre*, it is not so much the relationship between man and external nature that is stressed as a result of Goethe's scientific work, but morphological studies are applied to human life. The inner nature of man is described in terms of quality and development, and the course of natural change is depicted in terms of the process of the human personality. In *Die Wahlverwandtschaften*, nature is seen in a very different perspective. Its outward phenomena have symbolic significance. The characters more rarely identify themselves with nature, but they grasp what appears to them to be significant. Particularly important, however, is inner nature. It is less subjected to a process of development in stages; its tremendous power is depicted. Not biographical development but chemical laws are used for illustration, for culture is concerned with 'that which has been produced and that which is being produced'.[7] The disposition of the characters in the novel is fixed, but they develop their relations with one another and with society.[8] What is opposed to nature cannot flourish, but the characters are unable to carry on a fruitful activity since human life does not depend on natural laws alone; it is for the individual to channel the forces of nature according to the rules of custom and morality. Man's relationship with nature is also a central problem of the *Wanderjahre*. Nature demands that we follow its laws, and stop wherever it imposes limitations. On the other hand, we have to renounce our natural impulses when they come into conflict with society. Nature is the basis of all human activity, but it is nonetheless involved in a continuous interplay with social need. Neither nature nor society is constant; without awareness of their constant change it is impossible for man to attain real maturity.

The description of social life is developed in a similar manner. In *Werther* the hero is prepared to participate in it as long as he is happy; as soon as he despairs he is alienated from society. In the *Lehrjahre*, similar obstacles are described which stand in the way of the *Bürger*, but the possibility still exists for him to further his education and to be accepted in a sphere where noblemen carry on practical activity.

Society is unchanged, but Wilhelm succeeds in entering other social spheres. In *Die Wahlverwandtschaften*, there is no change in the social scene; close interchange between society and nature determines the structure and through its symbolism shows how profoundly society can affect personal life. In the *Wanderjahre*, social life is seen in the perspective of continuous change. Man is judged by his success in adapting himself to it. At the same time, he is confronted with forces which bring to the fore latent capacities, but his failure is not condemned by the same stern law of necessity as in *Die Wahlverwandtschaften*.

Human imperfection is mirrored in the shortcomings of the social order. In *Werther* the social order is seen from the point of view of a man who cannot adapt himself. His desire to develop his personality fully forces him into a conflict with the traditional forms of society[9] and there is no indication how this is to be resolved. In the *Lehrjahre*, however, constructive social thought is more fully disclosed. The political crisis which threatens feudal rule is to be countered by an active group of intelligent men, held together by intellectual bonds and personal friendship. Class differences become insignificant, for the novel ends with a series of marriages which break down the barriers at that time dividing the aristocracy from the middle class. The community does not wish to rule through an active intervention in daily politics. It believes in humanism and hopes that its ideals will be realized, even if with difficulty. The affinity to Schiller's political thought in the *Aesthetic Letters* is obvious.[10]

In the *Wanderjahre*, these ideas are developed even more fully through pedagogic attempts to incite men to political activity. It is assumed that such men would be free from political and social prejudice and could have a positive effect on social life and promote stability. *Die Wahlverwandtschaften*, on the other hand, makes it clear how society can be threatened if political open-mindedness and social equilibrium are not pursued. The political and social thought of the two *Wilhelm Meister* novels was of urgent significance for Goethe's own revolutionary age.

Education and religion are the forces which most of all further a willingness to accept change. For Werther, the problem of education hardly exists. His immediate feelings preoccupy him so much that he is not able to be extensively, or even systematically, concerned with his education. For Wilhelm, education is a major concern. Growing inner clarity becomes outwardly visible through his readiness and through his acquired capacity to embark upon practical realistic action. An educational process is thus described. In *Die Wahlverwandtschaften*, only Ottilie develops. A growth of maturity and of inner awareness characterizes her development. In the *Wanderjahre*, Wilhelm's education takes a practical turn: he trains for a profession. In the Pedagogic Province, practical training is considered essential. Equal rights and equal importance are ascribed to different religions: the view is not subjective as in *Werther*. Of course, Werther is not an orthodox Christian, but his attitude is determined by the Christian style of thinking. He compares his sufferings even to those of Christ, believing that he has to bear the sufferings of mankind vicariously. In the *Lehrjahre*, Wilhelm encounters Christianity as an educative force essential for his spiritual and emotional development. In *Die Wahlverwandtschaften*, Charlotte's and Ottilie's actions are determined by Christian ideas of marriage, but none of Goethe's novels is inspired by a truly Christian outlook. The most important figure of the *Wanderjahre*, Makarie, radiates saintly qualities, but we do not know if she is a practising or believing Christian.

Religion is one of the forces which permit man to accept life's vicissitudes. Without this acceptance, on which renunciation is based, no activity has any meaning for the later Goethe. In the *Wanderjahre* the characters are judged according to the criteria of renunciation. It is particularly necessary in *Die Wahlverwandtschaften*. It is possible only with increasing maturity, for the force of love is absolute, and determines the fate of a human being. The editor intimates that Werther has put forward a one-sided point of view. In the *Lehrjahre*, on the other hand, Wilhelm experiences that love can be lasting only if it also permits practical activity, for a man who is not bound by the demands of society and ethics cannot prosper.

In the *Wanderjahre*, love is decisive; attention is focused less on the experience of one single person or of a group, but rather on the experience of the various individuals at different stages and levels of life. Love, here, is seen as one of the forces of life which bind men together but also separate them. Without it, communal life is impossible, but it is not the only power: custom, convention and religion are equally essential.

For Werther, love ends in death which grants what life denied. Death for him is fate; for the editor, however, it is part of the process of living. In the *Lehrjahre*, for the most part and in the *Wanderjahre*, a positive view prevails: death is not granted dominion over man's thinking. In *Die Wahlverwandtschaften* on the other hand, the thought of death comes again and again, in accordance with the tragic spirit of the work, but a detached mode of narration prevails.

A novel can be an attempt to find a satisfactory attitude to reality.[11] *Werther* is still conditioned by the conflicting views of reality held by the hero and the editor. The *Lehrjahre* leads from confusion to clarity. The vision of reality is still further differentiated in *Die Wahlverwandtschaften*, but the main characters do not succeed in finding a satisfactory attitude to reality in their relation to one another. Goethe's view of the world is here more complex than in the *Lehrjahre*. In the *Wanderjahre*, only Makarie even approaches a level of living which affords an all-embracing view of reality. No one view can ever do justice to the complexity of life. The criterion of useful, practical activity allows us to gauge here and also in *Die Wahlverwandtschaften*, the degree of realism achieved.

The organization of the novels also shows a distinct development.[12] In *Werther*, the incidents and the images are interrelated and are at first misinterpreted by Werther as guarantors of his hope. When his mood darkens, the outward world grows dark too. The *Lehrjahre* is so organized that many characters and events allow us to gauge what perils lurk in Wilhelm's way and what possibilities are open to him. Hamlet, Werner, the Melina family, Friedrich, and even the Harper, are warnings to Wilhelm, yet they also allow us to see him more clearly. Friedrich's conviction of being a father and his lack of direction, Hamlet's use of a play in order to understand the situation in which he finds himself, Lothario's love-affair, the Harper's instability, Werner's pedantry and Melina's social decline, all place Wilhelm's endeavours in an ironic setting. They tell us as much of what he might have become as of what he did become.

The organization of *Die Wahlverwandtschaften* is much more complex. Goethe created a highly complex work of fiction, whose structure is akin to drama. The large number of incidents, of details and of images which illustrate the development show the different states of mind of the protagonists and reveal how closely experiences and mutual relations are linked.

The open form of the *Wanderjahre* produces much looser organization. The stories and experiences are like a series of portraits or mirrors that illuminate one another. The principle of analogy is at work.

The form of the individual novels had to be different because Goethe saw the world differently at different stages of his life. The material (*Stoff*) was different, but this is also true of the significance of the work, its import (*Gehalt*). The vision of the poet as a young man was directed towards the individual, extreme case; intensity of experience where feeling and convention, experience and practice were still in flux demanded that reality be presented in a concentrated manner. The lengthy gestation of the *Lehrjahre* is a sign of the change and development of Goethe's image of reality. The way from the special to the typical could not be found too quickly; it needed time. Emphasis was no longer laid on the individual, but on the group, and finally on a series of groups which demanded new forms; for instance, the compactness of *Die Wahlverwandtschaften* with its intense concentration, or the open form of the *Lehrjahre*, where the events reflect the differences between the various groups of individuals.

Goethe never stood still. In each novel, he created new modes of fiction. His contemporaries partly recognized this, but they also misunderstood him much of the time. *Werther* evoked many imitations.

The influence of the *Lehrjahre*, however, was more extensive. As the outstanding example of the German pedagogic novel, it overshadowed German fiction in the nineteenth and twentieth centuries. The Romantics, and many of their successors such as Stifter, Keller, Thomas Mann and Hermann Hesse, saw it as a forerunner of their own work.[13] Yet this novel had in one respect a fate similar to that of *Werther*; it met with both sympathetic appreciation and misunderstanding. Novalis, for example, was at first enthusiastic, and considered it as a model[14] hardly capable of being surpassed.[15] Later on he called it a 'fatal and foolish, pretentious and precious' book – a *Candide* directed against poetry.[16]

Die Wahlverwandtschaften was a *succès d'estime*, many critics seeing in it only an attack on marriage. The *Wanderjahre* was not well received; it was set aside as the strange work of an old man. It is not difficult to see why. *Werther* and the *Lehrjahre* speak directly to a wide circle of readers, but Goethe must have been aware from the very beginning that *Die Wahlverwandtschaften* and the *Wanderjahre* would not become popular. In his youth and in the first years of his friendship with Schiller, he was anxious to reach a wide reading public. He hoped that culture could be furthered from Weimar through important work like his own and that of Schiller.[17] The failure of their common plans disappointed him greatly. Only through education can a genuine culture arise and last: for 'many thoughts only stand out from a great culture like the blossoms from green branches. At the time of rose-blossom we see roses everywhere.'[18] The discontinuation of Schiller's journal *Die Horen* was a symbol of this failure. In *Literarischer Sansculottismus* (1795) Goethe had castigated his age, which did not appreciate his efforts. It became clearer and clearer to him that he wrote for a few people only:

> My writings cannot become popular. Whoever hopes and strives for this end is mistaken. My works are not written for the mass – only for the individual who desires and seeks something similar. . . .[19]

He had to hope from the future for what the literary public of the day had refused him.

> What we write, we should devote to the distant, to the future.[20]

Werther and the *Lehrjahre* formed the intellectual tendencies of the time and were representative of many trends, but the two later novels stimulated only a few writers, and are of much less importtance in the intellectual history of the age, though their influence may well be more enduring.

Nonetheless, Goethe was fully aware of the literary tendencies of his time. All his novels are closely associated with the rise of prose fiction.[21] *Werther* is inconceivable without Goethe's encounter with the English sentimental novel, with Rousseau, with Pietism. Wieland's *Agathon*, Karl Philipp Moritz's *Anton Reiser*, the rise of the theatre, Pietistic writings, the literature of the Enlightenment and Lessing's attempt to create a vital German drama, all had a noticeable influence on the *Lehrjahre*. *Die Wahlverwandtschaften* and the *Wanderjahre* are closely linked to Romantic aspirations. *Die Wahlverwandtschaften* even supplies an answer to Romantic ethics by refuting the views of the Romantics on marriage and personality;[22] for Goethe, who took a broad-minded view about many things, marriage was sacred. The *Wanderjahre*, on the other hand, could be considered as a symbolic work such as the Romantics sought in vain to create.[23]

In the context of contemporary theories of fiction, it becomes clear that although Goethe was in practice a pioneer, his fiction in fact carried out what the theorists had demanded, even though no definite link can be established between them and Goethe. Blanckenburg's theory, for instance, justified the passive hero in fiction, although there is no reason to believe that his *Versuch über den Roman* influenced *Werther*. Blanckenburg's views on the hero's inner development through the impact of events on his mind are more likely to have left their mark on the *Lehrjahre*, though again no proof of any direct influence can be substantiated. Furthermore, in the *Lehrjahre*, Goethe certainly defined the nature of the hero of fiction in a manner which agrees with Blanckenburg: i.e. as mainly passive.[24] Jean Paul's demand for formal rigour in the dramatic novel is adhered to in *Die Wahlverwandtschaften*. On the other hand, the open form of the *Wanderjahre* may well agree with contemporary conceptions of fiction.[25] Close as these parallels appear, Goethe himself did not venture to support his innovations as a novelist by bold theoretical argument. In his writings on literary criticism and theory, he did not speak out in defence of the novel.

What does the literary world of today think of Goethe's novels? It is difficult to ascertain, even in Germany, whether Goethe's novels still find enthusiastic readers. Goethe may be the favourite author of the university teacher of German, but he is certainly not the most popular German novelist – even for the educated German, let alone for the non-German reader of fiction. The *Lehrjahre* is still, both in Germany and elsewhere, more popular than the *Wanderjahre*. Yet in English-speaking countries, despite Carlyle's translations, it is less frequently read than *Werther*; a recent translation has done nothing to alter the situation.

The academic historian of literature, especially if he be a German scholar, may be tempted to ignore public opinion. Has not Goethe scholarship become an institution of modern academic, if not modern intellectual, life? And do the many publications about the individual novels of Goethe not prove that they belong to the front rank of fiction? For the historian of literature the gulf between significance and popularity may be beside the point, yet it exists. The scholar should not ignore the views of his own age; he ought to ask himself the question whether he does not represent vested interests. Academic literary critics are always in danger of becoming outsiders so that one day their views and even they themselves will be swept away by the tide of general culture. But this question is very complicated. What constitutes the intellectual life of an age? How and where is it found? And who has a right to assume the role of its speaker?:

> Was Ihr den Geist der Zeiten heisst,
> Das ist im Grund der Herren eigner Geist,
> In dem die Zeiten sich bespiegeln.[26]

Still, it can be argued that the critic has the duty to believe in and follow the criteria of his discipline. He must not lose contact with educated readers in so far as they still exist, i.e. if specialization has not obliterated them. The educated reading public may be mistaken and need further education, but the taste of the day must encourage the interpreter to revise his views.

Goethe's major dramas are part of the traditional repertory in German-speaking countries, but his novels are not a major topic of intellectual discussion. If they are read, it is mainly because, in Germany, they belong to the classical heritage. Outside Germany, they are perhaps revered but scarcely read. *Faust* alone of his major works has acquired both a position of respectability and a wide audience.

What are the reasons for this apparent neglect? If overwhelmed by the material, we disregard the form – as some critics did – we are likely to consider *Werther* sentimental[27] and, here as in other novels, miss the tension; by comparison with the immediate impact of other novels, much in the *Lehrjahre*, the *Wanderjahre* and *Die Wahlverwandtschaften* appears remote.

Such critical objections are mistaken. They are based on two false presuppositions. Firstly Goethe, except in his *Sturm und Drang* work, is not a poet who overwhelms the reader at first sight. Insight comes only after repeated reading: the deeper the experience of his work, the richer it appears.

Secondly, the historical conditions of his writings are easily ignored. Although his novels are of general human interest, they deal essentially with contemporary problems. The conceptions of sentimental love and of social conflict are different today. We live in an age which generally prefers a more sober tone of expression, but the basic problem facing a sensitive individual in a hostile world remains the same. The sentimentality of the late eighteenth century may be out of date. To many, if not to most readers, inner experience in an age of heightened awareness and excessive self-criticism will appear different from what it did to the eighteenth-century view. If we avoid these prejudices and concentrate upon the structural qualities of *Werther*, we cannot miss its powerful quality. Anyone who has experienced the destructive force of passion can be affected by the unique form which Goethe found for it in *Werther*. Anyone who forms an objective judgement of life in its fullness must accord passion and *taedium vitae* a place in life, but will not hold them to be the essential forces of life. Even Goethe, whose positive attitude to life cannot be in doubt, addressed these to Werther almost half a century after he published his first novel:

> Zum Bleiben ich, zum Scheiden du erkoren,
> Gingst du voraus und hast nicht viel verloren.[28]

This allows us to assume that he believed that Werther represented a fundamental human possibility, and in a conversation with Eckermann, he expressed this same view more fully:

> The age of Werther, which has been so much discussed, does indeed occur, if we look at it more closely, not in the course of world history, but in the course of the life of every individual, who, endowed with an innate and free natural bent, has to learn to adapt himself to the confining forms of an out-of-date world. Thwarted, inhibited activity and unsatisfied wishes are not the failings of a particular age, but of every individual human being, and it would be very wrong, indeed, if every one were not to have, at some time or other in his life, a period in which 'Werther' affected him as if it had been written for him specially.[29]

The *Lehrjahre* represents a more comprehensive achievement. It is difficult not to concede that the novel lacks tension, even if the individual scenes are most effective. This lack of tension is a result partly of the rambling nature of the action, and partly of the lack of force of the plot. By way of contrast to *Werther*, the reader is not shaken; the narrator's irony prevents this. Yet the ironic tone does not fail to arouse the reader's interest. There are thus both strength and weakness in this feature; for it also raises him to a higher intellectual level, the level of critical understanding. The situation is not powerful enough to shock the reader. Above all, the character of Wilhelm is not dynamic. Despite all his amiability, sensitivity and urbanity, he is colourless by comparison with, for instance, the heroes of Balzac and Dostoevsky. On the historical plane, the political and social fermentation is missing. Somerset Maugham characterized these features in a rather ironic manner:

> I suppose few people in England read it now, unless for scholastic reasons they are obliged to, and I don't know why anyone should – except that it is lively and amusing, both romantic and realistic; except that the characters are curious and unusual, very much alive and presented with vigour; except that there are scenes of great variety, vivid and admirably described, and at least two of high comedy, a rarity in Goethe's works; except that interspersed in it are lyrics as beautiful and touching as any that he ever wrote; except that there is a disquisition on Hamlet which many eminent critics have agreed is a subtle analysis of the Dane's ambiguous character; and above all, except that its theme is of singular interest. If, with all these merits, the novel on the whole is a failure, it is because Goethe, for all his genius, for all his intellectual powers, for all his knowledge of life, lacked the specific gift which would have made him a great novelist as well as a great poet.[30]

We need not agree with this view, though these flaws – if they can be called flaws – may have prevented many an interested reader from studying the work. However, it is precisely in the so-called flaws that the strength of the novel is found; for the calm enlightened tone produces an objective, typical image and shows us the turns which the development of a sensitive man can take. Occasionally, the modern reader may be disturbed by certain improbabilities in the action, but, by comparison with the richness of thought and the masterly fashion in which Wilhelm's experience was presented, they are of minor importance. The deeper we penetrate into the novel, the more connections we see. An inexhaustible work, it still fascinates readers: its impact on German literature has lasted from romanticism to the present day.

Die Wahlverwandtschaften, on the other hand, depicts the gestation of an elemental experience of tragic quality. The depth of symbolism cannot be recognized on a superficial reading. It is possible, with Somerset Maugham, to hold that the characters are shallow and the situations artificial, that there is no genuine development of the action, that whole chapters, like the episodes concerning the architect or Luciane, are tedious,[31] but nonetheless we should be prepared to probe more deeply. Once we grasp the symbolism, the inevitability of the catastrophe produces the tautness otherwise found only in a great tragedy. *Die Wahlverwandtschaften* must be read as a psychological tragedy. It is the first great European novel with a carefully elaborated and compact form. It is a precursor of the closely knit novels of Flaubert and Henry James, which have set the tone for much of modern fiction, though admittedly, it did not serve as a model for these French and English novelists.

The *Wanderjahre* lacks a strict form, and the action does not convey the sense of necessity found in *Die Wahlverwandtschaften*. Its didactic tone and lack of tension have been adversely criticized. Mainly for that reason only a few readers of the *Lehrjahre* turn to the *Wanderjahre*. But if we read it as an experiment, as the forerunner of many modern novels, we shall find it interesting. The *Wanderjahre* may lack the structural coherence and the inner consistency of the modern novel, however, if a reader is prepared to read it again and again and thus to absorb the atmosphere of the work, he will gain much.

In all these novels, the reader who has been brought up in the tradition of the realistic, psychological novel of the nineteenth and twentieth centuries will find many strange features. Goethe, however, was indifferent to the demands of realism. He wrote in a non-deterministic tradition of the novel and had no scruples about introducing, for instance, many accidental events which are not psychologically motivated. Goethe wrote his novels in order to entertain an audience which differed from the reading public of today and which did not expect the measure of probability characteristic of the modern realistic novel.

A more serious drawback is that few characters in Goethe's fiction possess the precious blend of forcefulness and originality which is the mark of striking literary characters. What are the reasons for this muted impact? No simple answer can be given, for they are different in each novel. In each, his delineation is sure and his portraits are plausible, but each presents a markedly different approach to characterization. Werther dominates Goethe's first novel to such an extent that the other characters, even Lotte and Albert, never fully emerge from his orbit. Werther alone is treated in depth. He, and he alone, possesses the complexity and originality which put him among the great figures of European literature. In the *Lehrjahre*, Goethe was mainly interested in the impact of the environment on the individual and in the problems of the individual's education, and Wilhelm thus became a passive figure who does not wish to mould his environment. The other characters are not explored in depth and are too close to the conventional novel to be original. Mignon alone is original (it is not surprising that she became the heroine of an opera); yet her early death prevents the further growth of her personality. The main characters of *Die Wahlverwandtschaften* are much more carefully analysed. However, they are not interesting people in themselves; they excite interest only on account of the emotional conflicts engendered by their relationships. Ottilie is potentially interesting, but, like Mignon, she dies too early to lead a full adult life. In the *Wanderjahre*, on the other hand, several of the characters have interesting ideas and lead unusual lives, but the emphasis is, in the main, not on the personalities, but on ideas and attitudes of mind. On the whole, there is little concern with detail of characterization. The characters also lack the dynamism and power which great literary characters normally exude.

In a quite different, but always appropriate, manner, each of these novels offers us something that is 'significant, true, beautiful, something that is a whole cosmos with its own laws'; it thus satisfies Goethe's own criteria of literary excellence[32] and guarantees his achievement. No other German novelist has shown a similar originality in all of his great narrative work. The power and dignity of the style and the intensity and breadth of the themes in the four novels surpass that of all German writers of fiction of his day. It has not been very different in our century. Did not Thomas Mann, the most versatile German, if not European writer of this century, create his novels and short stories in the tradition of Goethe? What could be a more striking example of the lasting power of his fiction? But Goethe is unique not only in the sphere of German writing. There are many other European novelists whose narrative power and creative vigour is greater, whose immediate impact has been more significant and who are more widely read, but Goethe need yield to none with regard to variety and originality of form and depth of content. No other novelist has embraced wider spheres of experience and thought, no one has been more comprehensive in the whole of his creative work. Lyric poetry and scientific thought became part of his fiction. *Werther* and *Die Wahlverwandtschaften* offer intensity of experience, and the *Wilhelm Meister* novels a breadth of vision, which make them rank as equals with the other great European novels.

The objections which have been raised against Goethe as a novelist are, in the last resort, of as little significance as his own considerations about the impurity of the form of fiction, if we compare them with the powerful, many-sided achievement of his epic work. Goethe's novels confirm the experience which he gained as a scientist and conveyed as a poet.

They are protean and offer us a new view each time we read them. They force us to re-examine our experience. There can be no greater proof of their continued vitality; and the words of Goethe's poem *Parabase* may well be applied to them:

Und es ist das ewig Eine,
Das sich vielfach offenbart;
Klein das Grosse, gross das Kleine,
Alles nach der eignen Art,
Immer wechselnd, fest sich haltend,
Nah und fern und fern und nah;
So gestaltend, umgestaltend –
Zum Erstaunen bin ich da.[33]

Notes

1. Ronald Peacock, 'Goethe's Version of Poetic Drama', *PEGS*, xvi (1947), p. 51.
2. Cf. Lange, 'Goethe's Craft of Fiction', *PEGS*, xxii (1953), who considers this aspect fully.

3. Cf. E. L. Stahl, 'Goethe as Novelist', *Essays on Goethe* (ed. William Rose), London, 1949, p. 70.

4. W.A., i, 3, p. 271.

'He who wrote Werther at XXII
how can he live at LXXII!'

5. Cf. Letter to Adolph Müllner, 6 April 1818.

6. Cf. Steer, '*Goethe's Social Philosophy as revealed in* Campagne in Frankreich *and* Belagerung von Mainz', University of Carolina Studies in the Germanic Languages and Literature, 15, Chapel Hill, 1955, who makes this point for the latter two works.

7. W.A., ii, 6, i, p. 9 (*Zur Morphologie*, i).

8. Cf. Stahl, 'Goethe as Novelist', p. 67; cf. also E. Kohn-Bramstedt, *Aristocracy and the Middle Classes. Social Types in German Literature 1830–1900*. London, 1937, pp. 29 ff. for a sociological analysis of Goethe's fiction.

9. Cf. Georg Lukács, 'Wilhelm Meisters Lehrjahre', *Goethe und seine Zeit*, Berne, 1947, pp. 40 ff.

10. Cf. L. A. Willoughby, 'Schiller on Man's Education to Freedom through Knowledge', *GR*, xxix (1954); cf. also H. S. Reiss, 'The Concept of the Aesthetic State in the Work of Schiller and Novalis', *PEGS*, xxvi (1957).

11. Cf. Trilling, *The Liberal Imagination*, London, 1951, p. 209.

12. Cf. Liselotte Dieckmann, 'Repeated Mirror Reflections: The Technique of Goethe's Novels', *Studies in Romanticism*, i, Boston, 1962, pp. 154 ff. for a full account of this aspect of Goethe's novels, excluding the *Wanderjahre*.

13. Cf. Roy Pascal, *The German Novel*, Manchester, 1956, for a study of the main trends of the German novel.

14. Novalis, *Werke*, ed. Ewald Wasmuth, Berlin, 1943, iii, pp. 271 ff.

15. Ibid., p. 275.

16. Ibid., p. 278.

17. Cf. Bruford, *Culture and Society in Classical Weimar 1775–1805*, Cambridge, 1962, for a penetrating analysis of Goethe's views on culture and his cultural leadership.

18. H.A., 8, p. 486, No. 177.

19. Conversation with Eckermann, 11 October 1828.

20. H.A., 12, p. 512, No. 1035.

21. Ian Watt, *The Rise of the Novel. Studies in Defoe, Richardson and Fielding*, London, 1957.

22. Cf. Walzel, 'Goethes "Wahlverwandtschaften" im Rahmen ihrer Zeit', *GJB*, xxvii (1906), pp. 166 f.

23. David, 'Goethes "Wanderjahre" als symbolische Dichtung', *Sinn und Form*, viii (1956), pp. 126 ff.

24. W.A., i, 22, p. 177 (v, 7).

25. I owe this observation to Friedrich Sengle, who informs me that one of his students is expected to publish soon a dissertation arguing this point.

26. W.A., i, 14, p. 35 (*Faust* 577–9): 'What you call the spirit of the times is basically the spirit of men themselves in which the times are mirrored.'

27. Cf. Leonard Forster, 'Goethe und das heutige England', *Euph.*, xlv (1950), p. 36, who quotes A. J. P. Taylor, *The New Statesman and Nation*, 26 February 1949.

28. W.A., i, 3, p. 19:

> 'I was chosen to stay, you were chosen to leave.
> You went first – and did not lose much.'

29. Conversation with Eckermann, 2 January 1824.

30. W. Somerset Maugham, 'Three Novels of a Poet', *Points of View*, London, 1958, p. 2.

31. Ibid., p. 48.

32. Jolles, *Goethes Kunstanschauung*, Berne, 1957, pp. 223 ff.

33. W.A., i, 3, p. 84: 'And it is the eternal unity which reveals itself in manifold forms. Whatever is great is small, whatever small is great. Everything after its own kind, always changing, yet keeping its identity, near and far, far and near, thus shaping and reshaping. I am here to be – astonished.'

Select Bibliography

(*a*) *Goethe: Collected Works*

Goethes Werke. Vollständige Ausgabe letzter Hand, Stuttgart and Tübingen, 40 vols., 1827–30.

Goethes Werke, 133 vols. (in 143), Weimar, 1887–1919 (Weimarer or Sophien-Ausgabe).

Goethes Sämtliche Werke (ed. E. von der Hellen), 40 vols. (and one index vol.), Stuttgart and Berlin (1902–12) (Jubiläumsausgabe).

Goethes Werke (ed. Robert Petsch), 18 vols., Leipzig, 1926–7 (Festausgabe).

Goethe. *Gedenkausgabe der Werke, Briefe und Gespräche* (ed. Ernst Beutler), 24 vols., Zürich, 1948–60.

Goethes Werke (ed. Erich Trunz), 14 vols. (and one index vol.). 1948–64. *Goethes Briefe*, 3 vols. to date, Hamburg, 1962 ff. (Hamburger Ausgabe).

Werke Goethes (ed. Deutsche Akademie der Wissenschaften), Berlin, 1952 ff.

Der junge Goethe (ed. Max Morris), 6 vols., Leipzig, 1909–12 (revised ed. by Hanna Fischer-Lamberg, 3 vols. to date, Berlin, 1963 ff.).

Graef, Hans Gerhard (ed.), *Goethe über seine Dichtungen* (3 parts in 9 vols.), Frankfurt/Main, 1901–14.

(*b*) *Goethe: individual works and translations*

Der wahre Werther (edition of 1774 with introduction by Alexander Leynet-Holenia), Hamburg-Vienna, 1959.

The Sorrows of Young Werther (ed. and trans. William Rose), London, 1929.

Goethe's Die Leiden des jungen Werthers (ed. E. L. Stahl), Oxford, 1942.

Wilhelm Meisters Theatralische Sendung (ed. Harry Maync), Stuttgart and Berlin, 1911.

Wilhelm Meisters Theatralische Sendung (ed. Günther Weydt), Bonner Texte, 7, Bonn, 1949.

Kindred by Choice [*Die Wahlverwandtschaften*] (trans. H. M. Waidson), London, 1960.

Wilhelm Meisters Wanderjahre oder die Entsagenden. Ein Roman von Goethe, Teil I, Stuttgart and Tübingen, 1821 (first version) (2nd ed. by Max Hecker, Der Domschatz, 4, Berlin, 1921).

(*c*) *Other primary sources*

Blanckenburg, Christian Friedrich von, *Versuch über den Roman*, Leipzig und Liegnitz, 1774 (2nd facsimile edition by Eberhard Lämmert, Sammlung Metzler, 39, Stuttgart, 1965).

Engel, Johann Jacob, *Fragmente über Handlung, Gespräch und Erzählung*, Leipzig, 1774 (reprinted *Schriften*, iv, pp. 254 ff., Berlin, 1802); facsimile ed. of 1774 edition by Ernst Theodor Voss, Sammlung Metzler, 37, Stuttgart, 1965.

Lessing, Gotthold Ephraim, *Hamburgische Dramaturgie* (1767–8) (*Sämtliche Schriften* ed. by Karl Lachmann [3rd ed. by F. Muncker], Stuttgart, 1886–1900).

Lichtenberg, Georg Christoph, 'Vorschlag zu einem orbis pictus für deutsche dramatische Schriftsteller, Romanen-Dichter und Schauspieler', *Göttingisches Magazin der Wissenschaften und Literatur* (ed. G. C. Lichtenberg and Georg Forster), i, 3, 1780.

Merck, Johann Heinrich, 'Über den Mangel des epischen Geistes in unserm lieben Vaterland', *Teutscher Merkur*, xxi, 1778.

Nicolai, Friedrich, *Freuden des jungen Werthers*, Berlin, 1775.

Novalis (Hardenberg, Friedrich von) *Werke* (ed. Ewald Wasmuth), Berlin, 1943.

Pustkuchen, Johann Friedrich Wilhelm, *Wilhelm Meisters Wanderjahre*, Quedlinburg and Leipzig, 1821–8 (new impression ed. Ludwig Geiger, Berlin, 1913).

Richter, Jean Paul Friedrich, *Vorschule der Aesthetik*, *Sämtliche Werke*, i, 11, Weimar, 1935.

Schlegel, Friedrich, 'Fragmente', *Athenäum*, i, Berlin, 1798.

— 'Über Goethes Meister', ibid.

(*d*) *Secondary Literature*

Abeken, Rudolf, 'Über Goethes Wahlverwandtschaften', *Morgenblatt für gebildete Stände*, 22, 23 and 24 January 1810 (reprinted *Graef*, i, 1, pp. 438 ff.; H.A., 6, pp. 627 ff.).

Amann, Paul, *Schicksal und Liebe in Goethes 'Wahlverwandtschaften'*, Basler Studien zur deutschen Sprache und Literatur, 25, Berne and Munich, 1962.

Anstett, J. J., 'La crise religieuse de Werther', *ÉG*, iv, 1949.

Appell, J. W. von, *Werther und seine Zeit*, 4th ed., Oldenburg, 1896.

Appelbaum-Graham, Ilse, 'Minds Without Medium: Reflections on *Emilia Galotti* and *Werthers Leiden*', *Euph.*, lvi, 1962.

Arndt, Karl J. R., 'The Harmony Society in *Wilhelm Meisters Wanderjahre*', *Comparative Literature*, x, 1958.

Atkins, Stuart Pratt, *The Testament of Werther in Poetry and Drama*, Cambridge, Mass., 1949.

— 'J. G. Lavater and Goethe. Problems of Psychology and Theology in *Die Leiden des jungen Werthers*', *PMLA*, lxiii, 1948.

Aulhorn, Edith, 'Der Aufbau von Goethes "Wahlverwandtschaften"', *Zeitschrift für den deutschen Unterricht*, xxxii, 1918.

Barnes, H. G., 'Bildhafte Darstellung in den "Wahlverwandtschaften"', *DVLG*, xxx, 1956.

— 'Ambiguity in *Die Wahlverwandtschaften*', *The Era of Goethe. Essays presented to James Boyd*, Oxford, 1959.

— 'Goethes "Wahlverwandtschaften" vor der katholischen Kritik', *Literaturwissenschaftliches Jahrbuch*, Neue Folge, i, 1960.

Barnes, H. G., *Die Wahlverwandtschaften. A Literary Interpretation*, Oxford, 1967.

Bauer, Georg Karl, 'Makarie', *Germanisch-Romanische Monatsschrift*, xxv, 1937.

Baumhof, H., *Die Funktion des Erzählers in Goethes 'Wilhelm Meisters Lehrjahre'* (unpublished 1958 Diss.), Heidelberg, 1959.

Beaujean, Marion, *Der Trivialroman in der zweiten Hälfte des 18. Jahrhunderts. Der Ursprung des modernen Unterhaltungsromans*, Abhandlungen zur Kunst-, Musik- und Literaturwissenschaft, 22, Bonn, 1964.

Becker, Eva D., *Der deutsche Roman um 1780*, Germanistische Abhandlungen, 5, Stuttgart, 1964.

Benjamin, Walter, 'Goethes Wahlverwandtschaften', *Neue Deutsche Beiträge*, ii, 1, 1924 (reprinted in *Schriften*, i, Frankfurt/Main, 1955).

Berend, Eduard (ed.) *Goethe, Kestner und Lotte*, Munich, 1914.

Beriger, Hanno, *Goethe und der Roman. Studien zu Wilhelm Meisters Lehrjahre* (Diss.), Zürich, 1955.

Beutler, Ernst, 'Wertherfragen', *G*, v, 1940.

Bimler, Kurt, *Die erste und die zweite Fassung von Goethes Wanderjahren*, Beuthen, 1907 (Diss. Breslau, 1907).

Blackall, Eric A., *The Emergence of German as a Literary Language 1700–1775*, Cambridge, 1959.
— 'Wilhelm Meister's Pious Pilgrimage', *GLL*, xviii, 1965.
— 'Sense and Non-Sense in *Wilhelm Meisters Lehrjahre*', *Deutsche Beiträge zur geistigen Überlieferung*, v, Berne and Munich, 1965.
Borcherdt, Hans Heinrich, *Der Roman der Goethezeit*, Urach, 1949.
Böschenstein, Hermann, *Deutsche Gefühlskultur*, i, Berne, 1954.
Boucke, Ewald, *Goethes Weltanschauung auf historischer Grundlage*, Stuttgart, 1907.
— *Wort und Bedeutung in Goethes Sprache*, Literarhistorische Forschungen, 20, Berlin, 1911.
Brandes, Georg, *Goethe* (German trans. Erich Holler and Emilie Stein), 4th ed., Berlin, 1922.
Brinkmann, Hennig, 'Zur Sprache der Wahlverwandtschaften', *Festschrift für Jost Trier*, Meisenheim/Glan, 1954.
Brinkmann, Richard, *Wirklichkeit und Illusion. Studien über Gehalt und Grenzen des Begriffs Realismus für die erzählende Dichtung des neunzehnten Jahrhunderts*, Tübingen, 1957.
Broch, Hermann, 'James Joyce und die Gegenwart', *Dichten und Erkennen*, *Essays*, i, Zürich, 1955.
— 'Das Weltbild des Romans. Ein Vortrag', ibid.
Bruford, W. H., ' "Goethe's Wilhelm Meister" as a Picture and Criticism of Society', *PEGS*, i, 1933.
— *Germany in the Eighteenth Century*, Cambridge, 1935.
— *Theatre, Drama and Audience in Goethe's Germany*, London, 1949.
— 'Goethe's Reputation in England since 1832', *Essays on Goethe* (ed. W. Rose), London, 1949.
— 'A Foot-Note on Wilhelm Meister', *German Studies presented to L. A. Willoughby*, Oxford, 1951.
— *Culture and Society in Classical Weimar 1775–1805*, Cambridge, 1962.
Butler, E. M., 'The Element of Time in Goethe's *Werther* and Kafka's *Prozess*', *GLL*, xii, 1959.
Catholy, Eckehard, 'Karl Philipp Moritz. Ein Beitrag zur Theatromanie der Goethezeit', *Euph.*, xlv, 1950.
— *Karl Philipp Moritz und die Ursprünge der deutschen Theaterleidenschaft*, Tübingen, 1962.
Clark, Robert T., Jr., 'The Metamorphosis of Character in *Die Wahlverwandtschaften*', *GR*, xxix, 1954.
— 'The Psychological Framework of Goethe's *Werther*', *JEGP*, xxix, 1954.
Croce, Benedetto, 'Die beiden Fassungen des Wilhelm Meister', *Goethe* (trans. Werner Ross), Düsseldorf, 1949.

David, Claude, 'Goethes "Wanderjahre" als symbolische Dichtung', *Sinn und Form*, viii, 1956.

Delp, Wilhelmine, 'Goethe und Gessner', *MLR*, xx, 1925.

Diamond, William S., 'Wilhelm Meister's Interpretation of Hamlet', *Modern Philology*, xxiii, 1925–6.

Dichler, Gustav, ' "Wilhelm Meisters Wanderjahre" im Urteil Deutscher Zeitgenossen', *Archiv für das Studium der neueren Sprachen*, 87 Jg., 162 Bd., 1932.

Dickson, Keith, 'Spatial Concentration and Themes in *Die Wahlverwandtschaften*', *Forum for Modern Language Studies*, i, 1965.

— 'The Temporal Structure of *Die Wahlverwandtschaften*', *GR*, xli, 1966.

Dieckmann, Liselotte, 'Repeated Mirror Reflections: The Technique of Goethe's Novels', *Studies in Romanticism*, i, Boston, 1962.

Diez, Max, 'The Principle of the Dominant Metaphor in Goethe's *Werther*', *PMLA*, li, 1936.

Düntzer, Heinrich, *Goethes 'Die Leiden des jungen Werthers'*, 6th ed., Leipzig, 1880.

Dvoretzky, Edward, 'Goethe's *Werther* and Lessing's *Emilia Galotti*', *GLL*, xvi, 1962.

Eichner, Hans, 'Natalie and Therese: Some Remarks on Goethe's Conception of Love and Marriage', a paper read at the 78th meeting of the M.L.A. at Chicago, December 1963 (unpublished).

— 'Zur Deutung von Wilhelm Meisters Lehrjahren', *JbFDH*, 1966.

Ellis, J. M., 'Names in *Faust* and *Die Wahlverwandtschaften*', *Seminar. A Journal of Germanic Studies*, i, 1965.

Emmel, Hildegard, *Weltklage und Bild der Welt in der Dichtung Goethes*, Weimar, 1957.

Emrich, Wilhelm, 'Das Problem der Symbolinterpretation im Hinblick auf Goethes "Wanderjahre" ', *DVLG*, xxxvi, 1952.

Enright, D. J., 'Wilhelm Meister and the Ambiguity of Goethe', *Cambridge Journal*, vi, 1952–3.

Fairley, Barker, *Goethe as revealed in his poetry*, London, 1932.

— *A Study of Goethe*, Oxford, 1947.

— *Goethe's Faust. Six Essays*, Oxford, 1953.

— 'Goethe's Last Letter', *University of Toronto Quarterly*, xxvii, 1957.

Feise, Ernst, 'Zur Enstehung, Problem und Technik von Goethes "Werther" ', *JEGP*, xiii, 1914.

— 'Lessing's *Emilia Galotti* and Goethe's *Werther*', *Modern Philology*, xv, 1917.

— 'Goethes Werther als nervöser Charakter', *GR*, i, 1926 (reprinted in *Xenion. Themes, Forms and Ideas in German Literature*, Baltimore, Maryland, 1950).

Fischer-Hartmann, Deli, *Goethes Altersroman. Studien über die innere Einheit von Wilhelm Meisters Wanderjahren*, Halle, 1941.

Fittbogen, Gottfried, 'Die Charaktere in den beiden Fassungen von Werthers Leiden', *Euph.*, xvii, 1910.

Flitner, Wilhelm, 'Aus Makariens Archiv. Ein Beispiel Goethescher Spruchkomposition', *Goethe-Kalender auf das Jahr 1943*, xxxvi, Leipzig, 1943.

— *Goethe im Spätwerk*, Hamburg, 1947.

Forster, E. M., *Aspects of the Novel*, London, 1927.

Forster, Leonard, 'Goethe und das heutige England', *Euph.*, xlv, 1950.

— 'Werther's Reading of *Emilia Galotti*', *PEGS*, xxvii, 1958.

François-Poncet, André, *Les Affinités Électives de Goethe*, Paris, 1910.

Fries, Albert, *Stilistische Beobachtungen zu Wilhelm Meister*, Berliner Beiträge zur germanischen und romanischen Philologie, 44, Berlin, 1912.

Funck, Heinrich (ed.), *Die schöne Seele. Bekenntnisse, Schriften, und Briefe der Susanne Katharina von Klettenberg*, Leipzig, 1911.

Geerdts, Hans Jürgen, *Goethes Wahlverwandtschaften*, Weimar, 1958.

Gerhard, Melitta, *Der deutsche Entwicklungsroman bis zu Goethes 'Wilhelm Meister'*, *DVLG* Buchreihe, 9, Halle/Saale, 1926.

Gibelin, J., 'Une source possible des *affinités électives de Goethe*', *Revue de Littérature Comparée*, xxvii, 1953.

Gilg, André, *Wilhelm Meisters Wanderjahre und ihre Symbole*, Zürcher Beiträge zur Deutschen Literatur und Geistesgeschichte, 9, Zürich, 1954.

Gloel, Heinrich, *Goethes Wetzlarer Zeit*, Berlin, 1911.

Gose, Hans, '*Goethe's Werther*', Bausteine zur Geschichte der Literatur, 18, Halle, 1921.

Graefe, Johanna, 'Die Religion in den "Leiden des jungen Werthers" ', *G*, xx, 1958.

Gregorovius, Ferdinand, *Goethes Wilhelm Meister in seinen socialistischen Elementen entwickelt*, Königsberg, 1849.

Greiner, Martin, *Die Entstehung der modernen Unterhaltungs-Literatur, Studien zum Trivialroman des 18. Jahrhunderts*, Reinbek near Hamburg, 1964.

Grimsley, Ronald, *Rousseau. A Study in Self-awareness*, Cardiff, 1961.

Grosser, Alfred, 'Le jeune Werther et le Piétisme', *ÉG*, iv, 1949.

Gundolf, Friedrich, *Shakespeare und der deutsche Geist*, Berlin, 1911.

— *Goethe*, Berlin, 1916.

Hankamer, Paul, *Spiel der Mächte*, Tübingen, 1943.

Hass, Hans-Egon, 'Werther-Studie', *Gestaltprobleme in der Dichtung* (*Festschrift für Günther Müller*) (ed. Richard Alewyn, Hans-Egon Hass and Clemens Heselhaus), Bonn, 1957.

Hass, Hans-Egon, 'Wilhelm Meisters Lehrjahre', *Der deutsche Roman*, i (ed. Benno von Wiese), Düsseldorf, 1963.

Hatfield, Henry, 'Towards the Interpretation of *Die Wahlverwandtschaften*', *GR*, xxiii, 1948.

— *Goethe. A Critical Introduction*. Norfolk, Conn., 1963 (Cambridge, Mass., 1964.)

Havuck, J., 'Psychoanalytisches aus und über Goethes "Wahlverwandtschaften" ', *Imago*, i, Vienna, 1913.

Henkel, Arthur, *Entsagung*. Hermea. Germanistische Forschungen, N.F. 3, Tübingen, 1954.

— 'Versuch über den Wilhelm Meister', *Ruperto-Carola*, xlv, Heidelberg, 1962.

Hennig, John, 'Englandkunde in "Wilhelm Meister" ', *G*, xxvi, 1964.

Herbst, Wilhelm, *Goethe in Wetzlar*, Gotha, 1889.

Hering, Robert, *Wilhelm Meister und Faust und ihre Gestaltung im Zeichen der Gottesidee*, Frankfurt/Main, 1952.

Heun, Hans Georg, *Der Satzbau in der Prosa des jungen Goethe*, Palaestra, 172, Leipzig, 1930.

Hirsch, Arnold, 'Barockroman und Aufklärungsroman', *ÉG*, ix, 1954.

— *Bürgertum und Barock im deutschen Roman. Ein Beitrag zur Entstehungsgeschichte*, 2nd ed. by Herbert Singer, Literatur und Leben, N.F. 1, 1957.

— 'Die Leiden des jungen Werthers. Ein bürgerliches Schicksal im absolutistischen Staat', *ÉG*, xiii, 1958.

Hofmannsthal, Hugo von, 'Der Urmeister', *Prosa III*, Frankfurt/Main, 1952 (first published *Neue Freie Presse*, Vienna, 1911).

Hohlfeld, A. R., 'Zur Frage einer Fortsetzung von "Wilhelm Meisters Wanderjahre" ', *PMLA*, lx, 1945.

Höllerer, Walter, *Zwischen Klassik und Moderne*, Stuttgart, 1958.

Huinandeau, O., 'Les Rapports de Goethe et de Lavater', *ÉG*, iv, 1949.

Ittner, Robert T., '*Werther* and *Emilia Galotti*', *JEGP*, xli, 1942.

Jantz, Harold, 'Die Ehrfurchten in Goethes "Wilhelm Meister". Ursprung und Bedeutung', *Euph.*, xlviii, 1954.

Jenisch, Daniel, *Über die hervorstichendsten Eigenthümlichkeiten von Meisters Lehrjahren, oder über das, wodurch dieser Roman ein Werk von Göthen's Hand ist*, Berlin, 1797.

Jolles, Matthijs, *Goethes Kunstanschauung*, Berne, 1957.

Jungmann, Karl, 'Die pädagogische Provinz. Eine Quellenstudie', *Euph.*, xiv, 1907.

Kayser, Wolfgang, 'Die Entstehung von Goethes "Werther" ', *DVLG*, xix, 1941.

Kestner, A. (ed.), *Goethe und Werther*, Stuttgart and Tübingen, 1854.

Killy, Walther, 'Wirklichkeit und Kunstcharakter. Goethe: "Die Wahlverwandtschaften" ', *Wirklichkeit und Kunstcharakter. Neun Romane des 19. Jahrhunderts*, Munich, 1963.

— *Wandlungen des lyrischen Bildes*, Göttingen, 1956.

Kindermann, Hans, *Theatergeschichte der Goethezeit*, Vienna, 1948.

Klotz, Volker (ed.), *Zur Poetik des Romans*, Wege der Forschung, 35, Darmstadt, 1965.

Knauth, Paul, *Goethes Sprache und Stil im Alter*, Leipzig, 1898.

Knudsen, Hans, *Goethes Welt des Theaters*, Berlin, 1949.

Koester, Albert, 'Wilhelm Meisters Theatralische Sendung', *Zeitschrift für den deutschen Unterricht*, xxvi, 1912.

Kohn-Bramstedt, Ernst, *Aristocracy and the Middle Classes. Social Types in German Literature 1830–1900*, London, 1937.

Köpke, R., *Ludwig Tieck*, Leipzig, 1885.

Lange, Victor, 'Goethe's Craft of Fiction', *PEGS*, xxii, 1953.

— 'The Language of the Poet Goethe 1772–1774', *Wächter und Hüter. Festschrift für Hermann J. Weigand*, New Haven, Conn., 1957.

— 'Erzählformen des Romans im achtzehnten Jahrhundert', *Anglia*, 1958, reprinted in *Zur Poetik des Romans* (ed. Volker Klotz), Wege der Forschung, 35, Darmstadt, 1965.

— 'Die Sprache als Erzählform in Goethes "Werther" ', *Formenwandel. Festschrift zum 65. Geburtstag von Paul Böckmann* (ed. W. Müller-Seidel and W. Preisendanz), Hamburg, 1964.

Langen, August, *Der Wortschatz des deutschen Pietismus*, Tübingen, 1954.

Lauterbach, Martin, *Das Verhältnis der zweiten zur ersten Ausgabe von Werthers Leiden*, Quellen und Forschungen zur Sprach- und Kulturgeschichte der germanischen Völker, 110, Strassburg, 1910.

Leitzmann, Albert, 'Studien zum Urmeister', *G*, x, 1947.

Leppmann, Wolfgang, *The German Image of Goethe*, Oxford, 1961 (*Goethe und die Deutschen*, Stuttgart, 1962).

Lewy, Ernst, *Zur Sprache des alten Goethe. Ein Versuch des Einzelnen*, Berlin, 1913.

Lissau, R., *Wilhelm Meisters Wanderjahre. A critical re-examination and revaluation* (M.A. diss., London, 1943, unpublished typescript).

Lockemann, Theodor, 'Der Tod in Goethes "Wahlverwandtschaften" ', *JbGG*, xix, 1933.

Lockemann, Wolfgang, *Die Entstehung des Erzählproblems. Untersuchungen zur deutschen Dichtungstheorie im 17. und 18. Jahrhundert*, Meisenheim/Glan, 1963.

Lubbock, Percy, *The Craft of Fiction*, London, 1921.

Lukács, Georg, 'Die Leiden des jungen Werthers; "Wilhelm Meisters Lehrjahre" ', *Goethe und seine Zeit*, Berne, 1947.

Mann, Thomas, 'Zu Goethes "Wahlverwandtschaften" ', *Die Neue Rundschau*, xxxvii, 1925.

Martini, Fritz, 'Der Bildungsroman. Zur Geschichte des Wortes und der Theorie', *DVLG*, xxxv, 1961.

Maugham, W. Somerset, 'Three Novels of a Poet', *Points of View*, London, 1958.

Maurer, Friedrich, *Die Sprache Goethes im Rahmen seiner menschlichen und künstlerischen Entwicklung*, Erlanger Universitäts-Reden, 14, Erlangen, 1932.

Maurer, K. W. 'Goethe's "Elective Affinities" ', *MLR*, xlii, 1947.

Maurer, Karl, 'Die verschleierten Konfessionen. Zur Entstehungsgeschichte von Goethes Werther', *Die Wissenschaft von Deutscher Sprache und Dichtung. Festschrift für Friedrich Maurer*, Stuttgart, 1963.

Mautner, Franz H., Feise, Ernst, and Vietor, Karl. 'Ist fortzusetzen . . .', *PMLA*, lix, 1944.

May, Kurt, ' "Wilhelm Meisters Lehrjahre". Ein Bildungsroman?', *DVLG*, xxxi, 1957.

— 'Die Wahlverwandtschaften als tragischer Roman', *JbFDH*, 1936–40.

— 'Goethes "Wahlverwandtschaften" als tragischer Roman', *Form und Bedeutung. Interpretationen zur deutschen Dichtung des 18. und 19. Jahrhunderts*, Stuttgart, 1957.

Meyer, Eva Alexander, *Goethes Wilhelm Meister*, Munich, 1947.

Mayer, Herman, 'Mignons Italienlied und das Wesen der Verseinlage im "Wilhelm Meister". Versuch einer gegenständlichen Polemik.', *Euph.*, xlvi (1952).

— 'Kennst Du das Haus? Eine Studie zu Goethes Palladio – Erlebnis', *Euph.*, xlvii (1953).

Michelsen, Peter, *Laurence Sterne und der deutsche Roman des achtzehnten Jahrhunderts*, Palaestra, 232, Göttingen, 1962.

Monroy, Ernst Friedrich von, 'Zur Form der Novelle in "Wilhelm Meisters Wanderjahre" ', *Germanisch-Romanische Monatsschrift*, xxxi, 1943.

Muir, Edwin, *The Structure of the Novel*, London, 1938.

Müller, Günther, *Gestaltung-Umgestaltung in Wilhelm Meisters Lehrjahren*, Halle, 1948.

— 'Die Goethe-Forschung seit 1945', *DVLG*, xxvi, 1952.

— *Kleine Goethe-Biographie*, Bonn, 1947.

Müller, Joachim, 'Phasen der Bildungsidee im "Wilhelm Meister" ', *G*, xxiv, 1962.

Nitzschke, O., *Goethes pädagogische Provinz* (Diss.), Heidelberg, 1937.

Oakeshott, Michael, *Rationalism in Politics and other Essays*, London, 1962.

Ohly, Friedrich, 'Zum *Kästchen* in Goethes "Wanderjahren" ', *Zeitschrift für Deutsches Altertum*, 1961–62.

Ohly, Friedrich, 'Goethes *Ehrfurchten* – ein *ordo caritatis*', *Euph.*, lv, 1961.

Olzien, O. H., *Der Satzbau in Wilhelm Meisters Lehrjahren*, Von deutscher Poeterey, 14, Leipzig, 1933.

Oppel, Horst, *Das Shakespeare-Bild Goethes*, Mayence, 1949.

Pascal, Roy, *The German Sturm und Drang*, Manchester, 1953.

— *The German Novel*, Manchester, 1956.

Pasternak, Boris, *An Essay in Autobiography*, trans. Manya Harari, London, 1959.

Peacock, Ronald, 'Goethe's Version of Poetic Drama', *PEGS*, xvi, 1947.

Peschken, Bernd, 'Das Blatt in den Wanderjahren', *G*, xxvii, 1965.

Petersen, Julius, *Das Deutsche Nationaltheater*, Leipzig, 1919.

Popper, Karl R., *Logik der Forschung*, Vienna, 1935 (Engl. transl. *The Logic of Scientific Discovery*, London, 1959).

Raabe, August, 'Das Dämonische in den "Wanderjahren" ', *G*, i, 1936.

Radbruch, Gustav, 'Wilhelm Meisters sozialpolitische Sendung', *Logos*, viii, 1919–20.

— 'Wilhelm Meisters sozialistische Sendung', *Gestalten und Gedanken*, Leipzig, 1944.

Rasch, Wolfdietrich, 'Die klassische Erzählkunst Goethes', *Formkräfte der deutschen Dichtung vom Barock bis zur Gegenwart*, ed. Hans Steffen, Göttingen, 1963.

Rausch, Georg, *Goethe und die deutsche Sprache*, Leipzig, 1909.

Rausch, Jürgen, 'Lebensstufen in Goethes "Wilhelm Meister" ', *DVLG*, xx, 1942.

Reiss, Hans, – 'On some Images in *Wilhelm Meisters Lehrjahre*', *PEGS*, xx, 1951.

— 'Bild und Symbol in "Wilhelm Meisters Wanderjahren" ', *Studium Generale*, vi, 1953.

— '*Die Leiden des jungen Werthers*. A Reconsideration', *Modern Language Quarterly*, xx, 1959.

— *Goethes Romane*, Berne and Munich, 1963.

— 'Wilhelm Meisters Wanderjahre. Der Weg von der ersten zur zweiten Fassung', *DVLG*, xxxix, 1965.

— (ed.) *The Political Thought of the German Romantics 1795–1815*, Oxford, 1955.

— *Das politische Denken in der deutschen Romantik*, Berne and Munich, 1966.

Riemann, Robert, *Goethes Romantechnik*, Leipzig, 1902.

Riess, Gertrud, *Die beiden Fassungen von Goethes 'Die Leiden des jungen Werthers'*, Breslau, 1924.

Robertson, John George, *The Life and Work of Goethe*, London, 1932.

Rose, William, *From Goethe to Byron. The Development of Weltschmerz in German Literature*, London, 1924.
— 'The Historical Background of Goethe's "Werther" ', *Men, Myths and Movements in German Literature*, London, 1931.
— (ed.) *Essays on Goethe*, London, 1949.
— 'Goethe's Reputation in England during his Lifetime', ibid.
Rötscher, Heinrich, *Die Wahlverwandtschaften von Goethe in ihrer weltgeschichtlichen Bedeutung, ihrem sittlichen und künstlerischen Werthe nach entwickelt. Abhandlungen zur Philosophie der Kunst*, Pt. ii, Berlin, 1838.
Sagave, Pierre-Paul, 'Les "Années de Voyage de Wilhelm Meister" et la critique socialiste', *ÉG*, viii, 1953.
— 'L'Economie et l'Homme dans "les Années de Voyage de Wilhelm Meister" ', *ÉG*, vii, 1952. (Both articles are reprinted in *Recherches sur le roman social en Allemagne*, Aix-en-Provence, 1960.)
Sarter, Eberhard, *Zur Technik von Wilhelm Meisters Wanderjahren*, Bonner Forschungen, N.F. 7, Berlin, 1914.
Schaeder, Grete, *Gott und Welt. Drei Kapitel Goethescher Weltanschauung*, Hameln, 1947.
Scherer, Wilhelm, *Geschichte der deutschen Literatur*, 3rd ed., Berlin, 1885.
Schiff, Julius, 'Mignon, Ottilie, Makarie', *JbGG*, ix, 1922.
Schlechta, Karl, *Goethes Wilhelm Meister*, Frankfurt/Main, 1953.
Schlegel, Friedrich, 'Über Goethes Meister', *Athenäum*, i, Pt. 2, Berlin, 1798.
—'Athenäum-Fragmente', ibid.
Schmidt, Erich, *Richardson, Rousseau und Goethe*, Jena, 1875.
— 'Der erste Wilhelm Meister. Auszüge und Bemerkungen', *Internationale Monatsschrift für Wissenschaft, Kunst und Technik*, vi, 1912.
Schneider, Franz Josef, *Die Freimaurerei und ihr Einfluss auf die geistige Kultur in Deutschland am Ende des 18. Jahrhunderts*, Leipzig, 1909.
Schöffler, Herbert, 'Die Leiden des jungen Werthers. Ihr geistesgeschichtlicher Hintergrund', *Deutscher Geist im 18. Jahrhundert*, Göttingen, 1956.
Scholz, Felix, 'Der Brief Wilhelm Meisters an Mariane', *JbFDH*, 1928.
Schrimpf, Hans Joachim, *Das Weltbild des späten Goethe*, Stuttgart, 1956.
Schumann, Detlev, 'Some notes on Werther', *JEGP*, lv, 1956.
Schweitzer, Christoph, 'Wilhelm Meister und das Bild vom kranken Königssohn', *PMLA*, lxxii, 1957.
Seidlin, Oskar, 'Zur Mignon-Ballade', *Euph.*, xlv, 1950.
Sengle, Friedrich, *Wieland*, Stuttgart, 1949.

Sengle, Friedrich, 'Der Romanbegriff in der ersten Hälfte des neunzehnten Jahrhunderts', *Arbeiten zur deutschen Literatur 1750–1850*, Stuttgart, 1965.

Seuffert, Bernhard, *Goethes Theaterroman*, Graz, Vienna, Leipzig, 1924.

Singer, Herbert, *Der galante Roman*, Stuttgart, 1961.

Solger, Karl Friedrich Wilhelm, 'Über die Wahlverwandtschaften', *Nachgelassene Schriften* (ed. Ludwig Tieck and F. Raumer), Leipzig, 1926. (Reprint, *Graef*, i, 1, p. 474 ff. and H.A., 6, p. 634 ff.)

Sommerfeld, Martin 'Romantheorie und Romantypus der Aufklärung', *DVLG*, iv, 1926.

— 'Goethes Wahlverwandtschaften im neunzehnten Jahrhundert', *Goethe in Umwelt und Folge, Gesammelte Studien*, Leiden, 1935.

Spranger, Eduard, 'Der psychologische Perspektivismus im Roman', *JbFDH*, 1930.

— 'Goethe über die menschlichen Lebensalter', *Goethes Weltanschauung*, Wiesbaden, 1949.

— 'Die sittliche Astrologie der Makarie in "Wilhelm Meisters Wanderjahren" ', ibid.

Stahl, E. L., *Die religiöse und die humanitätsphilosophische Bildungsidee und die Entstehung des deutschen Bildungsromans im 18. Jahrhundert*, Sprache und Dichtung, 56, Berne, 1934.

— 'Die Wahlverwandtschaften', *PEGS*, xv, 1946.

— 'Goethe as Novelist', *Essays on Goethe* (ed. William Rose), London, 1929.

Staiger, Emil, *Die Zeit als Einbildungskraft des Dichters*, Zürich, 1939.

— *Goethe*, 3 vols., Zürich, 1952–9.

— 'Ein Satz aus der Winckelmannschrift', *Schweizer Monatshefte*, xxxvii, 1957.

Staroste, Wolfgang, 'Zur Ding "Symbolik" in Goethe's "Wilhelm Meister" ', *Orbis Litterarum*, xv, 1960.

— 'Zum epischen Aufbau der Realität in Goethes "Wilhelm Meister" ', *Wirkendes Wort*, xi, 1961.

— 'Raumgestaltung und Raumsymbolik in Goethes *Wahlverwandtschaften*', *ÉG*, xvi, 1961.

Steer, Alfred G., '*Goethe's Social Philosophy as revealed in "Campagne in Frankreich" and "Belagerung von Mainz"* ', University of Carolina Studies in the Germanic Languages and Literatures, 15, Chapel Hill, 1955.

Steiner, Jacob, *Sprache und Stilwandel in Wilhelm Meister*, Zürcher Beiträge zur deutschen Sprache und Stilgeschichte, Zürich, 1959 (2nd ed., Stuttgart, 1965).

Stock, Irvin, 'A view of *Wilhelm Meister's Apprenticeship*', *PMLA*, lxxii, 1957.

Stöcklein, Paul, 'Stil und Sinn der Wahlverwandtschaften', *Wege zum späten Goethe*, Hamburg, 1949.

— 'Stil und Geist der "Wahlverwandtschaften" ', *Zeitschrift für Deutsche Philologie*, lxxxi, 1951.

Stopp, F. J., ' "Ein wahrer Narziss". Reflections on the Eduard—Ottilie relations in Goethe's *Wahlverwandtschaften*', *PEGS*, xxix, 1960.

— 'Ottilie und das "innere Licht" ', *German Studies presented to Walter Horace Bruford*, London, 1962.

Storz, Gerhard, 'Der Roman "Die Leiden des jungen Werthers" ', *Goethe-Vigilien*, Stuttgart, 1953.

— 'Zwei Beispiele des Tagebuch-Romans', ibid.

— 'Wilhelm Meisters Lehrjahre', ibid.

— 'Die Lieder aus Wilhelm Meister', ibid.

— 'Wilhelm Meisters Lehrjahre in den Briefen Goethes und Schillers', *Figuren und Prospekte*, Stuttgart, 1963.

Thalmann, Marianne, *Der Trivialroman des achtzehnten Jahrhunderts und der romantische Roman*, Germanische Studien, 24, Berlin, 1923.

— *Johann Wolfgang von Goethe. Der Mann von Funfzig Jahren*, Vienna, 1948.

Trevelyan, Humphry, 'Ottilie und Sperata', *G*, xi, 1949.

Trilling, Lionel, *The Liberal Imagination*, London, 1951.

Trunz, Erich, 'Altersstil', *Goethe-Handbuch*, 2nd ed. (ed. A. Zastran), Stuttgart, 1955 ff.

Ulrich, Oskar, *Charlotte Kestner*, *Ein Lebensbild*, Bielefeld, 1921.

Vietor, Karl, *Goethe*. Berne, 1949.

— *Der junge Goethe*, Munich, 1950.

— 'Goethes Gedicht auf Schillers Schädel', *PMLA*, lix, 1944. (Reprinted in *Geist und Form*, Berne, 1952.)

— 'Zur Frage einer Fortsetzung . . . (Antwort)', *PMLA*, lx, 1945.

Waidson, H. M., 'Death by Water: or the Childhood of Wilhelm Meister', *MLR*, lvi, 1961.

Walzel, Oskar F., 'Goethes "Wahlverwandtschaften" im Rahmen ihrer Zeit', *GJb*, xxvii (1906).

Watt, Ian, *The Rise of the Novel. Studies in Defoe, Richardson and Fielding*, London, 1957.

Weber, Walter, 'Zum Hauptmann in Goethes "Wahlverwandtschaften" ', *G*, xxi, 1959.

Wiese, Benno von, 'Der Mann von fünfzig Jahren', *Die Deutsche Novelle von Goethe bis Kafka*, ii, Düsseldorf, 1962.

Wilkinson, Elizabeth M., 'Goethe's Conception of Form', *Proceedings of the British Academy*, xxxvii, 1951 (reprinted in Wilkinson, Elizabeth M. and Willoughby, L. A., *Goethe: Poet and Thinker*, London, 1962).

Wilkinson, Elizabeth M., ' "Form" and "Content" in the Aesthetics of German Classicism', *Stil- und Formprobleme in der Literatur* (ed. Paul Böckmann), Heidelberg, 1960.

— '*Tasso — ein gesteigerter Werther*' in the Light of Goethe's Principle of *Steigerung*. Some Reflections on Critical Method', *MLR*, xliv (1949) (reprinted in *Goethe: Poet and Thinker*, London, 1962).

Wilkinson, Elizabeth M. and Willoughby, L. A., *Goethe: Poet and Thinker*, London, 1962.

— 'The Blind Man and the Poet. An early state in Goethe's Quest for Form', *German Studies presented to Walter Horace Bruford*, London, 1962.

Willoughby, L. A., 'The Image of the Horse and the Charioteer in Goethe's Poetry', *PEGS*, xv, 1946.

— 'On some Problems of Goethe's Imagery', *Bulletin of the Modern Humanities Research Association, 1949* (reprinted as 'On the Study of Goethe's Imagery', *Goethe: Poet and Thinker*, London, 1962).

— 'The Cross-Fertilization of Literature and Life in the Light of Goethe's Theory of "Wiederspiegelung" ', *Comparative Literature*, i, 1949 (reprinted as 'Literary Relations in the light of Goethe's Principle of "Wiederholte Spiegelungen" ', *Goethe: Poet and Thinker*, London, 1962).

— 'The image of the "Wanderer" and the "Hut" in Goethe's Poetry', *ÉG*, vi, 1951.

— 'Schiller on Man's Education to Freedom through Knowledge', *GR*, xxiv, 1954.

— ' "Name ist Schall und Rauch": On the Significance of Names for Goethes work', *GLL*, xvi, 1963.

Wittich, Werner, 'Der soziale Gehalt von Goethes Roman "Wilhelm Meisters Lehrjahre" ', *Hauptprobleme der Soziologie*, *Erinnerungen für Max Weber*, ii, Munich and Leipzig, 1923.

Wolff, Eugen, *Mignon. Ein Beitrag zur Geschichte des Wilhelm Meister*, Munich, 1909.

— 'Die ursprüngliche Gestalt von Wilhelm Meisters Wanderjahren', *GJb*, xxxiv, 1913.

Wolff, Hans M., *Goethes Weg zur Humanität*, Berne, 1951.

— *Goethe in der Periode der Wahlverwandtschaften, 1801–9*, Berne, 1952.

— *Goethes Novelle 'Die Wahlverwandtschaften'. Ein Rekonstruktionsversuch*, Berne, 1952.

Wundt, Max, *Wilhelm Meister und die Entwicklung des modernen Lebensideals*, Berlin and Leipzig, 1913 (2nd ed., 1931).

Zeydel, Edwin H., 'Goethe's Reputation in America', *Essays on Goethe* (ed. W. Rose), London, 1949.

Index

A. *Persons (mentioned in text)*

B. *Places*

C. *Goethe: Werke*

Page references in italic figures refer to the main treatment of the works

D. *Subjects*